S0-AVD-752

microprocessor systems design

microprocessor systems design

Edwin E. Klingman,
President
Cybernetic Micro Systems

prentice-hall, inc. englewood cliffs, new jersey 07632

Library of Congress Cataloging in Publication Data

KLINGMAN, E   E
  Microprocessor systems design.

  Bibliography: p.
  Includes index.
  1. Microprocessors—Design and construction.
I. Title.
TK7885.K544   621.3819′52   76-45190
ISBN   0-13-581413-8

© 1977

by PRENTICE-HALL, INC., Englewood Cliffs, New Jersey   07632

All rights reserved. No part of this book
may be reproduced in any form
or by any means without permission
in writing from the publisher.

Printed in the United States of America

10 9 8 7 6 5 4 3 2

PRENTICE-HALL INTERNATIONAL, INC., *London*
PRENTICE-HALL OF AUSTRALIA PTY. LIMITED, *Sydney*
PRENTICE-HALL OF CANADA, LTD., *Toronto*
PRENTICE-HALL OF INDIA PRIVATE LIMITED, *New Delhi*
PRENTICE-HALL OF JAPAN, INC., *Tokyo*
PRENTICE-HALL OF SOUTHEAST ASIA PTE. LTD., *Singapore*
WHITEHALL BOOKS LIMITED, *Wellington, New Zealand*

To my sons,
Eddie and David

contents

preface

This book is not concerned with designing toys or mere teaching models, but is directed toward the design of powerful computer systems which are orders of magnitude better than the best that major universities could afford little more than a dozen years ago. That a serious student can understand the design and application of such a system today—and then build his/her own system—would not even have been good science fiction a few years ago.

The book is intended to serve both as an introduction to computer systems in general and to the design of systems based on microprocessors in particular. The presentation is self-contained. All relevant techniques are developed, and their range of application is described. The emphasis is evenly divided between the concepts and the state-of-the-art devices with which one may fashion a computer. The design of a general purpose computer is used as a vehicle for developing all of the basic concepts required for understanding the spectrum of microprocessors available today. The choice of processor was based on the following criteria: 1) a simple basic instruction set and 2) a control structure that embodies most of the features that are employed in processors. The second criterion argues against the highly integrated second and third generation families of devices that have been designed with compatible timing. Although the trend toward integrated sets of devices will surely continue, it is absolutely necessary that the digital systems designer be capable of interfacing any of the thousands of devices which are available, and this requires an understanding of timing and control structures.

Processors of this type include the Intel 8008, RCA COSMAC, General Instruments CP-1600, Intersil IM6100, Mostek MK5065P, National PACE, and others. Of these, the Intel 8008 possesses a very simple instruction set of 48 instructions which is a subset of the 8080/8085 microprocessors's 78 instructions and the Zilog Z-80's 158 instructions. The coded state signals and multiplexed bus structure allow development of the necessary timing/control concepts required for most processor design. Historically, as the first eight bit central processor unit, it has influenced the design of several later processors.

The book is organized in three sections as follows: The first section, consisting of Chapters 1–4, treats the basic concepts of digital building blocks and presents typical examples of such. The second section, Chapters 5–8, designs a computer based around the 8008, developing computer concepts as needed. The final section, Chapters 9–14, treats specific topics in terms of the spectrum of microprocessors; i.e., concepts are developed and their implementations in various microprocessors are presented. Such topics include software structures, addressing structures, Input/Output structures, Interrupt structures, Direct Memory Access structures, and architectural structures. In addition to all relevant concepts, this portion of the book is rich in detail and the design data required for using these processors.

The philosophy of design will consist of defining a goal and then concentrating upon the simplest means of realizing the goal. The economic premise underlying this philosophy is that the typical reader is assumed to be interested in understanding, acquiring, and applying a general purpose computer in a specific problem area. Each application is therefore considered to be one of a kind. Thus the cost function to be minimized is design time in contrast to the commercial situation in which unit cost is to be minimized at the expense of design time, thereby maximizing the profit over a large number of systems.

This philosophy is felt to be realistic in the assessment of the needs of a typical reader and also to provide the most sensible approach to a very complex subject. This objective will be met primarily by choice of the most convenient and/or simplest building blocks. In this vein a choice between random access memory blocks, for example, would be made in favor of the simple static RAM rather than the slightly cheaper but much more complex dynamic RAM if both RAMs satisfy the requirements of the design.

The treatment of software is consistent with the assumed 'applications oriented' bias of the reader. The most powerful tool for applying computers in most environments is the *interpreter*, and a simple, expandable interpreter is developed which is capable of serving as the basis for a number of applications. In addition, the concepts concerning assemblers, macro-assemblers, and conditional assembly are developed in Chapter 9 and in the appendices.

Although written primarily for computer scientists, electronic engineers, and physicists, the book is designed to be useful in many disciplines. Information processors are multi- and inter-disciplinary and, as such, are of interest to growing numbers of people. Once the principles of digital building blocks have been grasped, they should prove as useful to an experimental psychologist as to an experimental physicist.

Digital design is obviously of use to engineers who need to apply computer based systems to specific problems, particularly the monitor/control problems of transportation, factory automation, or communication systems and to the physicists, chemists, and biologists who need to automate their laboratories for tight control of experimental parameters and programmed data acquisition and analysis. Others who may wish to utilize digital building blocks include a growing number of artists who appreciate the dynamic medium afforded by the computer, particularly in conjunction with, but not limited to, video displays. As mentioned above, the experimental psychologist should welcome the computer to his laboratory, and a large number of nonexperimental psychologists today feel that an understanding of the computer is a valuable asset to those who think about thinking. Architects who wish to design adaptive and interactive living environments will find the necessary tools described herein. Selected portions of this text can form a course for business oriented students who need to understand the operation and effect of automation in sufficient detail to plan for, rather than just respond to, events.

The unique feature of this book lies in its *complete* treatment of real, non-trivial, digital systems made possible by the emergence of Large Scale Integrated (LSI) microprocessors. By treating microprocessors at the system level and treating subsystems at the component level, it becomes possible to cover entire systems in one book and to place the extremely detailed treatment of particular systems in a conceptual context of sufficient scope to apply to both current and future systems.

In order to gain some appreciation of microprocessors and the rate at which technological change is occurring today, we may contrast typical microprocessor characteristics with the first major processor that I had the opportunity to work on: an IBM 650. In 1960 this system leased for about $10,000 per month. If we consider only parts cost, a microprocessor-based system will today range from $50 to $1000. Although these processors differ vastly in architecture and implementation (vacuum tubes versus LSI) it is possible to draw a rough comparison between them.

The IBM 650 had 60 instructions; most microprocessors possess 70 to 100. The 650 possessed a 20-millisecond instruction execution time; today's microprocessors possess two micro-second instruction execution times—ten thousand times faster! Although the power requirements of the 650 are unknown, it did require heavy-duty air conditioning facilities, whereas microprocessors use only a few watts and are roughly one hundred times smaller in volume. The 650 used 2000 words of drum memory; most microprocessors address 65,000 words of semiconductor memory.

Although this book covers state-of-the-art digital design and in places predicts some developments to be expected in the next few years, it is impossible to predict very far downstream. A thorough coverage of the hardware available today and the trends in hardware is presented, and concepts that are unlikely to change are expounded. But rather than list innumerable applications of computer systems, which are already well-documented elsewhere, the stress here is on the capability of such systems. Each reader is assumed to bring with him his own applications requirements.

Chapter One presents an overview of information processing and digital design in an attempt to shed some light on the significance of the transformations occurring in the field of computer science.

Chapter Two introduces binary arithmetic, Boolean algebra, logic gates, and Venn diagrams. The TTL family characteristics are presented and discussed. Combinatorial logic is described and examples are presented. A brief summary of the building blocks to be used throughout the book concludes Chapter Two.

Chapter Three introduces flip-flop storage elements. Clocked flip-flops are discussed; and the R-S, T, D, J-K Master-Slave flip-flops are presented in detail. The development of memory cells and their organization into arrays is covered. Shift registers are derived and discussed.

Chapter Four deals with coding and MSI and LSI building blocks. The space/time concept of coding is developed in detail. A representative digital building block from each class of building blocks is treated. This chapter is essential to any course in computer design, as these are the blocks from which the system will be built. The final sections describe the interfacing between families of blocks.

Chapter Five treats the instruction set of the CPU. The internal architecture of the CPU is analyzed in detail as preparation for a meaningful treatment of the instructions. Examples are developed in the form of short programs both in the machine language and assembly language.

Chapter Six treats the state transition and timing for a central processor unit. This material is balanced between the general concepts that are applicable to most processors and the specific details that are necessary for design work. Emphasis is placed on time/space multiplexing and on the need for, and interpretation of, status information. State timing and the state transition diagram are covered.

Chapter Seven begins the hardware design of a computer system. The circuitry that effects information transfers between the CPU and memory is designed. Particular attention is paid to an analysis of timing. Often several alternatives are considered before arriving at a final design.

Chapter Eight analyzes the I/O instructions and develops the I/O port selection circuitry.

Chapter Nine traces the use of symbols from the elemental hardware level through macro-assemblers and interpreters.

Chapter Ten treats the addressing structures that are associated with microprocessors. The first half of the chapter provides detailed coverage of the address presentation mechanisms currently in use while the second half covers address formation mechanisms now used in microprocessors. The duality of procedure/data structure is discussed and then used as a framework for the introduction of computed addressing techniques.

Chapter Eleven provides an extensive coverage of Input/Output structures and techniques. Examples using Teletypes and analog-to-digital converters attempt to balance hardware, software, and timing concepts. The status-checking techniques lead quite naturally to interrupt structures which are treated in the following chapter.

Chapter Twelve presents interrupt structures as an event-driven symbol replacement technique. The wide range of interrupt structures and techniques that are available with microprocessors is given detailed treatment. A single level interrupt system is expanded to a general multi-level interrupt system, and the software that is required is developed in detail.

Chapter Thirteen treats direct memory access structures and techniques and covers microprocessor DMA subsystem design, both integral and additive.

In Chapter Fourteen, treating architectural themes, the concepts of bundled and orthogonal structures are defined and used to place current architectures in perspective, as well as to predict future trends. This chapter ends with a brief introduction to multi-processing concepts as applied in microprocessor architectures.

For three years prior to publication of this text, I taught survey courses and seminars on microprocessors, consulted on microprocessor developments, and designed commercial systems. These activities brought me into contact with well over 1,000 engineers and programmers working in every imaginable application area. Although it is impractical to list all of these people by name, they have together contributed far more to this book than any individual. Yet there are specific individuals who deserve mention: Dr. Robert Naumann, who supported my minicomputer and microprocessor work at NASA. Drs. Ron McNutt and Bill Short, who arranged for me to teach a microprocessor course at Athens College in late 1972. Dr. John Peatman at Georgia Tech, who encouraged this undertaking at a critical time. Jerry L. Ogdin, Dr. Roger Camp, John Harris, and Scott McPhillips, with whom I conducted some of the first seminars, have influenced my thinking on microprocessors. I have had helpful conversations with Tampy Thomas at Intersil and Hash Patel at National. The support given me by Intel Corporation has been tremendous, and I am indebted to many Intel employees, particularly Juris Brempelis, Dane Elliot, Ken McKenzie, Hal Feeney, Jim Lally, and Dr. Bill Davidow. I am also grateful for enlightening and enjoyable conversations with Chuck Peddle and Will Mathys of MOS Technology, Inc. Dr. John Gault of North Carolina State has been most helpful in reviewing the manuscript and suggesting a number of changes in organization. I feel that the changes have improved the presentation and I appreciate his efforts. Finally I wish to thank my production editor, Margaret McAbee, for her gracious assistance in producing this book.

EDWIN E. KLINGMAN

1 *microprocessor systems design: an overview*

> *"A science of design. . . would depend upon the relative simplicity of the interface as its primary source of abstraction and generality."*
>
> *Herbert Simon*
> The Sciences of the Artificial,
> *The MIT Press, 1969*

The utilitarian value of technology lies in the effectiveness of tools and techniques in accomplishing desired goals. The most effective and widely applicable technology today is that of micro-electronics, in which the ability to fabricate integrated circuits on a dielectric base has culminated in the monolithic microprocessor, or "computer on a chip." Our goal is to develop an understanding of and a facility with these integrated circuit "building blocks" that are revolutionizing the field of digital design. Our vehicle will be the design of a general-purpose digital computer that uses a basic Large-Scale Integrated (LSI) circuit central processor unit. This system will allow the introduction of both hardware and software structural features that enhance the power of an information processor. Emphasis will be placed on the design of real-time interactive systems.

ADVANTAGES OF MICROPROCESSORS

Unquestionably the major advantage of microprocessors is that of cost. They are now inexpensive enough for thousands of applications, and prices are dropping as their capabilities increase.

In applications limited to pure number crunching associated with large-scale scientific calculations, and those of file management associated with large-scale data bases, the information processors must of necessity be large scale. This is primarily due to the fact that long word lengths and high execution speeds facilitate long calculations and rapid data searches. These factors are of lesser importance for smaller calculations and data banks, and even less so in monitor/control applications. They will become still less important as the word lengths and speeds of microprocessors increase.

A distinct advantage of microprocessors over large processors is that, whereas large processors are shared by many people and tasks, microprocessors are dedicated to one person and/or one task. The attendant decrease in operating system complexity is enormous. The software required to keep track of multi-user environments presents huge overhead costs on top of rather formidable hardware costs. These costs are absent in dedicated microprocessor systems. The prefix *micro-* used in the preceding discussion should be interpreted in terms of size and cost rather than capability. The microprocessors of today are superior in most aspects to the major processors of a dozen or more years ago. The decrease in size and cost of processors by several orders of magnitude has correspondingly increased the range of practical applications of processors by several orders of magnitude.

ESSENTIAL FUNCTIONS OF PROCESSORS

Before proceeding to discuss the design of processor-based systems, it is appropriate to define a processor in terms of its function. The essential function of a processor can be specified by five operations:

1. READ the input symbol x.

2. COMPARE x with z, the internal state of the processor.

3. WRITE the appropriate output symbol y.

4. CHANGE the internal state z to the new state z'.

5. REPEAT the above sequence with a new input symbol x'.

The power inherent in this set of operations is well known to those familiar with automata theory. Heinz von Foerster has given an exceptional introduction to the processor for physicists by pointing out that Maxwell's Demon can be simply described by five equivalent operations. Maxwell's Demon was the mechanism postulated by James Clerk Maxwell to cause heat to flow from a cold container to a hot container in apparent violation of the Second Law of Thermodynamics. This was to be achieved by positioning a "demon" or mechanism between the two containers to channel selectively the most energetic or "hottest" molecules from the cold gas into the hot container. The operations performed by the Demon are:

1. READ the velocity, v, of the approaching molecule with mass m.

2. COMPARE the energy $(mv^2/2)$ with the mean energy $\langle mv^2/2 \rangle$ (or temperature T) of the cooler container (intend state T).

3. OUTPUT this molecule (to the hotter container) if $(mv^2/2)$ is greater than $\langle mv^2/2 \rangle$; otherwise close the channel.

4. CHANGE the internal state T to the new (cooler) state T'.

5. Repeat the above sequence for a new approaching molecule m'.

Maxwell's Demon was designed a century ago, long before the advent of quantum mechanics and information theory. The concept of entropy as a measure of disorder in a system is today central to many fields, and the ability to increase order *locally* at the expense of energy is widely recognized. Thus, the microprocessor, operating from a power supply or energy source, can retard the increase of entropy in a local system to an arbitrarily slow rate. This remarkable ability characterizing the information processor can be used to optimize or increase the efficiency of almost any imaginable process.

The primary problem facing a world of finite *resource* and finite *sinking* capabilities is that of waste. The pollution that accompanies all life was, in the prehuman world, recycled naturally. Some human societies such as the Hopi Indians, having lived on the same plateau for approximately 5000 years, also maintained an ecologically efficient relationship. The invention of agriculture, the city, and industrial civilization, combined with unnatural population densities, have aggravated and emphasized the problem of waste. It may be in this area that the information processor, in its capacity as an entropy retarder, will be of most value in the immediate future.

The ecological applications of information processors to retard the growth of entropy (i.e., minimize waste) range from the system simulations of Jay Forrester et. al. at MIT to process regulation systems designed to increase efficiency. Increased efficiency in any process equates to less waste. There can be little doubt that as energy costs rise and processing costs decline the applications of microprocessors to increase efficiency will continue to grow.

The concept of increasing entropy, like most of the concepts of physics, applies to closed systems. In an open system it is possible to decrease entropy or hold it constant. The application of processors in adaptive or learning processes brings about a decrease in entropy by removing redundancy in a system. Learning processors or pattern recognition systems remove redundancy by disclosing structure in a system. The development of learning systems must unquestionably be considered a process of endowing our environment with intellegence. That it is currently a low order of intelligence is of little consequence. We will not pursue this theme as the vast possibilities that open up are mind-boggling, but subject to considerable controversy. We, therefore, limit our discussion to increases in efficiency of processes.

We hesitate to be specific about microprocessor applications simply because the list is endless. We prefer rather to consider two categories in which efficiencies are achievable: physical and social. Under physical we include efficiencies in transportation, manufacturing, and such areas as physics, chemistry, and biology laboratories, as well as medical applications. The social category consists of communications efficiencies achievable in education, government, management, and entertainment. Aside from the obvious computer/TV cable linkups and other purely communications-oriented applications, there is a less well-publicized aspect known to every person lucky enough to have unrestricted access to a modern minicomputer: the computer is beyond doubt THE SUPERTOY and is capable of providing as such a new, expressive medium for creative drive. It is entirely plausible that of all the uses to which information processors may be put, this—in the long run—may be the most important to mankind.

THE NEW DUALISM

The preceding discussion introduces the idea of inseparable opposites, growth/ decay, referred to as a dualism or dualistic pair. The use of the concept *recycle* in this discussion illustrates the most important aspect of this dualism, i.e., the dualistic opposites are mutually transformable. The products of decay contribute to the growth process, which in turn maintains the decay process.

This idea of opposites that *define* each other, i.e., have no meaning alone, and yet are mutually transformable, we refer to as *dualism* or dualistic process. The relation between dualistic opposites is one of complementarity rather than negation.

There seems to be an increasing awareness of the complementarity in dualistic descriptions of the world: on/off, up/down, light/dark, hot/cold, happy/sad, and on and on. The realization that these inseparable opposites *define* each other has come with an increased awareness of, and interest in, Eastern consciousness and understanding of Western science.

Einstein's Dualisms

The fundamental dualism of the twentieth century has been that symbolized by $E = mc^2$, i.e., the matter/energy dualism. The unexpected discovery that matter could be transformed into energy, and that energy could be transformed into matter, has changed both practical and philosophical aspects of our life.

Yet another dualistic transformation of categories once believed to be mutually exclusive was conceived and formalized by Albert Einstein. The relativistic transformation in which the space/time dualism appears relates spatial to temporal quantities, and vice versa, through a four-dimensional equation. This transformation has been experimentally confirmed and practically applied by scientists in several fields of physics.

A less well-publicized complementarity is that symbolized in the Schroedinger equation of quantum physics. Reconciling deterministic world views with non-deterministic, this famous equation rigorously and deterministically states the laws governing the quantum mechanical wave function while the wave function itself is *probabilistic*. i.e., indeterministic. A few practical consequences of this interpretation are found in atomic energy, the laser, and the integrated circuits of solid-state physical electronics. Micro-electronic technology is a direct consequence of the probabilistic interpretation of the wave function determined by Schroedinger's equation. The philosophical consequences of this interpretation may be no less significant, if less recognized.

An even more radical dualistic transformation is coming to be understood and is every bit as earthshaking as the fundamental dualisms of the twentieth century: space/time, probabilistic/deterministic, matter/energy, particle/wave. The *hardware/software* dualism will have much more profound effects, both practical and philosophical, than these. This dualism can be stated as:

> *Any software process can be transformed into an equivalent hardware process, and any hardware process can be transformed into an equivalent software process.*

The nature of this dualism is at the very root of PROCESS and is the defining relationship for cybernetic processes. Neither hardware nor software has independent existence; therefore, the transformation can never be complete. There must always be software to direct hardware processes, and there must always be hardware to process software algorithms. This statement is experientially evident. We accept it as a metaphysical *given*. The analogous requirement in the matter/energy dualism states that there is a relativistic mass associated with every field, and that the energy/matter transformation can occur only in the presence of a momentum-conserving mass field.

The short history of the hardware/software trade-off has been primarily an economic trade-off. In this respect, the governing rule was: hardware is fast, software is cheap; so we accepted the simple, slow, predominantly software systems. The evolution occurring for the past quarter-century has seen the economic ground rules change. Before proceeding with the discussion of this change, it is well to define our terms more closely.

Algorithm: An algorithm, or algorithmic activity, is a procedure for carrying out a task.

Hardware: A relatively permanent physical embodiment of an algorithmic process.

Software: A relatively impermanent, informational embodiment of an algorithm.

Information: The entity that makes the difference between knowing and not knowing that which makes possible a decision.

Context: That character of the environment which gives meaning to a decision. That which allows an interpretation of a given quantity of information.

These terms, like *collection* or *set* in mathematics, are purposefully defined in a very intuitive manner in order to avoid the constraints imposed by tighter definitions and the consequent restrictions on their range of application. Specific examples of hardware, for instance, may take the form of simple logic gates or of adders that carry out processes determined by their physical electronic structure. More sophisticated hardware executes processes determined by the permanent physical structure of the device and by the momentary information structure presented to the device. An example of the former would be the AND gate that produces an output defined to be TRUE when both inputs are TRUE and a FALSE output under any other input conditions. The latter type of hardware is exemplified by the 74181 Arithmetic Logic Unit that executes a large number of logical or arithmetical operations on two-word inputs to different ports in the device, and outputs the resulting word from a third port. The operation executed at a given time is determined by an instruction word input to the device through a separate instruction port. An even more sophisticated hardware processor is the Central Processor Unit. This is the device with which this book is most concerned. Further discussion is postponed until the preliminaries have been completed.

Software can exist as patterns of light, sound, holes in a medium, or charges or voltage distributions. Information streams in the form of current densities in specially structured solids are transformed in hardware and often halted and stored as static charge distributions in readiness for the moment when use will be made of the informational pattern. A single unit of information is called a bit. Bits may be separated in either time or space, or both. Bits separated in space, but "simultaneous" in time, require separated paths or require separate propagation channels or paths in space. Between devices the paths are normally pins and wires or layered wires as on printed circuit boards. Internally there are several ways of forming channels; however, to discuss them in any depth would take us too far afield. The use of one space channel over which separate bits are transferred during successive time intervals is known as serial transmission of information. The simultaneous (i.e., within the same time interval) transmission of information over a number of distinct paths is called parallel transmission of information. A collection of bits of information which, taken as a whole, is considered a new unit, a character, or word, is always interpreted, i.e., given meaning, in the context of its environment. The environment provided by an instruction port, for example, attaches different meaning to a 4-bit word than the same word would have if placed on input lines to a data input port. The meaning of any given bits of stored information is always determined by the use that is made of this information.

CHARACTERISTICS

Several contrasting characteristics of hardware and software may be mentioned. Ease of alteration of an algorithm vastly differs for the two. A change of arbitrary magnitude can normally be made in an existing software algorithm, whereas the possibility of changing an existing hardware algorithmic processor is almost nil. The manner of implementation of the two types often differs; the hardware process is a continuous one-step parallel execution, while the software process is more likely to consist of a series of discrete serial execution steps. An example is found in the multiplication of two binary numbers. This multiplication can be performed in one step in a hardware multiplier with no intermediate states appearing, whereas a software multiplication algorithm that uses hardware adders consists of several separate steps, each producing an intermediate result.

Partly as a consequence of this, a hardware process is normally much faster than a software process. A very dynamic economic relationship between hardware implementation and software implementation has come about due to the rapid technological change occurring in the field. A blend of hardware and software that is now commonly called "firmware" has resulted in changes in architecture within only the last few years. A descendant of such forms as punched paper tape and cards, firmware consists of storing software algorithms in fast access, relatively permanent hardware (integrated circuit storage devices). Both permanent nonerasable firmware in the form of Read Only Memory (ROM) and semipermanent but specially re-PROgrammable Memory (PROM) now exist. The forms offer ease of design and flexibility over a wide range of speeds. Used in microprogramming applications, they allow custom system implementation by using standard universal hardware devices combined with special-purpose software algorithms. Although advances in computer-aided design techniques will probably lead to fully hardware implementation of custom microprocessors, the immediate future belongs to the universal processor—implemented in hardware and combined with special software. This book attempts to present, in a realistic and understandable manner, the ways in which such processors are used.

The field of digital design is demanding in that successful design requires a simultaneous view both of the forest, i.e., the whole of available technology today and in the near future, and the trees, i.e., detailed understanding of the specific hardware devices and software techniques available today. We attempt to maintain this perspective and to remember, too, that the forest is growing and changing many of its characteristics as we work our way through it. Jumping from tree to tree requires above all a sense of timing, and a primary goal of this book is the development of just this sense. If by working through the concepts and the problems presented here the reader sharpens his sense of timing, it will stand him in good stead, regardless of the direction technology may take several years hence.

The hardware/software duality applies only to digital systems. The connection between hardware and software is discussed in Chapter 9. The transformation from analog building blocks to digital building blocks is developed in the following section.

ANALOG BUILDING BLOCK TO DIGITAL BUILDING BLOCK TRANSFORMATIONS

The analog building blocks, i.e., resistors, capacitors, inductors, and transistor devices, require mathematical treatment of necessity. Exponential rise and decay curves and derivatives or rates of change are expressed poorly in words, and any serious attempt to design analog circuitry without the use of equations would severely restrict the complexity obtainable. (See Fig. 1-1.) The current and voltage relations so easily mapped onto the mathematical framework of the calculus resist description in natural languages such as English.

The digital integrated circuit building blocks, on the other hand, are not susceptible to easy description in terms of calculus. Semimatrix methods, such as Karnaugh maps and Quine-McCluskey techniques, are quite successful in combinational logic design; however, their useful range of applications is extremely limited. Once complex time relationships enter the picture, they become worthless rapidly. State transition diagrams are excellent tools for system analysis, but in terms of digital building block design they leave much to be desired. The classical techniques have been designed to minimize the number of gates. The cost of gates is now so small, and still falling, that there remains little relevancy in this goal. In most cases, the pin count or package count is a more realistic parameter. (See Figures 1-2 through 1-5 for examples.)

To summarize, there is no known technique based on mathematics that is of much value to the designer of systems based on digital integrated circuits. Having worked as a mathematical physicist for a decade, the author realizes that the preceding statement may drive away some readers who feel that anything not basically mathematical cannot be worth much. There is a tendency sometimes among those who appreciate the beauty and power of unambiguous mathematical statement to lose sight of some of the limitations inherent in the use of mathematical language as opposed to a natural language. In many fields, the mathematics becomes so abstruse that diagrammatic techniques are employed as aids to intuitive analysis. This has long been the case in chemistry and in electrical engineering, and more recently in the Feynmann and Goldstone diagrams of theoretical physics. The use of logic circuit diagrams combined with natural language descriptions is largely sufficient for digital system design. The more powerful semimathematical techniques will almost surely evolve on the computer-aided design systems now in use in several companies and universities. This book assumes that the average reader does not have access to these powerful, but unfinished, systems. It is even hoped that this book may contribute to the development of such.

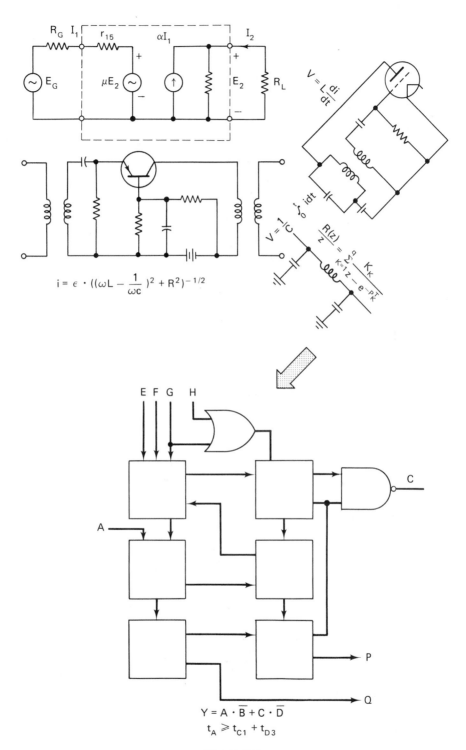

$$i = \epsilon \cdot \left(\left(\omega L - \frac{1}{\omega c}\right)^2 + R^2\right)^{-1/2}$$

$$V = L\frac{di}{dt}$$

$$V = \frac{1}{C}\int_0^t i\,dt$$

$$\frac{R(z)}{z} = \sum_{K=1}^a \frac{K_K}{z - e^{-p_K}}$$

$$Y = A \cdot \overline{B} + C \cdot \overline{D}$$
$$t_A \geqslant t_{C1} + t_{D3}$$

Figure 1-1

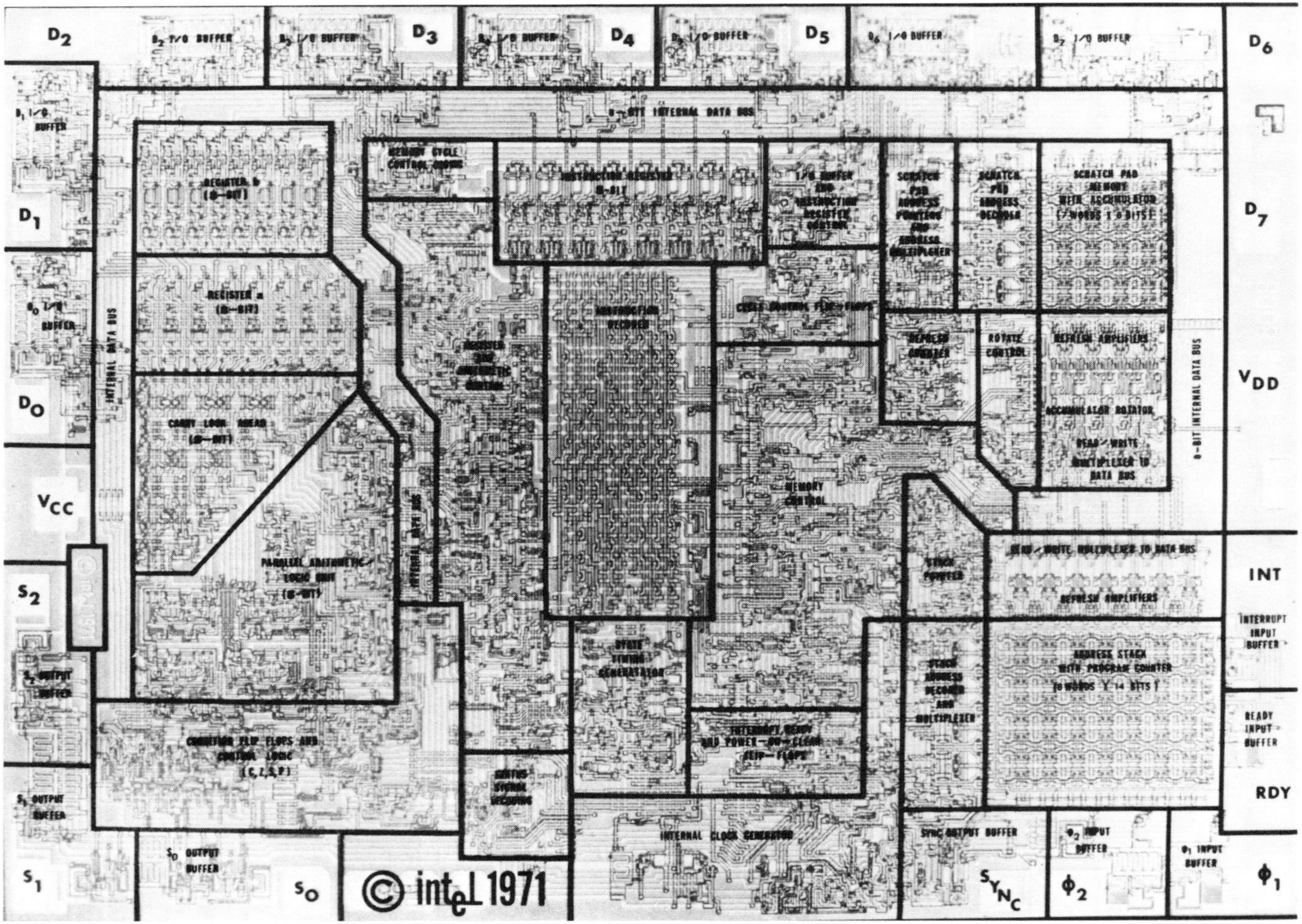

Figure 1-2 Design Prototype of Intel 8008 (Photo courtesy of Intel Corp.)

Figure 1-3 Design Prototype of Intel 8080 (Photo courtesy of Intel Corp.)

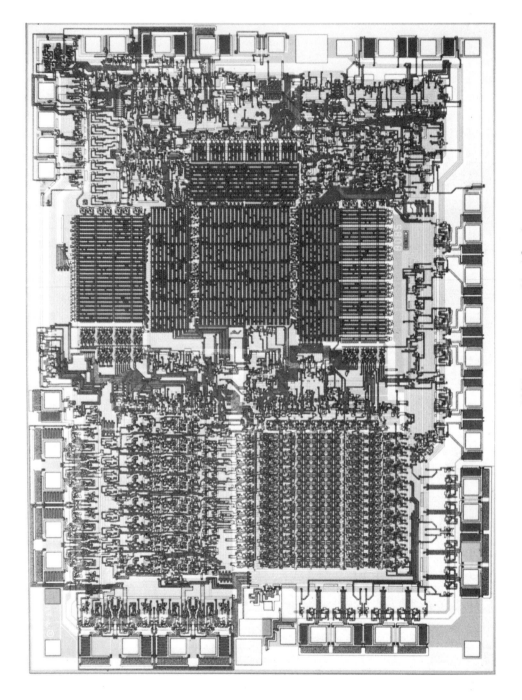

Figure 1-4   *Design Prototype of Intel 8085 (Photo courtesy of Intel Corp.)*

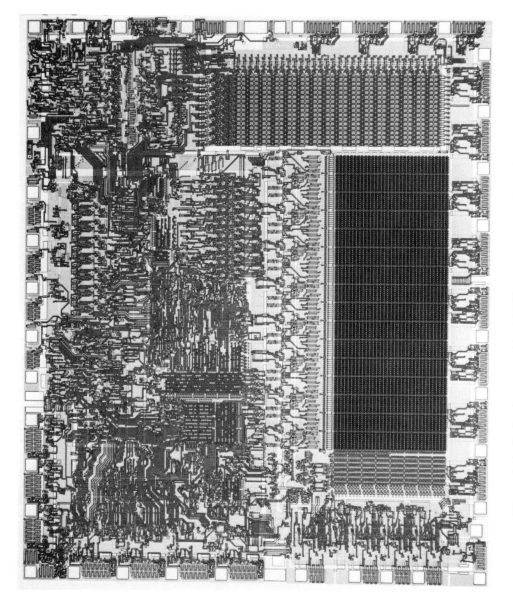

Figure 1-5 Design Prototype of Intel 8748 (Photo courtesy of Intel Corp.)

The primary transformation has been a topological one on the elements with which systems are built. The older building blocks—the resistors, capacitors, inductors, and nonlinear active devices—obeyed complex equations. For example, the voltage across an element may be described by:

1. A linear relation $\qquad e = iR \qquad\qquad$ resistor

2. An integral $\qquad\qquad e = \dfrac{1}{C} \int i\, dt \quad$ capacitor

3. A derivative $\qquad\quad e = L\dfrac{di}{dt} \qquad\quad$ inductor

4. A nonlinear function $\quad e = f(i) \qquad\qquad$ transistor

The consequence of these relations is that a designer who wishes to connect these basic elements together must deal with integro-differential equations, a nontrivial process. In place of these elements, the topologically transformed integrated circuits can be connected to each other and the states of interest are described by Boolean algebra and binary arithmetic. The time-dependence relations are normally simple inequalities. The relevance of this to the designer's task is great. In contrast to the effort required to build working analog systems, digital design is play.

SUMMARY

The intent of this chapter has been to develop an overview of microprocessor systems design. This was begun by describing the essential functions of processors. The essential function of a processor in any application is to improve the efficiency of a process. The range of applications is limitless and is determined, in most cases, solely by economic factors. The plummeting prices of microprocessors are resulting in exploding markets for these devices. Microprocessors were invented in 1971 by Intel Corporation.* Second-generation devices were introduced in late 1973, and third-generation processors in late 1975. The availability of a variety of processors and the "second sourcing" of the most popular processors generated competitive pressures that caused prices to fall from $360 per device at the beginning of 1975 to less than $30 at the end of 1975. By the beginning of America's 200th birthday, the price of the most basic machines had dropped to less than $10.

It is difficult to discuss the implications of this technology since there are no precedents from which we can draw analogies. One viewpoint holds that microprocessors are "just small computers" and will not affect mankind greatly. The counter argument states that changes in scale of several orders of magnitude are

---

*Several other companies developed microprocessors inhouse, including Honeywell and Collins Radio; however, these devices were never available on the open market.

radical and generally alter the very nature of a system. Some intuitive feel for this point of view may be obtained by contemplating the effect of a scale change in human size, either 1000 times larger or 1000 times smaller! Microprocessors represent scale changes of several orders of magnitude in size, cost, and power consumption. The extrapolated effect of these scale changes points to this conclusion:

Microprocessor technology is developing toward the point where it will be economically feasible to design "intelligence" into the environment at any desirable point.

If we take as a meaningful distinction between animal and human the *storage* of *symbolic* information in the environment, it is interesting to speculate upon the implication of *processing symbolic* information in the environment. Such speculation leads far beyond the scope of a design text, so we will only present —not pursue—this line of thought.

As a conservative statement we can say that the designer of digital systems has capabilities today that were seen before only in science fiction. Today one person working alone can design and build in a workshop a computer that far surpasses those available anywhere only a dozen or so years ago. The intent of this book is to present all of the information presently needed to use these wondrous tools.

2 *information devices*

INTRODUCTION

The transformation from analog building blocks to digital devices radically alters design techniques by simplifying the relations that describe the interconnections between devices. These devices must be fabricated by using analog elements: resistance, capacitance, and inductance. In practice, however, only resistance and capacitance are employed in integrated circuits. The development of digital devices from analog components is treated in the first part of this chapter, and a brief introduction to the properties of these basic devices, called *logic gates*, is presented. Circuits that consist of several gates are termed Small-Scale Integrated circuits (SSI). More complex arrangements of gates into digital subsystems are termed Medium-Scale Integrated (MSI) circuits. The chapter ends with a descriptive summary of available MSI building blocks.

BINARY DEVICES FROM ANALOG COMPONENTS

The resistance to the flow of current in a medium is a parameter of central importance in most electrical circuitry. One of the first practical uses of variable resistance was Alexander Graham Bell's microphone; the variations in air pressure compacted the carbon grains and changed the resistance in such a way that the varying electrical current through the carbon reproduced the pressure variations. The relation that describes the dependence of current on resistance is Ohm's law, $V = IR$, where V represents voltage, and I and R represent current and resistance, respectively. If the resistance R is replaced by two discrete resistors R_1 and R_2 in series, then we may write:

$$V = IR = I(R_1 + R_2) = IR_1 + IR_2 = V_1 + V_2$$

When the voltage across the pair is constant and one resistance changes, then each voltage drop must change in such a manner that the drop across the pair is constant. This is shown diagrammatically in Fig. 2-1.

In order to obtain some feel for the variation of V_{out} with resistance we examine a few cases. The case where $R_1 = R_2$ results in the trivial case $V_{out} = \frac{1}{2}V$.

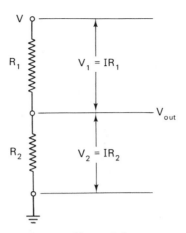

Figure 2-1

A more interesting case obtains when $R_1 = 99R_2$ in which case $V = I(R_1 + R_2)$ $= I(100R_2)$ and, therefore, $I = V/100R_2$. Thus, the voltage drop across R_2 is given by $IR_2 = (V/100R_2) \cdot R_2 = 0.01$ V. If we let $R_2 = 99R_1$, we obtain the voltage across R_2 equal to 0.99 V. Thus, by holding the resistance R_1 constant and varying R_2 over four orders of magnitude, we can vary the output voltage from 1% to 99% of the impressed voltage. Much of the field of linear electronics is concerned with the use of small voltages to vary resistance such that large changes occur at the output. This is the means by which amplification of signals is achieved. In digital electronics we are less concerned with behavior over the entire range of voltages and, instead, concentrate on the fact that the output may be made approximately equal to the impressed voltage V, or to ground. The first case is described by saying the output is HIGH and the second by saying it is LOW or in the LOW state. Alternate terminology includes ON/OFF, TRUE/FALSE, 1/0, and others.

Due to the existence of excellent texts on the solid-state physics underlying the electrical processes with which we are concerned, we offer only a brief statement of the device physics. Methods of inserting foreign atoms into a crystalline lattice to alter the energy band structure have been perfected such that the application of control voltages to the crystal can bend these bands. The resistance to current flow through the lattice is strongly a function of these energy bands; therefore, altering the band structure effectively alters the resistance. Since the silicon crystal is overlaid with a metal oxide layer, the device is referred to as a Metal Oxide Semiconductor (MOS) device. The change in resistance derives from the application of an electrical field to this metal oxide "gate," and thus the MOS Field Effect Transistor (MOSFET) gates current as a function of applied field. Descriptive terminology is used with MOSFETs: the "gate" controls the flow of current between the "source" and the "drain." The physical structure and the diagrammatic representation are shown in Fig. 2-2.

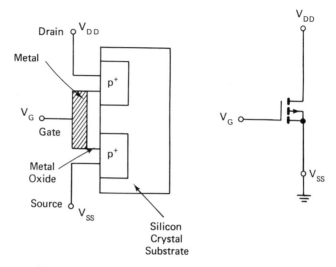

Figure 2-2

Since we prefer to think of the MOSFET as a variable resistance controlled by the gate voltage, we may replace the variable resistance of the resistor pair by the MOSFET and obtain the circuit shown in Fig. 2-3. By observing that the resistance of the MOSFET is a function of the gate voltage, we conclude that any resistance (within the MOSFET range) can be achieved by the application of the proper gate voltage to a MOSFET. Thus, the fixed load resistor represented by the conventional resistor, R, can be replaced by a MOSFET, as shown in Fig. 2-3. So we have a resistor pair formed by MOSFETs, in which the top, or load resistor is fixed by application of a constant gate voltage, and the bottom,

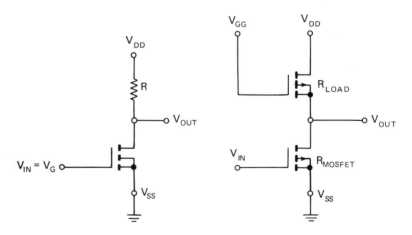

Figure 2-3

or variable resistor is controlled by a variable gate voltage. By restricting the values of V_{in} to those that cause the resistance R_{MOSFET} to satisfy one of the following conditions

$$R_{MOSFET} > 9R_{LOAD}$$

or

$$R_{MOSFET} < (1/9)R_{LOAD}$$

we obtain output voltages, V_{out}, either greater than $0.9\,V_{DD}$ or less than $0.1\,V_{DD}$, respectively. We ignore the transitions between these regions for now. The outputs will be characterized as HIGH ($V_{out} > 0.9\,V_{DD}$) or LOW ($V_{out} < 0.1\,V_{DD}$), and the device shown in Fig. 2-3 will be the basic element in MOS circuitry. In Large-Scale Integrated (LSI) circuits, thousands of similar devices are fabricated on a single (monolithic) silicon crystal. The LSI technology that used P-channel MOS made possible the first monolithic Central Processor Unit (CPU), the subject of this book. The relations between the input signals and the output voltages have logical analogs, as may be seen from the following analysis. Since the devices are to be implemented on a single crystal, we explicitly show the common substrate as in Fig. 2-4. The operation of the circuit is such that a LOW input voltage will produce a HIGH output, while a HIGH input will produce a LOW output. The inverse character of this physical device has a logical analog in the NOT function, i.e., the logical description of this relation is OUTPUT = NOT (INPUT).

While the logical function is insufficient to perform a variety of logical operations, we can extend the usefulness of MOSFET devices by considering the action of *two* variable resistances, R_a and R_b, in series. Since the only conditions of interest are very high resistance and very low resistance (relative to load resistance), we see that the sum of the two is low, relative to the load, only when R_a AND R_b are in the low-resistance state. By using two MOSFETs in series with a load MOSFET as shown in Fig. 2-5, an output voltage is obtained that is LOW

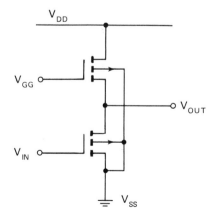

Figure 2-4

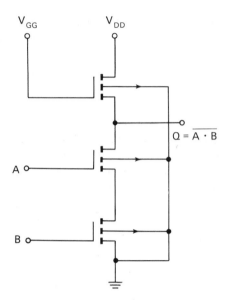

Figure 2-5

only when input voltage V_a AND V_b are HIGH. Since the inversion remains, the logical equation describing this relation is $V_{out} =$ NOT $(V_a$ AND $V_b)$.

This condition is so common that it has been renamed the NAND function, a contraction of NOT-AND. The standard logic notation in electronics uses a bar above a symbol for negation, a plus sign ($+$) for logical OR, and a dot ($\cdot$) for logical AND. In this notation, OUT $= \overline{A \cdot B}$ where the cumbersome Vs have been dropped since we are interested in logical relations first and voltages only secondarily. Figure 2-5 represents the physical device that accomplishes this function and shows the common substrate lines explicitly. Since we are concerned solely with MOSFETs on a common substrate, the substrate lines are redundant and are omitted. The last two figures are reproduced in Fig. 2-6 without these substrate lines. Each electrical diagram is accompanied by its logic equivalent diagram.

The ability to implement the logical OR circuitry by placing two MOSFETs in parallel follows from the previous discussion. The actual implementation is in the inverted, or NOR, form for the same reason that the NAND is implemented. By feeding the output voltage into an inverter, the AND and OR can be achieved, but the cost of doing this, i.e., the extra inverter, is not justified.

Having derived the electronic circuits needed to implement logical functions, we now discuss briefly the algebra of these functions: Boolean algebra. The reader has probably been exposed to a course in Set Theory in which Venn diagrams and the terms *union* and *intersection* were employed. Rather than use these diagram-oriented terms, we prefer the signal-oriented AND and OR

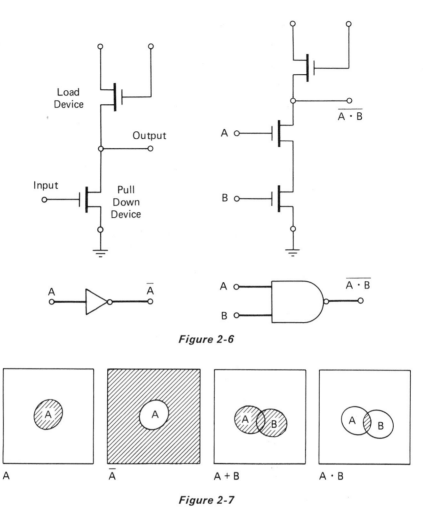

Figure 2-6

Figure 2-7

terminology. The term *intersection* will be replaced by AND and the term *union* by OR. The NOT function is the complement.

The standard Venn diagrams are shown in Fig. 2-7 with the logic notations used in electronics. The basic postulates of our algebra are:

Basic Postulates

1. If the subset A is contained in a universe U, and the subset B is contained in U, then A AND B ($A \cdot B$) is contained in U.

2. If the subset A is contained in U, and the subset B is contained in U, then A OR B ($A + B$) is contained in U.

3. There is an element "0" such that $A + 0 = A$ for every element A contained in U.

4. There is an element "1" such that $A \cdot 1 = A$ for every element A contained in U.

5. Assume A, B, C are always in U.
   a. $A + (B + C) = (B + A) + C = (A + C) + B =$ etc.
   b. $(A \cdot B) \cdot C = A \cdot (B \cdot C) =$ etc.
   c. $A + (B \cdot C) = (A + B) \cdot (A + C)$ left distributivity with respect to $+$
   d. $A \cdot (B + C) = (A \cdot B) + (A \cdot C)$ left distributivity with respect to $\cdot$

6. If "0" and "1" are unique, then for every element A there is an element $\bar{A}$ such that $A \cdot \bar{A} = 0$ and $A + \bar{A} = 1$.

7. A, B, and C are such that $A \neq B \neq C$.

Given these postulates, the theorems that emerge are:

Theorems

1a. $A + A = A$
1b. $A \cdot A = A$

2a. $A + 1 = 1$
2b. $A \cdot 0 = 0$

3a. $A + 0 = A$
3b. $A \cdot 1 = A$

4a. $\overline{(A)} = \bar{A}$
4b. $\overline{(\bar{A})} = A$

5a. $A + \bar{A} = 1$
5b. $A \cdot \bar{A} = 0$

6a. $\overline{A + B + C + \cdots} = \bar{A} \cdot \bar{B} \cdot \bar{C} \cdots$
6b. $\overline{A \cdot B \cdot C \cdots} = \bar{A} + \bar{B} + \bar{C} + \cdots$ De Morgan's theorem

7a. $A \cdot (A + B) = A + A \cdot B = A$
7b. $A + (A \cdot B) = A \cdot (A + B) = A$

The postulates indicated with an "a" are the duals of the postulates indicated with a "b". Duality in this case is defined as the interchange of all AND and OR signs and of all "1"s and "0"s. If a Boolean equation is true, then its dual is true.

Example: Prove by two different methods that $A \cdot (\bar{A} + B) = A \cdot B$.

Method 1. Venn Diagram

Method 2. Postulates

$$A \cdot (\bar{A} + B) = A \cdot \bar{A} + A \cdot B$$

$$A \cdot \bar{A} = 0 \text{ by Postulate 6}$$

Therefore, $A \cdot (A + B) = A \cdot B$

If the only applications of computers were to solve problems in pure logic and to obtain answers of the type "True" or "False," then the theorems just given would be sufficient for the design of systems. However, we know that many,

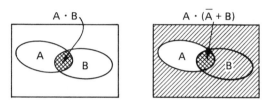

Figure 2-8

if not most, problems to which computers are applied are of a mathematical nature and, therefore, we investigate the nature of a base-two, or binary number system and think in terms of the allowed states of the system, "1" and "0". This will be a positional number system similar to the decimal number system in that the position of an integer refers to the power of the base used as a multiplier of that digit; for example, the decimal number 987.32 can be considered a shorthand notation for:

$$(9 \times 100) + (8 \times 10) + (7 \times 1) + (3 \times 0.1) + (2 \times 0.01)$$

or $\quad (9 \times 10^2) + (8 \times 10^1) + (7 \times 10^0) + (3 \times 10^{-1}) + (2 \times 10^{-2})$

In the last notation the numbers 9, 8, 7, 3, and 2 are coefficients, and the number 10 is the base (or radix) of the decimal system. The exponent simply indicates the power of the radix associated with the position. In general, any number can be represented by the expression

$$\sum_{j=m}^{j=n} a_j x^j$$

where m and n are limits on the powers involved. The basis of automatic computation is generally the binary number system for reasons that are discussed later in this chapter. In this base the coefficients are simply one and zero. An example of a number expressed in the base two number system can be easily obtained by first expressing the number using the powers formulation. For any number, say, 28, we may write:

$$1 \times 2^4 + 1 \times 2^3 + 1 \times 2^2 + 0 \times 2^1 + 0 \times 2^0 = 28$$

$$16 \qquad 8 \qquad 4 \qquad 2 \qquad 1$$

Therefore, the expression in binary is $(11100)_2 = (28)_{10}$. The natural progression of this number system is shown is this table:

Decimal	Binary	Hexadecimal
0	00000	0
1	00001	1
2	00010	2
3	00011	3
4	00100	4
5	00101	5
6	00110	6
7	00111	7
8	01000	8
9	01001	9
10	01010	A
11	01011	B
12	01100	C
13	01101	D
14	01110	E
15	01111	F
16	10000	10
17	10001	11
.	.	.
.	.	.
.	.	.

For generality, the hexadecimal number system (base 16) is included because it is widely used as a more convenient number system for humans who have to work with the binary system due to the fact that each hexadecimal number can replace, or be replaced by, a unique binary number composed of four bits. Thus, the binary number 1110011001110001 may be rewritten 1110 0110 0111 0001, and then rewritten by inspection of the previous table as E671. This is easier to write and speak of than the binary form.

The rules for addition of binary numbers are extremely simple and are best presented by displaying all possible combinations. The arithmetic rules and examples are:

Rule 1. Binary ADDITION

$$0 + 0 = 0$$

$$0 + 1 = 1$$

$$1 + 0 = 1$$

$1 + 1 = 0$ plus a carry of 1 to the next higher column

$1 + 1 + 1 = 1$ plus a carry of 1 to the next higher column

Example: Binary   Decimal

$$
\begin{array}{rr}
01101 & 13 \\
+01010 & +10 \\
\hline
10111 & 23 \\
\end{array}
$$

Rule 2.   Binary SUBTRACTION

$$0 - 0 = 0$$
$$1 - 0 = 1$$
$$1 - 1 = 0$$
$$0 - 1 = 1 \text{ with a borrow of 1 from the next higher column}$$

Example: Binary   Decimal

$$
\begin{array}{rr}
01110 & 14 \\
-01011 & -11 \\
\hline
00011 & 3 \\
\end{array}
$$

Rule 3.   Binary MULTIPLICATION

$$1 \times 1 = 1$$
$$1 \times 0 = 0$$
$$0 \times 0 = 0$$
$$0 \times 1 = 0$$

Example: Binary   Decimal

$$
\begin{array}{rr}
01101 & 13 \\
\times 01001 & \times \ \ 9 \\
\hline
01101 & 117 \\
\end{array}
$$

$$
\begin{array}{l}
01101 \\
00000 \\
\hline
001101 \\
00000 \\
\hline
0001101 \\
01101 \\
\hline
01110101 \\
00000 \\
\hline
001110101 \\
\end{array}
$$

Note: Whenever a zero appears in the multiplier, no addition is required, only a left shift.

64 32 16 4 1 $= 117$

Example: Using shift method of multiplication:

$$
\begin{array}{l}
01101 \\
\times 01001 \\
\hline
01101 \\
01101SS \\
\hline
01110101 = 117 \\
\end{array}
$$

(S) $=$ left shift

Rule 4. Binary DIVISION

$0/1 = 0$

$1/1 = 1$

$1/0$ is undefined

$0/0$ is undefined

Rule 5. Binary-to-Decimal conversion: Simply add the decimal weight of each binary digit.

Rule 6. Decimal-to-Binary conversion: Divide by two and *list* the remainders as the binary number.

Example: Convert $(125)_{10}$ to $(X)_2$

$125/2 = 62 + 1$

$62/2 = 31 + 0$

$31/2 = 15 + 1$

$15/2 = 7 + 1$

$7/2 = 3 + 1$

$3/2 = 1 + 1$

$1/2 = 0 + 1$ Note that remainders are listed in reverse order.

$(125)_{10} = (1111101)_2$

Definition 1: The ONE's COMPLEMENT of a binary number is obtained by changing all 1s to 0s and all 0s to 1s.

Example: The one's complement of 110111 is 001000.

Definition 2: The TWO's COMPLEMENT (or true complement) of a binary number is obtained by adding one to the least significant digit (LSD) of the one's complement.

Example: Two's complement of $110111 = 001000 + 000001$

$= 001001$

The principal use of the complement of a number is to perform either subtraction or division by the process of addition. To perform subtraction, the subtrahend is put in its two's complement form and the minuend and (complement) subtrahend are added. The result of this addition turns out to be the difference of the two numbers, i.e., a subtraction results. The significance of this is that complements of binary numbers are very easily obtained with the inverter circuitry we have seen, and the use the of these complements allows us to build circuitry that will ADD, SUBTRACT, MULTIPLY, and DIVIDE by the simple process of addition! Thus, we need only figure out a circuit that will perform binary addition.

Example: Subtract 10 from 16 (using eight-bit words)

$$
\begin{array}{rl}
16 & 00010000 \\
-10 & -00001010 \\
\hline
6 &
\end{array}
\Longrightarrow
\begin{array}{l}
00010000 \longleftarrow 16 \\
+11110110 \longleftarrow \text{two's complement of 10} \\
\hline
1)00000110
\end{array}
$$

Carry bit is ignored; it indicates that subtraction was performed. Note that the answer is an 8-bit word.

The preceding review of binary arithmetic is intended as a refresher. Should the reader require more detail, there are a number of introductions to binary arithmetic to fill this need.

The reasons for going to binary systems are varied, but the most immediately obvious gain is a relaxation in the output requirements of a binary circuit as compared to an analog circuit. The information in the analog circuit is given by the magnitude of the voltage (or current), and any variation from the desired value—no matter how small—results in a loss of information. In a binary circuit there is only one bit of information, and this is determined according to which of two possible regions the binary output falls in.

Consider the problem of conveying a fixed amount of information, say 20 bits, by electronic signal. Each bit of information allows us to choose between two equally likely alternatives; therefore, 20 bits would represent one of 2^{20} or 1,048,576 possible alternatives. Thus, we could divide the range of an output signal into 2^{20} equal parts, and by determining in which part of this range the analog output occurs, we extract 20 bits of information.

For a range of 0 to 10 volts, the increments are 10 microvolts, and the design of a usable circuit with this accuracy over a realistic range of temperatures and noise environments is next to impossible, or at least prohibitively expensive. One alternative is to use 20 binary circuits, the output of each one carrying one bit of information. Although we are multiplying the number of circuits that we must use, we are greatly decreasing the cost of each circuit. By considering the case in which we desire 40 bits of information requiring 10-picovolt generating *and* detecting capability for analog circuitry versus 40 cheap, simple binary (ON/OFF) circuits, it becomes evident that the costs involved dictate that binary devices are superior to analog devices for handling large amounts of information. Figure 2-9 illustrates the information capabilities of an analog circuit and one binary circuit.

A glance at the figure shows that a noise voltage of one increment added to the output *at any level* would represent false information, whereas the only place this would occur in a binary device is within one increment of the threshold.

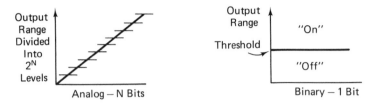

Figure 2-9

Added to any other value of the binary output, the noise would have no effect!

Even this critical region for binary circuits can be eliminated by establishing a "forbidden zone" separating the two regions and requiring that (except for times of transition) the output voltage always lie above (ON) or below (OFF) this zone. The zone is forbidden in the following sense. The manufacturer of the device guarantees that, if certain rather simple rules are followed in using the device, the ON voltage will never fall below a minimum value, and the OFF voltage will never rise above a certain value (in the absense of noise). Since most of the Medium-Scale Integrated circuits (MSI) that will be used (at this writing) to interface with MOS/LSI are bipolar devices known collectively as TTL (for transistor-transistor-logic), the voltage levels for this popular family of devices are shown in Fig. 2-10.

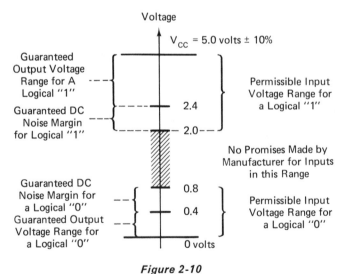

Figure 2-10

The simplest circuits with which we will be concerned are called "gates," known as AND gates, OR gates, NOR gates, and NAND gates. This terminology derives from the manner in which the devices are commonly used. The AND

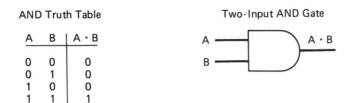

AND Truth Table

A	B	A · B
0	0	0
0	1	0
1	0	0
1	1	1

Two-Input AND Gate

Figure 2-11

gate is a circuit with N inputs and one output such that the output is HIGH only if all inputs are HIGH (i.e., input_1 AND input_2 AND input_3 AND . . .). Such a device is *defined* by the truth table shown in Fig. 2-11 and represented schematically. For simplicity, a two-input AND gate is shown.

The term "gate" is applied to the device because, as can be seen from the truth table, one input signal can be used to "gate" another signal through the device. Although the circuit is completely symmetrical, we will arbitrarily consider the A input to be the control signal, and the output will then be controlled by A. Consider B to represent a pulse string and A to be a much longer pulse. The output is shown in Fig. 2-12 as a function of the inputs.

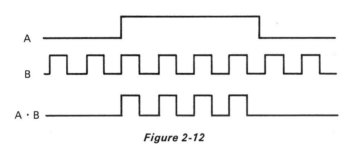

Figure 2-12

Another basic binary gate is the OR gate. This is a circuit with N inputs and one output such that the output is HIGH if *any one* of the input lines is HIGH (i.e., input_1 OR input_2 OR input_3 OR . . .). The defining truth table and the logic diagram are shown in Fig. 2-13. The response of this gate to the same string of pulses is shown in Fig. 2-14.

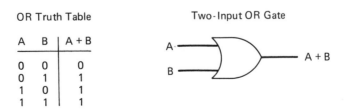

OR Truth Table

A	B	A + B
0	0	0
0	1	1
1	0	1
1	1	1

Two-Input OR Gate

Figure 2-13

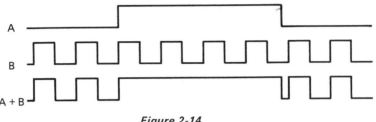

Figure 2-14

The simplest gate is the inverter, or NOT gate, defined by the truth table and shown schematically in Fig. 2-15. Inverters may be placed anywhere in a circuit as shown in Fig. 2-16.

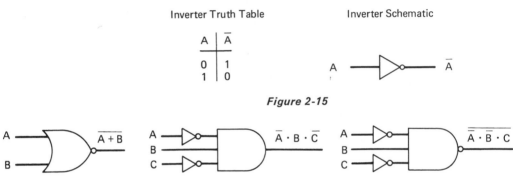

Figure 2-16

The device on the left represents an OR gate followed by an inverter and is known as a NOR gate. The other devices are two- and three-input AND and NAND gates, respectively, with inverters in several of the input lines. For reasons of economy and efficiency, the basic gates of the TTL family are NOT, NOR, and NAND gates. With very little practice it is as easy to think in terms of NOR and NAND as it is to think OR and AND; however, for reasons of simplicity, ORs and ANDs will be used in this book when desirable.

Yet another basic gate is the EXCLUSIVE-OR gate. The output of the EXCLUSIVE-OR (XOR) gate is LOW if both inputs are the same and HIGH if the inputs differ from each other. The defining truth table and schematic diagram are shown in Fig. 2-17. It is obvious from examination of the XOR truth table that the gate can be used as a comparator to test for equality, yielding a HIGH output if the inputs are unequal. The manner in which an XOR gate can be implemented from the previously introduced gates is shown in Fig. 2-18.

The comparison function is important in artithmetic and logic; however, the EXCLUSIVE-OR gate offers even more. In the following circuit we make the identification S = sum and C = carry. By examining all possible combina-

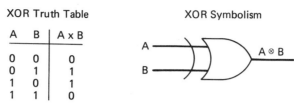

Figure 2-17

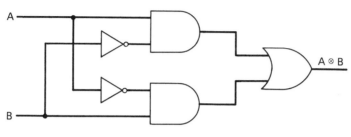

Figure 2-18

tions of inputs to the circuit, it is easily seen that the circuit adds the two inputs in that the proper sum and carry are generated. Such a circuit is called a half-adder and is usually shown as a block in the form shown on the right in Fig. 2-19.

The circuit is called a half-adder because it adds only first-order numbers. For addition of higher-order numbers there must be a provision for accepting and adding a carry that may result from addition of the previous order. By using two half-adders, as shown in Fig. 2-20, and comparing the results with the truth table, we see that we have designed a circuit that will yield the proper result in all additions. These can be combined in parallel to any order. Using

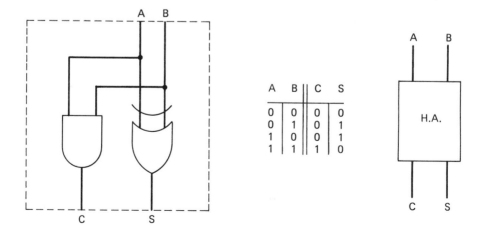

Figure 2-19

C$_{in}$	A	B	C$_{out}$	SUM
0	0	0	0	0
0	0	1	0	1
0	1	0	0	1
0	1	1	1	0
1	0	0	0	1
1	0	1	1	0
1	1	0	1	0
1	1	1	1	1

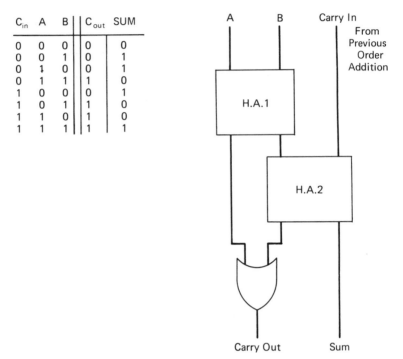

Figure 2-20

this circuit and our earlier result that subtraction, multiplication, and division can be achieved through inversion and addition, we see that we already possess the basic circuitry to perform binary arithmetic!

While on the topic of simple gates, notice that De Morgan's theorem says that a NOR function can be implemented with ANDs and NOTs—that is, only two basic functions are necessary for any logic implementation, either AND-NOT or OR-NOT. This is shown in Fig. 2-21.

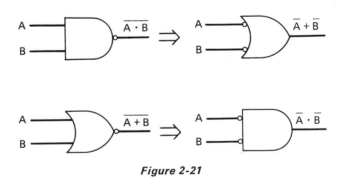

Figure 2-21

The actual hardware at the gate level is called Small-Scale Integration (SSI). Almost all imaginable two-, three-, and four-input functions are available at a cost of approximately 10 cents per gate. With higher-scale integration, the cost drops to a fraction of a cent per gate; however, the individual gates are no longer available at this level, but are dedicated to a certain function within a device. The basic members of the 7400 TTL family are shown in Fig. 2-22.

As can be seen by considering all four input cases, the circuit shown in Fig. 2-23 is an EXCLUSIVE OR formed from NAND gates.

By means of such examples, it can be shown that either the NAND or the NOR function can serve as the basis for Boolean algebra in that all other functions can be generated by using NANDs or NORs alone. This can be shown

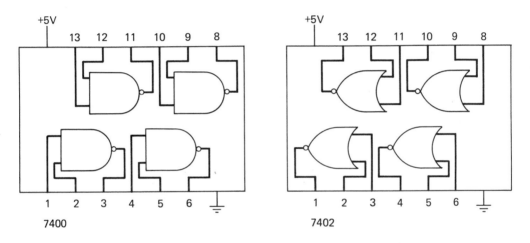

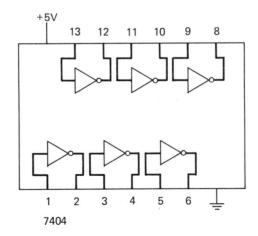

Figure 2-22

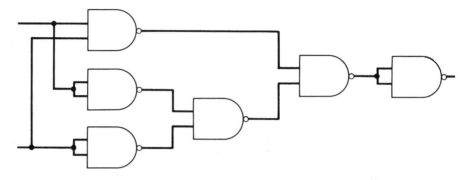

Figure 2-23

analytically by considering the NAND function defined as $f(a, b) = \overline{a \cdot b}$; then:

$$\bar{a} = f(a, a)$$
$$a \cdot b = f(f(a, b), f(a, b))$$
$$a + b = f(f(a, a), f(b, b))$$

This result was pointed out by H. M. Scheffer in 1913.

The conversion from Boolean algebra to logic circuitry is so straightforward that we can question the utility of even bothering with Boolean theorems. Consider the equation

$$y = \bar{A} \cdot \bar{B} \cdot (\overline{C + D}) + (\overline{A + B})$$

that is implemented in Fig. 2-24. There are four input variables and one result or output line. It is not immediately obvious from an examination of the circuit

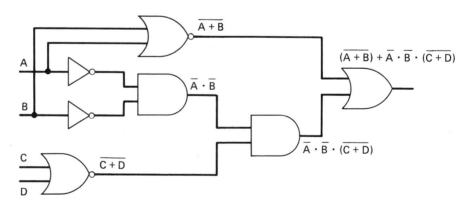

Figure 2-24

whether this might have been accomplished more simply. By studying the logic equation in the light of our Boolean theorems, we may proceed as follows:

$$y = \bar{A} \cdot \bar{B} \cdot (\overline{C + D}) + (\overline{A + B})$$
$$= (\overline{A + B}) \cdot (\overline{C + D}) + (\overline{A + B}) \qquad \text{by applying Theorem 6a.}$$
$$= \overline{A + B} \qquad\qquad\qquad\qquad \text{by applying Theorem 7a.}$$

Thus a simpler, less costly way to obtain the same output would be to NOR A and B because the output is independent of C and D.

For combinational logic circuits of this sort, techniques have been developed to "automate" the reduction of logic expressions; however, most of the building blocks available today do not lend themselves to these methods. In fact, the manufacturers of these devices have already put much work into this area of automated simplification. Thus the methods are either the tools of the past or the wave of the future, but, having little relevance to systems design with MSI and microprocessors, they will not be covered in this book.

As a final example of the use of discrete gates we treat the following simple problem:

> *I will go to the movies if there is a good movie showing and the car will start, or if the TV is broken and it is not raining. Design a circuit that will give me the answer as to whether I go to the movies when I input the appropriate conditions.*

We can put the problem in Boolean form:

$$F(A, B, C, D) = (A \cdot B) + (C \cdot D)$$

$A =$ good movie showing
$B =$ car will start
$C =$ TV is broken
$D =$ not raining

from which we see the circuit in Fig. 2-25. By placing switches at *A, B, C,* and *D,* and a display light at the output, we easily obtain answers to the problems

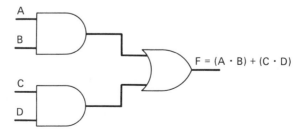

Figure 2-25

of the form:

F(YES, NO, NO, YES).

We will get into more sophisticated and more realistic design problems rather quickly, but there are several other general concepts we must consider first. The basic problem of storage of information is treated in Chapter 3.

The concluding paragraphs of this chapter consist of very brief natural language descriptions of classes and types of building blocks that are available, most of which cost from $1 to $10, and none of which costs more than $50.

PURELY DIGITAL BUILDING BLOCKS

The simplest blocks available today are those that perform logical operations such as AND, NAND, OR, NOR, and EXCLUSIVE OR on from two to twelve 1-bit binary words. There are blocks that ADD binary coded words of various lengths to produce a binary coded sum word, and blocks that count binary pulses appearing at an input to produce a binary coded sum at an output port. There are divide-by-N pulse devices that produce one output pulse for every N input pulses.

Comparator blocks compare the magnitudes of two binary coded words present at two input ports and produce an output at a third port that either signals equality or specifies the relative order of their magnitudes. Multiplier blocks multiply two binary numbers and add a third number to produce a binary arithmetic result.

There are building blocks that decode a binary instruction word n bits long to select one of 2^n output lines and similar functional blocks capable of sampling any one of 2^n input lines. Latching blocks capture and store n-bit long words for use at a later time. Serial storage registers capture serial bit streams and store these in the form of a recirculating loop. There are blocks that receive n-bit serial words on an input line and present the same word in parallel forms on n outputs, or the same word serially on an output line. Also available are building blocks that combine both of the above operations. There are priority encoder blocks that determine the highest priority signal present in any combination of signals on 2^n input lines and output an n-bit binary coded word identifying this line. An increasing number of blocks of all types are characterized as tri-state devices having, in addition to the normal binary ON/OFF states, a third, "disappearing," state in which the device effectively becomes invisible to the rest of the system.

There are blocks capable of transforming each of 2^n n-bit words into an m-bit word, where m is any integer, and blocks that store up to 16,384 bits of information with the capability of randomly accessing any one of these bits in one cycle of time. Many of the various devices can be grouped in a manner to extend either the number of words under consideration or the length of the words, or both.

Some blocks emit a number of pulses determined by an input word, while others either generate a parity bit for transmission or check the parity of words being received. Some storage registers can increment or decrement their contents according to a control instruction applied at a control port, while content address-able memory blocks are capable of associatively retrieving information based upon certain characteristics of the information itself.

Multi-function blocks, such as arithmetic logic units and central processor units, are capable of receiving data words and instruction words that execute operations and output results.

Asynchronous Receiver/Transmitter blocks exist, which in the transmit mode, accept parallel words, append start, parity, and stop bits, and transmit serially to a similar block in another (asychnronous) system that is operating in the receive mode. The receiver detects the start bit, receives the serial word, checks the parity, looks for the stop bits, strips the appended bits, and outputs a word-received-indicator flag and the word itself in parallel form. Other intersystem blocks accept up to n m-bit words at one rate and transmit them at another rate. Pulse synchronizer blocks synchronize arbitrarily occurring pulses to a system clock or other sync command.

INTERFAMILY INTERFACE BLOCKS

There are families of building blocks defined by characteristics that are common to all members of the family and, therefore, allow direct interfacing between elements of the same family. There are also interfamily interface blocks whose inputs have the characteristics of one family and whose output characteristics match those of another family. The list of blocks in the popular families grows monthly and, in the most popular families, weekly.

SEMIDIGITAL BUILDING BLOCKS

In addition to the purely digital blocks that have been described, many semi-digital blocks are available. These include digital-to-time converters, digital-to-analog voltage converters, and analog-to-digital converters. They are compatible on one or more inputs or outputs commonly with some integrated circuit family of digital devices, while other inputs or outputs are analog-voltage compatible. These devices can readily be used to interface digital systems to the nondigital world.

A powerful example of such blocks is the digitally selected Light-Emitting Diode (LED) that displays by a pattern of lighted dots or bars either a numeric or an alphabetic character. The inverse type of block exists in the form of an array of photodiodes that output a binary one or zero, depending on the intensity of light on the appropriate diode. Still another such device is the self-scanning photo-array, which consists of many rows of elements that are scanned in a TV-like manner. The input is the light intensity, and the output is a series of charge pulses, the magnitude of which is proportional to the light intensity of the appropriate photodiode. The self-scanning array must be driven by clock pulses, and these clock inputs are compatible with the devices in the proper digital family. There exists, then, a variety of light-to-digital and digital-to-light transforming devices that can be considered as basic building blocks to be used by the designer.

Digital-to-analog voltage blocks map n-bit binary numbers present at digital inputs into the corresponding magnitude out of 2^n possible voltage levels. Analog-to-digital blocks, on the other hand, determine in which of 2^n voltage increments an input voltage falls, and output an n-bit binary word that contains this information.

Other blocks sense threshold crossings, changing their output from binary zero to binary one as the threshold is crossed. Zero-crossing detectors change state as an input voltage swings through zero volts. Some of the threshold detectors are instantaneous in that the output is at every moment indicative of the state of the input, whereas others sense the crossing and remember that it has occurred until commanded to forget by an "erase" instruction.

More sophisticated blocks measure an analog input voltage and output four Binary-Coded-Decimal (BCD) digits to drive display or other digital blocks. A digital compatible timer, capable of producing pulses from microseconds to hours duration, is an extremely versatile building block.

LINEAR BUILDING BLOCKS

Although this book is little concerned with such devices, there is an appreciable family of purely linear circuits. Some, quite useful for digital circuits, are precision voltage regulators that can serve to interface the digital building blocks to an unregulated power supply. Other linear devices, which are seldom used with digital systems, include power amplifiers, operational amplifiers, differential amplifiers, video amplifiers, and phase-locked loop building blocks. An FM detector and limiter block and a TV Chroma system consisting of three building blocks are also available, as well as a balanced Modulator-Demodulator, for use as a communication system building block. The family of linear building blocks is growing rapidly and a complete treatment is already beyond the scope of this text.

SUMMARY

The use of variable resistance elements in a voltage divider network provides the means of obtaining a two-state, or binary, circuit element. Although varieties of implementations are possible, the use of field effect transistors was considered for simplicity. Using these devices, several simple configurations were presented and output voltages were seen to be related to input voltages via the logical operators: NOT, AND, OR, etc. The logic gates were then combined to implement a *comparator* (EXCLUSIVE OR) and an ADDER. These basic circuits can be used to perform the Boolean algebraic and binary arithmetic operations required by digital computers. They can also be used to build more complex MSI components. Representative classes of MSI components were listed at the end of this chapter. These will be described in detail in Chapter 4.

Before leaving the discussion of basic gates, it should be emphasized that the logical interpretation of a gate function is left to the designer. In the "positive logic" convention, the 5-volt input is considered HIGH or TRUE, and zero-volt input is LOW or FALSE. In this case, the devices function as described in this chapter. If we assigned the opposite meaning to the zero and 5-volt signals, we would use De Morgan's theorem to find that the positive logic NAND gate becomes a negative logic OR gate, etc. Either assignment is valid as long as it is used consistently. Normally we will use the positive logic convention for simplicity.

3 *information storage devices*

The devices considered in Chapter 2 have been instantaneous in the sense that the output instantaneously follows the input.* It is highly desirable in many situations to be able to retain information that an *event* has occurred. A pulse counter that returned to its original state when the pulse went LOW would be of very little use. What is needed is a circuit that can be pushed from its original state into a second *stable* state, i.e., a bistable device that will remain in the second state after the triggering event has passed. Since we have seen that all combinational logic can be implemented by using only NAND gates, we attempt to build a storage device using only NANDs. The approach to be taken is that of coupling the devices in such a way that an input to one is "felt" by the others. This coupling is necessary, since a single NAND is unable to store information. The output of one NAND will be fed back to the input or inputs of other NANDs in the circuit. Having discussed the necessity of feedback, we now address the problem of the minimum number of NANDs required. Some problems are best solved by trial and error, and in this case intuition would suggest that bistable *may* imply symmetrical and, for the simplest possible combination of two NAND gates, the feedback of the output of each to an input of the other. This cross-coupled circuit is shown in Fig. 3-1. Assume that the bottom input is "1" and the output Q is "0." $\bar{Q}$ is "1" and if R is "1," the system is stable. If R is considered to be the controlling input, we ask what will happen when R goes LOW. According to the NAND truth table, Q will go HIGH, and this will force $\bar{Q}$ LOW. The fact that $\bar{Q}$ has gone LOW will not affect Q, which remains HIGH. This state is also stable. The interesting result is that when R returns to a HIGH state, the output Q is unaffected. Thus, the system as a whole stores the information that "R has gone to 0 at some time in the past." The complete symmetry, of course, allows the mirror image operation. Rather than hold the bottom input to "1," we can allow it to take any value S. The truth table for such a device, called an R-S flip-flop, is shown beside the circuit symbol in Fig. 3-2.

With an ingenious and unbelievably simple and economical circuit we have achieved information storage! The basic circuit is called a *latch* because the

---

*Actually, the propagation delays are major concerns in computer systems design but are not relevant to this discussion.

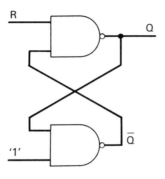

Figure 3-1

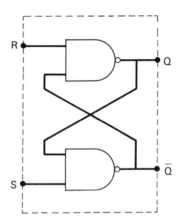

R	S	Q	$\overline{Q}$
0	0	Indeterminate	
0	1	1	0
1	0	0	1
1	1	No Change	

Figure 3-2

occurrence of certain changes at either input latches the circuit in a new state. Many more versatile circuits have been designed, but all share the basic latch behavior.

The latch adds a new dimension to our systems, that of *history*. Prior to its introduction, the output of any system formed with logic gates was dependent only on the inputs to the system at any given time. Now, circuits can be built whose output is a function of the inputs *and their history*. With this ability to "remember," a new problem becomes quite serious. In earlier discussions we have implicitly assumed that, like so many electrons, our basic elements were identical. The fact that manufactured devices are never identical means that some will change state more quickly than others and, therefore, unplanned-for *intermediate* states may occur. Previously, this was no problem because of the fleeting nature of such events; however, we now have the capability of storing the information that these (unwanted) states have produced. Thus, the problem of design becomes, in many cases, formidable.

This feature is characteristic of large combinational logic systems and is termed the *race* problem. Before treating this problem we wish to redefine our basic R-S flip-flop in terms of cross-coupled NOR gates as shown in Fig. 3-3. In the truth table, Q_n represents the state of the output of the flip-flop just before the inputs change, and Q_{n+1} represents the state of the output of the flip-flop that results from the input change. It can be seen that no change occurs when both inputs are LOW. A pulse on the SET input sets Q to the HIGH state, and a pulse on the RESET line resets Q to LOW. If both inputs are HIGH simultaneously, the last one removed determines the state of the device, essentially an indeterminate situation. We will arbitrarily consider this to be our standard R-S flip-flop rather than the NAND device shown earlier. This device will be used to illustrate variations on the theme.

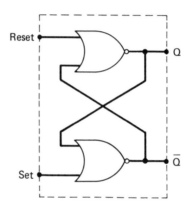

R	S	Q_n	Q_{n+1}
0	1	0	1
1	0	1	0
0	0	0	0
0	0	1	1

Figure 3-3

The race problem in combinational circuitry resulted from the fact that signals propagating through different levels of logic gates can differ from path to path by an amount sufficient to (momentarily) cause a false state to occur. Such a case is shown in exaggerated form in Fig. 3-4. If all of the devices in one path have appreciably shorter signal propagation delay times than those in another path, the false state is almost certain to occur and will be recorded. An obvious way to prevent this behavior is to lock the flip-flop out of the circuit until the maximum delay has occurred. One means of accomplishing this lockout is shown in Fig. 3-5 and is referred to as a clocked R-S flip-flop. The clocked R-S flip-flop will respond to either the SET or RESET lines going HIGH during the time when the clock pulse is HIGH.

This gating of signals through a circuit is an effective way of solving the race problem. Systems using this scheme divide the continuous time of purely combinational logic into discrete time intervals associated with clocked systems. The new type of circuit is called *sequential*, since the changes are sequenced

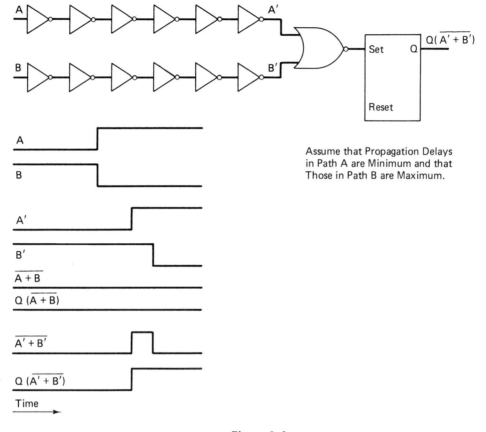

Assume that Propagation Delays
in Path A are Minimum and that
Those in Path B are Maximum.

Figure 3-4

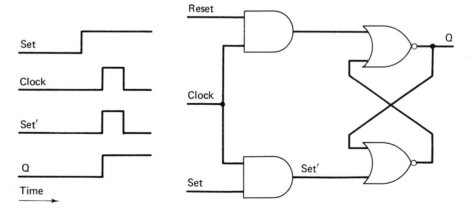

Figure 3-5

through the system rather than racing through it. A system with only one clock is called synchronous sequential. If there are several independent clocks, the system is called asynchronous sequential. The ability to handle information in a sequential circuit is a function of the clock frequency. High frequencies with narrow clock pulses are utilized to obtain the maximum information throughout. The highest permissible frequency is approximately the sum of the worst case propagation delays occurring at each level. This is the part of the period during which the inputs to the flip-flop must be held OFF. Most clocked devices require a minimum pulse-width, and this time should be added to the above to determine the approximate minimum permissible clock period. The device times are published by all manufacturers.

Figure 3-6 illustrates the minimum clock period found according to the above prescription. The hold-off time is determined for n levels of combinational circuitry. The general diagram of a synchronous sequential system with n levels of combinational circuitry is shown in Fig. 3-7.

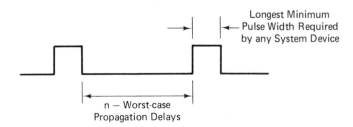

Figure 3-6

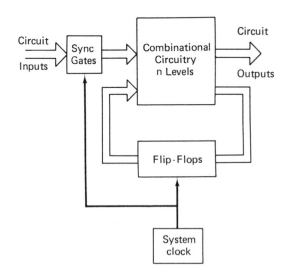

Figure 3-7

This system is remarkably general and could serve as the archtype of digital computers. We are concerned almost exclusively with sequential systems, both synchronous and asynchronous. With this in mind we return to consideration of clocked flip-flops.

A very popular variation of the clocked R-S flip-flop is the D-type or data flip-flop shown in Fig. 3-8. This flip-flop will set if the data line is HIGH when the system is clocked. If the data line is LOW, then the clock pulse clears the device. Thus, the output will follow the data on the data line while the clock pulse is HIGH and retain this data after the clock goes LOW. The D-type flip-flop is used primarily for implementing temporary data storage. It is available in a variety of configurations.

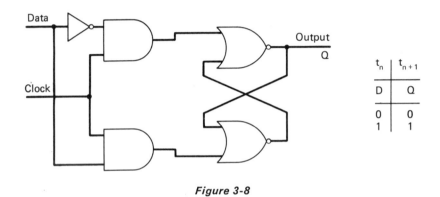

t_n	t_{n+1}
D	Q
0	0
1	1

Figure 3-8

One simple configuration is given by the TTL device 7477, which is the quadruple D-type latch shown in Fig. 3-9.

A more useful D-type flip-flop would provide additional control lines that could be used to set or clear the device as desired, independently of the data input. Such a device is pictured schematically in Fig. 3-10. Two such devices are in the TTL 7474 integrated circuit.

In addition to situations where we wish to *set* the output state, there are those in which we wish to *change* the output state. A device with this capability must have a means of sensing the current state: i.e., some feedback path must exist from the output of the flip-flop back to its input. Since we wish to change the state of Q, we feed back its complement, $\bar{Q}$. The new device with this property is called a Toggle or T-flip-flop. The symbolism for the T-flip-flop, its truth table, and a variation of this circuit formed with a D-type flip-flop are shown in Fig. 3-11. When the T input is LOW prior to receipt of the clock pulse, the Q output will not change with clocking. When the T input is HIGH, the device toggles with the clock pulse. The D-type flip-flop shown with its $\bar{Q}$ output feedback will toggle with every clock pulse.

A device in which the data inputs are *never* directly connected to the outputs

7477

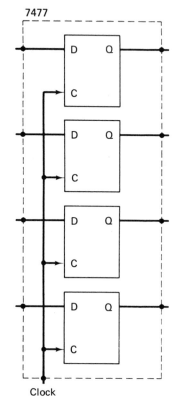

Clock

Figure 3-9

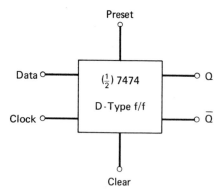

Figure 3-10

at any time during clocking may be made by using two latches connected serially. These devices are not sensitive to changes on the input lines while the clock is HIGH. Such a device might be used to prevent noise pulses from propagating into a counter. The use of separate clocks for each of the latches ensures the

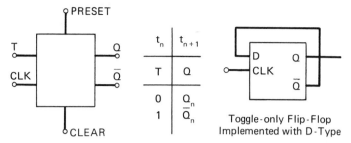

Figure 3-11

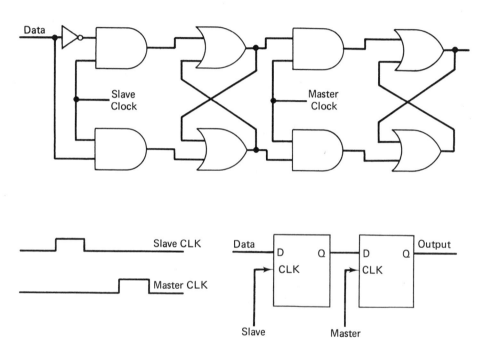

Figure 3-12

isolation of the input from the output. The provision of a D-type slave to hold the data until the master flip-flop is clocked gives rise to the name Master-Slave flip-flop. The Master-Slave flip-flop is shown in Fig. 3-12 in two formats and includes the clock relations.

Finally, we consider the J-K flip-flop, a two-input, single clock device that is extremely flexible. (See Fig. 3-13.) This device has been implemented in a number of integrated circuit configurations. As indicated in the accompanying truth table, the J line sets the output if it is HIGH when the device is clocked. If the K line is HIGH, the output line is reset with the clock. When both the J and the K inputs are HIGH, the device toggles, and when both are LOW, there is no change at the output.

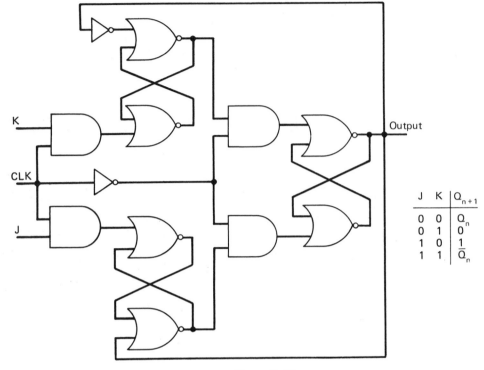

J	K	Q_{n+1}
0	0	Q_n
0	1	0
1	0	1
1	1	$\bar{Q}_n$

Figure 3-13

Three popular implementations of J-K flip-flops are the 7470, 7472, and the 7473 TTL devices. Numerous higher-numbered devices provide variations on these themes. The 7470 is a J-K flip-flop with gated inputs, direct clear and preset inputs, and complementary Q and $\bar{Q}$ outputs. Input information is transferred to the outputs on the positive edge of the clock pulse. The 7472 is a Master-Slave flip-flop in which the slave section sets on the positive edge of the clock pulse and the transfer is completed when the clock goes LOW, thus preventing noise pulses from propagating through the system while the clock is HIGH. The 7473 is a dual J-K Master-Slave flip-flop. There are more than a dozen different integrated circuit configurations of flip-flops and latches in every major logic family. The number is still growing in most families.

MEMORY CIRCUITS

The need to store large quantities of information has led to the development of integrated circuits containing large numbers of storage devices. The basic storage element in such circuits is called a memory cell. Memory cells can be implemented by using one, three, four, six, or more transistors. The simplest cell is the one-transistor cell shown in Fig. 3-14. This device uses the MOSFET

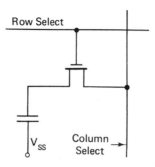

Figure 3-14

as a transmission gate; i.e., when gated ON, the device is considered a closed circuit with zero resistance; and when gated OFF, the MOSFET is treated as an open circuit with effectively infinite resistance. Thus, charge can be deposited on the capacitor from the column line by turning the MOSFET ON or OFF with the Row Select. The capacitor is charged to a "1" or a "0" level by the Column line when it is accessed during a WRITE cycle (Row Select enabled). During a READ cycle, the charge on the capacitor modifies the voltage on the floating column line, and this change is sensed by an amplifier whose output provides the data read from the cell. The trade-offs involved with this cell are large capacitance for readable signal versus small capacitance for packing density. The cell requires refreshing to prevent the charge from leaking off and, since the readout is destructive, the cell contents must be rewritten following each READ cycle. Memory cells that must be refreshed to prevent loss of stored data are referred to as *dynamic* as opposed to *static* cells that do not require the extra timing and control circuitry associated with this operation.

From our treatment of flip-flops we recognize that the static cell shown in Fig. 3-15 should require no refresh logic. When the Row Select line of

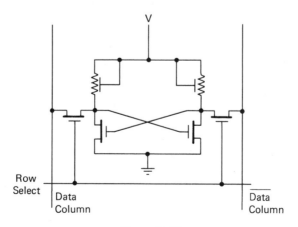

Figure 3-15

this cell is made HIGH, the corresponding row of cells is available for connection to the data lines. The Column Select line is used to determine which cell of this row is actually connected to the data lines. Writing is accomplished by forcing the appropriate data line to change the state of the flip-flop. To prevent flipping the cells while reading, both data lines, DATA and $\overline{\text{DATA}}$, are initially charged HIGH prior to activating the select line.

Before completing this circuit let us see how a four-transistor cell can be used to replace the six-transistor cell shown in Fig. 3-15. The fact that there is always capacitance associated with each gate allows information to be stored temporarily in the form of stored charge. The amount of charge needed to hold a gate ON or OFF is much less than that required for the sense amplifier of the one-transistor cell. This physically small capacitance is desirable and allows us to delete the two load MOSFETs that ordinarily control the gates, at the cost of dynamic operation. This cell is shown in Fig. 3-16 and provides the basic cell for Fig. 3-17.

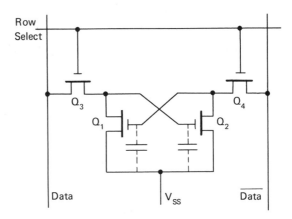

Figure 3-16

Again, the data lines are precharged to V_{DD}. The Row Select line opens the transmission gates Q_3 and Q_4. If Q_1 conducts, the DATA line discharge to the V_{ss} potential is as shown in Fig. 3-17. This automatically "refreshes" the gate of Q_2. Since Q_2 is held OFF, the gate of Q_1 is also refreshed. Thus, the cell "refresh" occurs with each access to the cell. If the cell is to be read, the DATA line is used to gate the DATA OUT line that is tied to V_{ss} through a series gate controlled by the Column Select line. A WRITE operation gates the data lines which are connected to the DATA IN line in a D-type configuration. This circuitry is shown for an arbitrary two-by-two submatrix of a general N cell array.

The number of storage cells available in memory chips is a function of the design. Memories built with static cells are readily available with 4096 bits organized in a matrix of 32 by 32 storage cells. Memories with 16,384 dynamic cells on a chip are standard.

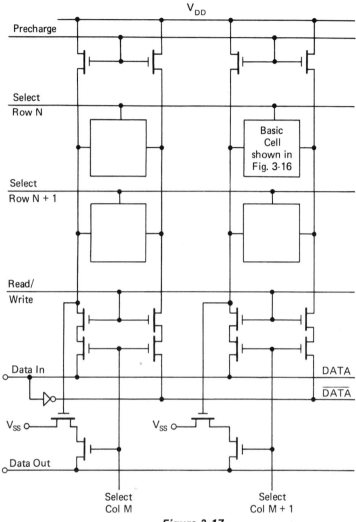

Figure 3-17

The static devices are easier to use in systems at the cost of more power and chip area. The dynamic MOS cells use the parasitic capacitance with the circuit to store data temporarily in the form of charge. This eliminates the need for load devices, but adds the problem of charge leakage. Since the charge will leak off the capacitor in milliseconds, circuitry must be provided to restore or refresh the charge. The refresher circuits normally require special clocks and timing circuitry that increases the cost and complexity. These can be justified only if the savings in load devices will pay for the extra circuitry. Since two load devices are associated with each bit of storage, significant savings occur only for large numbers of bits ($>$20,000).

Thus, memories of 16K words or larger should be implemented with dynamic chips, whereas smaller memories can be made by using static devices. Many memories can also be operated at reduced voltages, thus minimizing power without loss of data. This is termed a "standby" mode and is useful in many applications. Speeds associated with MOS memories range from 0.1 to 2.0 μsec. Memories using TTL technology offer speeds from 50 to 150 nsec, but use more power and offer fewer bits per chip at higher cost. Power consumption is a function of speed as well as design. Typical figures are 10 mW/bit for TTL, 0.5 mW/bit for MOS, and 0.1 mW/bit for MOS in the standby mode.

COUNTERS

In Fig. 3-18 we compare the output of a toggle or T-flip-flop with the clock input. It is easily seen that there is only one output pulse for every two input pulses. Such a relationship is characteristic of a divide-by-2 circuit. If we recall that dividing by two and displaying the remainder was a recommended technique for converting from decimal to binary, we may guess that a series of such divide-by-2 circuits can be made to yield a binary representation of an arbitrary number of pulses. This is illustrated in Fig. 3-19 in which three divide-by-2s have been placed in series to form a divide-by-8 circuit. In this figure, J-K flip-flops are used with both inputs HIGH to produce the toggle action. The outputs of each stage are shown, illustrating the count. Since the clock inputs are not tied to one clock, the system is asynchronous. TTL flip-flops are normally negative-edge-triggered devices; therefore, the output of each stage changes as the clock pulse returns to ground. As the clock pulse input to the first stage goes LOW, the output of the first stage goes HIGH. This output provides the clock input to the second stage; however, no change will occur in the output of the second stage until its clock goes LOW. The output of the first stage will not change

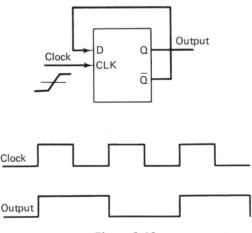

Figure 3-18

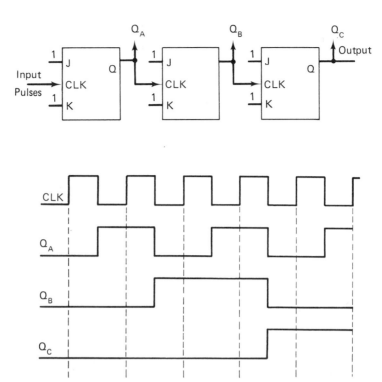

Figure 3-19

until the next pulse occurs, at which time it goes LOW, thereby clocking the second stage output HIGH. In this manner each stage produces only one pulse at its output for each two pulses on the clock input. Thus, N stages will result in a 2^N division of the input pulses.

Let us assume that all of the outputs are initially cleared, i.e., all are in the LOW state. A most interesting characteristic of the divide-by-N circuit appears when the outputs of all the stages are examined before the first pulse and before every succeeding pulse occurs. The accompanying table is a summary of the states of Q_A, Q_B, and Q_C sampled before each pulse. The outputs are seen to provide a binary count of the number of pulses input to the circuit! The counter cycles when it reaches 2^N. By judicious choice in feeding back outputs into preceding inputs it is possible to design a circuit that will count up to an arbitrary number and then cycle, rather than be constrained to powers of 2. Such counters and frequency dividers are available in many configurations, one of the most popular being the TTL 7490 Decade Counter that is normally used in a mode that counts from zero to nine and then cycles back to zero. Another extremely useful device is the 74190 UP/DOWN counter that will either count UP in binary numbers or count DOWN (subtract one with each pulse), depending upon the state of the control lines on the chip. The number of different counters is almost as great as the number of different flip-flops, and the designer is almost guaranteed to find the particular type of counter desired in integrated circuit form.

Number of Input Pulses	Q_C	Q_B	Q_A
0	0	0	0
1	0	0	1
2	0	1	0
3	0	1	1
4	1	0	0
5	1	0	1
6	1	1	0
7	1	1	1
8	0	0	0

SHIFT REGISTERS

The configuration in which a series of toggle flip-flops have the nth output connected to the $n + 1$st clock input was shown to yield a pulse counter with binary coded count available to drive displays or other digital circuitry. So useful was this circuitry that we are tempted to look for other useful configurations of flip-flops in series. The most obvious alternative configuration is one in which the output of the preceding stage is fed into the input of the following stage. Such a system, using Data or D-type flip-flops, is shown in Fig. 3-20.

This system is synchronous due to the common clock. We also assume that this system initially has all outputs cleared. An analysis of the behavior of this system indicates that the input bit to the first stage will be passed to the first stage output, Q_A, with the first clock pulse. The second clock pulse will transfer this data to the output of the second stage, Q_B. In this manner the initial data bit is shifted right with each successive clock pulse. Since every bit of input

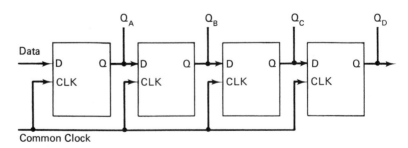

Figure 3-20

data is handled in this fashion, the outputs of the flip-flops maintain a sequential record of the data inputs at each clock time, with the first input being stored farthest to the right. After n clock pulses, an n-bit word is stored in the circuit. Temporary storage elements are called registers and, due to the fact that data can be shifted into and out of this type of register, they are also called shift registers.

As with other useful components, there are literally dozens of integrated-circuit shift registers available in many different configurations. The lengths of the registers range from four stages to over 1000 stages, i.e., over 1000 bits of serial storage per package. Shift registers with only a few stages are used for calculations and temporary storage, whereas long shift registers are used to implement cheap storage devices. The short registers normally provide an output from each stage, while only the input and final output bit are accessible on long registers. The table shown illustrates a 4-bit shift sequence when the data word 1101 is clocked in serially with four clock pulses.

	Data in	Q_A	Q_B	Q_C	Q_D
Initially	0	0	0	0	0
Clock pulse 1	1	1	0	0	0
Clock pulse 2	0	0	1	0	0
Clock pulse 3	1	1	0	1	0
Clock pulse 4	1	1	1	0	1

The recirculating loop is a means of storing data in shift registers with repeated access to each bit of storage. The output is fed back to the input, and the data are shifted in an endless loop. Obviously there must be a way to break the loop and insert data into the storage subsystem. This insertion is accomplished via the use of a WRITE pulse that serves to control a gate in the input circuit. A shift register in which this gate is built into the package is shown in Fig. 3-21. The recirculation loop is created with an external jumper wire between the appropriate pins.

It is necessary to keep track of the clock pulses in order to address a particular bit in the shift register storage. As mentioned before, counters are readily available that can be employed to provide binary addresses corresponding to the number of pulses required to reach a particular bit in storage. We have also discussed the fact that EXCLUSIVE-OR circuits can be used as comparators that provide a signal indicating when two words are equal. With these devices we can conceptually implement a system that will read any bit in storage. Such a system is shown in Fig. 3-22 based around the Signetics 2533 lK static shift register with integral stream select. Selection of any desired bit is accomplished by presenting the address to the comparator. The output of the pulse counter is also input to the comparator. When the two words are equal, the comparator output gates the selected bit out.

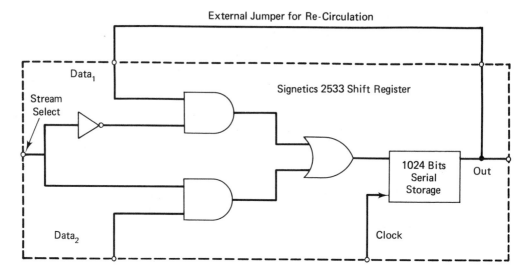

Figure 3-21

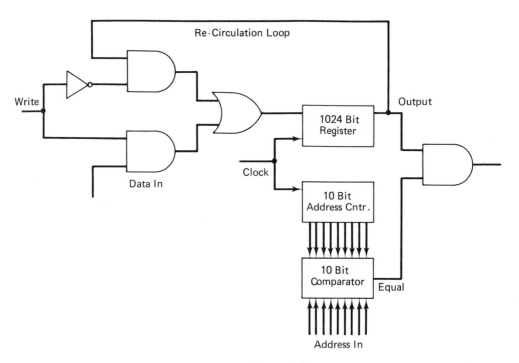

Figure 3-22

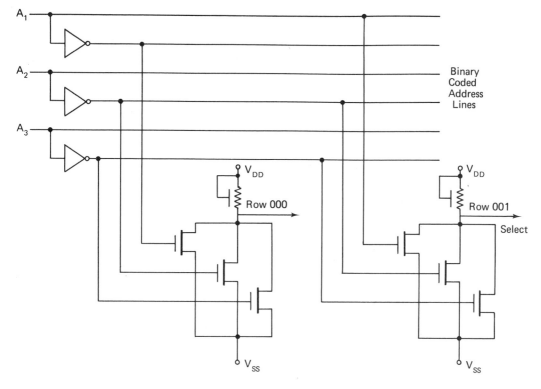

Figure 3-23

Bit selection circuitry used with random access memory cellular arrays is shown in Fig. 3-23. The general cell selection scheme will be treated in more detail in Chapter 4.

MOS Implementation of Shift Registers

The implementation of shift registers based on static cells is straightforward. However, the dynamic MOS shift register, based on capacitive storage, is particularly elegant and is shown in Fig. 3-24. The cell is comprised of two transmission gates with nonoverlapping clocks, two inverters, and two capacitors (normally parasitic). When ϕ_1 goes HIGH, the input capacitor C_1 charges according to the state of the input data line. These data appear inverted at the output of inverter I_1. Clock pulse ϕ_1 then returns to LOW, trapping the charge and holding the output of I_1 constant. When ϕ_2 goes HIGH, the action is repeated with C_2 charging and I_2 providing a second inversion. Any number of these cells can be lined up to form a serial shift register. The inverters are the simple MOS types first described. Figure 3-25 explicitly depicts the MOS

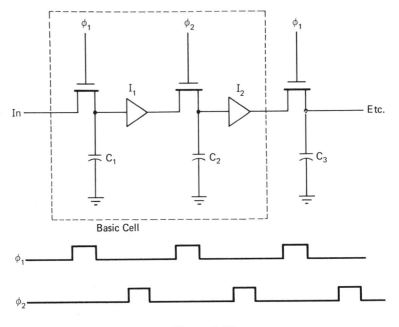

Figure 3-24

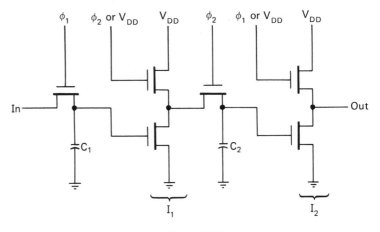

Figure 3-25

inverters. If static inverters are used, the load gates will be held at V_{DD}. These loads will be dissipating power constantly. This power dissipation can be minimized by going to the configuration in which the load devices are clocked and conduct only when the clock is HIGH. By feeding back the output of I_2 to the input of I_2, a static cell can be formed. Shift registers with dynamic cells

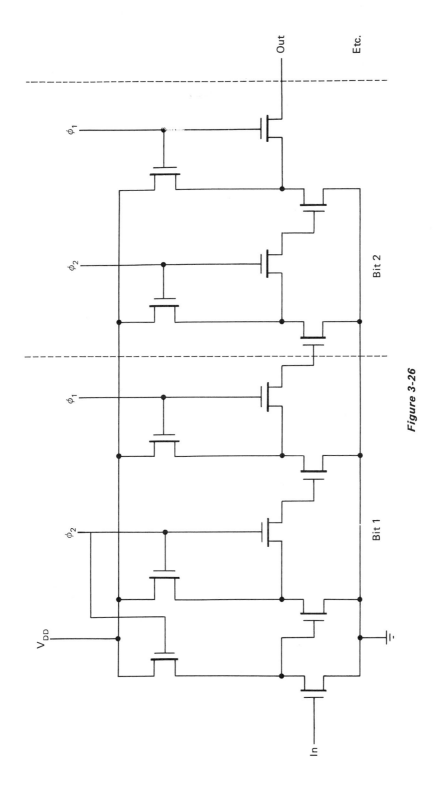

Figure 3-26

must be clocked approximately 10 KHz or higher to prevent data loss, whereas the clock frequency for static shift registers may go down to DC. The implementation of the Signetics 2506 shift register is shown in Fig. 3-26.

The WRITE line on the 2533 shift register was used to steer either new data or recirculated data into the register. As a worthwhile exercise in using gates to steer signals, we consider the implementation of a bidirectional shift register, i.e., one that will shift either left or right. In addition to the bidirectional shift capability, we also specify that the register must be able to accept parallel input data. Since each parallel bit requires a separate pin, we are constrained to a few stages and, therefore, make available the outputs of each stage as well. The device we are designing will be able to function in these modes:

Parallel in—shift left serial out

Parallel in—shift right serial out

Parallel in—parallel out

Serial in (left)—shift out (right)

Serial in (right)—shift out (left)

Serial in (either)—parallel out

The bidirectional shift capability means that the output of each stage must have a path to both the input of the preceding stage (for left shift) and the input of the following stage (for right shift). Only one of these paths may be open at once; therefore, each path must contain a gate. Figure 3-27 indicates a possible gating arrangement.

Since each stage must be able to accept data from either the preceding stage *or* the following stage, there must be an OR gate included in the input to each flip-flop, as shown in Fig. 3-28.

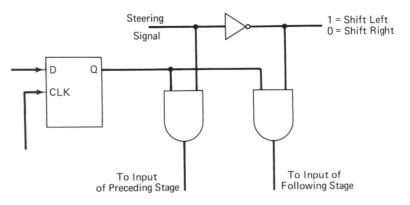

Figure 3-27

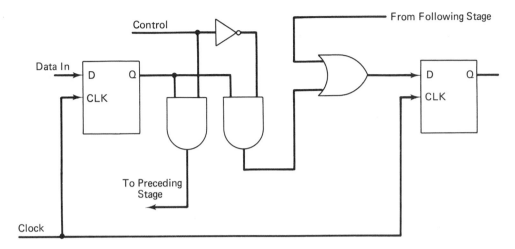

Figure 3-28

The use of a three-input OR gate allows parallel input data to be loaded into the register. Another gating signal is required to hold this data OFF until desired. An implementation of a three-stage universal shift register is shown in Fig. 3-29. The scheme can be extended to N stages. The TTL 74194 is a four-stage universal shift register that is very similar to the circuit just designed. An additional feature on this device is provided by a common CLEAR line that allows all stages to be reset to zero upon command. It should be noted that the use of two steering signals allows four modes of operation; therefore, in addition to the left and right shifts and the broadside load, there is a clock INHIBIT mode that prevents shifting although the clock is still running. The mode control signals are enumerated in Fig. 3-29.

Feedback Shift Registers

The ease with which we are able to route signals from stage to stage leads us to consider less orthodox feedback. For example, the output of one or more stages may be fed back to the input stage. We label the left input signal a_n, the output of the first stage a_{n-1}, the second stage output a_{n-2}, and the jth stage output a_{n-j}. With this notation we can describe the input of a k-stage Feedback Shift Register (FSR) with specific outputs fed back by the functional relation:

$$a_n = f(a_{n-1}, a_{n-2}, \ldots, a_{n-k})$$

This is a recurrence relation that is completely general and may take a variety of specific forms. By using n as the input, rather than 1, the same relation can be used to describe feedback to *any* stage in the device. An example of a specific

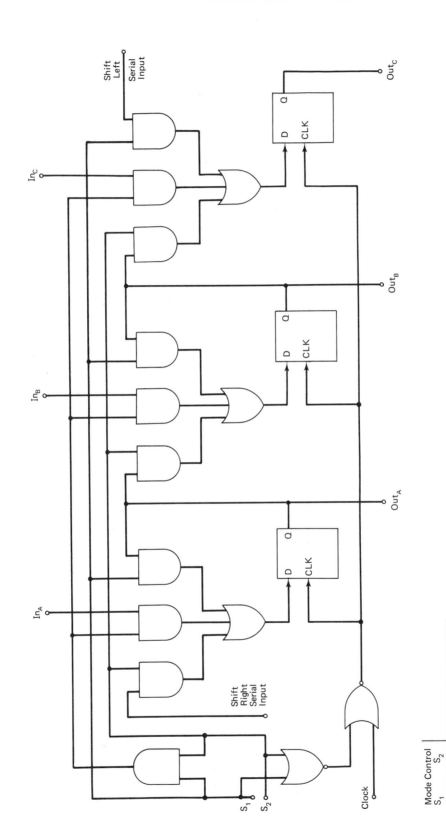

Figure 3-29

Mode Control		
S_1	S_2	
1	1	Parallel (Broadside) Load
0	1	Shift Right
1	0	Shift Left
0	0	Inhibit Clock

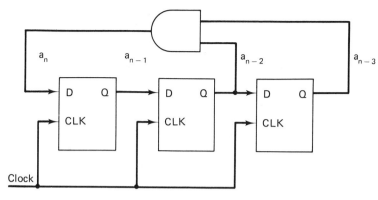

Figure 3-30

recurrence relation is given by

$$a_n = a_{n-2} \cdot a_{n-3}$$

which would describe the FSR shown in Fig. 3-30.

We describe the *state* of the FSR by writing the values of $a_{n-1}, a_{n-2}, a_{n-3}$ and observe that each clock pulse causes a state transition that is easily obtained by inspection. If we assume the initial state to be 110, then we can draw a state transition diagram by enclosing the state in a circle and drawing an arrow to the successor state as shown in Fig. 3-31.

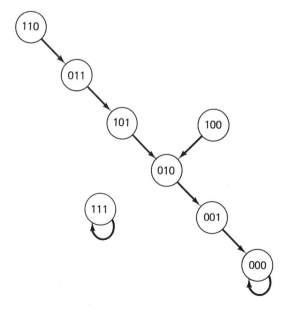

Figure 3-31

We observe that all states occur and lead unambiguously to a successor state, which may be the same state. The feedback can be altered by changing the bits that are fed back or by changing the function, or both. Most changes result in an entirely new state transition diagram. The function

$$a_n = a_{n-1} \otimes a_{n-3}$$

for the feedback shift register shown in Fig. 3-32 leads to the state transition diagram in Fig. 3-33.

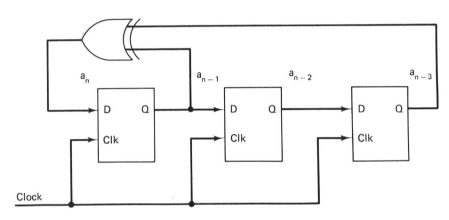

Figure 3-32

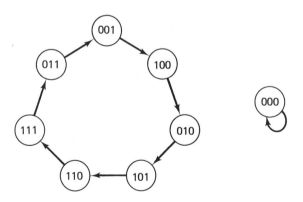

Figure 3-33

By altering the feedback configuration, an indefinite number of specific examples of FSRs can be obtained. A more interesting transition diagram occurs when a control signal is employed in the feedback path. Quite complicated state transition diagrams can be easily obtained from quite simple systems. Consider the use of the control bit, c, in the feedback shift register with feedback function

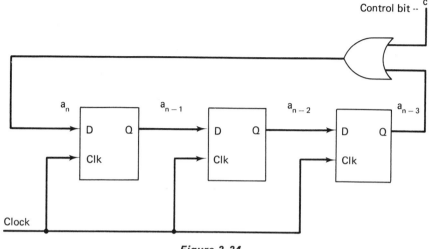

Figure 3-34

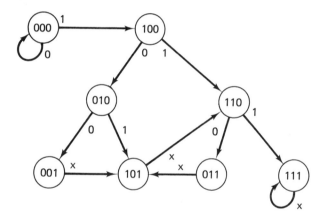

Figure 3-35

$$a_n = a_{n-3} + c$$

and FSR diagram in Fig. 3-34. This system yields the transition diagram in Fig. 3-35.

In Fig. 3-35 the value of the control bit is indicated beside each path by a 0, a 1, or an x, where x represents a "don't care" condition. This ability to control branching in the transition diagram is extremely important for finite-state machines. We will see later that the Intel 8008 microprocessor has the state transition diagram in Fig. 3-36. In this machine the feedback paths are controlled by bits from the current instruction, and the transition diagram is implemented via a 5-bit feedback shift register.

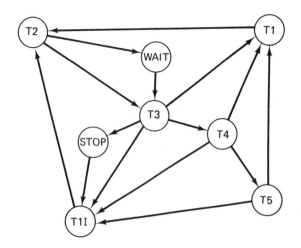

Figure 3-36

SUMMARY

The logic gates that serve as the most basic digital building blocks can be combined by utilizing feedback to obtain basic "memory cells" or storage flip-flops that can record the occurrence of certain past events. The ability to record past events introduces "hazards" associated with the momentary occurrence of undesirable events. This problem can be solved by clocking the system that is then referred to as a sequential system. A side effect of this is to break up the vague "past" into specific time periods, with each of which we may associate a "state" of the system. The state is defined as the minimum amount of information necessary to predict the response of the system to known inputs. Transitions between states then become important, and the study of machines that have a finite number of states, i.e., *finite-state machines*, provides the central theme of digital electronics.

An elementary introduction to state transitions was given in terms of feedback shift registers. These devices, however, do not play a large role in finite-state machines and were discussed because of the fact that the 8008 microprocessor utilizes an FSR, and because the treatment of shift registers in general led quite naturally into the development of the feedback shift register. The most general form of a finite-state machine, and the one that the reader should keep in mind, consists of combinational logic, some of whose outputs are stored in flip-flops and are subsequently fed back to certain inputs.

Chapter 4 treats coding and decoding, and extends the list of basic digital building blocks.

4 coding and MSI building blocks

Previous chapters have dealt largely with means of combining a number of inputs to obtain an output consisting of fewer bits that are a function of logical connections between the input bits. Thus, an equation of the form

$$y = \overline{A \cdot B} + \overline{C \cdot D}$$

replaces the four bits A, B, C, D with one bit, y, that indicates the truth or falsity of the logical relation between the four bits symbolized in the equation. Yet this relation is only one of many possible logical relations that can exist with A, B, C, and D. Consistent with the binary logic interpretation of these four variables, we can systematically consider all possible combinations of values by using the customary convention: $1 = $ true, $0 = $ false. Thus, between the "all false" input, $(A, B, C, D) = (0, 0, 0, 0)$, and the "all true" input, $(1, 1, 1, 1)$, we find a spectrum containing every possible combination. We have already noted the one-to-one correspondence possible between these states and the binary number system, and we observe now that it is possible to generate at least one equation that would be true for each combination, and *only* for that combination. The simplest illustration of this is probably the AND function shown in this table:

Binary Count	Possible AND Function of Four Variables
0000	$y_0 = \overline{A} \cdot \overline{B} \cdot \overline{C} \cdot \overline{D}$
0001	$y_1 = \overline{A} \cdot \overline{B} \cdot \overline{C} \cdot D$
0010	$y_2 = \overline{A} \cdot \overline{B} \cdot C \cdot \overline{D}$
0011	$y_3 = \overline{A} \cdot \overline{B} \cdot C \cdot D$
etc.	etc.

From this table it is apparent that, for N input bits, it is very easy to derive 2^N unique logic equations that can be used to specify which input combination has occurred. Here we are concerned with circuitry that generates many output bits from a few input bits. This type of circuit is invaluable for selecting or addressing purposes and will be elaborated upon later in this chapter.

The preceding discussion treated inputs presented to a circuit simultaneously, i.e., in parallel. There are many situations in which the input occurs
in serial form, and it is possible to associate a binary *code* with each serial input
in a manner similar to the coding of the parallel input case. The binary pulse
counter̄developed in Chapter 3 provides one such encoder. If we assume that
an input gate is held open for eight periods or time slots, each of which can
contain a pulse, then the possible inputs can be put in one-to-one correspondence
with the 8-bit binary numbers, as shown in Fig. 4-1.

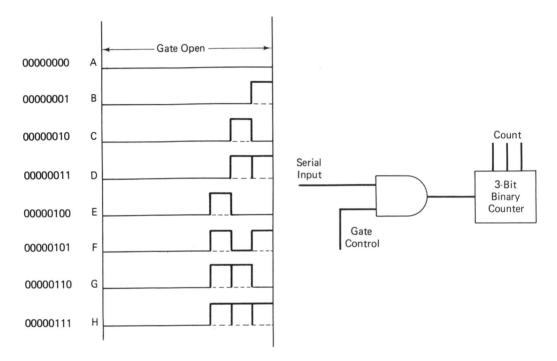

Figure 4-1

The output of the binary counter is a binary code that contains information
about the input combination of pulses. Yet this simple encoding scheme maps
the inputs *D*, *F*, and *G* into the same image point, thus destroying information
contained in the input stream. A more conservative coding scheme would preserve the differences found in permutations at a cost in the number of bits
required to store such information. Whereas three bits suffice to describe the
situation in which *n* ones and $(8 - n)$ zeros were presented to the input, eight
bits are required to preserve their relative order of occurrence. By a clever
arrangement of flip-flops we could easily record *all* of the information in the
pulse train in just eight bits. This is exactly what we achieved in the shift register;

however, the emphasis here is on the fact that the *counter* does not record all of the information. In an analogous fashion, the logic equations at the beginning of this chapter fail to distinguish between all of the $2^N - 1$ false possibilities while invariably signalling the occurrence of the one true condition. The loss of information entailed in the use of any one logic equation of more than one variable is characteristic of many digital systems and should be kept in mind by the designer.

The fact that most systems today are parallel means that this is the area that receives attention with respect to optimization techniques. The logic equations at the beginning of this chapter could be implemented with combinational circuitry whose output(s) corresponds to only one input (TRUE) while ignoring all other (FALSE) input combinations. This is essentially a discrete binary number filter: i.e., the system will pass only one signal that corresponds to a unique binary number. It is precisely the ability to repond to only one input combination that allows us to use combinational circuits for timing and control.

In particular, the coding of 2^N choices into N-bit binary numbers requires just such circuitry in order to be useful: i.e., a decoder can be implemented only if there exists a circuit that will recognize the appropriate number and ignore all the rest. Due to the exponential character of 2^N, it is obvious from space/time considerations that the use of either 2^N time slots or 2^N space channels can become an extremely expensive way to transmit information for large N. Thus, the ability to encode 2^N combinations with N bits, transmit the coded information, and then decode to physically select the proper one of 2^N cases allows much more economical system design. Even with the coded information, there is some question as to whether serial or parallel transmission of information should be employed. The answer is usually scale dependent.

For small-scale systems, such as computers, the answer is almost universally parallel; however, for large-scale systems, such as computer networks connected by cables or telephone lines, the answer is twofold. The intracomputer communications conserve time at the expense of space channels, whereas inter-computer communications minimize spatial channels with the attendant cost of cables by transforming from the parallel to the serial mode for transmission, and then reconverting to parallel at the receiver. The cost in time is considered to be cheaper than the cost of implementing a fully parallel network.

The space/time question also arises in information storage. Until quite recently serial storage media have been the cheapest to implement, and the change-coupled-diode (CCD) and magnetic bubble technologies are currently restoring this condition. As we saw with the recirculating shift register, the single access point requires that a selected (addressed) bit be present at the output of the shift register. In general, this will not be the case; therefore, a time delay will occur before the desired bit can be shifted to the output. In order to avoid this time delay, a parallel storage system can be used in which any bit at random can be addressed as rapidly (by selecting its channel) as any other bit in storage.

The ability to address directly and access a random bit within any clock cycle leads to the name Random Access Memory (RAM), which is associated with parallel storage.

The ability to store large amounts of information in parallel (16,384 bits in one chip) demands that coding and decoding be utilized. The physical impossibility of attaching 16,384 wires to a chip implies that the address must be presented to the chip in coded form and decoded on the chip itself. Since $16,384 = 2^{14}$, a 14-bit binary representation of the address will be presented to the chip, a much more feasible number of connections. Spatial channels going to each of the storage locations must exist, but these are implemented as "micro-wires" by using LSI techniques, and even here we will find tricks to cut down on such large numbers. We should note here that scale dependence is entering again.

The use of coding achieves another economy: the ability to use a particular piece of information requires that we know where to find it, i.e., an address must be provided. For any process that is not instantaneous, we must provide a means of storing the addresses of information that will be called for. This requirement also favors the use of coded N-bit addresses over the fully parallel 2^N-bit form of addressing. In addition to the space/time economies associated with binary coding, there are important side effects. The use of binary numbers allows easy address modification by using binary arithmetic circuitry. Such modifications allow addressing modes that would probably not exist in fully parallel form.

The way in which an address decoder can be implemented follows from the discussion on the first page of this chapter. The binary number coding scheme that uses N-bit words can easily be put into one-to-one correspondence with the N-variable logic equations shown in the table (as well as with other, equivalent, systems of equations). The simple nature of each equation requires one AND gate and from zero to N inverters, as shown in Fig. 4-2.

The 4-bit address bus would allow the selection of each one of 16 target

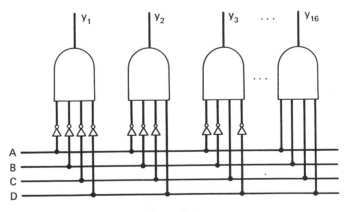

Figure 4-2

devices. For a wider bus, corresponding to a large number of targets, decoding rapidly becomes expensive, even with LSI technology; therefore, a variation on this theme is usually employed. Rather than use lines to address a target device, we use nodes or connected line pairs. Since the number of nodes in a square matrix is proportional to the square of the size, this can achieve great economies, as shown in Fig. 4-3.

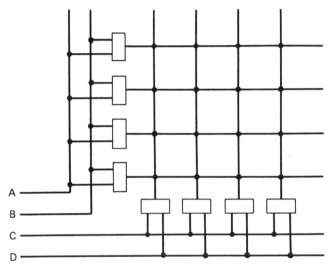

Figure 4-3

Of course, the lines are not actually connected together as indicated in the figure. They are used in pairs to select a target cell. The use of this scheme for an 8-bit bus would consist of organizing a four-by-four decoder with 16 *plus* 16 lines and 16 *times* 16 nodes. In general, the use of $2N$ lines in the matrix yields N^2 nodes.

Most memory chips contain decoding circuitry that selects the addressed memory cell via the X-Y scheme described above. There are numerous applications that involve selection of a particular device or subsystem and require the use of a discrete decoder. Such decoders are available in medium-scale integrated circuits.

MEDIUM-SCALE INTEGRATED CIRCUITS

Preceding sections of this book have been concerned with the background necessary for understanding the principles behind the operation of integrated circuits. The remainder of this chapter is devoted to a presentation of the basic types of digital building blocks available. The devices number in the hundreds.

We, therefore, will treat only categories of integrated circuits and illustrate each with a representative example.

Decoders

A primary application of digital systems is in a control mode. For complex systems, control automatically entails selection, and the devices that are to be selected are often indicated by a binary word. Thus, the decoder chip that will accept an N-bit binary number and place a signal on one of 2^N output lines is extremely useful. The Intel 3205 1-of-8 binary decoder is shown in Fig. 4-4. It is implemented with Schottky TTL, requires very low input current (0.25 mA), and has very little propagation delay (18 nsec). Three enable lines are simply wired to the proper voltage.

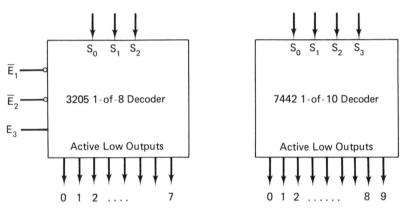

Figure 4-4

Many devices, particularly those with keyboard inputs, utilize only the decimal digits 0 through 9. Although four binary bits are required for the Binary-Coded Decimal (BCD) numbers, there are six unused binary combinations. An example of a BCD decoder is shown on the right in Fig. 4-4. It is the 7442 decade decoder with four input lines and 10 output lines.

Decoders are normally active LOW devices, i.e., the selected line goes LOW, while unselected lines remain HIGH. This is based on both speed and power consumption. More power is required when the outputs are LOW. Therefore, the normal state is HIGH.

Latches

Parallel systems utilize busses consisting of parallel wires such that the data word is distributed over the bus one bit per wire at any time. We speak of 4-wide busses, 8-wide busses, etc. The sequential nature of the systems with which we are most concerned implies that data are placed on the bus in some sequence. There often exists a need to catch and save a particular word of data, and the building blocks that perform this function are called latches. The latch must have an input port and an output port, and a control (or latch enable) line. Sometimes more than one latch enable line is provided so that the latch action can be made a function of several variables. Often there is a need in digital systems to be able to reset the system to a starting configuration, and this is usually done by forcing all latch outputs to zero. Thus, a *clear* signal or asynchronous *master reset* line can be provided. The Fairchild 9308 Dual 4-Bit Latch, shown in Fig. 4-5, provides all of the above features with two independent 4-bit latches in one package. The device has a 25-nsec delay associated with it: i.e., the output will follow the input as long as both enable lines are LOW, with no more than a 25-nsec propagation delay. When either enable line on either 4-bit section goes HIGH, the data at the input is latched and the outputs do not respond to further inputs until both enable lines are returned to LOW. The two lines allow for easy *X-Y*, or matrix, addressing: i.e., the latch can be easily selected from a group of latches in the same way that a storage cell is selected by using a matrix of wires.

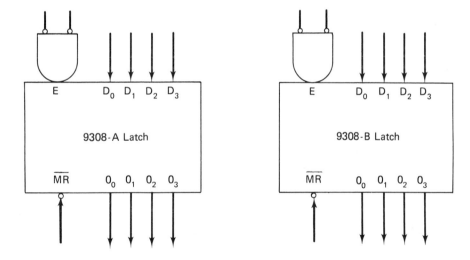

Figure 4-5

Adders

The ability to perform all arithmetic operations through complementation and addition makes the integrated adder circuit a valuable device. The device should conceptually feature two input ports for the words to be added, and an output port for the sum. In addition, there should be a carry input line from less significant figures and a carry output to more significant figures. The TTL

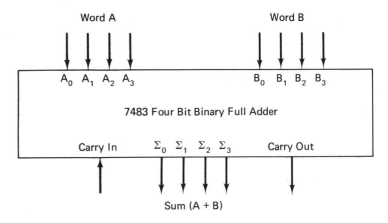

Figure 4-6

7483 shown in Fig. 4-6 provides these features. All TTL devices will be assumed to have a $+5$-V input and a ground line. These will normally be omitted from diagrams.

Comparators

In addition to the performance of arithmetic operations, there is often a need for equality tests between two words. This is provided by a comparator with two input ports and an output port containing the result of the comparison. Two types of comparisons can be made: identity and magnitude. The simple identity comparator has one output line: EQUAL/$\overline{\text{EQUAL}}$. The 9324 5-bit magnitude comparator shown in Fig. 4-7 has two 5-bit inputs each for word A and word B, and three output lines that indicate either $A > B, A < B$, or $A = B$. The device has an active low enable line. When the device is disabled, all outputs are forced LOW.

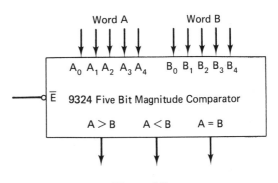

Figure 4-7

Multiplexers

Whereas the action of the 1-of-N line decoder was to select a specified line to be used as an output, we may also wish to input from 1-of-N lines. This is termed multiplexing and is quite common in digital systems. Multiplexers have also been used extensively for function generation, although with microprocessor-based systems this is often performed in software. The Fairchild 9312 8-input multiplexer shown in Fig. 4-8 has an active LOW enable line, three channel select bits, eight input channels, and an output channel. A complementary output is also included. Note that the active LOW enable line that enables the device is compatible with the active LOW outputs of decoders that are used to select devices. The data present at the input channel selected by the address lines, S_0, S_1, and S_2, are passed through the chip to the output(s) with a propagation delay of about 24 nsec. The device consumes approximately 135 mW of power.

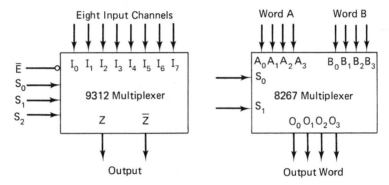

Figure 4-8

Often we desire to select words rather than single bits of data. The Signetics 8267 has two 4-bit input ports and a 4-bit output port. Two SELECT lines are provided on the chip. When both lines are HIGH, the chip is disabled and the outputs are forced HIGH. The device is shown on the right in Fig. 4-8.

Counters

The dozens of different types of counters may be divided into two classes: UP counters and UP/DOWN counters. The first type increments with each input pulse until the maximum count is reached, and then recycles. The second type of counter has the ability to increment or decrement with each pulse, depending upon the state of a control line. A variation on this deletes the control line and inputs "up" pulses to one port and "down" pulses to a different port. The "granddaddy" of the counters is the Texas Instruments 7490 Decade Counter,

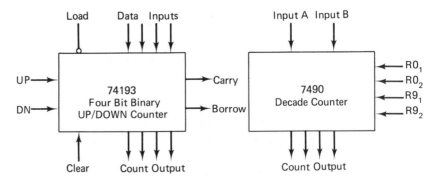

Figure 4-9

shown in Fig. 4-9, that counts from zero to nine and then recycles. The counter is split internally into a divide-by-2 stage and a divide-by-5 stage so that an external jumper is required for divide-by-10 operation. The device has four RESET lines, two of which force all outputs to zero, and two of which force all outputs to a BCD nine count. These lines also inhibit the count action. The average power consumed by the 7490 is 160 mW.

The 74193 is a 4-bit Binary UP/DOWN Counter with preset inputs. It is a synchronous counter, and all inputs change at once: i.e., the OUTPUT lines do not have any spikes occurring, as do the ripple through-type asynchronous counters. The direction of counting is determined by the input used. A CLEAR line is provided to force the outputs to zero. Data can be entered from the preset inputs when the LOAD line goes LOW. BORROW and CARRY outputs allow 74193s to be cascaded for 4-by-N-bit counts. The carry is fed to the count-up input of the succeeding counter, and the borrow is fed to the count-down input. The term "Binary" in the description of the counter indicates that the device counts from zero to 15, and then recycles. A Decade version, the 74192, is also available.

TIME OUT . . .

At this point it should be worthwhile to consider the control power available with even the most basic building blocks. We will use three devices, the 9312 Multiplexer, the 74193 UP/DN Counter, and the 3205 1-of-8 Decoder. The circuit we will design will be capable of stepping through a sequence of operations, each of which will initiate a test of some sort. The controller will advance to the next test only upon receipt of a positive result from the current test. It will be able to cycle through any portion of the sequence and jump, conditionally or unconditionally, to any other step in the sequence. (This design is found in the *Fairchild TTL Applications Handbook*.) We will use only eight steps; therefore, the full range of the 74193 will not be utilized. The output of the counter serves two functions: it addresses the 3205 Decoder whose output initiates the test, and it also selects the channel of the 9312 Multiplexer that will receive the test result. The output of the 9312 is fed to the UP count input of the 74193, as shown in Fig. 4-10. Until the test result is positive, this input is low and no change will occur in the controller. When the test is completed successfully, the indication appears at the selected multiplexer input and is routed through to the output, and from there to the UP-count input of the 74193 where it causes the count to change, therby initiating the next step in the sequence. The sequence can be initiated at step zero by using the 74193 CLEAR line. Steps can be omitted by

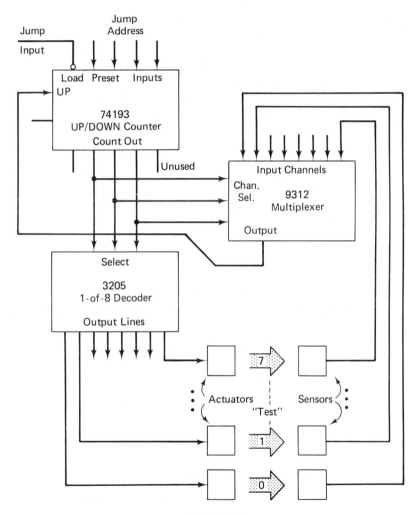

Figure 4-10

tying the appropriate input to the 9312 permanently HIGH. Conditional or unconditional jumps can be achieved by using the appropriate test result to jam in a new count via the preset inputs of the 74193: i.e., the test result is fed back to the LOAD line of the 74193, and the desired step is presented at the preset input port. Many useful variations can be derived from this basic circuit. This is an excellent system for the reader to work with because many non-trivial systems can be achieved with minor variations on this basic scheme.

Parity Checker/Generators

Although digital circuits are much less susceptible to noise than analog circuitry, their application is often in a noisy environment. For this reason it is desirable to provide a check on the validity of a word: i.e., attempt to assure that the word that has been received is the same word that was transmitted. Error-detecting and error-correcting codes have been devised for this purpose. The simplest error-detecting system counts the number of binary 1s in a word and determines whether this number is even or odd. An extra bit, indicative of this factor, is then appended to the word and is called a "parity bit."

The parity bit is normally 1 for even parity and 0 for odd parity. If the parity of the received word does not agree with the parity bit sent with the transmitted word, then it is assumed that an error has occurred somewhere in transmission. The code is not foolproof in that errors that will cancel can occur; for example, two 1s could be dropped without changing the parity of the word. This is considered so unlikely in most systems that a single parity bit is often used. The 9348 12-input Parity Checker/Generator accepts up to 12 inputs and produces both even and odd parity outputs. The appropriate bit is then placed on the parity line and the full word *plus* parity bit is transmitted. Another 9348 is used at the receiver end and checks the parity of the incoming word. The output of this 9348 is then compared with the received parity bit. Several 9348s can be arranged to form a Hamming circuit for a 20-bit word. The Hamming code uses more than one bit to detect an error and determine *where* it occurred, thus allowing for correction. The 9348 is shown in Fig. 4-11.

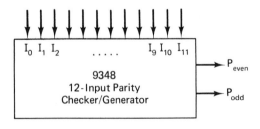

Figure 4-11

Priority Encoders

The sequential nature of most digital circuitry breaks time into pieces, and each time slot is then dedicated to one task or function. Often there are several devices or subsystems that compete for a given time slot, and some priority must be established to determine which subsystem gains control at a given time. Although the priority determination must be decided by the system designer, once it has been decided, some means of implementing it must be provided. The 9318 8-input Priority Encoder serves to select the highest priority input from a number of simultaneous inputs, and to produce a 3-bit code indicative of which device is requesting service. In addition to the eight active LOW inputs and the three binary-coded outputs, there are two ENABLE lines, one for the input and one for the output, and an active LOW output line that specifies whether any of the inputs are active. These allow for cascading 9318s to handle more than eight inputs. The 9318 is shown in Fig. 4-12.

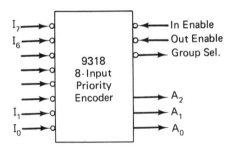

Figure 4-12

Addressable Latches

The 9312 8-input multiplexer possesses eight input channels and one output channel. A 3-bit address selects which input is to be routed to the output. We reverse this scheme and specify one input channel and a 3-bit address to route the data at the input to 1-of-8 output ports. This circuit is called a demultiplexer. A latch can also be provided at each output port to store the data after the input has disappeared. The 9334 8-bit addressable latch possesses these characteristics. Eight bits can be stored by presenting the data at the input and the address of the latch to be written into. The data are written into the latch when the ENABLE line is active (LOW), and data entry is inhibited when the ENABLE line returns HIGH. A CLEAR line is present for resetting all outputs except the addressed output; this will follow the data input when the ENABLE line is active. Thus, the CLEAR line provides for a demultiplexing mode of operation. When the CLEAR line is inactive, the 9334 operates in the memory mode. The device is shown in Fig. 4-13.

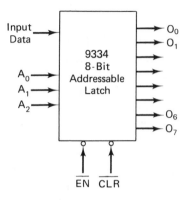

Figure 4-13

Multiport Memories

For high-speed applications it is sometimes desirable to access two words from a memory at the same time. Even higher speed can be obtained if a word can be written into memory at the same time that two words are being accessed. The 9338 8-bit Multiport Memory, shown in Fig. 4-14, provides these capabilities. The A address selects the bit to be written into, while B and C address the two bits to be read. The data to be stored is placed on the D_A input line, and the output data appear at ports Z_B and Z_C. The CLOCK line enters data in a Master-Slave arrangement so that the data being entered on the rising edge are isolated from that being read out. When the clock falls LOW, the new data are stored in the cell addressed by A. This Master-Slave action can be defeated by using the Slave Enable (SLE) input that allows immediate transfer of information to the selected Master to the outputs.

Binary Multipliers

By its very nature, multiplication can be accomplished via a series of additions. In sequential systems, each addition takes a certain amount of time and, thus, multiplication of large numbers becomes impractical. The binary system allows the SHIFT AND ADD technique; however, this technique often requires two orders of magnitude more time than a simple ADD. Thus, for high-speed systems that perform many multiplications (examples: matrix inversion and Fast Fourier Transforms) there is a dire need for a multiplier circuit. A basic multiplier building block is the 9344 Binary 4-bit $\times$ 2-bit Full Multiplier shown in Fig. 4-15. One input port accepts a 4-bit binary number $X = X_0 X_1 X_2 X_3$, and another port accepts a 2-bit number $Y = Y_0 Y_1$. There also exist two other ports, K (4 bits) and M (2 bits). The output of the device is a 6-bit number defined as $S = X \cdot Y + K + M$. The two numbers are multiplied and an additive constant is operated on at the same time. All inputs and outputs are

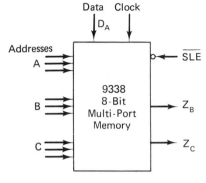

Figure 4-14

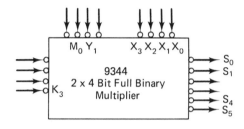

Figure 4-15

active LOW. Multiple 9334 chips can be used to provide wider word multiplication. All manufacturers of this device provide schematics for wide-word circuits, but these will not be shown here.

Using 9334s, an 8×8-bit multiplier circuit can be built to operate in approximately 150 nsec. A 16×16-bit multiplication requires about 350 nsec. These times are appreciably shorter than the ADD time for most microprocessors. A single chip TTL 16×16 bit multiplier is available from TRW. The MPY16A operates in less than 200 nsec. and draws 850 ma.

Bidirectional Bus Driver/Receivers

As will be discussed in following chapters, a bidirectional port offers an efficient way to design bus-oriented systems. The internal circuit of the Signetics 8T26 will be shown in Chapter 7; therefore, we present only the block diagram in Fig. 4-16. The 8T26 is a tri-state device with HIGH output drive capability (40 mA) and LOW input loading (200 μA). It is a very high-speed device with a 17-nsec maximum propagation delay. The electrical characteristics make it an ideal MOS-to-TTL interface device. Two control lines, $\overline{\text{RCVR ENABLE}}$ and DRIVER ENABLE, can be tied together to implement a one-line directional control that determines the direction of data flow through the device.

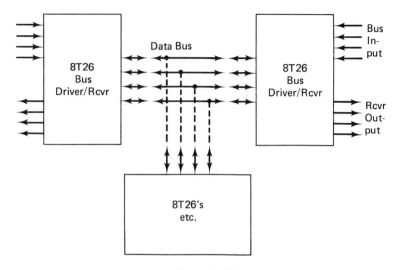

Figure 4-16

Monostable Multivibrator (One-shot)

Although sequential digital systems provide repetitive clock pulses of a fixed pulse width, there are many applications that require one pulse of a nonstandard pulse width. The use of a circuit that can be pushed momentarily into a second, unstable state allows the generation of such pulses. External components can be used to determine the pulse width. The 74121 one-shot pulse generator is shown in Fig. 4-17. R and C are resistive and capacitive elements that may be

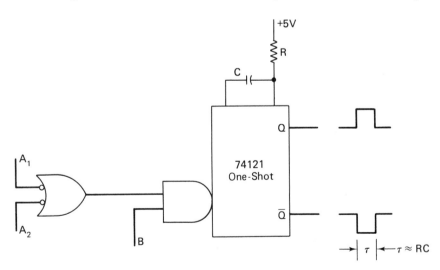

Figure 4-17

chosen to provide a pulse width of approximately $R \cdot C$ seconds when R is given in megohms and C in microfarads. The A-inputs are negative edge triggerred TTL gates, and the B-input is level sensitive. Once fired, the output is independent of the input conditions. Both positive- and negative-going output pulses are available.

Schmidt Triggers

The level-sensitive action mentioned in the description of the one-shot is a very convenient feature. TTL circuits require certain rise and fall times on inputs and will not respond to slowly changing signals. A circuit that will react to threshold crossings is available as the 7413 Schmidt Trigger. The input can vary at any speed (1 V/sec), and when the threshold is crossed the TTL output goes LOW and remains there until a negative-going threshold is crossed. The positive threshold is nominally 1.7 V, and the negative threshold is nominally 0.9 V; thus, the device exhibits some hysteresis. The 7413 Dual NAND Schmidt Trigger provides four level-sensitive inputs for slowly changing signals and provides a NAND function TTL output. There are two such devices in the package. The device in Fig. 4-18 has three inputs tied permanently HIGH and one tied to the input signal.

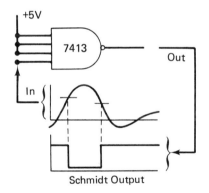

Figure 4-18

High-Voltage Open-Collector Buffer/Drivers

The ability to drive devices at a higher voltage than the TTL supply voltage is provided by open-collector circuits. The 7407 Hex Buffer/Driver shown in Fig. 4-19 accepts TTL input signals and provides high-voltage, high-current, open-collector outputs for interfacing with MOS devices, lamps, and relays. The outputs will handle up to 30 V at 40 mA. Open-collector devices can also be wire-ORed together.

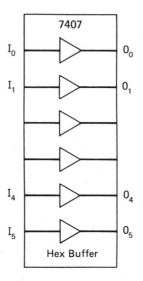

Figure 4-19

Opto-Isolators

The use of computers as control devices often results in electrical connection to systems that operate at extremely high voltages. The requirement for electrical isolation can be met by using an opto-isolator of the type shown in Fig. 4-20. The input signal is converted to a light beam, and the information is carried, via the light beam, to the receiving light-sensitive transistor. Since it is

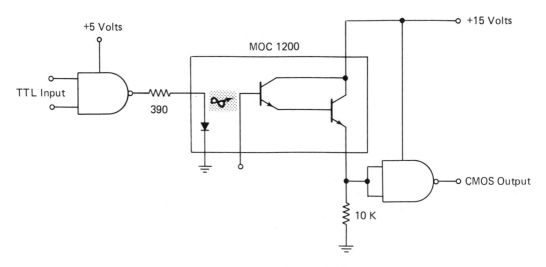

Figure 4-20

impossible for voltage to leak across this path, the package itself provides the minimum resistance path, normally about 10^{11} ohms isolation. The output is a linear function of the input and there is virtually no feedback to the input. The device has an effectively infinite life. The device shown is typical of the Texas Instruments TIL100 series of opto-isolators and the Motorola MOC series. It is shown as an interface element between 5-V TTL and 15-V CMOS circuitry.

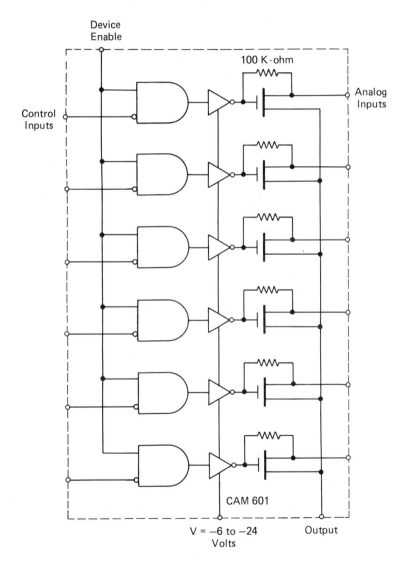

Figure 4-21

Analog Multiplexers

The ability to electrically switch analog signals in and out of a circuit has been discussed in terms of transmission gates, both in MOS and CMOS. This function is so important that many such devices are available today. A particularly convenient configuration is that of the Teledyne Crystalonics CAM601 6-Channel Analog Multiplexer depicted in the schematic in Fig. 4-21. The device has a "break-before-make" action to guarantee that two signals will not be passed at the same time (thus providing a path for shorting between two circuits). In addition, the control inputs are TTL compatible for ease of interfacing to digital circuitry. The analog inputs can be AC or DC, and the input range is ± 10 V.

STORAGE DEVICES

A vast number and variety of storage devices exist for use in computer systems. One viewpoint holds that the memory is paramount and the processor(s) is simply a memory controller. The actual cost of storage in digital systems today is approximately an order of magnitude greater than the processor cost at the very minimum, and this is likely to be the case indefinitely. In the following pages we examine a variety of storage devices and explain where each is used.

Shift Registers

Having already discussed shift registers in some detail, we will say very little about them at this point. The registers shown in Fig. 4-22 include the 7491 8-bit register that is implemented in TTL and the 2533 $1k$-bit static shift register implemented with MOS. A package containing six 32-bit static shift registers on a common clock is shown in the Signetics 2518 in Fig. 4-23. This device can be clocked at frequencies up to 3 MHz and is TTL compatible. Each register has a recirculation path on the chip. At this time dynamic RAMs provide less expensive storage than dynamic shift registers, although charge-coupled device (CCD) shift register prices are falling more rapidly than RAMs.

Random Access Memories

The largest percentage of semiconductor storage devices is implemented as Random Access Memory (RAM), both static and dynamic. The static devices are much easier to use; however, the dynamic memories are less expensive for medium-to-large storage systems. For years the RAMs have been organized as 1-bit wide and N-bits long. This is shown in Fig. 4-24 in the static 2102 $1k \times 1$ RAM and the dynamic 2107 $4k \times 1$ dynamic RAM in Fig. 4-25. The static RAM is simplicity itself! Ten ADDRESS inputs are on the chip, as well as the

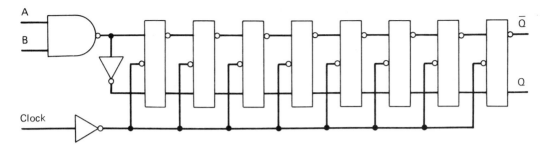

7491 8-Bit Shift Register TTL

2533 1 K-Bit Shift Register MOS

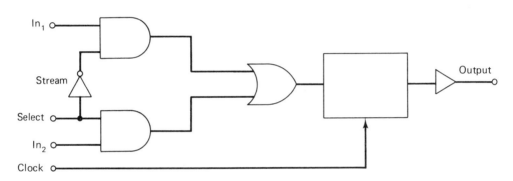

Figure 4-22

DATA-IN and DATA-OUT ports. A READ/WRITE control line is required and a CHIP SELECT line is available for sending the outputs into the tri-state mode. Thus, banks of memory can easily be switched in and out of a system.

The 2102 is 100% TTL compatible on all lines and requires only a +5-V power supply for operation. The device has a 500-nsec access time, which is respectably fast for most systems. A variation on the Intel 2102 is the Signetics 2606 that has 1024 bits organized as 256 4-bit words. This is an ideal package for 4- and 8-bit microprocessors because it cuts down the package count considerably for systems that require minimal memory. The inputs and outputs are common and are selected by the READ/WRITE control line. This organization is ideal for bus-structured systems, and the N-MOS implementation requires only +5 V power and allows easy interface to TTL. The tri-state device has a chip enable line that must be activated before reading or writing can occur. The ACCESS and READ cycle times are less than 750 nsec, making it well suited to most microprocessors.

The $4k \times 1$ RAM shown in Fig. 4-25 is the Intel 2107. This RAM and those

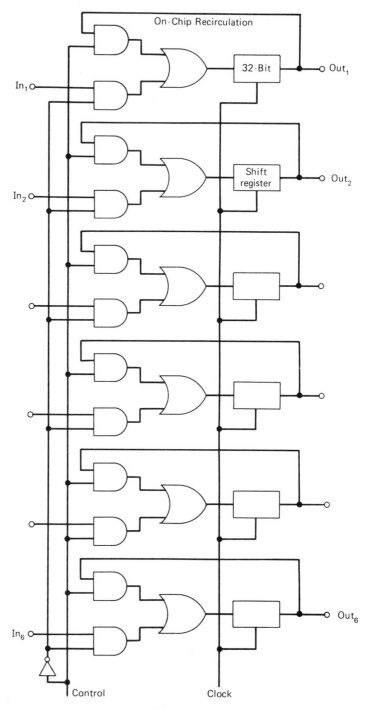

Figure 4-23

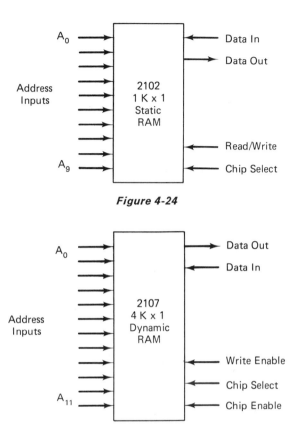

Figure 4-24

Figure 4-25

of 10 other semiconductor memory manufacturers were available for less than two years when Intel introduced an N-MOS RAM with 16,384 bits of READ/ WRITE storage on one chip, organized as $16k \times 1$. The basic cells in these devices vary from manufacturer to manufacturer, as do the speed and printouts of the devices. The average speed is approximately 300 nsec, with some devices clocked below 200 nsec. A $64k$-RAM has been implemented by using Charge Coupled Device (CCD) technology. The existence of dynamic refresh-memory controller chips simplifies memory design with these dynamic RAMs.

Read Only Memory

Systems that are dedicated to a particular function or purpose are likely to require that certain programs and/or data structures be relatively permanent and unchanging. For example, the values stored in a trig table will not change with time. Many control programs for a particular process are fixed, and operation consists of initializing the system, then cycling through a series of instructions. Storage of this information in RAM suffers from the volatile nature of semiconductor RAM, i.e., when the power vanishes, the information is lost. Thus, systems that store fixed information structures in RAM must reload after every power-down event. Since the fixed information will not be changed, there is no need for a WRITE facility associated with its storage. The development of storage consisting of Read Only Memory (ROM) has solved the problem of volatility. The information is permanently stored in most ROM via one of two techniques. During the actual manufacturing of the memory, the transistors are designed to be either ON or OFF permanently. Thus, a flip-flop is not needed because there is no need to flop. The basic static storage cell is simpler (consisting essentially of a diode), and thus the ROM, contains more cells than the RAM.

The tooling of the masks required to build a special memory is expensive, however, and can be justified only when large numbers of the same ROM are needed. To get around this problem, the field-programmable ROM was developed. These units usually are built with *all* cells reading one, but with a fusible link associated with each cell. By setting up the cell address and then "blowing the fuse," a particular cell can be altered to read zero. Thus, information can be written *once* into each cell of the device through the use of a special WRITE circuit. Although these ROMs are more expensive in quantity than masked ROMs, they are much cheaper for small quantities. In particular, they allow us to make mistakes without paying a tremendous price. Even so, the fact that few programs run correctly the first, or even the second, time can cost hundreds of dollars in fusible ROM expenditure.

The need for a reusable ROM was met by Intel's development of the Field Alterable MOS (FAMOS) device that can be written into by using approximately 30 V, and then erased with ultraviolet light. Although costlier than any other type of ROM, their reusability makes them ideal devices, and in very many applications they are undoubtably the cheapest ROM. Any development of a new digital system requiring ROM should be done with such Programmable ROMs (PROMs). The ROMs shown in Fig. 4-26 are the Intel 2708 $1k \times$ 8-bit FAMOS PROM and the Electronic Arrays EA 4800, the first $16k$-bit ROM. The 4800 is mask programmable and has an access time of 2 μsec. It is static with all address decoding on the chip and requires $+5$ and -12 V. The ROM is organized as 2048 8-bit words. In large quantities, the cost per word is approximately 1 cent. Power is 0.032 mW per bit. The $16k$ ROMs are also available with access times under 1 μsec. Both $32k$-ROMs and $64k$-ROMs are becoming available. The latter allow $8k$-bytes of instruction or data to be stored *in one chip*.

It should be pointed out that most memories come in several speeds. The Intel 2102, for example, can be bought with access times ranging from 250 to 650 nsec. These are all the same memories, but have been graded as they come off the production line and divided into three categories. The price of the device is generally a function of its speed.

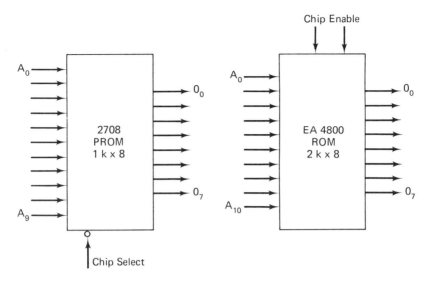

Figure 4-26

The cost of ROM is approximately 1 cent per byte. Thus, it is often cheaper to perform a given function in software, using penny instructions, than in hardware, using dollar devices. For cost savings, PROMs are usually available as masked ROMs; i.e., after the system has been proven with PROMs, large numbers of a system are more economically produced by using cheaper masked ROMs that are identically configured to the PROM. Finally, there are data structures that do not change, such as trig tables, code converters, character codes, and others. These are manufactured in large quantities and sold cheaply relative to any other ROM containing the equivalent amount of information.

First-In-First-Out Buffers

As the trend toward multiprocessor systems continues, there is more need for buffer memories that can be used to hold information being transferred between processors or between a processor and an asynchronous peripheral device. The use of standard memories shared between asynchronous devices is awkward at best. The flexible buffer best suited for this function would allow words to be entered in one port at almost any speed, and removed from another port at a completely unrelated speed. Thus, loading of information and accessing of information would occur at the natural frequency for each system. The Signetics 2535 MOS First-In-First-Out (FIFO) Buffer shown in Fig. 4-27 exhibits the following characteristics.

The device functions from DC to 1 MHz, and is fully TTL compatible. It will operate in either a parallel or a serial mode, and contains logic that provides flags to indicate the presence of data and the availability of empty storage

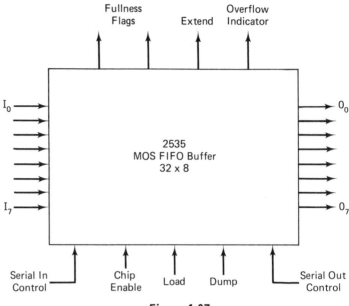

Figure 4-27

locations. It is designed so that data entered at the input will "fall through" to the lowest unoccupied location. Particularly convenient is the fact that several buffers may be configured to expand the buffer in either the bit or the word direction. The 2535 provides 32 8-bit words of elastic storage. A similar device that provides 64 words of storage is available from Texas Instruments.

Content Addressable Memories

The ability to retrieve data based on content rather than on an address is valuable because it apparently mimics human information storage more than the fixed address structured memories. Many applications would probably be achieved much more easily by using Content Addressable Memories (CAMs); however, the cost is usually prohibitive. The devices require "keys" or identifiers to allow addressing a particular data item, resulting in a more complex cell structure. The use of large arrays of CAM is economically prohibited today. Certain small problems, however, are ideally solved by using CAMs. The best use to date is probably the minicomputer virtual paging system developed at the University of Massachusetts. In this scheme, large, cheap, slow storage is combined with small, costly, fast storage, and the data currently in use are moved by the "page" into the fast-memory section. A CAM is used to record which "pages" are in fast memory. Each address sent to memory also addresses the CAM, and if the addressed page is present, no action occurs. If the CAM indicates the page is not present, then execution ceases until the page is fetched from mass storage. This hardware virtual memory system allows the programmer to pretend (or even believe) that he has relatively unlimited directly addressable storage, and thereby relieves him of the task of keeping track of page storage. The Fairchild 93402 (not shown) is a 4 × 4 CAM. CAMs are sometimes called Associative Memories.

ARITHMETIC LOGIC UNIT

A central component of any computer is the arithmetic logic unit that performs the arithmetic and logical operations upon data. These units have evolved from serial vacuum tube units to discrete transistors, and then to systems implemented with small-scale integrated circuits. The medium-scale integrated Arithmetic Logic Unit (ALU) served for several years as the epitome of TTL integrated technology. The Texas Instruments 74181 ALU provides separate input ports for two 4-bit data words and an output port for the 4-bit result of the operation. Another port serves as an input for the control word or instruction used to select one of 32 possible operations. In addition, several lines indicate special conditions, such as equality of the operands and the occurrence of a carry bit as the result of the operation. The presence of a carry-in line, in addition to the carry-out line, allows the 74181s to be cascaded to form 4 × N-bit ALUs. The devices are quite fast with the ability to add or subtract in 36 nsec. Although the 74181 has the capability of performing 32 operations, only a portion of these are considered useful. These are shown in Fig. 4-28. The 74181 has been used to build the Arithmetic Logic Units of many of the computers on the market.

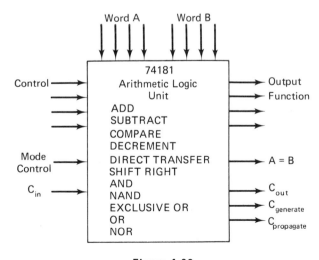

Figure 4-28

Accumulator

The ALU just discussed is normally associated with a temporary storage register where the results of additions or other operations are accumulated. This register is (strangely enough) called the accumulator. Although this has been implemented with latches in most computers, in 1973 Texas Instruments developed their second-generation ALU, the 74S281, which includes a storage matrix on the chip. This device is called a monolithic accumulator and is an example of Large-Scale Integrated (LSI) TTL technology. The S in 74S281 stands for Schottky circuitry, a high-speed version of TTL. With four 74S281s and a CARRY-LOOK-AHEAD chip, a 16-bit addition can be performed in 27 nsec. This is impressive speed and amounts to almost 40 million additions per second! Additional features of the '281 include both logical left shift and right shift capability, and arithmetic left and right shifts. The storage register is on the chip and features multiplexed tri-state output/input cascading lines. The device is shown in Fig. 4-29.

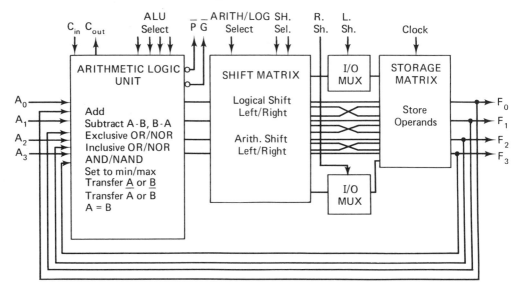

Figure 4-29

Microcontrollers

The evolution of the 74181 ALU resulted in the second-generation ALU/Accumulator, the 74281. The third generation of this continuing evolution is represented by the Monolithic Memories 6701 Microcontroller. This device and the Texas Instruments 74481 are best discussed in terms of micro-programming, and this treatment is therefore postponed.

ANALOG / DIGITAL / ANALOG DEVICES

A great number of applications require the conversion of analog voltages in digital numbers. This conversion is accomplished by using analog-to-digital converters. An example is given in Chapter 10, which treats input-output structure of microprocessors. The inverse operation of converting digital numbers into analog voltages is also possible by using digital-to-analog converters. Both of these building blocks are available in monolithic form.

Universal Asynchronous Receiver/Transmitters

Communications-oriented building blocks, such as UARTs, will be presented in Chapters 10 and 14.

INTERFACING BETWEEN TTL AND MOS CIRCUITS

Most large-scale integrated circuits are implemented by using MOS technology, while most small- and medium-scale circuits use TTL, although Complementary MOS (CMOS) is rapidly encroaching. The different characteristics of TTL and MOS must, therefore, be considered when interfacing between these two families. There are far too many MOS configurations to treat all cases; however, it is possible to state some fairly general rules about interfacing.

The voltage specifications for TTL circuits apply universally to all devices in the family. These are presented in Chapter 2. MOS circuits operate with a wide variety of voltages, normally more widely spaced than TTL, with logic levels close to the values of the high and low power supplies. The inputs to TTL sustain current flow, whereas MOS gates are essentially capacitive, and gate current will flow only until the capacitor is charged or discharged. Thus, the ability to drive an MOS input requires sufficient voltage swings and adequate current capability to drive the gate capacitance at the required speed. The drive capability of TTL is sufficient to provide the speed for most MOS capacitive loads. Many MOS devices do not possess sufficient drive capability for standard TTL; however, they can drive Low Power TTL (LPTTL). The LPTTL supplies only 0.18 mA to the MOS driver, however, as compared with 1.6 mA for standard TTL gates.

The TTL-to-MOS Interface

The use of a $+5$-V power supply for TTL and from -5- to -30-V power supplies for MOS devices often requires interface devices that specifically perform the level translation needed. These are readily available and are listed in parts catalogs under the heading *Interface Devices*. A more desirable situation can be obtained if there is a positive MOS voltage greater than, or equal to, the TTL supply voltage. Since the MOS substrate potential, V_{SS}, is the most positive MOS voltage, this can often be made positive to allow direct interfacing with TTL. For the simplest case, $V_{SS} = +5$ V, we can attempt to drive an MOS input from the TTL outputs as shown in Fig. 4-30.

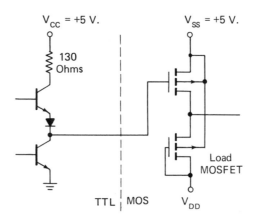

Figure 4-30

The gate voltages are referenced to the substrate potential, and the MOSFET is typically OFF for gate voltages in the range V_{SS} to $V_{SS} - 2$ V, and ON when the gate is more than 4 V below the substrate potential. The guaranteed output levels of TTL circuits are less than 0.4 V and greater than 2.4 V. These correspond to gate voltages at the MOSFET input of $V_{SS} = 4.6$ V and $V_{SS} = 2.6$ V, respectively. This is not sufficient to guarantee the MOS device will be in the OFF state; therefore, additional steps are necessary. The simple expedient of adding a "pull-up" resistor, R, between the TTL output and V_{SS} will solve this problem by rasing the TTL voltage for a logic "1" output. The logic "0" output is less critical and requires no extra precautions. This setup is shown in Fig. 4-31.

The same solution applies when V_{SS} is at a higher potential than V_{CC}. The situation for $V_{SS} = 10$ V is shown in Fig. 4-32. The pull-up resistors are normally 1000 Ω or less.

For those cases where the logic swings cannot be met by the TTL outputs, the use of discrete transistors is required. These configurations are treated in many manufacturers' application notes, however, the trend is toward systems that can be directly interfaced with only a pull-up resistor. For most clock inputs to shift registers and dynamic RAMs, the capacitive loading is enormously increased by the many gates that must be driven. Although we can

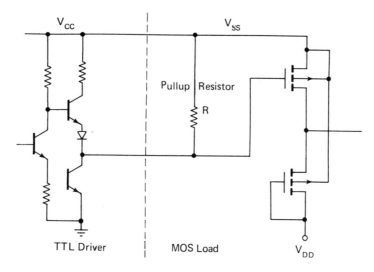

Figure 4-31

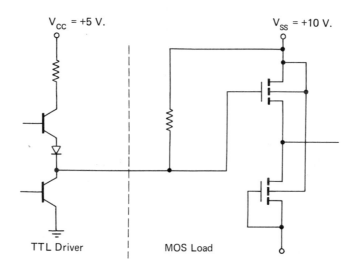

Figure 4-32

design transistor driver circuits, there are numerous clock-driver chips that are specifically designed for this task. The use of these devices is recommended.

The MOS-to-TTL Interface

The use of an external resistor may be required also when driving a TTL input from an MOS output. The resistance to ground seen by the TTL input

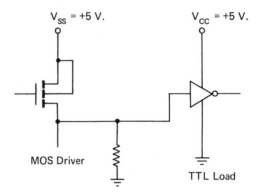

Figure 4-33

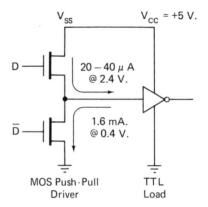

Figure 4-34

must be 250 ohms or less; therefore, the resistance in parallel with the MOS device is usually about 500 ohms. Such a circuit is shown in Fig. 4-33. The MOS output that is most widely used is the push-pull circuit, shown in Fig. 4-34, which does not require an external resistor.

Although such outputs can be designed to drive one TTL load, it is far more common to find P-channel MOS (P-MOS) drivers that will drive one low-power TTL device.

N-Channel MOS

The use of N-channel MOS provides higher packing density and more TTL-compatible input-output characteristics. Although the first MOS devices were universally P-MOS, most second-generation microprocessors are implemented with N-channel MOS (N-MOS). These ordinarily require no special precautions and will interface directly to one standard TTL device.

TRI-STATE DEVICES

We have seen that the two-state, ON/OFF, nature of digital devices allows their use in systems designed to work with both binary arithmetic and two-valued logic. From a purely systems point of view, a third state becomes extremely useful. Although this third state is termed the HIGH-Z state, it is perhaps better thought of as the "invisible" state. The Z stands for impedance, and the principle is illustrated in Fig. 4-35.

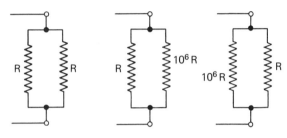

Figure 4-35

The left-hand circuit contains two resistors with value R. These are of equal weight and provide twice the load of either alone. In the center and right-hand diagrams the impedance of one of the pair has been increased enormously, to the point where the path containing the large resistance approximates an open circuit. The large resistor provides almost no loading and, in effect, becomes nearly "invisible" to the rest of the circuit, i.e., the smaller resistor determines the impedance seen by the driver. The ability to greatly increase the resistance of a parallel circuit element provides a means of effectively removing the element from the circuit. Thus, a device that possesses this property can electrically be switched in and out of a system—a highly useful feature for any device.

By examining the push-pull output of the preceding section, we can fairly easily see how such behavior may be accomplished. The push-pull output shown in Fig. 4-36 uses two MOSFET variable resistances instead of one variable and one fixed load device. By gating the devices with complementary signals, one device will always be in the low-resistance state and the other in the high-resistance state, as required. This circuit also provides the possibility of sending *both* MOSFETs into the high-resistance region, effectively creating an open circuit. This can be accomplished by tying the gates to V_{ss} through another pair of MOSFETs used as transmission gates. When these output disable gates

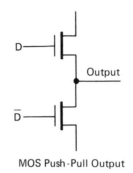

MOS Push-Pull Output

Figure 4-36

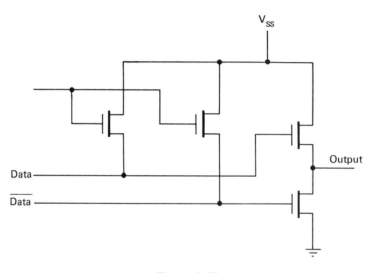

Figure 4-37

are in the low-resistance state, they hold teh output gates at V_{SS}, thus cutting off both output MOSFETs. This circuit is shown in Fig. 4-37.

As we will later discover, there is strong economic incentive to minimize the number of pins on a package, and one means of achieving this is through bidirectional data transfer over common pins. Thus, by sending the output into the Hi-Z mode the output line can then be used for inputting data to another MOSFET. Such a scheme is shown in Fig. 4-38. The particular circuit shown is the bidirectional data bus of the Intel 8008 microprocessor. It is directly low-power TTL compatible.

Although the device physics are different for TTL, the tri-state operation is the same. A tri-state circuit may be disabled with a control line and effectively switched out of the system. Tri-state devices characteristically require very low

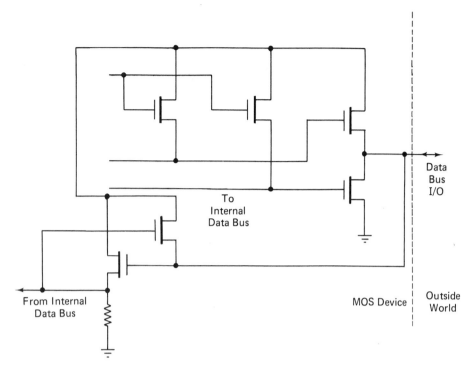

Figure 4-38

input currents and provide very hefty drive capability. They are ideal for bus-structured systems, as will be seen in Chapter 7.

CMOS DEVICES

The push-pull output described in the preceding section leads quite naturally to one of the newest logic families, Complementary MOS or CMOS. The CMOS family uses both P-MOS and N-MOS, as shown in Fig. 4-39. Since the substrates are at different potentials, we no longer speak of V_{SS} and V_{DD}, but use the TTL terminology, V_{CC} and ground. The devices are designed so that each transistor has the same threshold value, but is otherwise complementary. Thus, the input signal passing through the threshold turns one device OFF as it turns the other ON. Since only one device can be conducting at a time, and the OFF resistance is extremely high, virtually no current will flow from V_{CC} to ground. Actually, the thresholds are never exactly equal; therefore, there will be some current flow as the input signal swings through the threshold region.

At this point, both MOSFETs are low resistance and a large current will momentarily flow. If the signal passes through this region quite often, i.e.,

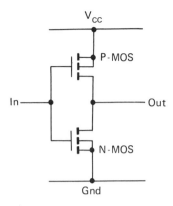

Figure 4-39

if the device is operated at high frequencies, then appreciable power will be dissipated here. At high frequencies, the effect of the input capacitance also increases power dissipation. At low frequencies, and in static operation, the current is barely measurable and CMOS will operate well off batteries in this situation. As an example, electronic wristwatches use CMOS circuitry that is powered by tiny batteries for months. The first CMOS devices were produced by RCA and are known as the 4000 series. National Semiconductor has introduced a pin-for-pin TTL-compatible family known as the 74C series. Although the cost of CMOS is higher than TTL, the ratio is declining.

The advantages of CMOS include very low power consumption at the low operating frequencies, on the order of 10 nanowatts for static operation. Low propagation delays are on the order of 25 to 50 nsec, and noise immunity is very high due to the fact that the logic levels are effectively equal to the power supply voltages. The speed of CMOS and the power consumption both go up as the power supply voltage is increased. Unlike TTL, which must operate at 5 V, plus or minus 10%, CMOS will operate over a range of 3 to 15 V (3 to 18 for the Motorola devices). The noise immunity is approximately 45% of the power supply voltage, i.e., a 6-V noise spike should not affect a flip-flop operating at 15 V. The range of usable power supply voltages facilitates interfacing to other logic families. For P-MOS operating over a 15-V range, the coupling is direct; however, a pulldown resistor is required to compensate for the fact that the lower P-MOS threshold is nowhere near ground.

An alternate solution, and one that is necessary when the P-MOS operates above 15 V, consists of biasing the CMOS as shown in Fig. 4-40. The low power drain of CMOS makes this solution relatively economical, and a battery or small power supply made with discrete parts is often sufficient for this bias source. If TTL is also present, the high voltage will be the TTL supply and the P-MOS will be more negatively biased. CMOS interfaces quite readily to N-MOS, although in some cases a pullup resistor is recommended on the N-MOS output. The same statement applies to TTL, i.e., a pullup resistor may

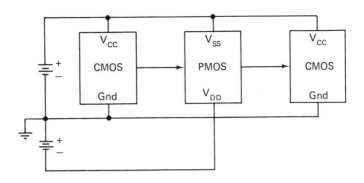

Figure 4-40

be required on the TTL output. CMOS will readily interface to LPTTL and can be paralleled to obtain sufficient drive capability for standard TTL. The ability to obtain increased drive capability by using two or more inputs of a multi-input NAND gate may be seen by examining the structure of the NAND gate shown in Fig. 4-41.

The disadvantages associated with CMOS are higher cost and decreased ruggedness. The high input impedance is especially susceptible to static charge buildup, and voltages sufficient to cause electrical breakdown can result from

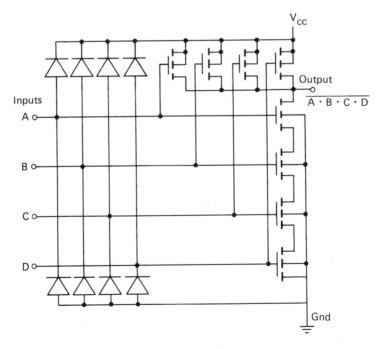

Figure 4-41

simply handling the devices. CMOS also appears to fail during operation at a higher rate than TTL, particularly when operating at higher voltages. For very high-frequency operation, the power loss is of the same order of magnitude as that of TTL.

In addition to TTL-like circuitry there is a clever and exceedingly useful CMOS device that has no analog in TTL. This is the transmission gate shown in Fig. 4-42. As can be seen, both of the parallel devices are either ON or OFF, presenting either a low resistance (ON) or an effectively open circuit (OFF). Thus, unlike TTL, CMOS can switch analog signals as well as digital signals.

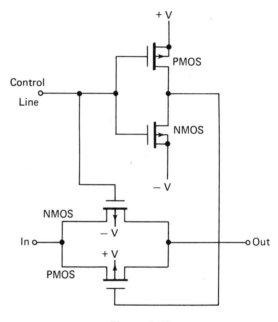

Figure 4-42

In summary, for many applications, CMOS has no competition. The low power and ease of interfacing with MOS circuits make CMOS especially attractive for microprocessor-based systems. The number of MSI components in the family is growing rapidly, and the series is certainly destined to play a major role in digital electronics.

SUMMARY

The digital universe is divided into two parts: space and time. Each of these can be subdivided into pieces or channels, and information conveyed over these channels. Although classically the time channels have been the cheapest to use, the ever-decreasing cost of hardware makes the spatial, or parallel, path system economical in many applications. The cost of transmitting fully parallel (one channel per choice) information is prohibitive, however, and a compressed information, or coding, scheme is generally employed. The coded information oftens serves as addresses of information storage cells, and access to the appropriate cell requires decoding of the address. By organizing cells in matrix configurations and addressing each cell by using a *pair* of address lines, the cost and number of required lines are decreased appreciably. The cells themselves are designed in a variety of configurations, with each configuration chosen to optimize some parameter, such as space, speed, cost, power consumption, etc. The use of either static or dynamic memories is usually dependent upon the size of the memory and is based purely on economic grounds. Large memories are implemented with dynamic devices and small memories are static, although for one-of-a-kind systems the design time may offset the price advantage of dynamic memories for medium-size systems.

The digital building blocks have been designed as an extremely compatible family, with the TTL specifications serving as the standard to which others are compared. Any function that is performed quite often in digital systems may be bought in packaged form as an integrated circuit. This includes such functions as coding, decoding, arithmetic operations, comparisons, latching, routing, counting, and other operations.

Various features of MOS and CMOS logic families may dictate that a system be designed using elements from different families. Thus, a general knowledge of the family characteristics aids in the design of interfaces between these elements. The nonuniformity of MOS devices means that no fixed interfacing rules can be stated and then followed; however, the general methods described in this chapter apply to most of the applications we expect to encounter. The manufacturers of the different devices usually provide interface rules and guidelines, as well as examples and even specific information such as the values of pullup resistors. Many, if not most, of the recently designed MOS devices are TTL compatible or at least low-power TTL compatible. The emergence of N-MOS technology has increased this trend considerably.

This chapter provides the background necessary for the design of digital systems by using available building blocks. Future chapters will develop architectural concepts with specific examples and applications of digital systems.

5   *a central processor unit instruction set*

Up to this point, the functioning of digital systems has been viewed primarily from the hardware perspective. This is the preferred viewpoint when designing digital subsystems, and we shall return to it in Chapter 6. However, the software perspective is to be preferred for viewing a complex system such as the LSI microprocessor. The instruction set of a processor serves to highlight the functional aspects of the system rather than the functioning of subsystems. The complementarity of the two descriptions is somewhat analogous to the particle/wave duality of quantum physics, and is interesting in its own right. However, we will not delve into this topic any further in this chapter.

THE ORIGIN OF "SOFTWARE"

In previous chapters a number of functional elements have been presented and a means of steering data along prescribed paths has been developed. The functional elements are remarkable in themselves, but when combined to form a central processor unit, these basic hardware devices assume a flexibility and fluidity that has given rise to the term "software."

The ability to "steer" data along a chosen path was demonstrated in the Signetics 2533 shift register recirculation path and also in the universal shift register developed in Chapter 3. Via the use of storage registers composed of latches and arithmetic logic units similar to the Texas Instruments 74181, it is possible to access stored data, perform prescribed operations on the data, and store the result in a register. In general, such operations require three information *fields*: one to specify the data source, one to specify the operation, and one to specify the destination register. It is possible to arrange the basic functional elements and data paths so that these three functions are independent or orthogonal. Thus, the circuit can be effectively "rewired" by altering one or more of the control fields!

The ability to electrically "rewire" a circuit by changing a control word is the basis of all digital information processors. It allows certain pieces of hardware to be used repeatedly in various configurations. This is obviously a sequential process, and the sequence of control words is called a "program." The individual control words are called "instructions." This chapter presents the instruction set of the Intel 8008 microprocessor, a subset of the instruction sets of Intel 8080 and 8085 microprocessors.

STORED-PROGRAM MACHINES

The ability to apply one piece of hardware to an incredible variety of problems is provided via custom-tailored instruction sequences or programs. These programs are stored in a "program store" that is often physically separate from the processor unit. The retrieval and interpretation of these instructions are handled by the Central Processor Unit (CPU) via instruction fetch and instruction decoding and control subsystems.

THE BASIC PROCESSOR CYCLE

The essential function of processors has been summarized in Chapter 1 in terms of five basic operations:

1. READ the input symbol X.
2. COMPARE X with Z, the internal state of the processor.
3. WRITE the appropriate output symbol Y.
4. CHANGE the internal state Z to the new state Z'.
5. REPEAT the above sequence with a new input symbol X'.

This definition obviously refers to a *sequential* processor. The internal state of the processor refers to the configuration of data paths and latching signals determined by the control signals from the instruction decoder. This state is altered as prescribed in step 4 above, by fetching a new instruction from the instruction store. The lack of this instruction-fetch mechanism prevented the arithmetic-logic units described in the previous chapter from qualifying as full-fledged microprocessors. The Intel 8008 described in this chapter possesses all of the properties needed to execute the operations that define a processor.

In general, the basic cycle of stored program machines is:

EXECUTE   FETCH
INSTRUCTION   INSTRUCTION

In the 8008 CPU, each cycle is divided into five subcycles or *states*: T1, T2, T3, T4, T5. States T1 and T2 are associated with the instruction FETCH phase of the cycle and states T3, T4, and T5 are associated with the EXECUTION phase. (States T4 and T5 are optional as explained later.)

The instruction FETCH mechanism is treated in detail in following chapters. This chapter treats intraCPU processes, i.e., those functions that occur *within* the CPU. In particular, we develop the control word set or instruction set associated with the Intel 8008, 8080, and 8085.

The 8008 CPU possesses a register file that consists of seven 8-bit registers, each of which can serve either as a source of data or a destination register. These registers are individually labeled A, B, C, D, E, H, and L. The organization of the register file in the CPU provides for register-to-register transfers of data. Since the source and destination registers must be specified in the instruction, the 8008 register file instructions are also two-address instructions and have this format:

Two-Address Transfer Instruction Format	Opcode Field	Destination Reg. Field (3)	Source Reg. Field (3)

The address fields are shown as three bits wide since there are only seven registers to be addressed. The two opcode bits are used to specify the class of register-register instructions as distinct from other classes of instructions. They instruct the processor to access a source register and transfer the contents of this register to a destination register. The contents of register *r* are denoted by (r). Thus, the above process may be described symbolically by writing:

$$(r_{dest}) \longleftarrow (r_{source})$$

By convention the source register is specified on the right and the destination register on the left. This convention is followed throughout this book. All of the data-transfer instructions are called MOVE instructions and are denoted by writing MOV and specifying the source and destination registers as follows:

MOV D, S

11	DDD	SSS

The register file internal to the processor is used for temporary storage of data that are currently being processed in much the same manner as a scratchpad for intermediate results and, for this reason, are termed scratchpad registers.

The hardware design of the CPU precludes a direct transfer from register to register during a single state. The transfer is effected via a temporary storage register (reg. b) that cannot be addressed by any instruction and is, therefore, invisible to the programmer. The CPU executes an intraregister-file transfer, MOV D, S, during states T4 and T5 as follows:

T4:   (reg. b) ⟵ (SSS)
T5:   (DDD) ⟵ (reg. b)

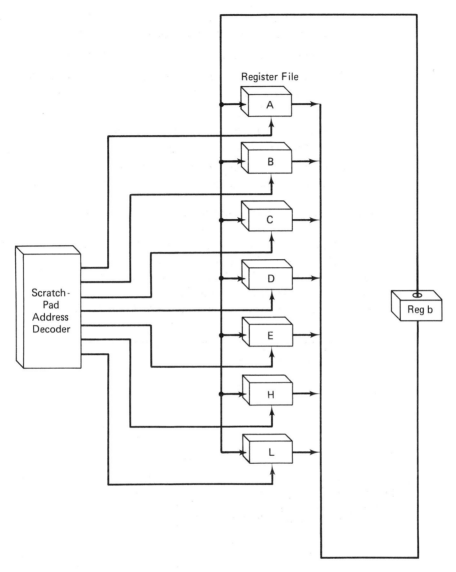

Figure 5-1

This discussion has disclosed a partial view of the internal architecture of the central processor unit which is shown in Fig. 5-1.

The receipt of the MOV D, S instruction initiates the "data transfer" operation that executes the following algorithm in hardware:

1. Select, during T4, the address bits of the source register field and multiplex these bits via the scratchpad address multiplexer to the scratchpad address decoder.

2. Access the data stored in the source register and place the data on the internal data bus via the memory data multiplexer.

3. Latch the data on the bus into temporary register b.

4. Select, during T5, the address bits of the destination register and send the bits via the scratchpad address multiplexer to the scratch pad address decoder.

5. Access the data stored in temporary register b and place the data on the internal data bus.

6. Latch the data on the internal data bus into the destination register in the scratchpad register file via the memory multiplexer.

The subsystems that accomplish the execution of the above algorithm are shown in Fig. 5-2.

There are additional subsystems that may be inferred from our discussion of the CPU. The 8-bit data transfer instruction must enter the CPU via an 8-bit wide port through which all data, addresses, and instructions are input or output, and the $\overline{CPU}$ data bus must be buffered from the internal data bus. From the discussion we expect to find an Instruction Register (IR), an instruction

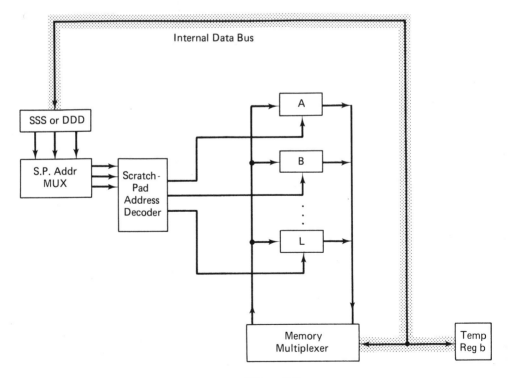

Figure 5-2

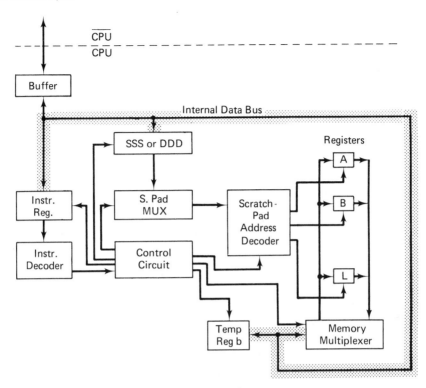

Figure 5-3

decoder, and control circuitry. The expanded system that includes these subsystems is shown in Fig. 5-3.

The path to the outside world leads to external random access memory. The CPU can access and store data in either the internal scratchpad memory or the external RAM, and we would expect that a means of transferring data between internal registers and external memory registers might exist. Such is the case, and we now consider it in detail.

In order to either access or store data in external memory, it is necessary, first, to send the address of the appropriate external memory register to the $\overline{\text{CPU}}$. This 14-bit address is time multiplexed over the data bus during T1 and T2 as an 8-bit, low-order address and a 6-bit, high-order address. These are latched and sent to the RAM address decoder for selecting the memory register to be used during state T3. The R/W signal, which determines whether the register is to be accessed or loaded, is derived from the two-cycle control bits sent out on the data bus lines D_6 and D_7 during T2. These bits are placed on the data bus by the machine cycle-control subsystem and are derived from the instruction via the instruction decoder. The data are transferred between the CPU register and RAM register during state T3. These subsystems are shown in Fig. 5-4.

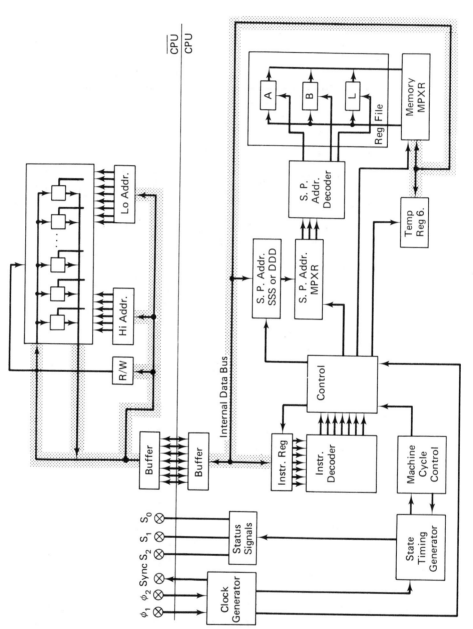

Figure 5-4

The instruction that accomplishes the CPU/$\overline{\text{CPU}}$ register-to-register data transfer is a MOV instruction and has the same 11 opcode as the internal register-register transfer instructions. A two-register transfer instruction must contain two address fields and, as in the previous MOV instruction, the CPU register is specified by a 3-bit register address field. This internal register may serve as either the source or the destination register. The requirement that 14 bits of RAM address be used to select the external register presents something of a problem. If these 14 bits are included in the instruction proper, a 19-bit instruction will result. This awkward length would require three 8-bit words of storage and be wasteful of storage since there would be 5 unused bits of storage per instruction. To avoid this situation the Intel designers made the following trade-off. The use of seven registers in the internal register file requires 3 bits of register address, but does not exhaust the possible 3-bit codes. The eighth code (111) is, therefore, designated as a special code that addresses not one, but a *pair* of registers, the H and L registers. This pair is used as a pointer to the external register in RAM, i.e., the address of the external register is stored in the H-L register pair and sent to the RAM during T1 and T2 of the appropriate cycle. The instruction format is shortened in that only the 3-bit address of the H-L pair is required, and not the full 14 bits. The H-L pair is treated as a new register, the *M* pointer. Thus, an instruction that will send data from an internal register to an external register has this format:

MOV *M, r*

11	111	SSS
Opcode Field	Dest. Reg. (*M*) Field	Source Register Field

This instruction is 8 bits long and requires minimal space in the instruction storage area and wastes no bits. The cost associated with this solution is far from negligible, however. Before any word in external memory can be addressed, it is necessary to preload the H-L register with the pointer address. If this must be done very often, the overhead is tremendous and both time and storage space are wasted. This may be avoided, or at least minimized, by storing data in sequential locations so that the address must be changed by adding the number one to the previous contents of the *M* pointer. This is a weak point associated with the 8008 CPU, and one that has been remedied in the second-generation microprocessor, the 8080, and in the third generation 8085.

We should also make note of the terminology that applies to this type of addressing. Normally the use of an intermediate register to hold the address of a destination register is referred to as *indirect* addressing. If the intermediate register is one of the scratchpad registers, then it is permissible to refer to this addressing scheme as *direct* addressing. The use of the term *direct* more commonly is taken to mean that the address is contained within the instruction proper, i.e., had we included all 14 bits of address in the instruction, this would have been direct addressing in the usual sense. Addressing modes are quite important and differ from processor to processor; therefore, it is necessary to know what is being referred to when the term "direct" is used.

The execution of the CPU/$\overline{\text{CPU}}$ data transfer requires another cycle, during which the address of the external register is sent to RAM. The fetch and execution of the MOV M, r instruction are shown below. It is assumed that the M pointer has been preloaded with the proper address of the external RAM register.

MOV M,r

Cycle	State	Process
	T1	Low-order instruction address sent to RAM address latch.
PCI	T2	High-order address sent to RAM address latch.
	T3	MOV M,r is fetched from memory to instruction register.
	T4	Move contents of register r into temporary register b.
	T1	Contents of register L sent to RAM address latch.
PCW	T2	Contents of register H sent to RAM address latch.
	T3	Contents of register b written into RAM.

It is instructive to compare the execution of the MOV M, r with that of a MOV r, M instruction in which the transfer is from RAM to the scratchpad register r. The format is shown below. The M register is now the source and r is the destination register.

MOV r, M

11	DDD	111
Opcode Field	Dest. Register Field	Source Reg. (M) Field

The algorithmic execution of this instruction is outlined below:

MOV r,M

Cycle	State	Process
	T1	Low-order instruction address sent to RAM.
PCI	T2	High-order address sent to RAM.
	T3	MOV r,M instruction fetched from RAM.
	T1	(L) sent to RAM address latch.
	T2	(H) sent to RAM address latch.
PCR	T3	Data read from RAM and stored in temporary register b.
	T4	Idle state
	T5	Contents of register b loaded into register r.

The execution of the MOV M, r instruction sends data from the internal register r to the RAM. This data is available as soon as the instruction is fetched and, therefore, the T4 state of the PCI instruction fetch cycle is used to load the data into the temporary register b. The RAM address is then sent out and the register b data is written into RAM. Compare this with the PCI cycle of the MOV r, M instruction. Here the instruction is fetched at T3 and the cycle ends. This is necessary because there is no data immediately available for loading into the temporary register. Only after the address has been sent to RAM during the PCR DATA-READ cycle can the data be accessed and loaded into the temporary register. The relevant point here is that the CPU "knows" what states are needed. There is no need for the programmer to concern himself/herself with the actual execution states. The state sequence is presented for insight into the workings of the CPU and not because this information is necessary to use the device. Only when we are concerned with execution times is knowledge of the sequence of states needed; however, this is available for all instructions in the relevant data books. The mechanism by which the 8008 CPU "knows" what action is needed is the feedback shift register that was discussed in Chapter 3.

IMMEDIATE DATA INSTRUCTIONS

The MOV r_1, r_2, MOV M, r, and MOV r, M instructions have been 1-byte instructions that transfer data from a source register to a destination register. The transfers between the CPU and RAM have required that the H-L register pair be preloaded with the pointer address to the RAM register. It is possible, via the use of 2-byte instructions, to effect a data transfer from RAM without preloading the M pointer. The MOVE DATA IMMEDIATE (MVI) instructions contain the data in the second byte of the instruction. The first byte contains the opcode and the destination register address. The execution of the instruction results in the data byte being loaded into the destination register in the CPU. The MVI r instruction has this format:

MVI r	00 DDD 110
DATA	b b b b b b b b

The CPU recognizes the MVI instruction as a 2-byte instruction and automatically fetches the second byte, DATA, requiring no action on the part of the programmer. In particular, the H-L register pair is not used and need not be preloaded. A variation that does use the H-L pair exists in the MVI M

instruction that loads the data byte immediately following the instruction byte into the RAM register addresses by the pointer in the *M* register.

THE PROGRAM COUNTER

In order to understand the execution of the MVI instructions, we consider the means by which the CPU sequences through the instructions stored in memory. The address of the current instruction is always stored in a special CPU register called the Program Counter. This register is 14 bits wide and is time-multiplexed as PC_L, the lower 8 bits, and PC_H, the higher 6 bits, during T1 and T2, respectively, of the PCI instruction fetch cycle. After an instruction byte has been fetched from memory, the contents of the program counter are normally incremented by one, thus maintaining the pointer to the next byte to be fetched from memory. This address is utilized in the MVI instructions by loading data at this address and thus using the program counter (PC) to point to the data rather than the *M* pointer. It is obvious that only data that are known when the instruction sequence or program is being written may be used in this manner. The MVI instructions provide a convenient means of storing constants in a program and eliminate the need to go through the *M* pointer. This frees the *M* pointer for use in the MVI *M* instruction that fetches the data byte from the instruction stream and stores it through the *M* pointer. The algorithm that executes this memory-to-memory transfer is:

MVI M

Cycle	State	Process
	T1	PC_L sent to RAM address latch.
PCI	T2	PC_H sent to RAM address latch.
	T3	First byte of MVI *M* fetched into instruction register and PC is incremented by one.
	T1	PC_L sent to RAM address latch.
PCR	T2	PC_H sent to RAM address latch.
	T3	Second (data) byte of MVI *M* instruction is fetched and stored in temporary register b.
	T1	Register L sent to RAM address latch.
PCW	T2	Register H sent to RAM address latch.
	T3	Register b sent to RAM register that is addressed by RAM address latch.

All of the previous instructions that move data from one location to another have involved the scratchpad registers and are known as the CPU Register Instructions. There are two other instructions in this class, the Increment Register and the Decrement Register instructions. The format of both of these instructions is:

$$\text{INr} \quad \boxed{\begin{array}{ccc} 00 & DDD & 000 \end{array}} \quad (r) \longleftarrow (r) + 1$$

$$\text{DCr} \quad \boxed{\begin{array}{ccc} 00 & DDD & 001 \end{array}} \quad (r) \longleftarrow (r) - 1$$

Each instruction contains the address of a single CPU register. The contents of the register is accessed during the execution of the instruction, one is added to or subtracted from the contents, and the result is restored in the register.

The last two instructions in the CPU register group have introduced a new capability, an arithmetic capability, into the CPU processes. There must then be an arithmetic subsystem that must be added to the previously developed CPU architecture. This subsystem consists of an 8-bit parallel arithmetic unit, and another temporary register, register *a*, along with the appropriate control circuitry. The temporary registers, *a* and *b*, are used exclusively by the CPU and cannot be accessed or loaded by the user. The expanded CPU architecture is shown in Fig. 5-5. The RAM is shown as a functional subsystem considered as a file or linear array of 8-bit registers which can be accessed or loaded as described above.

ACCUMULATOR GROUP INSTRUCTIONS

The inclusion of an arithmetic subsystem in the CPU architecture offers the possibility of not only transferring data between registers but of performing arithmetic transformations on the data while enroute. The use of a 1-byte instruction to specify a source register, one of several arithmetic transformations, and a destination register is clearly not feasible. Either a 2-byte instruction must be used, or some of the above information must be sacrificed to allow the use of only one byte. Since arithmetic instructions are quite common, the use of a 2-byte instruction is costly in terms of memory. A 1-byte instruction is achieved by sacrificing the generality that allows any of the registers to be used as a destination register. Instead, the results of the operation are accumulated in a special register called the *Accumulator*. The A register is designated as the accumulator and need not be specified in the instruction. The field that was previously used for specifying the destination register may now be used to specify the operation to be performed. The execution of an accumulator group instruction proceeds as follows: The data in the accumulator and the data in the source register are operated on by the arithmetic unit, and the result of the operation is accumulated in the A register. The contents of the source register are unchanged. The format is:

	Opcode	Function	Source Byte
Accumulator Group Instruction Format	bb	bbb	bbb

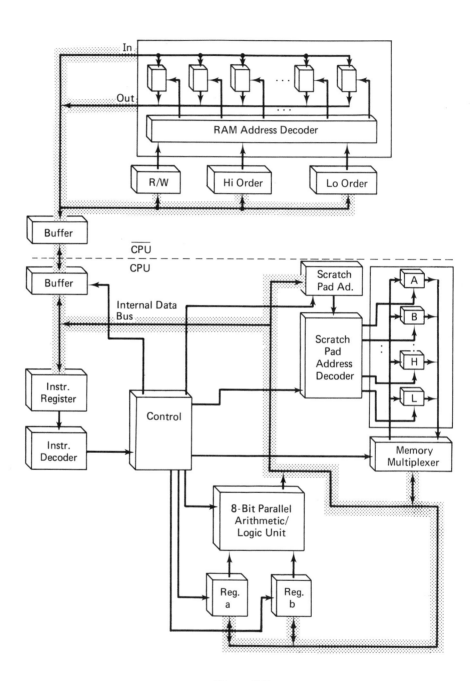

Figure 5-5

A partial listing of the processor capabilities is:

1. Fetch an instruction from memory and load the instruction register.

2. Transfer data from a memory register into the CPU register file.

3. Transfer data from the CPU register file into a memory register.

4. Transfer data between CPU registers.

5. Increment or decrement the contents of a CPU register.

6. Combine arithmetically the contents of two registers.

Previous discussion has indicated the desirability of these additional capabilities:

7. Compare the contents of two registers.

8. Use the result of the comparison to determine the next execution.

Central to the topic of branching is the existence of a condition bit or FLAG, the value of which is determined by the result of a specific operation. There are four such flags in the 8008 CPU (and five in the 8080 and 8085). They are associated with the accumulator group instructions. These condition flags, or status flip-flops, are generally set as a result of an operation performed on the contents of the accumulator. The accumulator group instructions always performs some operation on data and stores the result in the accumulator. Thus, answers to questions about the result of the operation may be found by examining the status of the contents of the accumulator. Several types of questions can be asked about the accumulator contents. The presence of a zero result is indicated by a ZERO flip-flop being set. Similarly, a CARRY flip-flop indicates the occurrence of a carry during an addition or a borrow during subtraction. The PARITY of the accumulator contents is available as is the SIGN of the twos complement result. The sign bit is the Most Significant Bit (MSB) of the word, and the magnitude of the word is given by the least significant seven bits of the word. The condition flags, or status flip-flops, their selection codes, and their interpretation when TRUE are summarized here:

Flag Symbol	Flag Code (c_4c_3)	Flag Name	Condition Indicated by True Flag
C	00	CARRY	Overflow, underflow
Z	01	ZERO	Result of operation is zero.
S	10	SIGN	MSB of result is "1."
P	11	PARITY	Parity of the result is even.

The flags are set by the accumulator group instructions. The discussion of the uses of these flags is postponed so the accumulator group instructions can now be discussed in detail. The symbols $\cdot$, $+$, and $\oplus$ are used to indicate AND, OR, and EXCLUSIVE OR, respectively. The notation, ( ), refers to the contents of a location or register. The symbols B2 and B3 refer to the second and third bytes, respectively, of multibyte instructions. Bit m of the A register is denoted by A_m and the program counter by P. The symbol $\leftarrow$ stands for "is transferred to." The symbol M stands for the external memory location pointed to by the contents of the H-L register pair. The notation SSS and DDD represent, as before, the address bits that designate the CPU source and destination registers, respectively, while XXX indicates the bits are "don't care," or irrelevant. The register codes are:

A	000	E	100
B	001	H	101
C	010	L	110
D	011	H-L	111

The accumulator group instructions may be divided into four subclasses, three of which are determined by the source of data used in the operation. These are:

ALU-Register Instructions— in which operations are carried out between the accumulator and the contents of one of the registers A through L. Only the contents of A are affected by the operation.

ALU-Operations with Memory—in which operations are carried out between the accumulator and the memory register M addressed by the H-L pair.

ALU Immediate Instructions— in which operations are carried out between the accumulator and the second (data) byte of the instruction.

The various arithmetic and logical operations from these subclasses are next described in detail.

Addition Operations

There are two addition processes that differ only in their treatment of the carry bit. The carry bit is always set or reset by an addition operation. In the first type of addition no use is made of the carry bit during the operation. In the second type the carry bit resulting from the previous addition is added to the current sum. These instructions are summarized below:

Mnemonic	Format	Function	Comment
ADr	10 000 SSS	$(A) \leftarrow (A) + (r)$	*r* is unaffected.
ADM	10 000 111	$(A) \leftarrow (A) + (M)$	*M* is unaffected.
ADI	00 000 100 ⟨B2⟩	$(A) \leftarrow (A) + \langle B2 \rangle$	2-byte instruction
ACr	10 001 SSS	$(A) \leftarrow (A) + (r) + (C)$	Carry bit is added.
ACM	10 001 111	$(A) \leftarrow (A) + (M) + (C)$	
ACI	00 001 100 ⟨B2⟩	$(A) \leftarrow (A) + \langle B2 \rangle + (C)$	

The add-with-carry instructions are useful for extended precision arithmetic in which multibyte additions are performed. A carry that occurs in a lower-order addition is automatically added in to the higher-order addition. If no carry occurs, then zero is added and there is no effect. All of the addition operations set or reset the C, Z, S, and P condition flip-flops, based on the result in the accumulator.

Subtraction Operations

The subtraction process is twos complement binary subtraction, and all of the condition flags are set, based on the result of each subtraction. Only the contents of the accumulator are affected by the operation. These operations are:

Mnemonic	Format	Function	Comment
SUr	10 010 SSS	$(A) \leftarrow (A) - (r)$	
SUM	10 010 111	$(A) \leftarrow (A) - (M)$	
SUI	00 010 100 ⟨B2⟩	$(A) \leftarrow (A) - \langle B2 \rangle$	2-byte instruction
SBr	10 011 SSS	$(A) \leftarrow (A) - (r) - (\text{borrow})$	Carry bit is
SBM	10 011 111	$(A) \leftarrow (A) - (M) - (\text{borrow})$	subtracted
SBI	00 011 100 ⟨B2⟩	$(A) \leftarrow (A) - \langle B2 \rangle - (\text{borrow})$	from accumulator.

The subtract-with-borrow operations are used for extended precision arithmetic in the same manner as the add-with-carry operations. The subtraction of a larger byte from a smaller results in a "borrow," i.e., the carry flip-flop is set. This bit is then subtracted from the higher-order bytes and the bookkeeping is automatically performed. If no borrow occurs, the carry bit is zero and the effect of the subtract-with-borrow instruction is the same as the ordinary subtraction.

Logical Operations

In addition to the arithmetic capabilities provided by the ALU, it is possible to perform logical operations between a word in the accumulator and a word from another source. These operations never result in a carry and always set the carry flag to zero. The repertoire of logical instructions for the Intel 8008 CPU is: (Note: 8080 and 8085 mnemonics and binary codes differ from the 8008 set.)

Mnemonic	Format	Function	Comment
NDr	10 100 SSS	$(A) \leftarrow (A) \cdot (r)$	Logical AND performed
NDM	10 100 111	$(A) \leftarrow (A) \cdot (M)$	and carry flip-flop reset
NDI	00 100 100 ⟨B2⟩	$(A) \leftarrow (A) \cdot \langle B2 \rangle$	to zero.
XRr	10 101 SSS	$(A) \leftarrow (A) \oplus (r)$	EXCLUSIVE OR performed
XRM	10 101 111	$(A) \leftarrow (A) \oplus (M)$	and carry flip-flop reset
XRI	00 101 100 ⟨B2⟩	$(A) \leftarrow (A) \oplus \langle B2 \rangle$	to zero.
ORr	10 110 SSS	$(A) \leftarrow (A) + (r)$	Logical OR performed
ORM	10 110 111	$(A) \leftarrow (A) + (M)$	and carry flip-flop reset
ORI	00 110 100 ⟨B2⟩	$(A) \leftarrow (A) + \langle B2 \rangle$	to zero.

The remaining function in the accumulator group instructions does not result in a transformation of data, but simply compares the data in the accumulator with a source word. The comparison is effected by subtracting the source word from the contents of the accumulator, but the result is *not* loaded back into the accumulator. All of the condition flags are set to the appropriate values by the operation, and these flags can then be tested to obtain information about the relation between the two words compared. For example, the ZERO flip-flop indicates equality or inequality of the operands, and the SIGN flip-flop indicates greater than or less than as shown in this table:

Mnemonic	Format	Function	Comment
CPr	10 111 SSS	$(A) - (r)$	Neither (A) nor (r) is
CPM	10 111 111	$(A) - (M)$	changed. The condition
CPI	00 111 100 ⟨B2⟩	$(A) - \langle B2 \rangle$	flags indicate:

Z	C	Comparison
1	0	(A) = source data
0	0	(A) > data
0	1	(A) < data

Rotate Accumulator Instructions

The last instructions belonging to the accumulator group do not affect any register other than the accumulator nor any flags except the CARRY flag. The effect of these instructions is to link the accumulators MSB with the LSB in a recirculating-shift-register-like arrangement and shift the contents of the accumulator either one bit right or one bit left. This may also be performed with the CARRY flip-flop inserted in the loop as shown in these diagrams:

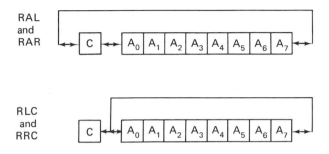

Figure 5-A

Mnemonic	Format	Function	Comment
RLC	00 000 010	$A_{m+1} \leftarrow A_m, A_0 \leftarrow A_7$ (carry) $\leftarrow A_7$	Rotate contents of accumulator left 1 bit.
RRC	00 001 010	$A_m \leftarrow A_{m+1}, A_7 \leftarrow A_0$ (carry) $\leftarrow A_0$	Rotate contents of accumulator right 1 bit.
RAL	00 010 010	$A_{m+1} \leftarrow A_m$ $A_0 \leftarrow$ (carry) (carry) $\leftarrow A_7$	Rotate contents of linked carry and accumulator left 1 bit.
RAR	00 011 010	$A_m \leftarrow A_{m+1}$ $A_7 \leftarrow$ (carry) (carry) $\leftarrow A_0$	Rotate contents of linked carry and accumulator right 1 bit.

The characteristic feature of the accumulator group instructions is the setting of the condition flags to indicate the condition of the result obtained from the operation performed. These flags can be tested by following instructions and the results of the test used to alter the program flow. This is achieved by using the instructions treated in the following sections.

TRANSFER OF CONTROL INSTRUCTIONS

The determination of the next instruction to be executed is normally accomplished by the program counter. This 14-bit register is incremented after each byte is fetched, and provides a pointer to the next byte. The program is stored in memory as a sequence of instructions, and the program counter automatically steps through the sequence as execution of the instruction stream proceeds. The instructions that bring the program counter under program control are referred to as "transfer of control" instructions. The Unconditional JUMP instruction is the simplest and most straightforward of this type. This JUMP from one place in the instruction sequence to another place is effected by altering the contents of the program counter. The current contents are replaced by the address of the next instruction to be executed, and this address is contained in the JUMP instruction in byte two and byte three. The format of the Unconditional JUMP instruction is:

JUMP	01 XXX 100	Opcode
$\langle B2 \rangle$	BB BBB BBB	LO order address
$\langle B3 \rangle$	XX BBB BBB	HI order address

The execution of the JUMP instruction is independent of the values of the "don't care" bits denoted by Xs.

The existence of a JUMP instruction allows economical use of memory in repetitive operations; rather than repeat a sequence of instructions, the program flows through a JUMP instruction back to a starting point in the sequence and loops through the sequence. An exit from the loop is accomplished through the use of a Conditional JUMP instruction that will jump out of the loop only when a specified condition obtains. The ability to alter program flow, based on conditions that occur, is essentially a *decision-making capability* and accounts for the tremendous power of computers.

Conditions that can be tested in the 8008 8080 and 8085 CPUs are, of course, the CARRY, ZERO, SIGN, and PARITY condition flags. An example that illustrates the use of these flags and of the Conditional JUMP instruction is provided by the problem of deciding whether the ratio of two numbers exceeds a certain threshold. Two integers, m and n, will be stored sequentially at locations M_m and M_n in memory. It is assumed that the pointer to M_n has been preloaded into the H-L pointer pair. An algorithm that should establish whether $m/n > 5$ is given below. Note that, in general, we would not wish to divide by successive subtractions. This example was chosen to illustrate the use of certain instructions and to avoid complexities that distract from the point under consideration.

Step	*Process*
1.	Load the constant 5 into the C register.
2.	Load n into register B.
3.	Increment register H-L.
4.	Load m into the accumulator.
5.	Subtract register B from the accumulator.
6.	If result is negative, go to step 11; else go to 7.
7.	Decrement the counter, register C.
8.	If result is not zero, go to step 5; else go to 9.
9.	Compare the accumulator with register C.
10.	If equal, go to step j; else go to 11.
11.	Begin execution of the YES routine.

.
.
.

$j-1$	End of YES routine
j	Beginning of NO routine

.
.
.

k	End of NO routine

The above algorithm will be executed as a subprogram or part of a MAIN program. This relation is shown schematically in the flow chart, Fig. 5-6. The MAIN program enters the decision algorithm and a branch occurs, depending upon the decision that is reached. In either case, an appropriate action is taken, and then control is returned to the MAIN program.

The two tests in the decision algorithm are performed on different conditions. A constant number, 5, is stored in a scratchpad register as a reference datum. The numbers m and n are also moved into temporary storage, and n is subtracted from m. The sign of the result is then used as a test for $m > n$. If the SIGN flip-flop is set to "1," the result is negative and $n > m$; therefore, $m/n < 5$ and the program executes a branch appropriate to this result. If the SIGN bit is not set, the result is uncertain and further tests must be performed. The same test can be repeated by jumping back to step 4 and again subtracting the B register from the contents of the accumulator, i.e.,

$$(A) - (B) = [m - n] - (B) = [m - n] - [n] = m - 2n$$

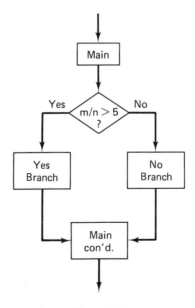

Figure 5-6

The SIGN flip-flop is once again tested to determine whether the result of the subtraction is negative, i.e., whether $m > 2n$ or not. If not, the loop counter, register C, is decremented and a test is made to determine whether the count has gone to zero. This action is performed every time the test in step 6 fails. This process is repeated until $(m - 4n) - n$ occurs. If the process has failed to yield a negative result, then it may be concluded that $m/n \geq 5$ since $m \geq 5n$. After the fifth pass through this loop, the loop counter contains zero and an exit from the loop occurs. The comparison of the contents of the accumulator with the contents of the counter is made to determine whether the equality holds, i.e., $m/n = 5$. If the accumulator contents are zero, the condition $m/n > 5$ fails and a branch to the NO routine occurs; otherwise, $m/n > 5$ and the program chooses the YES branch and executes whatever instructions are appropriate to this condition. A flow chart of this program is shown in Fig. 5-7.

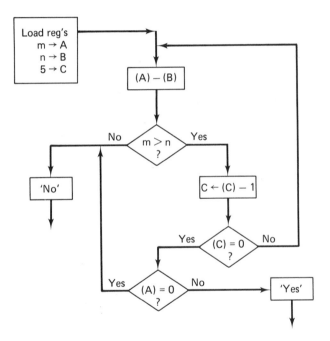

Figure 5-7

The Conditional JUMP instructions used for branching upon the results of a test must specify which condition flag is to be tested and the address of the instruction to which control is to transferred if the condition is met. The condition is specified in the first byte of the JUMP instruction, and the transfer address is contained in the second and third bytes. The format of the Conditional JUMP instructions is shown here.

Mnemonic	Format	Function	Comment
"Jump if condition TRUE"			Jump to location $\langle B3\rangle\langle B2\rangle$ if the
JTc	01 0C_4C_3 000 $\langle B2\rangle$ $\langle B3\rangle$	if (c) = 1 (P) $\leftarrow$ $\langle B3\rangle\langle B2\rangle$ if (c) = 0 (P) = (P) + 3	condition flag C_4C_3 is TRUE.
"Jump if condition FALSE"			Jump to location $\langle B3\rangle\langle B2\rangle$ if the
JFc	01 1C_4C_3 000 $\langle B2\rangle$ $\langle B3\rangle$	if (c) = 0 (P) $\leftarrow$ $\langle B3\rangle\langle B2\rangle$ if (c) = 1 (P) = (P) + 3	condition flag C_4C_3 is FALSE.
"Jump unconditionally"			Fetch the next instruction from
JMP	01 XXX 100 $\langle B2\rangle$ $\langle B3\rangle$	(P) $\leftarrow$ $\langle B3\rangle\langle B2\rangle$	location $\langle B3\rangle\langle B2\rangle$.

If the condition is not met, the program execution continues after the third byte of the JUMP instruction. The two address bytes are always fetched and the condition flag is tested after the fetch of the last byte. The bytes are stored in the temporary registers *a* and *b*, and transferred into the program counter only if the condition is met. This algorithmic execution of the JUMP instruction is detailed in this table:

Cycle	State	Process
PCI	T1	PC_L sent to RAM address latch.
	T2	PC_H sent to RAM address latch.
	T3	Fetch conditional Jump instruction to IR.
PCR	T1	PC_L sent to RAM address latch.
	T2	PC_H sent to RAM address latch.
	T3	Lower address byte B2 to register *b*.
PCR	T1	PC_L sent to RAM address latch.
	T2	PC_H sent to RAM address latch.
	T3	Higher address byte B3 to register *a*.
	T4	reg *a* to PC_H *if condition met* (T4 and T5 are not
	T5	reg *b* to PC_L *if condition met* present if failed)

As can be seen from the above algorithm, the Conditional JUMP instruction requires either 9 or 11 states for execution. If the condition fails, the last two steps, in which the jump address is jammed into the program counter, are omitted. The flow chart for this algorithm is shown in Fig. 5-8. Using instructions which have been presented in this chapter, it is possible to write the decision algorithm for the ratio test, $m/n > 5$. The instructions will begin at binary location 00..01000, which is meant to represent an arbitrary starting

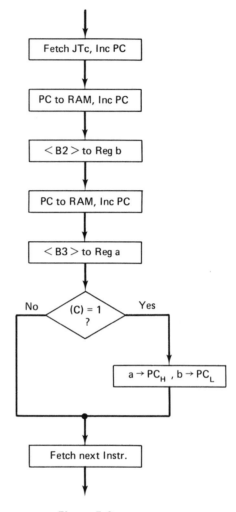

Figure 5-8

address. The H-L register pair is assumed to have been preloaded and points to *n*.

Location	Mnemonic	Machine Code	Comment
0..01000	MVI C,5	00 010 110	Load loop counter (C-reg)
01001		00 000 101	with the number 5.
01010	MOV B,M	11 001 111	Fetch *n* into reg B via H-L.
01011	INL	00 110 000	Increment the pointer L ≠ FF.
01100	MOV A,M	11 000 111	Fetch *m* into reg A via H-L.
01101	SUB	10 010 001	Subtract *n* from *m*.

01110	JTS 30B	01 110 000	If negative result (SIGN=1),
01111		00 011 110	begin executing the NO routine
10000		00 000 000	located at 30B (binary).
10001	DCC	00 010 000	Decrement the loop counter.
10010	JFZ 13B	01 001 000	If loop counter not zero,
10011		00 001 101	(ZERO=0) go to location 13
10100		00 000 000	and perform another subtraction.
10101	CPC	10 111 010	Compare reg C with reg A.
10110	JTZ 30B	01 101 000	If loop counter is zero,
10111		00 011 110	(ZERO=1) jump to location 30
11000		00 000 000	and begin the NO routine.
11001	BEGIN "YES" ROUTINE....		
.	.		
.	.		
.	.		
11110	BEGIN "NO" ROUTINE.....		

Although many useful decisions can be made with very few instructions, we have purposely chosen a decision that could not be based on only one test, in order to illustrate the use of several conditional transfer instructions in a realistic application.

CALLABLE SUBROUTINES

In the ratio decision algorithm described above, the subtraction of n from m was performed several times. Repetitious coding was avoided by looping through the instructions that were to be repeatedly executed. This is a very common software technique and is generally referred to as a form of "DO-LOOP" in which the desired action is "done," and then the program flow "loops back" and does the same action again. Changes occurring in one or more program variables are used to determine the proper time to exit from the loop. The loop is one of the most basic procedures in programming. The general structure involves a condition, C, and a procedure, P, defined by this statement:

$$\Rightarrow while\ C\ do\ P$$

The flow-chart representation of this algorithmic structure is shown in Fig. 5-9. The other two basic structures have already been presented, but they are also shown. They consist of the *sequential* structure, in which A is followed by B, and the *branch-on-condition* structure, in which control is transferred to one of two possible sequences of instructions.

By generalizing slightly we can consider a program in which an *algorithm* is to be repeatedly invoked. Although it may be possible to write some type of DO-LOOP involving the algorithm, this is in general not feasible. What is desired is a sequence of code that can be repeatedly called from different times

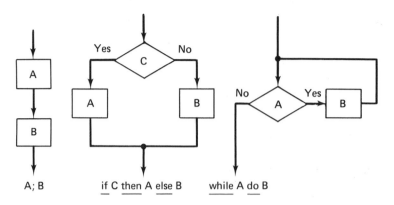

Figure 5-9

or places within the main program. This need is met via the introduction of a "callable subroutine." The special feature of the callable subroutine is the fact that it can be called at any time and from any location during program execution. Either the subroutine will provide a "deadend" to the program, or there must be a means of returning to the calling point in the main program. This latter alternative is the only acceptable one in most applications, and this feature will also be considered a characteristic of a callable subroutine. The ability to call subroutines from random locations and return is fundamental and should be provided for in the processor architecture. Thus, an addition to our list of processor capabilities might read something like this:

> *9. The processor should have the ability to transfer control to a nonsequential location and begin executing instructions sequentially from this point, and record where the transfer occurred so that a return to the main instruction sequence may be effected.*

The simple transfer of control, either conditional or unconditional, is provided via the JUMP instructions. The 2-byte address specifying the location to which control is transferred will also be required in the CALL instruction.

If a CALL instruction is fetched during an instruction fetch cycle, PCI, the location of the first byte (opcode) will be indicated by the contents of the program counter (PC) that are sent to the RAM address latches during T1 and T2 of PCI. The two address bytes are located at (PC) + 1 and (PC) + 2 and the next instruction in the calling program is located at (PC) + 3. In order to return to this instruction after the subroutine has executed, it is necessary to save the address given by (PC) + 3. This "housekeeping" may be viewed as shown in Fig. 5-10.

The "housekeeping" algorithm associated with calling a subroutine can be implemented either in software or in hardware. The essential difference between a JUMP instruction and a CALL lies in this return address that must be main-

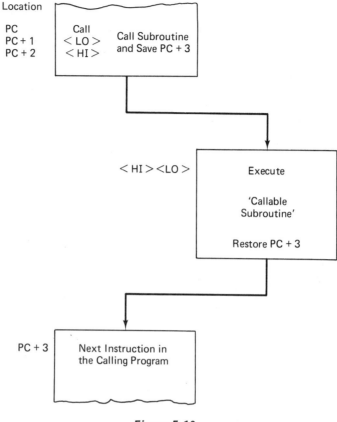

Figure 5-10

tained in the case of the CALL. Whereas the JUMP instruction simply jammed a new address into the program counter (which always points to the location of the next instruction to be fetched), the execution of a CALL instruction requires that the current program-counter contents be saved before the new address is jammed in. The final step in the called subroutine must be the restoration of the program-counter contents. Intel 8000 CPUs provide a hardware implementation of the save/restore-PC algorithm. Before introducing the specific CALL instruction, we will discuss two related concepts: namely NESTs and STACKs.

Nested Subroutines

The fact that a subroutine can be called from any location in the instruction store, and at any time during program execution, has been emphasized in the preceding section. It follows from this specification that a subroutine can be called *by another subroutine*. In the most general case, the subroutine can be called even by itself. This is known as a recursive call and will not be treated here. The fact that subroutines can call other subroutines which, in turn, can call other subroutines, etc., leads to the concept of *nested* subroutine execution. The execution of the lowest-level subroutine is nested within the execution of the next level that, in turn, is nested within the next level all the way up the hierarchy to the main routine. This is graphically evident when a block-structed style is employed to describe instruction execution. A subroutine or procedure that is called during the execution of another procedure is written indented. In the following example the main procedure is labeled P1, and other procedures are labeled Pn, where n is any positive integer. The instructions executed within procedure Pn are labeled Inm, where m indicates the order of occurrence during execution. An example of a nested execution sequence is:

```
I11   Begin P1
I12   -----
I13   -----
I14   Call P2
         I21   Begin P2
         I22   -----
         I23   -----
         I24   -----
         I25   Call P3
                  I31   Begin P3
                  I32   -----
                  I33   -----
                  I34   Return P2
         I26   Continue P2
         I27   -----
         I28   -----
         I29   Return P1
I15   Continue P1
I16   -----
I17   -----
I18   -----
I19   Call P5
         I51   Begin P5
         I52   -----
         I53   -----
         I54   etc.
```

The interest is not in the procedures themselves but in the hierarchical structure exhibited above. Each procedure may be identified with a purpose or reason for existing. The reason can be very simple, such as killing time by executing a delay loop, or more complex, such as inverting a matrix. In all cases, the procedure represents an algorithmic means of achieving a desired goal. In order to achieve a specific goal it may be convenient to execute a subroutine or procedure that will produce a partial result, necessary but not sufficient to accomplish the total goal. Any given procedure can call any number of sub-procedures where the modifier *sub-* is always attached to the *called* procedure. Thus, procedure B can be subject to A during one execution, while A can be subject to B during another execution in which different conditions arise.

Stack Architecture

Entrance into a subroutine requires that the contents of the program counter at the time of departure from the calling routine be stored so that, upon exiting from the subroutine, program execution may proceed from the proper location. Thus, the calling algorithm must provide a storage address as well as the address of the entry point into the subroutine. If the return address were stored anywhere in RAM, the instruction would require 4 address bytes in addition to the opcode byte. An alternative approach makes use of the space/time duality. Recognizing that addresses provide a sequential order mechanism in space, we look for the equivalent sequential order mechanism in time. The "order of occurrence" in time provides this mechanism. An attempt to illustrate the two addressing concepts graphically is made in Fig. 5-11. The spatial order is represented by dividing space into compartments such that the storage address of any data item is sufficient to retrieve the item. In the temporal case, there is only one spatial address, and all items are stored at this address, stacked on top of each other in the order of their storage. Therefore, to retrieve a given item from the stack, we must know the order in which the items were placed on the stack. Since the spatial address never changes, it can be made implicit in the opcode and, thus, no address information need be stored for the program-counter contents. The question then arises as to how the temporal order can be stored, and it is here that the concept of nested subroutines comes into play. By examining the block-structured example of the previous section, it may be seen that an exit from any subroutine always returns to the last location to be stored by

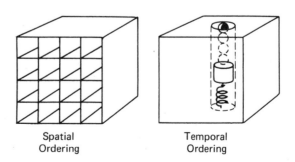

Spatial
Ordering

Temporal
Ordering

Figure 5-11

the calling algorithm. Thus, the last program-counter contents stored are the first program-counter contents to be retrieved, or, more simply, last in, first out. From this description it should be clear that this is the natural way in which a stack architecture should be used, and for this reason a stack is called a Last-In-First-Out (LIFO) buffer.

Thus, the stack provides the ideal storage mechanism for saving return addresses. The number of stored addresses is meaningless (until stack capacity is exceeded). Only the order of occurrence has meaning, and since this order is inherent in the structure of a program with callable procedures, there is no need to provide any stack address information in the CALL instruction proper!

LIFO buffers are commonly referred to as Push-down Stacks. This terminology arises from the way in which stack operation is visualized; the data added to the top of the stack "push" the entire stack down one level. Data recalled from the top of the stack are said to be "popped" off of the stack and the stack rises one level. This arrangement is shown in Fig. 5-12.

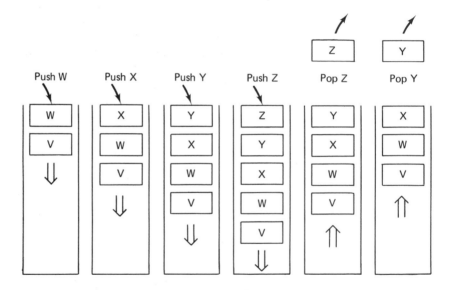

Figure 5-12

Prior to the advent of microprocessors, the majority of computers used push-down stacks implemented in software, if at all. In contrast, the majority of microprocessors possess stack-oriented architectures in which the Call and Return algorithms execute in hardware. The Intel 8008 contains a push-down stack capable of holding seven 14-bit return addresses. This stack is conceptually considered to be positioned just below the program counter. An alternate hardware perspective, in which the PC is one of eight registers with a moving pointer to the top of the stack, is developed in the problems at the end of this chapter. From the software perspective, the stack is full when it contains seven items, and the addition of an eighth address pushes the deepest stored address out the bottom of the stack. In the hardware view, the stack pointer recycles and the top of the stack is wrapped around so that the new entry is written over the oldest entry. The views are of course equivalent.

CALL and RETURN Instructions

The 8008 instruction repertoire contains both conditional and unconditional subroutine CALL and RETURN instructions. The seven-deep push-down stack implemented in the CPU allows seven-deep nested subroutine calls to be executed automatically. The CALL instruction contains an 8-bit opcode and two 8-bit address bytes specifying the location to which control is to be transferred, i.e., the subroutine entry point. Upon receipt of the CALL opcode, the CPU cycles twice through the PCR cycles and retrieves the two address bytes. These are temporarily stored in the a and b registers. The program counter is pushed onto the top of the stack to provide the return address and the a and b registers are loaded into the program counter. The next instruction FETCH cycle sends this address to RAM, and the subroutine execution begins. The three types of CALL instructions are:

Mnemonic	Format	Function	Comment
"Unconditional Subroutine Call"			
CAL	01 XXX 110	(Stack) ⟵ (PC)	Jump to subroutine.
	⟨B2⟩	(PC) ⟵ ⟨B3⟩⟨B2⟩	Save return address on top
	⟨B3⟩		of stack.
"Call subroutine if Condition satisfied"			
CTc	01 1C_4C_3 010	If (c)=1, then	If the conditions specified by
	⟨B2⟩	(Stack) ⟵ (PC)	C_4C_3 are met, the subroutine
	⟨B3⟩	(PC) ⟵ ⟨B3⟩⟨B2⟩;	is called. Otherwise, excution
		otherwise,	of the next instruction in
		(PC) ⟵ (PC) + 3.	the calling sequence occurs.
CFc	01 0C_4C_3 010	If (c)=0, then	
	⟨B2⟩	(Stack) ⟵ (PC)	
	⟨B3⟩	(PC) ⟵ ⟨B3⟩⟨B2⟩;	
		otherwise,	
		(PC) ⟵ (PC) + 3.	

Upon completion of the subroutine execution, a RETURN instruction is needed to get back to the calling routine. The execution of the RETURN instruction POPs the stack and loads the program counter with the POPed address. Thus, the effect of the RETURN instruction is similar to that of a JUMP instruction in which the jump occurs through the top stack address rather than through bytes B2 and B3 of the JUMP instruction. Both conditional and unconditional RETURN instructions are provided in the 8000 series CPUs as follows:

Mnemonic	Format	Function	Comment
RET	00 XXX 111	$(PC) \leftarrow (Stack)$	Unconditional return to calling routine.
RTc	00 1C_4C_3 011	If $(c) = 1$, then $(PC) \leftarrow (Stack)$; otherwise, $(PC) \leftarrow (PC) + 1$.	Return if condition is satisfied; otherwise, execute next instruction in subroutine sequence.
RFc	00 0C_4C_3 011	If $(c) = 0$, then $(PC) \leftarrow (Stack)$; otherwise, $(PC) \leftarrow (PC) + 1$.	Return if condition fails; otherwise, continue execution of subroutine.

HALT INSTRUCTION

The final instruction treated in this chapter is the HALT instruction that causes the CPU to enter the STOPped state and remain there until receipt of an INTERRUPT signal. The contents of all registers and external memory are unaffected by this instruction. The program counter is incremented and the on-chip dynamic storage is refreshed. The format of the HALT instruction is shown below. It is a 1-byte instruction that has two permissible formats:

$$\text{HALT} \quad \begin{array}{c} 00\ 000\ 00X \\ \text{or} \\ 11\ 111\ 111 \end{array} \quad \begin{array}{c} (PC) \leftarrow (PC) + 1 \\ \text{and} \\ CPU \longrightarrow \text{STOPped State} \end{array}$$

There are three other instructions in the 8008 instruction set and thirty-three more in the 8080 and 8085 sets. The instructions presented in this chapter have developed the architecture of the 8008 CPU, as shown in Fig. 5-13.

PARAMETER TRANSFERS

Subroutines are powerful programming aids to the development of hierarchically structured programs. The inherent modularity of the subroutines allows largely independent development of subprograms. The compartmentalization of algorithms, however, raises a problem—that of information transfer across module boundaries. This software Input/Output problem is normally solved in such a manner that each software subsystem will possesss an I/O structure that is compatible with all other subsystems. The interlevel address communication is handled in hardware by using the Call and Return algorithms.

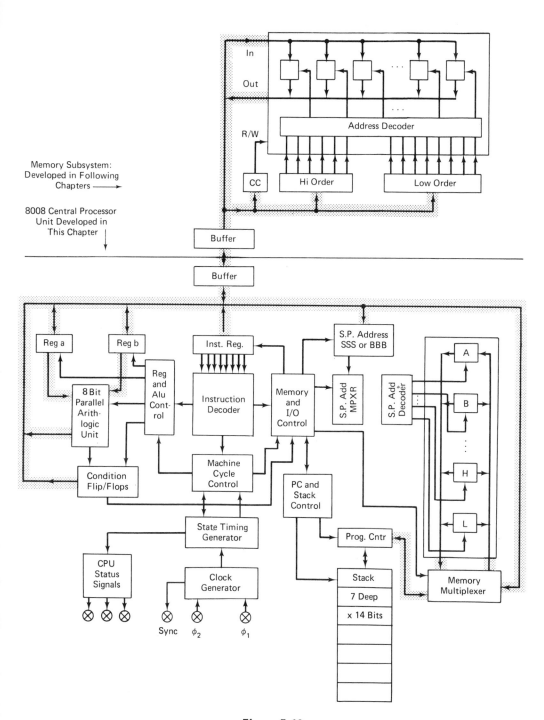

In

Out

R/W

Memory Subsystem:
Developed in Following
Chapters ⟶

8008 Central Processor
Unit Developed in
This Chapter ↓

Address Decoder

CC

Hi Order

Low Order

Buffer

Buffer

Reg a

Reg b

Inst. Reg.

S.P. Address
SSS or BBB

A

Reg
and
Alu
Cont-
rol

Instruction
Decoder

Memory
and
I/O
Control

S.P. Add
MPXR

S.P. Add
Decoder

B

8 Bit
Parallel
Arith-
logic
Unit

H

Condition
Flip/Flops

Machine
Cycle
Control

PC and
Stack
Control

L

State Timing
Generator

Prog. Cntr

Memory
Multiplexer

CPU
Status
Signals

Clock
Generator

Stack

7 Deep

x 14 Bits

Sync ϕ_2 ϕ_1

Figure 5-13

The transfer of data from calling routine to subroutine is referred to as parameter passing and is accomplished by the organized storage of parameters in "mutually agreed upon" locations by the sending routine, and retrieval of the data from these locations by the user routine. Use may be made of the CPU register file for the storage of parameters in a subroutine call. The parameter stored in the CPU can be a pointer to the table in external memory where a sequence of data items is located. This parameter will be stored in the H-L pointer pair before the call to the subroutine is made. If only one or two bytes of data are to be transmitted and execution times are critical, these bytes can be stored in the working registers of the CPU file.

SUMMARY

A concept that has emerged in this chapter is that of hierarchical structure. This structure consists of "levels" such that an algorithm, of nontrivial complexity when referred to its own level, is represented trivially as a symbolic "building block" at the next higher level. This is illustrated in Fig. 5-14. The algorithm on the right represents the Conditional JUMP algorithm described earlier in this chapter. When viewed from the next higher level, shown in the center of the figure, the internal features of the JFZ vanish and it is represented as a simple decision block. In similar fashion, the entire $m/n > 5$ algorithm is shown in the flow chart at the left as a simple decision block within the "Main" routine. The figure also graphically illustrates the hardware/software equivalence principle in that no distinction need be made in the flow chart between algorithms implemented in software and those in hardware. Today, the preferred means of designing a system consists in developing the algorithmic hierarchy from the highest level and filling in details by proceeding to lower levels. Only near the final stages of design need the designer consider the actual implementation of each algorithm.

This procedures is known as Top Down Structured design. The hierarchic levels correspond closely to the *general semantic* "levels of abstraction" in which consciousness of abstracting serves as a vital aid to clear and concise thinking. The distinction between goals and the means of achieving the goals allows the designer maximum flexibility insofar as the implementation of the system is concerned. The actual choice is a function of the particular problem. Only when a cost function or performance index has been specified can one particular implementation be characterized as superior to any other implementation.

The hierarchic structure also serves to prevent information overload from occurring by abstracting *only* the detail relevant to a process at a particular level, and thus minimizing the "forest-for-the-trees" type of confusion. This is very important for novice designers to keep in mind.

The practice of breaking up complex systems into subsystems is probably the most powerful design technique available to the designer. Implicit in such

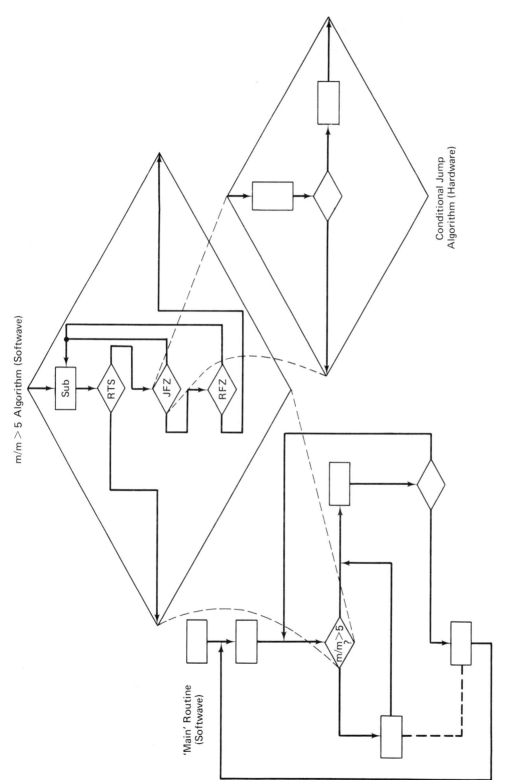

m/m > 5 Algorithm (Softwave)

Sub

RTS

JFZ

RFZ

Conditional Jump
Algorithm (Hardware)

'Main' Routine
(Softwave)

m/m > 5
?

Figure 5-14

a scheme is the existence of boundaries between subsystems. Information processing systems transmit information across these boundaries. The parameter transfer across the boundaries of software systems was described in this chapter. The transfer of information between hardware systems, the CPU and the memory system, is treated in Chapter 7. The following chapters treat the interface between the CPU and peripheral devices that transmit information from the "real world" to the CPU.

**NOTE: The 8008 instructions presented in this chapter form a subset of the 8080 and 8085 instruction sets. The functions are the same in the three processors, although the mnemonics and binary codes differ. The 8080 and 8085 utilize a stack pointer in the CPU and an external stack in RAM. The 8085 multiplexes the high address bytes, while the 8080 multiplexes the status byte over the data bus. These CPUs will be described in later chapters. The basic 8008 instruction set illustrates most important features associated with such sets. The 8008 timing and control signals, described in the next chapter, provide an ideal example of system timing concepts.

PROBLEMS

1. The Return Address/PC Stack in the 8008 has been implemented, using large-scale integrated circuitry (LSI). Design an MSI Push-Down Stack/Program Counter, using a binary up/down counter for the stack pointer and a RAM memory chip for the stack.

2. Design a software stack in RAM that is capable of storing data in FIFO fashion. Use the H-L register pairs to contain the pointer to the stack.

3. The 8008 instruction utilizes a very limited number of addressing modes. Discuss the significance of this fact in terms of declining memory costs.

4. Write a time delay loop. Two sequential loops are additive, while two nested loops are multiplicative. Compare the routines needed for long delay loops. Discuss how arbitrarily long delays may be written with no sacrifice in accuracy, using a combination of these two schemes.

5. Processor architects design an instruction repertoire consistent with a particular set of goals and implement this set in firmware. Each new processor is somewhat like a new alphabet that must be memorized before it can be applied. Does a knowledge of the instruction set tell us as much about the internal operations on symbols possible for a given processor as does a complete knowledge of the hardware inside the chip?

6 *an LSI central processor unit*

> *". . . . . technology evolves in a direction that is likely to subvert the classical modern notion of a* machine *no less than the ancient notion of* mind."*

> *David Hawkins*
> The Language of Nature

Information processors are physical machines in which both transfers of and transformations on *patterns* occur. From a hardware viewpoint these patterns are configurations and groupings of 1s and 0s, while the interpretation of these patterns as abstract symbols is preferable from a software perspective. In light of the hardware/software duality, the designer is well-advised to approach a goal from both of these directions.

The previous chapter dealt with the software viewpoint of the 8008 and treated intraCPU processes. This chapter considers the hardware details necessary for interfacing the device to other integrated circuits and subsystems. Since the details of interfacing between families have been covered in Chapter 4, we are now primarily concerned with interCPU functions and timing.

A MONOLITHIC CPU

The Intel 8008 CPU is a P-MOS LSI circuit that can be interfaced to any type or speed of semiconductor memory and address up to 16K (16,384) 8-bit words of storage. The processor is organized as an 8-bit parallel system that communicates with memory and input/output ports over an 8-bit data and address bus. These eight lines are used for transferring data and instructions in and out of the CPU, and also for sending address information to the memory, as shown in Fig. 6-1. Although it is possible to design an 8-bit microprocessor that uses only 8-bit wide instructions, the 8008 Central Processor Unit was designed with 8-, 16-, and 24-bit instructions and is capable of *directly* addressing all 16K words of storage. In order to provide such capabilities it is necessary to

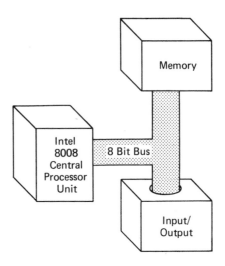

Figure 6-1

allow different types of information on the 8-bit data bus at different times. Such utilization of an n-bit wide bus to transmit $(m \times n)$-bit words is termed "time division multiplexing." Rather than a random policy of "grab the bus as you can," an orderly sequence has been established for determining what information will be on the bus at a given time. We later investigate the case in which "grab the bus" applies. Since the CPU is the major component of the information processing system being developed, it is the obvious place to determine the bus allocation. In order that the rest of the system that we must attach to the CPU can know what information is on the bus at any given time, the CPU must provide timing signals or information concerning the state of the CPU and, correspondingly, the data bus at all times. These signals are received and decoded by state control logic that then synchronizes the rest of the system to the CPU, as shown in Fig. 6-2.

Although it is possible to generate all system timing on the CPU chip, this was not very practical in this case for several reasons. The power required for clock signals that drive many gates is more easily handled outside the CPU chip. The critical timing that is essential to proper functioning of the system usually requires a capability of externally calibrating the basic timing signals with trimmer components. Since these trimmer components must be manually adjustable, they must be off the chip, requiring extra pins for connection. The number of pins that connect the micro-electronics on a chip to the external circuitry often serves as a cost function. Therefore, it is preferable to place the system clock entirely outside the CPU and simply send in timing signals through two pins (three, counting common-power supply). The CPU then derives its internal timing and sequencing information from an external clock and an internal

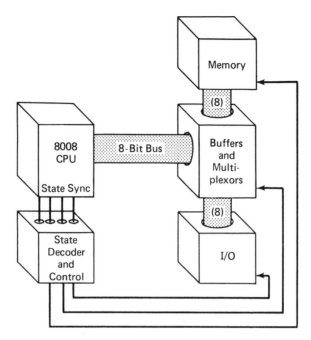

Figure 6-2

state-timing generator controls the state of the CPU and encodes this information in the status and synchronization (SYNC) signals that orchestrate the activity of the systems external to the CPU. The purpose in encoding and then decoding these status signals is again to save valuable pin connections between CPU and $\overline{\text{CPU}}$ circuitry.

The 8-bit data bus into the CPU is sufficient for transferring 8-, 16-, and 24-bit (one-, two-, and three-byte) instructions in separate time slots that can be stored in up to three memory locations, but are executed as one instruction in the CPU. The bus is wide enough to address only 256 words, whereas the system is designed to address 16K ($= 2^{14}$) words of storage requiring 14 bits of addressing information.

In order to select *directly* any one of the 16,384 (16K) words, 14 bits of address information are required. The 8008 CPU sends out one 8-bit word called the "low-order address" at one time, and immediately follows this with another 8-bit word that contains the six "high-order address" bits plus two extra bits.

The arrival of the address words during two different time slots requires storage facilities for the first (low-order) address bits until the high-order bits arrive. This storage is provided by buffers implemented with latches. The steering circuitry that latches the appropriate address bits in the appropriate storage buffers is shown in Fig. 6-3.

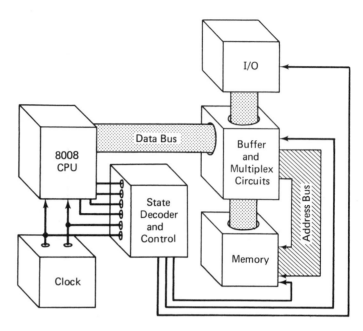

Figure 6-3

If we recall that the CPU's primary function is to execute instructions from a program (or sequence of instructions) stored in a memory (external to the CPU), then there must first occur a state in which the address of the instruction is sent to memory. The 8008 CPU performs this task in two separate steps, first sending out 8 bits of low-order address information, and then sending out 6 bits of high-order address information along with 2 bits of information that is to be used for control of the $\overline{\text{CPU}}$.

Summarizing, states T1 and T2 are used to send a 14-bit address word to the $\overline{\text{CPU}}$, plus 2 control bits. The STATE outputs used to inform $\overline{\text{CPU}}$ of the state of the processor consist of a SYNC signal that signals the beginning of a new state along with the state signals S_0, S_1, and S_2 that identify the state. State T1 is denoted by $(S_0, S_1, S_2) = (0, 1, 1)$, while T2 is denoted by $(0, 0, 1)$.

Although the address discussed above was specified to be that of an instruction, we note that there are two types of information stored in memory—instructions and data. Both are stored and fetched as 8-bit bytes. Instructions can be one, two, or three bytes long, whereas data words consist of one 8-bit byte. Instructions are analogous to verbs in natural language in that they specify an action to be performed, while data words are analogous to nouns in that they function as subject or object of an action.

Information is stored in memory external to the CPU in the form of 8-bit bytes. Such information must be brought into the CPU if it is to be used. In order to fetch a word from memory, the CPU must present the address of the word to the $\overline{\text{CPU}}$. This is done during T1 and T2. The transfer of an 8-bit byte from $\overline{\text{CPU}}$ to CPU occurs at state T3. This holds true for data words as well as instructions. Once in the CPU, the information can be treated as either an instruction or as data. The interpretation is done by the CPU; normally, $\overline{\text{CPU}}$ places no interpretation on the 8-bit bytes, merely presenting the requested word to the CPU during state T3, denoted by $(S_0, S_1, S_2)_{T3} = (1, 0, 0)$.

The Central Processor Unit not only receives information from external storage but also stores information externally. Whether sending or receiving information, it is obvious that every parcel of data sent must be accompanied by the appropriate address. There seems little point in creating special addressing circuitry merely to reverse the data flow; therefore the CPU has been designed so that *all* addresses are sent to CPU during states T1 and T2, regardless of whether the location specified by this address is to receive or transmit data.

The question that arises now is whether a new state T4 is needed to indicate that data flow is from CPU $\rightarrow$ $\overline{\text{CPU}}$, thus distinguishing from T3 in which the flow is $\overline{\text{CPU}} \rightarrow$ CPU. The answer is that all data flow between CPU and memory occurs during state T3. Since, therefore, the status signals S_0, S_1, S_2 do not indicate whether information is to be written into memory or read (fetched) from memory, there must be some other control information to inform CPU whether a READ or a WRITE is requested. This function is performed by the two control bits that are sent out at T2 with the six high-order address bits. The bits are present on lines D_6 and D_7 of the data bus, and are latched at T2. When both bits are high, i.e., $(D_6, D_7) = (1, 1)$, the $\overline{\text{CPU}}$ is being told to write the data that will follow at T3 into the address specified during T1 and T2. The succession of states required to effect such complete action is referred to as a cycle. The cycle-control coding bits D_6 and D_7, must be handled by specifically designed circuitry external to CPU, just as the state signals S_0, S_1, and S_2 are decoded by $\overline{\text{CPU}}$ circuitry.

We have assumed to this point in the discussion that the CPU interprets each incoming byte of information correctly as either a data word or as the first, second, or third byte of an instruction and that the $\overline{\text{CPU}}$ circuitry remains blissfully ignorant of the use made of this information. During normal program sequence, this is indeed true; however, there is an exceptional case that is of great significance. During normal execution of a program, the CPU fetches and executes instructions from memory. The instructions are stored sequentially and are retrieved one after the other. Special instructions can cause a jump to a new set of instructions where the regular sequential flow begins again.

The significant fact here is that program flow is determined by the program (including data) and can even be made up as it goes along! Although from time to time the program may test real-world (noncomputer dependent) conditions by inputting switch settings or instrument or other readings, no provision for *instantly* altering program flow exists in a normal program (as opposed to programmed means of altering program flow). The ability to interrupt normal program flow greatly enhances the utility of a computer and allows computers to be used in real-time applications.*

This interrupt capability has been designed into the 8008 microprocessor and allows an external signal present at the INTERRUPT pin to immediately alter program flow. As a consequence, it is necessary to inform the CPU circuitry whether each instruction is determined by normal program execution or is a special INTERRUPT instruction, possibly unrelated to the program being executed at the time the interrupt occurs.

An INTERRUPT signal *interrupts* normal program flow, but does not destroy it. After the INTERRUPT needs have been met, the program resumes normal program flow from the point at which it was interrupted. This return capability is built into the 8008 CPU and requires that the CPU receive the INTERRUPT signal directly. The CPU interprets the first byte of each instruction to determine whether a second or third byte is needed to complete the instruction. If so, these bytes are fetched during succeeding cycles automatically, i.e., the CPU cannot be interrupted in the middle of a multicycle instruction fetch. Another way of saying this is simply that the CPU does not have the ability to distinguish an INTERRUPT instruction from the second or third byte of a 16- or 24-bit instruction.

This means that INTERRUPT instructions can be "jammed" into the CPU only during times when the CPU is requesting the first byte of a new instruction. Thus, we must have a means of distinguishing the first cycle of an instruction fetch from additional bytes of instruction or data. The cycle control bits provide this means. The first cycle is always an instruction fetch cycle, designated PCI, and is coded during T2 by $(D_6, D_7) = (0, 0)$. This coding designates that the address is for a memory READ and is the first byte of an instruction. Obviously, interrupt instructions can be jammed in at this time, simply replacing the instruction that would normally be present at this point in the program. The other data fetch cycles are designated PCR cycles and are coded during T2 by (D_6, D_7) $= (0, 1)$. This coding designates the address for a memory fetch of additional bytes of instruction or of data.

Since the CPU places the coding bits on the data bus at T2, it means that the CPU is expecting the rest of an instruction or a word of data and would not properly interpret an INTERRUPT instruction jammed in at this time. Thus, we have seen that, during normal program flow, the $\overline{\text{CPU}}$ circuitry does not care whether the bytes fetched during T3 are instructions or data. Nevertheless, it is told by the CPU via $(D_6, D_7)_{T2}$ when a new instruction is being fetched,

---

*Real-time applications form a special class of problems for computers in that there is a maximum time allowable for solution. Although 10 seconds may be a reasonable time for a customer to wait for the result of a credit check, 10 milliseconds may be too much time for a computer to respond to a danger interrupt if the system being monitored is a nuclear power plant or jet aircraft. Thus, the nature of the problem defines real-time systems as distinct from those problems that merely massage data.

thereby allowing the $\overline{\text{CPU}}$ to jam the INTERRUPT instructions on the data bus during the appropriate cycle.

There is yet a further requirement to be met before jamming an INTERRUPT instruction into the CPU (thus disrupting normal program flow). The CPU must sense the interrupt condition and take the actions that will allow resumption of normal program flow after the interrupt demands have been satisfied. The CPU signals the $\overline{\text{CPU}}$ that an interrupt has occurred by outputting state signals $(S_0, S_1, S_2)_{T1I} = (0, 1, 1)$ to replace state T1 with T1I. State T2 followed T1I, but the normal sequential addressing operation of the CPU is inhibited. During state T3 of a successive PCI cycle following T1I, the INTERRUPT instruction may be jammed into the instruction register of the CPU.

Input/Output (I/O) operations can provide addresses to the I/O subsystem to select a specific input port or output port. An I/O cycle will be indicated by the PCC cycle code $(D_6, D_7)_{T2} = (1, 0)$. This code can be used to enable the I/O subsystem, as shown in Chapter 8. The table below summarizes the 8008 Cycle Control Coding that utilizes bits D_6 and D_7. This coding is present on the data bus only during T2. The PCC cycle will be treated in Chapter 8.

So far, we have discussed the states of the CPU in which addresses are sent to memory (T1 and T2) along with cycle coding (T2 only) and also the state during which data flow occurs to or from the CPU on the data bus. The state T1I signals the $\overline{\text{CPU}}$ that the CPU has detected an interrupt condition and will respond accordingly. There are four states remaining to be described.

D_6	D_7	Cycle	Function
0	0	PCI	Designates the address as a memory READ (1st byte of instruction)
0	1	PCR	Designates the address as a memory READ (additional bytes of instruction or data)
1	0	PCC	Designates the data as a COMMAND I/O operation
1	1	PCW	Designates the address as a memory WRITE data

States T4 and T5 are used for the execution of the instruction within the CPU. T4 and T5 do not occur in every cycle. They serve primarily to indicate to $\overline{\text{CPU}}$ that the CPU is busy. Special data are available from the CPU during T4 of the PCC cycle. These data consist of condition flags. (Discussion of this data at this time would be premature and is now postponed.) T4 is denoted by $(S_0, S_1, S_2)_{T4} = (1, 1, 1)$, and T5 is denoted by $(S_0, S_1, S_2)_{T5} = (1, 0, 1)$.

The CPU acknowledges receipt of a HALT instruction by entering the STOPped state that is denoted by $(S_0, S_1, S_2)_{\text{STOPped}} = (1, 1, 0)$. The CPU will remain in the STOPped state for an indefinite length of time, until the receipt of an INTERRUPT signal on the appropriate pin.

The final state that the CPU can enter is a WAIT state denoted by $(S_0, S_1, S_2)_{WAIT} = (0, 0, 0)$. The CPU will enter the WAIT state until the signal at the READY pin goes high. A CPU in the WAIT state responds to the READY signal by entering the T3 state. With fast memories the CPU will normally avoid the WAIT state. The READY line also provides a means of stepping through the execution of a program one cycle at a time. It is a very useful feature of the 8008, allowing the CPU to be easily incorporated into a hierarchial structure. It is perhaps best thought of as providing a "freeze" command in the same sense that children use the command in play; no special actions occur, the CPU just idles. Figure 6-4 summarizes the states and their coding, and presents the pin configuration of the 8008 CPU. The supply voltages $V_{DD} = +5\,V$ and $V_{cc} = 9\,V$ are shown also.

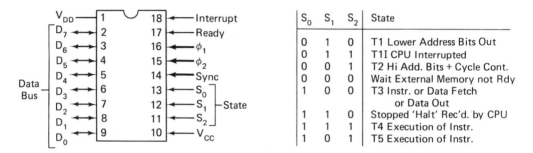

S_0	S_1	S_2	State
0	1	0	T1 Lower Address Bits Out
0	1	1	T1I CPU Interrupted
0	0	1	T2 Hi Add. Bits + Cycle Cont.
0	0	0	Wait External Memory not Rdy
1	0	0	T3 Instr. or Data Fetch
			or Data Out
1	1	0	Stopped 'Halt' Rec'd. by CPU
1	1	1	T4 Execution of Instr.
1	0	1	T5 Execution of Instr.

Figure 6-4

Every state is initiated with the leading edge of the SYNC pulse. The idealized timing diagram shown in Fig. 6-5 is representative of that occurring in any state. The nonoverlapping clock pulses ϕ_1 and ϕ_2 are input to the CPU and the SYNC pulse is derived from these, the rising edge of the SYNC pulse coinciding with the trailing edge of alternate ϕ_2 pulses. The timing diagram shown in Fig. 6-5 represents an ideal case. The presence of capacitance in the circuit will introduce delays or lags that are of some consequence and are treated in Chapter 7.

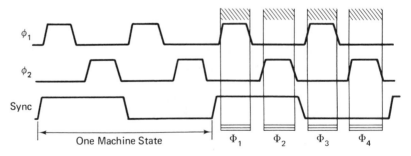

Figure 6-5

Also indicated in the figure is the division of every state into four nonoverlapping subperiods, Φ_1 through Φ_4, formed by logical combinations of the clock pulses and the SYNC pulse. These may be used in $\overline{\text{CPU}}$ to order events occurring within any given state of the CPU. This ability to arrange events within a state is extremely useful. We shall have to modify these clock phases somewhat in Chapter 7; however, the principle will remain the same. The state transition diagram for 8008 CPU is shown in Fig. 6-6. The diagram shows all allowable transitions and should be studied closely. It summarizes the relationships expounded upon in this chapter and provides in schematic form many of the guidelines to be followed in designing the $\overline{\text{CPU}}$ circuitry.

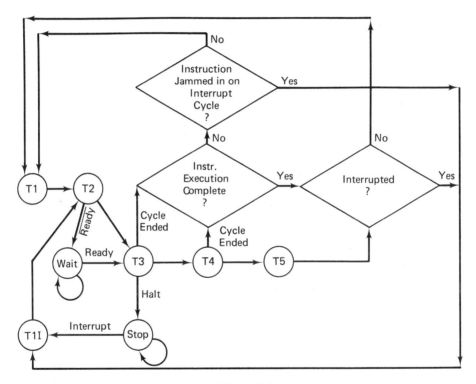

Figure 6-6

SUMMARY

The Intel 8008, introduced in 1971, was the first 8-bit monolithic central processor unit. One of the primary constraints at this time was the decision to use the proven 18-pin package rather than newer, as yet unproven, larger packages. The small number of information channels requires that several pieces of information be sent over the same space channel during different time slots, i.e., a space/time multiplexing scheme is used. The CPU is a finite-state machine, and each state of the CPU must be communicated to the $\overline{\text{CPU}}$ circuitry. The eight states are encoded by using three bits, and these are transmitted over three pins. The use of larger packages has reduced the need for time/space multiplexing in a number of second-generation 8-bit systems. However, several later CPUs are remarkably similar to the 8008. The technique is found in some form on almost every processor available, as will be seen in the chapters detailing specific addressing and I/O structures for the various machines. The following discussion eliminates detailed states and cycle codes and treats the universal aspects of space/time multiplexing.

A computer is essentially an information-processing device and, therefore, it can be looked at from an information-theory viewpoint. Information theory, in its simplest form, states merely that communication can occur only if there is a source, a receiver, and an information channel. This childishly simple statement would be of little interest except for two facts:

1. All real information channels are finite.
2. All real information channels generate noise.

Both of these facts are of tremendous importance to the total design and implementation of information-processing systems in general and computers in particular. The second is of primary importance to the designers of integrated circuits and of secondary interest to designers of systems based on integrated circuits.

We have discussed the solution to the noise problem in detail for the TTL logic family in Chapter 2 and observed that the TTL design rules tended to minimize the problem. Of particular interest to the systems designer is the finite information channel. This problem has twice occurred in the form of bottlenecks that have imposed limitations on our information channel capacity. The first finite channel was specified to be 8 bits wide and to serve as the channel along which all data and instruction flow occurs. The second channel was for transmitting the information specifying the internal state of the CPU to the $\overline{\text{CPU}}$ circuitry.

This status information, however, could not be transmitted on the 8-bit data channel. Rather than the constraint of a fixed channel width, we wished to minimize a cost function that almost amounted to simply minimizing the number of pin connections. There are eight internal states of the CPU. The possibility of using eight lines to transmit status information was rejected as being too costly in terms of pin connections. The problem was solved by encoding the status information by using a 3-bit binary code, thus reducing the channel width to three bits (pins) wide. Note that if minimum width were the *only* consideration, then a serial encoding scheme would be employed.

What trade-offs are involved in the optimal solution of a 3-bit channel width for a 3-bit code? Using a 3-bit code *and* a 1-bit wide channel would require sending at least three bits serially to specify each state. Thus, a clock rate three times higher than the system clock would be required to transmit the status information *by the end of each state*. To transmit the data in three pulses at the beginning of each state would require much higher clock rates. This can be achieved only by somehow building special circuitry, internal to the CPU, that would operate much faster than the rest of the CPU circuitry, or by slowing the rest of the CPU circuitry so that the CPU remained in each state much longer than the requirements dictated by physical parameters.

Either of these is very costly compared to the simultaneous propagation of three bits of information over the 3-bit wide information channel. Of the three solutions, 8-bit, 3-bit, and 1-bit channel widths, all were costly, i.e., the space/time product is never zero. The solution was an optimal, i.e., 3 bits wide plus coding rather than a minimal (1-bit wide, with or without coding). The coding prevents the solution from being minimal time since the gates used in encoding introduce finite time delays. A nonnegligible factor in the cost analysis is that the decoding in the receiver is easily achieved by cheap, readily available, MSI three- to eight-line decoders. Thus, the major cost is the eight-to-three encoder in the CPU itself. Such analyses are not academic questions, but will be faced by every system designer in some form or other. The best design will change according to the nature of the problem and the technology available for the solution.

The other information channel we have considered has been the 8-bit data bus. The width of this channel is insufficient to transmit the required 14 bits of address information at once, and rather than widen the data bus, a time-weighted trade-off was arrived at. The 14-bit address is broken into an 8-bit byte that is transmitted during one state of the CPU, and a 6-bit byte that is transmitted during a succeeding state of the CPU (along with two control bits). Thus, a serial (time) transmission of two parallel (space) words was chosen as the best solution to the bottleneck presented by the information channel, rather than the expedient of widening the information channel.

We see that time/space multiplexing consists of dividing a word into bytes and dividing the transmission time into periods. The process amounts to *dismembering* words, routing the parts to an information channel, sequentially transmitting the parts, receiving the parts, and routing the parts to appropriate locations where the word is *re-membered*.

The techniques of encoding/decoding and time/space multiplexing are standard methods used for transmitting information over narrow information channels. During the above analysis of the status information, it was implicitly assumed that we cannot predict the $(i + 1)$th state of the CPU from a knowledge of the ith state, i.e., information must be transmitted for each state. Were this not the case, only a START pulse and a SYNC need be transmitted to lock the

CPU and $\overline{\text{CPU}}$ in phase as they cycled through their predictable sequence of states. As it turns out, this is not the case due to two factors:

1. Different instructions lead to different state sequences.
2. The CPU can be interrupted by the $\overline{\text{CPU}}$ and, more specifically, by devices external to the computer.

These factors apply to *all* microprocessors. The following two chapters treat the 8008 specifically and design a system based on the state and cycle codes presented in this chapter. Later chapters present in detail the variations on these themes that are found in the other processors. The 8008 was chosen as a "worst case" design in the sense that the 18-pin-package constraint requires more external design than almost any other processor available and, therefore, serves as an ideal teaching tool. The multiplexed address/data bus in the second-generation, 16-bit PACE microprocessors (National Semiconductor) and the second-generation, 16-bit CP-1600 (General Instrument Corp.), the Intersil 12-bit IM 6100 and others, bear great resemblance to the 8008, as does the CP-1600 timing and control structure. Even more striking is the fact that, after providing a completely separate address bus in the second-generation 8080, Intel returned to address multiplexing in its third-generation 8085.

At this writing there are over two dozen microprocessors available, and the influence of the 8008 may be seen in most of them. A thorough knowledge of the 8008 is sufficient to allow us to understand most features of any nonmicroprogrammed CPU available today.

7 *the memory subsystem*

The goal of this chapter is to develop an intuitive feel for, and a facility with, the building blocks of earlier chapters via the design of a specific subsystem. As in algebra where the first step is usually a clear statement of the problem in natural language followed by translation into algebraic symbols, we wish whenever possible to state our problems in natural language and to follow this with translation into logic symbols. The existence of MSI and LSI building blocks makes this approach practical and often transparent. Examples of translation from words to logic symbols are shown in Fig. 7-1. The first example is very simply expressed in words, in Boolean algebraic terms, and in terms of logic symbols. The second example can also be expressed algebraically, although such an expression is more obscure than the original statement; i.e., $D \cdot E \cdot F \cdot S_1 \cdot S_2 \cdot S_3$ only hints at the relation between the S_is that are clearly stated to be lines that carry an octal code. The grouping of lines, which is not evident in the equations, is quite evident in the logic symbol diagram.

In the third example, the wording and logic symbols are quite clear. An attempt to describe this in Boolean algebraic form, however, would almost certainly be needlessly confusing. The fourth example clearly illustrates how readily a nontrivial word problem can be implemented in building-block symbolism. Should these examples prove unconvincing, then we could readily construct new ones organized around pulse synchronizers, priority encoders, multiple port register files, or majority logic—to name just a few possibilities.

PARTITIONING THE SYSTEM

The trend in systems software design has been toward modular development of programs. This approach both functionally defines the system and permits independent development of the system modules. In keeping with our assertion of hardware/software equivalence, we follow a similar strategy in design of our systems hardware. We first attempt to understand the entire problem, then to reduce this to subproblems that can be stated clearly enough that a logic implementation in terms of standard building blocks becomes immediately obvious. Seldom will we revert to algebraic expressions. The logic diagrams of

Word Formulation   Logic Symbolism

Example 1: The desired line, C,
goes Low when A is Low and
B is High.

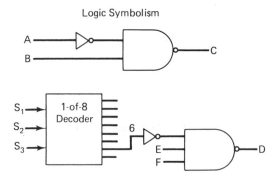

Example 2: The desired line, D,
is Low when the Octal Coded
State Lines (S_1 S_2 S_3) equal six
and lines E and F are High.

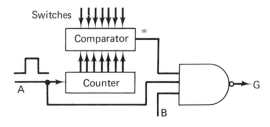

Example 3: Line G goes Low
when the nth pulse on Line A
coincides with Line B High for
arbitrary n Modulo m (m is
switch selectable).

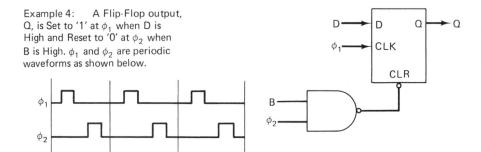

Example 4:   A Flip-Flop output,
Q, is Set to '1' at ϕ_1 when D is
High and Reset to '0' at ϕ_2 when
B is High. ϕ_1 and ϕ_2 are periodic
waveforms as shown below.

Figure 7-1 *Examples of word formulations and corresponding logic symbolism*

the computer systems designer are to be preferred to more artificial symbolic means of representation. It is necessary to understand fully the behavior of the building blocks, of course, in order to benefit from their symbolic representation. The symbolism for MSI functions provides a concrete, lucid means of translating our thoughts into patterns that others can interpret and understand quickly. One thing should be obvious, however: a poet who cannot spell and is unsure of the meanings of his words is likely to produce little great poetry. The designer who will not learn the details of each building block and only vaguely understands its function will surely dwell in the realm of mediocrity.

BASIC PATTERNS

The basic modules of which any information processor is composed have been discussed in the previous chapter and are presented again in Fig. 7-2.

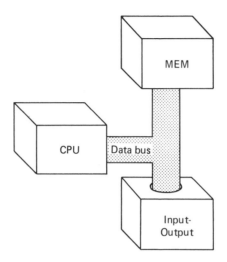

Figure 7-2   *The CPU/MEM/I-O modules*

Information transfers occur between the system modules and within the system modules. The intraCPU transfers are effected through software design and the interCPU/$\overline{\text{CPU}}$ transfers are effected through hardware design— specifically the design of the $\overline{\text{CPU}}$ circuitry. Thus, in attempting to gain an overall understanding of the general-purpose computer system, which we intend to implement with the CPU, and simultaneously to delineate the functional areas that have yet to be designed, we arrive at the following: The direction of our initial design effort should be toward the implementation of information-transfer circuitry that will interface in complementary fashion to the information channel that leads out of (and into) the CPU, i.e., the data bus. This interface must be electrically and functionally compatible with the CPU.

Our system consists of the CPU and both memory and I/O subsystems. The 8-bit wide data bus is used to communicate with both of these subsystems. We, therefore, state as our initial design goal:

> *Design circuitry capable of receiving and storing information transmitted from the CPU to the $\overline{\text{CPU}}$ during a normal process.*

To begin, we review the normal information transfers from the CPU. In particular, we are concerned with data that the CPU supplies to the $\overline{\text{CPU}}$ to be written into memory. These data must have an address associated with them, and also have two control bits that specify that the address is for memory

WRITE data. The address is present on the data bus during T1 and T2, while the control bits are present only during T2. The data word of interest is present on the data bus at T3. Since the address and control data are needed to route the data at T3, it is obvious that they must be stored and saved until T3. This is accomplished by latching the contents of the data bus at T1 and T2 into appropriate registers and using the contents of these registers at T3. We consider separately the electrical aspects and the functional aspects of the interface to the CPU.

The electrical parameters are specified in the design handbook, which states that all of the inputs to the 8008 CPU are TTL compatible, but recommends that pull-up resistors be used to ensure proper high levels. All outputs are low-

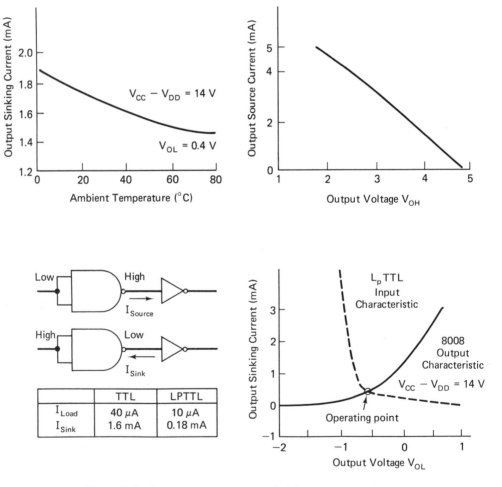

Figure 7-3 *Output source current and sink current capabilities of the 8008 shown with load and sink requirements for TTL and LPTTL devices*

power TTL compatible, with maximum output low voltage equal to 0.4 V at 0.44 mA, and minimum output high voltage equal to 3.5 V at 0.2 mA for $V_{cc} = +5.0$ V. From Fig. 7-3 it can be seen that the use of TTL circuitry interfaced to the 8008 would be marginal, whereas low-power TTL (LPTTL) is quite compatible with the CPU output capability. Low-power TTL devices are capable, in turn, of driving two TTL devices or ten LPTTL devices. The 33-nsec delays occurring with LPTTL gates are insignificant compared to the 500-nsec minimum clock pulse widths (Fig. 7-6). Therefore, it is permissible to buffer the 8008 data bus output with LPTTL inverters. We investigate several alternatives.

There are three data words that must be input to separate devices: the low-order address bits present at T1, the high-order address bits present at T2, and the data word itself present at T3. The first two are to be stored in a destination register in memory. One possible arrangement, shown in Fig. 7-4, provides a simple functional system. Low-power 8-bit latches are used, based on Fairchild 93L08 4-bit latch building blocks. Data are entered into the latch when the active low-enable line (Ē) goes LOW and is latched at the output when the line goes HIGH. By grounding the Ē line on one of the registers, we assure that the output lines will always follow the input, i.e., we simply use the device as a low-power 8-bit buffer between the 8008 and external memory. This is done in anticipation of the fact that most memory devices have TTL inputs rather than the LPTTL required by sinking-current considerations. By adding the sinking currents of the three devices, we obtain -1.92 mA, which total must be within the 8008 capability. However, it can be seen from Fig. 7-3 that at normal operat-

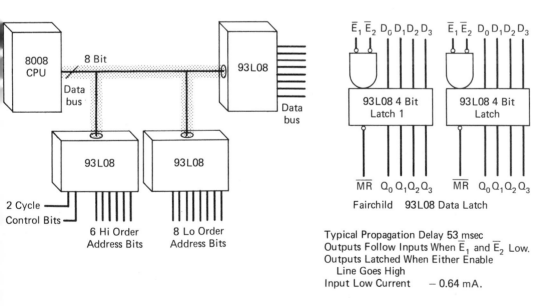

Figure 7-4 *Simple DATA OUT arrangement*

ing temperature this total exceeds the 8008 specifications and would thus be a poor design.

A latch that would satisfy the sink-current requirements is the Intel 3404. This latch has only 0.25 mA maximum input load current and, thus, three latches would require the 8008 to sink 0.75 mA, well within limits. The high speed latch has only a 12-nsec propagation delay. A slight disadvantage lies in its configuration—six latches per device—and in the fact that the device is inverting. By following each output with an inverter, we may recover the original information but only at the cost of twenty-four inverters. A better design would position the inverter before the latches, as shown in Fig. 7-5. The use of a low-power Schottky TTL inverter results in a buffer that does not exceed the 8008 sinking capability, and yet provides sufficient drive capability to handle the 3404s. Since the 74LS04 is a hex inverter, two packages will be required, thus providing several free LPTTL inverters for use with other 8008 outputs if needed.

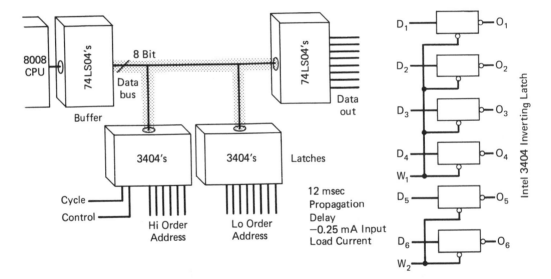

Figure 7-5 *DATA OUT circuitry that meets all of the electrical requirements*

The total delay is $12 + 10$ nsec $= 22$ nsec, which is less than that obtained with the 93L08s. The 3404 acts as a high-speed inverter as long as the WRITE enable is LOW, latching the inverted data when the line goes HIGH. An analysis of the clock timing shown in Fig. 7-6 indicates that the 22-nsec delay should be rather inconsequential since the typical periods occurring in the system are on the order of 500 nsec. There are, however, delays associated with the CPU that must be considered before our analysis is complete. The values given in Fig. 7-6 are typical ones; however, a range of variation is permissible. In particular, the clock period t_{cy} is specified to be from 2 to 3 μsec long, while

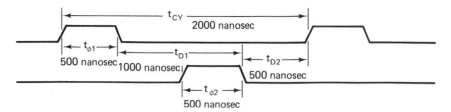

Figure 7-6   *Basic input clock pulse timing*

clock rise and fall times may not exceed 50 nsec. The clock delay from the falling edge of ϕ_1 to the falling edge of ϕ_2 must be from 900 to 1100 nsec long, while the clock delay from ϕ_2 to ϕ_1 must exceed 400 nsec and that from ϕ_1 to ϕ_2 must exceed 200 nsec.

A cognizance and understanding of the timing diagram presented in Fig. 7-7 are necessary prior to the design of the timing circuitry of the $\overline{\text{CPU}}$ subsystem. The following delays and hold times are discussed in some detail before proceeding: t_{DD}, t_{OH}, t_{IH}, t_{SD}, t_S. The figures for the various delays assume a capacitive load of 100 pF. The dependence of delay time on capacitive load is indicated in Fig. 7-7b.

t_{SD} —SYNC OUT DELAY—In Fig. 6-5 the timing is such that the leading edge of the SYNC pulse is coincident with the trailing edge of clock pulse ϕ_{22}, thus defining the beginning of a new CPU state. Although the CPU may be considered to enter the appropriate state at this time, there is actually a delay due to capacitive loading that may reach 700-nsec duration before the SYNC signal is output to the $\overline{\text{CPU}}$. This time is measured from the fall of ϕ_{22} through 1.5 V to the rise of SYNC through 1.5 V.

t_{SO} —STATE OUT DELAY—Although the beginning of each CPU state has been defined to be coincident with the rising edge of the SYNC pulse, there can be a delay of up to 1100 nsec between the trailing edge of ϕ_{22} and the actual output of state signals from the CPU. Consequently, the possibility of a large delay between the SYNC pulse out and the state signals out exists. Thus, we cannot assume that the proper state signals are present when the SYNC pulse goes HIGH. (An exception is that the state out delay for states T1 and TII is measured from the leading edge of ϕ_{11} and may not exceed 1000 nsec.)

t_{DD} —DATA OUT DELAY—This delay is measured from the trailing edge of clock pulse ϕ_{11} (when data is placed on the bus) to the time at which the voltage reaches 1.5 V. With a capacitive load of 100 pF the delay may reach 1000 nsec and *must* be considered when latching data from the data bus. Typical values of t_{DD} plotted against data bus capacitance are shown in Fig. 7-7.

The delays discussed above are guaranteed maximums that will not be exceeded when the appropriate lines are driving 100-pF capacitive loads. They

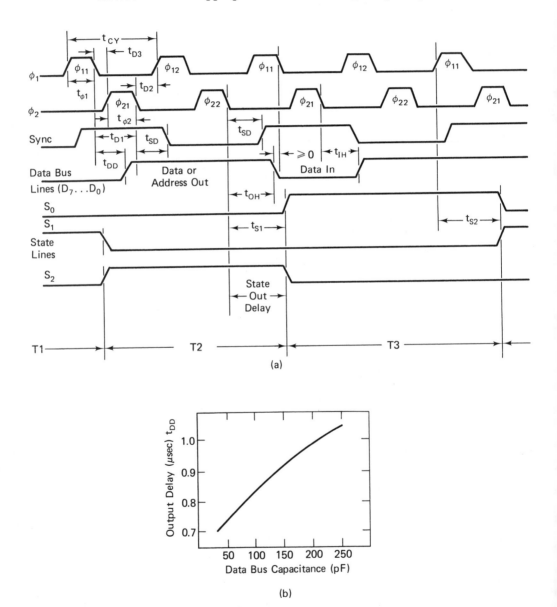

Figure 7-7 (a) CPU timing diagram; (b) DATA OUT delay vs. output load capacitance. (courtesy of INTEL Corporation)

complicate the design of the $\overline{\text{CPU}}$ circuitry and in one case must be circumvented by special anticipatory circuitry. The hold times discussed below are either guaranteed minimum time for the CPU or required minimum times for the $\overline{\text{CPU}}$ circuitry.

t_{OH} —HOLD TIME FOR DATA BUS OUT—This parameter is measured from the trailing edge of ϕ_{22} and specifies the minimum time elapsing before the data disappear from the data bus to be 100 nsec. Thus, if the trailing edge of ϕ_{22} is used to latch the data onto the data bus, the latching action must be completed within 100 nsec.

t_{IH} —HOLD TIME FOR DATA IN—This parameter specifies the amount of time that data must be held on the data bus following the falling edge of clock pulse ϕ_{21}. Although a numerical value is not given for set-up time, note that data input to the 8008 CPU during T3 must be on the data bus prior to the time at which clock pulse ϕ_{11} goes LOW.

With the above timing information we can complete our analysis of the data-out transfer circuitry. By choosing 74LS04 inverters to buffer the CPU, we optimize the relevant parameters, obtaining low delays through the choice of Schottky clamped TTL and low-power by specifying low-power Schottky. The input low current of -0.36 mA is well within the sinking capability of the 8008. The typical propagation delay of 9.5 nsec for the 74LS04 is several times faster than ordinary low-power TTL.

We consider, first, the transfer and latching of the address data. By adding the 10-nsec propagation delay through the buffer to the maximum delay, we obtain 1010-nsec delay compared to 1000 nsec without the buffer. This tells us that the buffer introduces an inconsequential delay and we need not have specified Schottky circuitry at this point. We overdesign with Schottky devices at this point, since there will be more delays entering into our design as we proceed. Note that $t_{\text{D1}} + t_{\text{D2}}$ yields a minimum of 1.3 μsec from the trailing edge of ϕ_{11} to the leading edge of ϕ_{12}, whereas t_{DD} specified from the same starting point is never greater than 1.0 μsec. This indicates that the data will definitely be on the data bus before the occurrence of ϕ_{12}. t_{OH} is guaranteed to be at least 100 nsec, i.e., the data will be on the data bus for 100 nsec after clock pulse ϕ_{22} goes LOW. Thus, we conclude that the desired data will be on the data bus during the periods Φ_3 and Φ_4 shown in Fig. 6-5. The definition of Φ_3 (and Φ_1) did not take into account any delay in the SYNC pulse, so we must now check to be sure the definitions are still valid. Referenced to the trailing edge of ϕ_2, the SYNC delay can be 700 nsec (t_{SD}), while the leading edge of ϕ_1 may occur only 400 nsec (t_{D2}) from the same reference. Thus, the SYNC pulse required to generate Φ_1 (and $\overline{\text{SYNC}}$ required for Φ_3) cannot be present at the beginning of ϕ_1. It can be seen from the definitions, $\Phi_1 = \text{SYNC} \cdot \phi_1$ and $\Phi_3 = \overline{\text{SYNC}} \cdot \phi_1$, that the SYNC out delay (and, of course, the $\overline{\text{SYNC}}$ out delay) does not allow Φ_1 and Φ_3 to be defined unambiguously. We must, therefore,

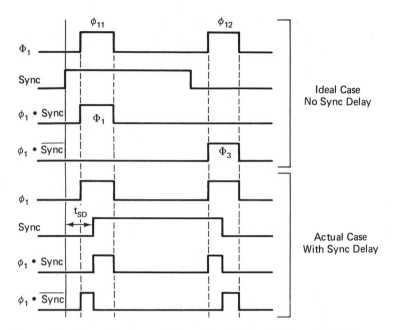

Figure 7-8 *Illustrating the ambiguity arising in the definition of clock phases* Φ_1 *and* Φ_3 *due to the SYNC delay* t_{SD}

restrict our $\overline{\text{CPU}}$ system design to a two-phase clock with nonoverlapping phases Φ_2 and Φ_4 that are not affected by the SYNC out delay. The ideal case with no SYNC delay is contrasted in Fig. 7-8 with the ambiguous case.

The conclusion we reach from analysis of the timing diagram is that data from the CPU that appear on the data bus can be latched at Φ_4. Our design problem can then be stated as:

> *design circuitry that will latch the low-order address during state T1 and period* Φ_4, *or T1I and* Φ_4, *and that will also latch the high-order address during state T2 and period* Φ_4. *The latches to be used are 3404s that act as high-speed inverters when the WRITE line is LOW, and latch the output when the line goes HIGH. T1 and T1I are one of eight decoder outputs.*

We consider first for the sake of simplicity the high-order address data that are to be latched at $T2 \cdot \Phi_4$. We desire the WRITE line to go LOW at this time in order to pass the new address bits at the latch inputs to the latch output, and then to go HIGH, thus latching the data. The WRITE line must be normally HIGH and must go LOW only when T2 and Φ_4 occur. This is logically accomplished through the use of a NAND gate with inputs T2 and Φ_4 and output $\overline{T2 \cdot \Phi_4}$. The logic symbolism is shown in Fig. 7-9a.

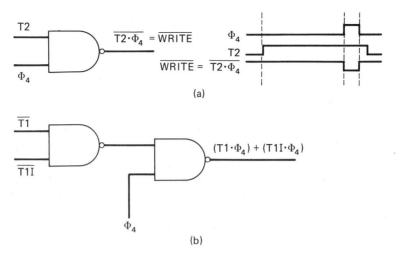

Figure 7-9 *(a) High-order address latching signal; (b) Low-order address latching signal*

The low-order address bits are to be latched when T1 and Φ_4, or T1I and Φ_4, occur. Although this condition could easily be drawn with logic symbols, it is worth writing down in equation form:

$$Y = (\text{T1} \cdot \Phi_4) + (\text{T1I} \cdot \Phi_4) = (\text{T1} + \text{T1I}) \cdot \Phi_4 = (\overline{\overline{\text{T1}} \cdot \overline{\text{T1I}}}) \cdot \Phi_4$$

The last relation is derived through application of De Morgan's theorem. Its significance derives from the fact that the signals T1 and T1I are state signals. Earlier discussion has described the encoded state information as that appearing on the three pins S_0, S_1, and S_2 of the CPU. This information must be transformed by a 1-of-8 decoder before use may be made of the individual state signals. One-of-eight decoders are active-low devices due to simple power considerations. Since no more than one line is active at any given time, and the devices in the output LOW state must sink the maximum current, such devices are always made active-low. This guarantees that at any given time at least seven inactive lines will be HIGH, thereby resulting in minimum power consumption. The 1-of-8 decoder thus effectively inverts the state signals. Well-designed MSI devices take this fact into account and all inputs that are most likely to be driven by the output of a 1-of-n decoder are made active LOW. For similar reasons we wish to take account of this fact in our circuit design. Thus, rather than T1 and T1I, the signals available at the outputs of the state decoder are $\overline{\text{T1}}$ and $\overline{\text{T1I}}$, and these are the inputs to the circuit we are now designing. We wish to NAND the two state inputs together and then NAND this output with the period Φ_4. The most economical circuit is shown in Fig. 7-9b.

Since the function Y in the Boolean equation is by convention TRUE, i.e., HIGH, we must invert it to obtain the active low WRITE line, $\overline{\text{W}}$. In terms of the WRITE line, $\overline{W}$, the relation becomes

$$\overline{W} = \overline{\overline{(\overline{T1} \cdot \overline{T1I}) \cdot \Phi_4}}$$

which is written down immediately in the NAND symbolism shown. A different circuit would have been most economical if the inputs had been assumed to be T1 and T1I. This design would have been compromised by two inversions necessary to obtain TRUE inputs from the decoder, or else a redesign would have been necessary, resulting in our solution. This example, occurring at the very beginning of our $\overline{CPU}$ design effort, should serve to emphasize that the designer should possess detailed knowledge of the elements that he uses. Such familiarity and attention to details should often result in economies, either in terms of number of gates used or number of design hours required.

A conclusion that may be drawn from the above discussion concerns the inputs and outputs of the subsystem that is being designed. It is seen that the interfaces between subsystems are excellent places to begin economical design. The designers of MSI devices have attempted to benefit those who design with MSI circuits by minimizing the power consumption of functioning MSI circuitry. An analysis of minimum power then becomes an essential aspect of digital design, as in some cases does an analysis of minimum propagation delay. These aspects are not inherent in any mathematical design technique and explain in part the relative uselessness of these techniques in design of MSI systems as opposed to their utility as demonstrated in the SSI design phase.

The design of the state decoder subsystem amounts to simply choosing an appropriate 1-of-8 decoder. One such building block that exhibits low input current and small propagation delays is the Intel 3205 decoder. The maximum input load current is 0.25 mA, and the maximum delay is 18 nsec; thus, the device is completely compatible with the 8008 CPU. The selection of the decoder completes the address latching subsystem design. The functional diagram of this subsystem is shown in Fig. 7-10. The detailed system that we have just

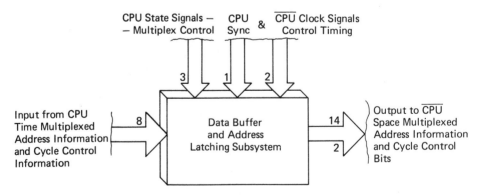

Figure 7-10   *Functional diagram of the address latching subsystem*

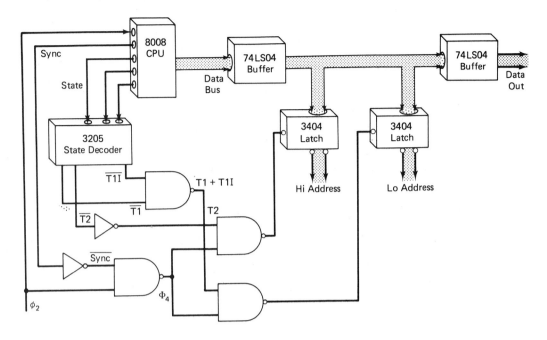

Figure 7-11 Preliminary design of address latching subsystem

designed is shown in Fig. 7-11. Our initial design goal was to develop circuitry capable of receiving and storing information transmitted from the CPU to the CPU during a normal, i.e., noninterrupt, process. This information consists of a data word plus the address words that designate where this word is to be stored in memory.

We now turn to the problem of storage of the data word sent out at T3. We choose the simplest storage element consistent with our address subsystem and with our desire to obtain a memory speed commensurate with the speed of the CPU. The speed criterion dictates random access memory (RAM). Maximum advantage is found in using RAM devices with on-chip address decoding because this relieves us of the burden of designing the address decoding circuitry, a simple but bothersome task both in terms of total number of devices used and in design effort. Most of the RAMs on the market possess on-chip decoding at very reasonable cost; therefore, this solution is the logical one. For the same reasons, we choose static random access memory rather than dynamic so that we have less timing to worry about. This choice means that the building blocks will cost more money, but this is more than offset by the economies in terms of device number and design effort. Only for very large memory systems that must be commercially competitive should we choose the more complicated dynamic memories that require quite critical timing circuits.

In addition to the static specification, we desire TTL compatability on both inputs and outputs, and a single $+5$-V power supply if possible. There should be at least 1024 bits (1K) of storage capacity or more, and an access time of 1 μsec or less.

The Intel 2102 1K static RAM, which is completely TTL compatible and requires only a single $+5$-V power supply, is organized as 1024 1-bit words (1K $\times$ 1) and includes an on-chip 10-bit address decoder plus one chip enable line used to send the tri-state outputs into the third, "invisible," state. The 2102 provides an ideal building block with nondestructive readouts of the same polarity as the input. The 500-nsec access time is sufficient for our system although a range of such time is available. This is a "workhorse" chip that has continued to decline in price. The simple timing constraints makes it well-suited to our example.

The use of 16,384 $\times$ 1 bit (16K $\times$ 1) dynamic RAMs is desirable for our system. However, the more complex timing required for the "refresh" circuitry detracts from its use as a teaching tool. The availability of refresh controller chips will simplify the use of such RAMs.

Since our purpose is to receive and store data from the CPU, we must fashion circuitry that provides the STORE or WRITE control signal to the 2102. We begin, as usual, with a statement of the problem:

design circuitry that will cause the RAM to store data from the CPU that appears on the data bus during state T3 of a PCW cycle.

The PCW cycle control coding indicates that the address appearing at T1 and T2 is for data that are to be written into memory. The PCW coding is $(D_6, D_7) = (1, 1)$; thus, the solution to the problem when timing is ignored requires simply that the WRITE signal occurs when T3 and PCW occur, i.e., T3·PCW. The presence of data out delays and the address and data set-up times required by the RAM demands that a timing analysis be made. We begin our analysis by considering the relevant RAM parameters, and limit our analysis to the WRITE cycle at this point. These parameters are shown in Fig. 7-12, and their description follows.

The 2102 random access memory stores data that are on the data input line when the active low R/W WRITE pulse makes a LOW-to-HIGH transition. The WRITE pulse must be at least 750 nsec in width, and the data that are to be stored must remain stable for at least 800 nsec prior to the LOW-to-HIGH transition and also be held for 100 nsec after the R/W line goes HIGH. A suggested order for application and duration of the required signals for the 2102 is shown in the nested diagram of Fig. 7-13. This is an acceptable, but not an absolute, order that can be modified if necessary. It merely gives a direction in which to proceed during the initial design stage. The diagram simply states that the four types of information can be applied in the following order and removed in the reverse order: Address, Chip Enable, Data, R/W.

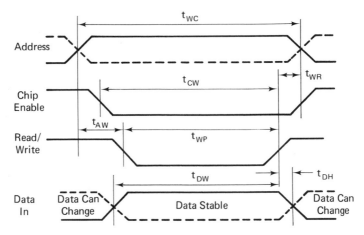

Figure 7-12   *Intel 2102 RAM WRITE cycle timing parameters*

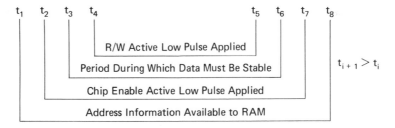

Figure 7-13   *Diagram illustrating acceptable order of application of signals to random access memory. Some changes can be made in this order if necessary, subject to the timing constraints.*

The timing parameters associated with the WRITE cycle are briefly described:

t_{WC} —WRITE CYCLE TIME—The total time associated with the write cycle is determined by summing the nonoverlapping times given by the rest of the timing parameters. The minimum period required for the presence of address data is 1000 nsec.

t_{AW} —ADDRESS TO WRITE SETUP TIME—the amount of time by which the address information must precede the application of the R/W WRITE signal is specified to be 200 nsec.

t_{WP} —WRITE PULSE WIDTH—the minimum width of the active low WRITE pulse is specified to be 750 nsec.

t_{WR} —WRITE RECOVERY TIME—the minimal time required after the WRITE pulse goes high before the chip enable line is allowed to go high, thereby disabling the RAM chip.

t_{DW} —DATA SETUP TIME—the amount of time preceding the low-to-high transition of the WRITE pulse, during which the RAM data must remain stable, is known as the data set-up time and is specified to be 800 nsec.

t_{DH} —DATA HOLD TIME—the amount of time following the LOW-to-HIGH transition of the WRITE pulse, during which the RAM data must remain stable, is called the data hold time and is at least 100 nsec.

t_{CW} —CHIP ENABLE TO WRITE SETUP TIME—the RAM chip must be enabled at least 900 nsec before the data are written into memory, i.e., before the LOW-to-HIGH transition of the active low R/W WRITE pulse.

The logic symbol and block diagram for the 2102 RAM storage device are shown in Fig. 7-14. Having specified the order and minimum durations that must be satisfied in designing with the 2102, it is possible to proceed with the design of the memory subsystem of the $\overline{CPU}$. The address latching circuits present the addressing information to the memory subsystem at time $T2 \cdot \Phi_4$. As just indicated, the chip enable pulse must occur next and be held for 900 nsec prior to the WRITE transition of the R/W line. Note that no set-up time is specified for the address information relative to the chip enable line and, therefore, it is possible to apply both the addressing information and the chip enable pulse simultaneously. This fact is quite useful and allows the address information to provide the chip enable signal as follows.

The address information available to the memory subsystem at $T2 \cdot \Phi_4$ consists of 14 bits capable of addressing directly 16K words of stored data. Of these 14 bits, only 10 are used to address the contents of a particular 2102 random access memory. Eight 2102s in parallel constitute a *bank* of 1K words of data. Sixteen such banks of RAMs would provide the maximum directly addressable storage for the 8008. The four address bits remaining are capable of selecting any one of 16 banks of RAMs. Thus, the somewhat obvious memory configuration suggested by these numbers is that which decodes the 4 bits using a 1-of-16 decoder and applies the active low output provided by such decoders to the appropriate chip enable lines, thereby selecting the desired bank of 1K RAMs. This configuration, in which all banks of 2102 RAMs are tied to the same address bus with all data inputs tied to the same data input bus and all outputs tied to the same output data bus, is shown in Fig. 7-15. The tri-state outputs of the 2102 provide that the 15 disabled RAMs are "invisible," i.e., represent a negligible load to the enabled RAM.

The completion of the preliminary design of the address and chip enable circuitry leads to consideration of the data bits to be written into the selected bank of RAMs. These data are placed on the data bus during T3 by the 8008 CPU and must remain stable for 300 nsec prior to the WRITE transition of the

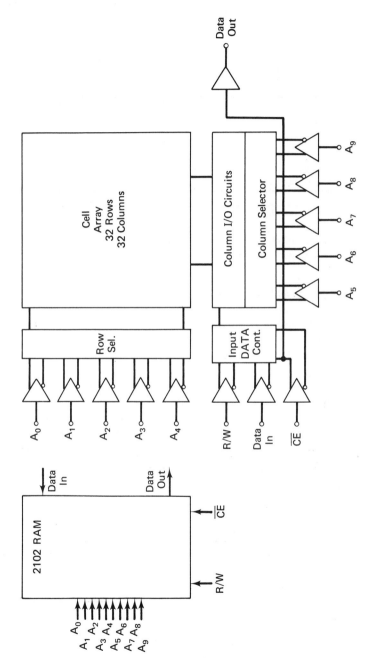

Figure 7-14 Logic symbolism and block diagram for the Intel 2102 RAM

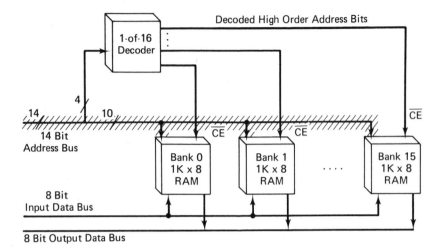

Figure 7-15 *16K memory subsystem configuration consisting of 16 1K RAM banks with common address and data busses*

R/W pulse, and for 100 nsec following this transition. The data can be put on the 2102 input lines at any time following the address and chip enable bits.

To establish the time at which the data are sure to be on the data bus, we note that the maximum data-out-delay is measured from the falling edge of the ϕ_{11} clock pulse and is less than, or equal to, 1 μsec. The clock delay from the falling edge of ϕ_{11} to the falling edge of ϕ_{21} is specified to be between 900 nsec and 1100 nsec, and the clock delay from ϕ_{21} to ϕ_{12} is at least 400 nsec; therefore, the data at T3 is guaranteed to be on the bus prior to ϕ_{12}, as shown in Fig. 7-16.

As discussed earlier, the SYNC delay prevents our being able to define four unambiguous clock phases Φ_1, Φ_2, Φ_3, and Φ_4. We are left with two usable time increments, Φ_2 and Φ_4, that are guaranteed to be valid by the timing constraint on the SYNC delay. A close study of Fig. 7-16 leads to this conclusion:

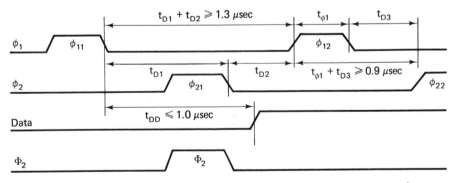

Figure 7-16 *Illustrating that data at T3 will be on the data bus prior to ϕ_{12}*

There are two clock phases that can conceivably be used to initiate the R/W HIGH-to-LOW transition, Φ_2 and Φ_4. If $\Phi_2 = \text{SYNC} \cdot \phi_2$ is used, then the R/W line will go LOW before the data is on the line, whereas when Φ_4 goes LOW, the data will be on the line, but the T3 state will be almost over. The latter is unsatisfactory due to the required data set-up times of 800 nsec plus the fact that we must then arrange for the R/W line to make a LOW-to-HIGH transition at some point before the address, the chip enable, or the data change. There appear to be few reasonable ways to accomplish this. Thus, we are led to consider the case in which the R/W line goes LOW *before* the data appear on the data input to the RAM. Although the WRITE cycle timing diagram (Fig. 7-12) shows the data appearing before R/W goes LOW, there is no timing constraint that governs this relation. The timing parameters relevant to this question merely state the minimum R/W pulse width allowable and the amount of time the data must remain stable prior to the WRITE transition of R/W. Since no timing constraint prevents the R/W pulse appearing before the data, this is an allowable order of occurrence. Note that the nest diagram of Fig. 7-13 is no longer applicable to this design.

Having decided that $\Phi_2 = \phi_2 \cdot \text{SYNC}$ will be used to initiate the R/W pulse, and tentatively decided that $\Phi_4 = \phi_2 \cdot \overline{\text{SYNC}}$ will effect the LOW-to-HIGH WRITE transition, we have only to check to see whether all set-up times are satisfied and then to design the appropriate circuit. Reference to Fig. 7-6 shows that the minimum width of the ϕ_{12} pulse plus the clock delay from ϕ_{12} to ϕ_{22} equals, or exceeds, 900 nsec. During this time the data have remained stable (appearing before ϕ_{12}) and the R/W line has been low (since $\Phi_2 = \phi_2 \cdot \text{SYNC} = \phi_{21}$); therefore, both the minimum R/W pulse width and the data set-up time requirements are met. It is obvious that the data will remain (latched) on the data input for a sufficient time after the R/W LOW-to-HIGH transition occurs any time during Φ_4. All relevant WRITE cycle constraints having been met, we now set out to design circuitry capable of generating such an R/W pulse. Such circuitry will initiate the pulse during the Φ_2 period and remove the pulse during Φ_4. We restate the problem in more specific terms:

> *design a circuit that will cause the R/W line to go LOW at T3·PCW·SYNC·ϕ_2.*

Although logically the triggering signals seem easily derivable with simple 4-input AND gates, it must be remembered that they are nonoverlapping. Thus, there must be a record that the first state has occurred and is only erased by the occurrence of the second state. This, of course, requires that a flip-flop be used as the memory. Recognizing this, let us further restate the problem:

> *design a circuit consisting of a flip-flop whose output state will be R/W line. Output will normally be HIGH; however, it should be cleared at T3·PCW·SYNC·ϕ_2 and set at T3·PCW·$\overline{\text{SYNC}}$·ϕ_2.*

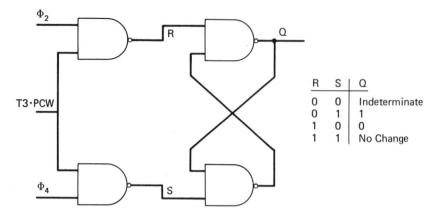

Figure 7-17 *Preliminary R/W circuit design using R-S flip-flop*

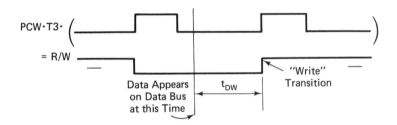

Figure 7-18 *Timing analysis of R/W circuit using R-S flip-flop*

The circuit shown in Fig. 7-17 consists of an R-S flip-flop with the appropriate gates connected to the SET and RESET lines. Assuming that the initial state of Q is "1," then it will remain so until PCW·T3·ϕ_2 occurs, causing the RESET line to go low and flipping the output, Q, to "0." When the RESET line returns high, the circuit remains in the Q = "0" mode. In this mode it "remembers" that PCW·T3·Φ_2 has occurred and will continue to do so until SET by PCW·T3·Φ_4 going LOW. This timing is shown in Fig. 7-18. Note that, due to the fact that Φ_2 and Φ_4 are nonoverlapping, the R/W flip-flop output is never indeterminate.

The only catch in this design is the assumption that the R-S flip-flop was initially in the state Q = 1. This, of course, must be provided for and, therefore, an initializing circuit must be designed. Although this is suggested as a worthwhile problem for the reader to consider, we will abandon the situation as unwieldy and investigate the use of other types of flip-flops. How, for instance, would we use a D-type flip-flop in an R/W circuit? We might arrange a 7474 dual D-type flip-flop, as shown in Fig. 7-19. The device is voltage triggered and insensitive to the transition time of the clock pulse. The input is locked out when the clock is either HIGH or LOW, but the D input is transferred to the output Q and latched on the positive going edge of the clock pulse. At first

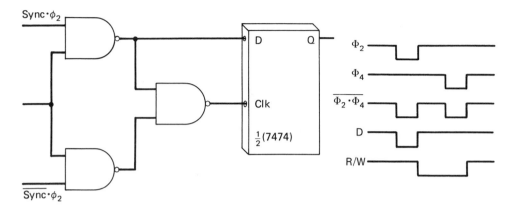

Figure 7-19 *Preliminary design of R/W circuit using 7474 D-type flip-flop*

glance this circuit looks good; however, a second glance shows that the delay caused by the NAND gate in the clock path would allow the D input to go high before the flip-flop triggered. This could be avoided by putting two inverters in the D line as a delay. The variations in propagation delay from gate to gate make this risky. We could put several more gates in to guarantee a sufficient delay, but this is a rather inelegant and costly solution. We, therefore, reject this approach before we even consider the question of initial state of the Q output (R/W line). We abandon the D-type flip-flop in favor of the most flexible, general-purpose latch, the J-K flip-flop. We use as our design vehicle the SN 7476 Dual J-K Master/Slave flip-flop with preset and clear. The device is shown in Fig. 7-20, along with the truth table and clock pulse action. In the first two tries at designing the R/W circuit there was a little problem in generating R/W

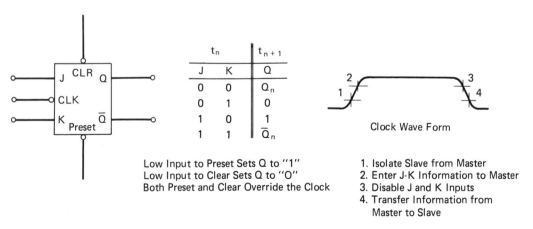

Figure 7-20 *TTL 7476 Dual J-K Master/Slave flip-flop logic diagram and relevant data*

transitions at the correct times. The weak point in both designs lay in the initial setting of the R/W time; therefore, this will be the direction of our approach: to guarantee that the R/W circuit is initially high and then worry about the transition times.

We begin by noting that if $J = 1$ and $K = 0$, then every clock pulse results in $Q = 1$. We might then simply use the SYNC line as the clock. Although this solves the specific problem, it is awkward because it does solve this problem and nothing else. Why not let SYNC$\cdot\phi_2$ serve as the clock line? This both sets R/W $= 1$ during the first PCI cycle (before the RAM can be enabled at T2), and also serves to effect the desired LOW-to-HIGH transition of R/W during

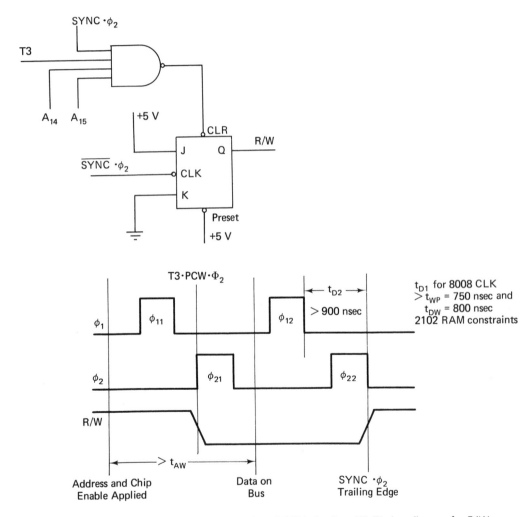

Figure 7-21   *(a) Final design of R/W circuitry; (b) Timing diagram for R/W circuitry*

the T3·PCW state. This is a nice solution and leaves us with only the task of sending R/W low at T3·PCW·ϕ_2. By noticing that the active low CLEAR line is independant of the clock, we can employ this line to initiate the R/W WRITE pulse. The final R/W circuit design is shown in Fig. 7-21a and the timing analysis in 7-21b. This elegant circuit is used in the Intel MCS-8 system that is based around the 8008 CPU.

With the completion of the R/W circuit design our subsystem now effects normal transfers *from* the CPU, i.e., CPU-to-memory transfers. We postpone until later the I/O transfer from the CPU to an output port. A reasonable goal at this time would be designing the circuitry for a normal transfer *to* the CPU, i.e., memory-to-CPU transfer. We now state the problem as:

> *design circuitry that will read data stored in memory and transmit these data to the CPU at the appropriate time during state T3.*

As pointed out earlier, there is no need to design new addressing circuitry; therefore, our task will largely be a timing analysis to ensure that the CPU and the memory timing are compatible. We need to employ the cycle control bits as before, of course, but this should be trivial.

As a starting point, we consider the READ cycle timing diagram for the 2102 RAM shown in Fig. 7-22. The timing parameters are described as:

t_{RC} —READ CYCLE TIME

t_A —ACCESS TIME—the time required to access data at any given address as measured from the application of address lines; typically, 500 nsec. Maximum time is 1000 nsec.

t_{CO} —CHIP ENABLE TO OUTPUT TIME—the minimum time from application of chip enable pulse to data out.

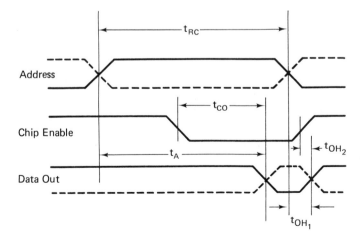

Figure 7-22 *READ cycle timing diagram for the 2102 RAM*

t_{OH_1} —the amount of time that data from the previous READ cycle is valid after removal of the address data.

t_{OH_2} —the amount of time that data from the previous READ cycle is valid after removal of the chip enable signal.

Having summarized the RAM timing parameters, we turn our attention now to the CPU input timing analysis. The relevant information is presented in Fig. 7-23. The first thing to notice about the "Data In" timing is that the CPU requires input data to be available much earlier in T3 than it does data out. Therefore, our first task is to decide whether the address set-up time for the 2102 RAM is compatible with the address-out-to-data-in time that is shown in the figure. This time is labeled t_{AD} and is equal to $t_{cy} - t_{D1}$. The worst case is min t_{cy} — max t_{D1}, or 2 μsec — 1.1 μsec = 900 nsec. Note that this is much larger than the typical 2102 address set-up time required, but just short of the max address set-up time. This presents a problem that can be solved in several different ways. By minimizing circuit capacitance and keeping temperatures low, we speed up the typical times; however, it is well to design to the maximum times. Another very simple solution is to make the minimum clock cycle 2.1 μsec long, thus bringing $t_{cy} - t_{D1}$ to the required 1000-nsec address set-up time. This simple solution means that our computer will run 5% slower than if we used 2.0-μsec cycle time, a drastic step indeed! We might arrange to latch the address on the leading edge of ϕ_{22}, rather than on the trailing edge, a move that will require redesign of the high-order address latching circuits. This is undesirable at best. When we reach such a dead end it is time to rethink the problem. Let us clearly restate the problem we are considering.

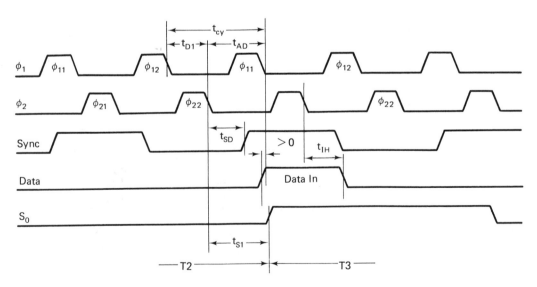

Figure 7-23 *DATA IN timing diagram for 8008 CPU*

The data READ from the 2102 RAM must be available to the CPU before the falling edge of ϕ_{11} during state T3. In order for this to occur, we must present the address to the RAM at least 1000 nsec (worst case analysis) prior to this time. The address is latched, however, only 900 nsec prior to this time, the latching occurring at the falling edge of ϕ_{22} during state T2.

This apparently messy problem is presented as a real problem that arises in the course of a design. We have discussed possible options a designer should consider, giving reasons why each was rejected. One solution that has not been mentioned is the use of the READY feature of the CPU that was designated for just such an event, i.e., the use of slow memories. The action of the READY line simply postpones the arrival of state T3 (an integral number of cycles) until the memories signal that all is in readiness. To use this line, however, would cause a much more drastic slowdown than the 5% stretchout discussed above, and would be ridiculous for a 100-nsec problem. The 2102 does not fall into the category of "slow" memories as far as the 8008 is concerned.

What is the solution, then? It lies in the realization that the problem is illusory. The problem here has arisen through the false assumption that the address data are available to the RAM *only after* it has been latched into the address storage register. For some latches, such as the J-K Master/Slave flip-flop of the R/W circuit, the output does indeed change state at the falling edge of the clock pulse. However, the 3404 latches that are used in the address register act as high-speed inverters as long as the WRITE line goes HIGH. Thus, the required address data are available to the 2102 RAM for an appreciable length of time (over 100 nsec) *before the latching action occurs*, and there is no problem.

The analysis that has been outlined illustrates the desirability of the designer having detailed knowledge of each building block. It is very likely that, given the above "problem," a nonzero percentage of designers would "solve" it.

We have determined that the address set-up time is satisfied for the 2102 so that the data out of the RAM are available to the CPU at the required time. We have implicitly assumed that the chip enable is presented concurrent with (and derived from) the address. Thus, the chip enable to output time, being shorter than the address set-up time, is automatically satisfied. Having determined that the 8008 CPU plus addressing circuitry is timewise compatible with the 2102 RAM, we must design the data path from the RAM output to the CPU input. We state the problem specifically as:

design circuitry capable of transferring data from memory to the CPU during the T3 of appropriate cycles, i.e., the PCI and PCR cycles.

Before beginning this design we should attempt to stand back and see where we are going. We have a central processor unit that is capable of inputting instructions or data from memory and from input devices, and is also capable of outputting data from the CPU to memory or to output ports. We have considered, so far, only the information transferred from CPU to memory and have given little thought to the problem of transferring data to output devices. Due to the limited drive (sink) capabilities of the CPU, we have buffered the output data path with a 74LS04 inverter. From earlier considerations of power it is obvious that, when we do consider output ports, we will of necessity place these on the $\overline{\text{CPU}}$ side of the buffer. Since the 8008 uses a common data bus for input and output data, we must present input data to the CPU data bus on the CPU side of the 74LS04 buffer. We have the choice of simply hanging all inputs to the CPU on the data bus at this point, or of using an input buffer. Even assuming that the 8008 has the current capability to withstand the presence of several outputs connected to the data bus, the resulting increase in load capacitance seen by the CPU immediately rules this out.

Therefore, we decide first to place a buffer between the CPU and all sources of data input to the CPU. When considering the output buffer we were severely restricted by the input requirements on the buffer. The requirements are much less strict on the input buffer and we have several types of outputs available for buffer devices: normal, open collector, and tri-state. By choosing tri-state we can disable, i.e., send into the HI-Z state, the input buffer when we are outputting data from the CPU and, thus, obtain a maximal decoupling of the devices from the output data bus. The tri-state buffer has only a 10-nsec propagation delay, a negligible amount. A suitable tri-state buffer is found in the Signetics 8T09. This is an inverting device and, therefore, requires that another inversion occur preceding the presentation of data at the 8T09 inputs. By buffering every input device connected to the input data bus with another 8T09, we obtain the double inversion at the same time that we take advantage of the tri-state common bus architecture. This scheme is shown in Fig. 7-24.

Although this scheme is satisfactory, we need not specify that tri-state buffers be used on each input device. Another buffered input scheme that would be quite acceptable is that shown in Fig. 7-25. This architecture utilizes an inverting data selector (or group of them) to achieve the necessary second inversion. Although we do not yet know the means by which a given input port is selected, we assume that it exists and can be transformed into a useful selection signal for either the architecture of Fig. 7-24 or that of Fig. 7-25. Thus, our choice of a tri-state inverting buffer at the input data bus of the 8008 is satisfactory in the sense that it achieves the isolation we desire while remaining compatible with several input selection schemes.

Before proceeding with the design of the memory-to-CPU data transfer circuitry we must choose the type of input selection circuitry we will use. The choices presented in Figs. 7-24 and 7-25 are the standard methods for gating data from several devices onto a common bus, i.e., we can either hang all devices on the bus by using open collector or tri-state buffers, or we can input each device separately to a multiplexer or data selector and tie the output of this

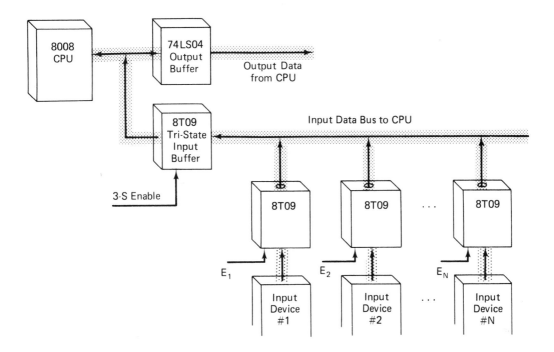

Figure 7-24 *Illustrating the use of tri-state device (8T09) that both buffers the CPU and provides second level of inversion needed for tri-state bus drivers on input devices*

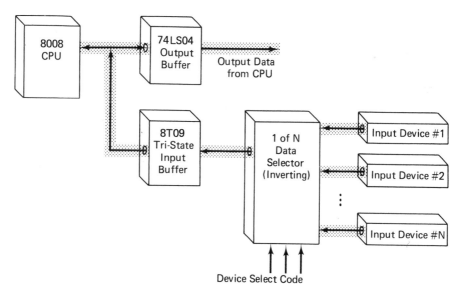

Figure 7-25 *Illustrating the use of tri-state device (8T09) that both buffers the CPU and provides second level of inverters needed for inverting multiplexer that selects input data*

selector to the bus. The use of open collector outputs is suitable where only a very few devices are to be hung on the bus and where propagation delay is of little concern; however, tri-state devices were developed specifically for bus-oriented systems and are generally preferable in this application. We will choose, then, between tri-state bus drivers and the use of a data selector. A cost analysis of a fixed number of devices or ports that will interface to the bus might turn out slightly in favor of the data selector; however, we are not ready to fix this number of ports at this time. If we should provide for the maximum number and then use fewer, our cost advantage would disappear. Our present choice of tri-state devices is based on simplicity, flexibility, and applicability.

The circuit shown in Fig. 7-24 buffers the CPU from the $\overline{\text{CPU}}$ input and output data buses by using the 74LS04 and 8T09 inverters. Since tri-state devices are ideal for bus driving applications, and since the 8T09 has at least ten times the driving power of the 74LS04 with the same propagation delay, it would seem very desirable to replace the 74LS04 buffer with an 8T09. Unfortunately, the 8T08 input load current is -2.0 mA and, therefore, exceeds the 8008 current sinking capacity; thus, we cannot interface directly to the CPU by using an 8T09. We could place an 8T09 on the $\overline{\text{CPU}}$ side of the 74LS04; however, the package count would be high and the design is awkward.

We find that our choice to utilize two extremely advantageous device types, low-power MOS/LSI and high-power bus-oriented tri-state TTL, is frustrated by incompatibility at the interface between the devices. It should come as no great surprise to learn that the designers of integrated circuit building blocks have solved our problem by building an MOS-to-TTL tri-state bus driver. The somewhat surprising feature of the device is that it is *bidirectional*, i.e., a tri-state bus driver/receiver.

The Signetics 8T26 quad bus driver/receiver is a Schottky TTL device designed for high-speed bus-oriented systems. The outputs are tri-state with high current drive capability, whereas the inputs are PNP transistors requiring only -200 μA "0" level input current compared to -1.6 mA for a standard TTL. This fact allows the 8T26 to drive up to 200 other 8T26s on the same bus. It also allows the 8T26 to interface directly to the 8008. The logic diagram for the 8T26 is shown in Fig. 7-26.

Although the bus driver enable line and the receiver enable line are both available for maximum versatility, we are interested only in situations in which they may be tied together. We refer to the connected pair simply as the BUS ENABLE (B/E) line and note that:

Mode	B/E	Function
RECEIVE	"0"	Driver Disabled/Receiver Enabled
TRANSMIT	"1"	Driver Enabled/Receiver Disabled

The configurations corresponding to both B/E HIGH and B/E LOW are shown in Fig. 7-27. The use of this device results in a highly desirable architecture and

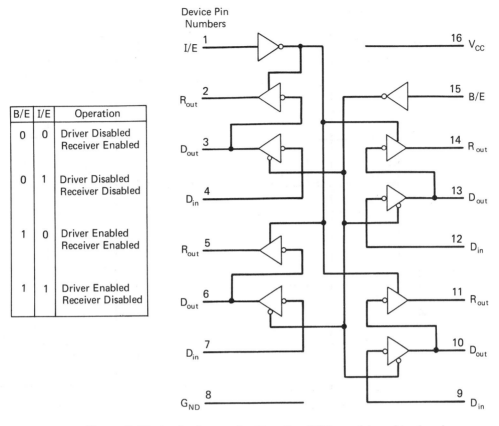

B/E	I/E	Operation
0	0	Driver Disabled Receiver Enabled
0	1	Driver Disabled Receiver Disabled
1	0	Driver Enabled Receiver Enabled
1	1	Driver Enabled Receiver Disabled

Figure 7-26 *Logic diagram for Signetics 8T26 quad bus driver/receiver (Courtesy of SIGNETICS Corporation)*

even reduces the package count, i.e., the two 8T26s replace four 8T09s and two 74LS04s. The CPU buffered by the 8T26s is shown in Fig. 7-28. We note that all devices communicating with the CPU will interface to this bus.

The design of the enable/disable circuitry for all of these devices is not unrelated to the B/E or TRANSMIT/RECEIVE control signal; therefore, we state the design of such circuitry at this point:

> *design circuitry that will enable the 8T26 "receiver" mode at PCI·T3, or PCR·T3, or PCC$_{IN}$·T3, and place the 8T26 in the "transmit" mode at all other times.*

The data input to the CPU consists of instructions and data read in during T3 of PCI and PCR cycles, and also instructions or data input to the CPU from an external device during T3 of the I/O cycle. Although we do not yet have the means of distinguishing between an "input" I/O command and an "output" I/O command, we assume that a signal PCC$_{IN}$ will allow us to select inputs of this type. The RECEIVE mode will be enabled by a signal derived

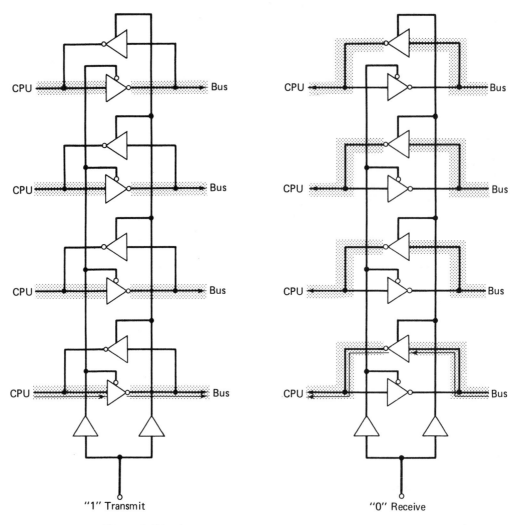

CPU ·············· Bus

CPU ·············· Bus

CPU ·············· Bus

CPU ·············· Bus

"1" Transmit

CPU ·············· Bus

CPU ·············· Bus

CPU ·············· Bus

CPU ·············· Bus

"0" Receive

Figure 7-27 *Illustrating the TRANSMIT and RECEIVE modes of operation of the 8T26 quad bus driver/receiver*

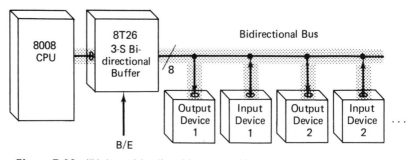

8008
CPU

8T26
3-S Bi-
directional
Buffer

/8

Bidirectional Bus

Output
Device
1

Input
Device
1

Output
Device
2

Input
Device
2

· · ·

B/E

Figure 7-28 *"Universal bus" architecture achieved with bidirectional 8T26 quad bus driver/receivers*

from the combination

$$(PCI + PCR + PCC_{IN}) \cdot T3$$

Since the cycle control signals are derived from A_{14} and A_{15} of the address latching subsystem, it is preferable to express the B/E receive signal in terms of these bits, i.e.,

$$((\overline{A_{14}} \cdot \overline{A_{15}}) + (\overline{A_{14}} \cdot A_{15}) + (A_{14} \cdot A_{15} \cdot X)) \cdot T3$$

where X is the signal distinguishing an input command from an output command. By using De Morgan's theorem, we transform this to

$$((\overline{A_{14} + A_{15}}) + \overline{(A_{14} + \overline{A_{15}})} + PCC_{IN}) \cdot T3$$

Another application of De Morgan's theorem yields the form

$$\overline{((A_{14} + A_{15}) \cdot (A_{14} + \overline{A_{15}})} + PCC_{IN}) \cdot T3 = (\overline{A_{14}} + PCC_{IN}) \cdot T3$$

Thus the expression for the "receive" signal becomes

$$\text{"receive"} = \overline{(\overline{A_{14}} + PCC_{IN}) \cdot T3}$$

where the logical expression has been inverted due to the fact that the "receive" signal is active low. The circuitry for this signal depends on the form of the inputs to the circuit. Since T3 will be used in several places throughout our system, we will use T3 here instead of the $\overline{T3}$ signal that is immediately available at the output of the state decoder. The signal A_{14} is immediately available from the address latching subsystem; therefore, we prefer it to $\overline{A_{14}}$. Since PCC_{IN} is as yet unknown, we accept either form for it. A suitable relation may be obtained through one more application of De Morgan's theorem:

$$\overline{(\overline{A_{14}} + PCC_{IN}) \cdot T3} = \overline{(\overline{A_{14} \cdot \overline{PCC_{IN}}}) \cdot T3}$$

in which two NANDs are employed as shown in Fig. 7-29.

The system at this point is capable of receiving any signal that appears on the bus at the proper time in the sense that the 8T26s will be placed in the RECEIVE mode. The circuitry involved in this mode selection is shown with

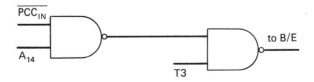

Figure 7-29 *Circuit that generates active LOW RECEIVE signal*

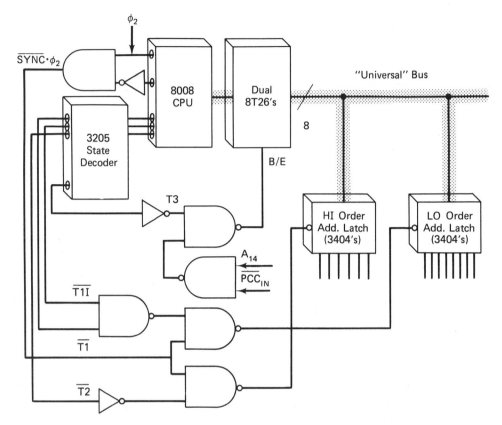

Figure 7-30 *Address latching and receiver enable circuitry*

the address latching subsystem in Fig. 7-30. The question of which of many possible devices will be allowed to place data on the bus at any given time will be treated later. Temporarily ignoring the problem of port selection, we assume that the memory port has been selected and proceed with our design of the memory-to-CPU data transfer circuit. Although the 2102 RAM is a tri-state device, we cannot assume that it will be disabled at the time some other input device can deposit data on the universal bus. Indeed, with the chip enable circuitry that we have designed, there will *always* be at least one RAM bank enabled. In addition to this, the 2102 RAM output is noninverting, whereas the bus receiver, i.e., the 8T26 buffer, is inverting. We must add an inversion level to compensate. For both reasons we must buffer the tri-state RAM outputs with another tri-state buffer. We choose the 8T09 for this purpose. The configuration described is shown in Fig. 7-31. In this configuration the memory assumes a "modular" form that is well suited to systems that are oriented around a universal bus. Such a concept is in keeping with our initial goal of partitioning the system into subsystems, thereby permitting independent

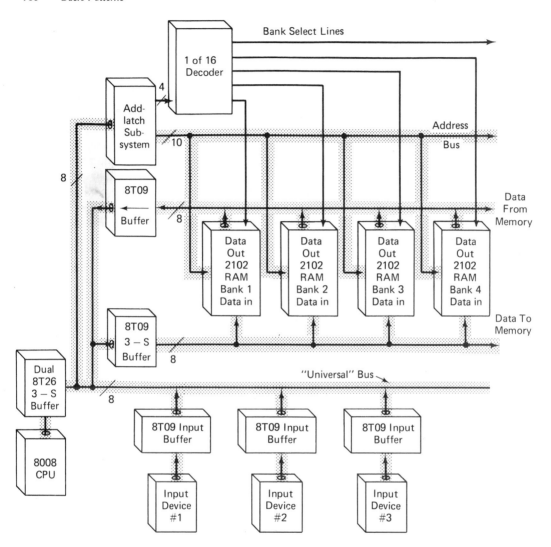

Figure 7-31 *Basic memory configuration, using tri-state input buffers and hung on a universal bus*

development of each of the system modules. We will find that the universal bus architecture will allow this treatment of all of the remaining subsystems. Our major design effort toward the module selector subsystem will be taken up in Chapter 8. We can note at this point, however, that the memory port buffer should be enabled during PCI·T3 and PCR·T3, whereas the other input buffers will be enabled only during the PCC cycle. There is yet a problem associated with the use of the state signal T3 to input data to the CPU that is independent of the rest of the circuitry. This problem may be seen by close examination of the CPU timing diagrams of Fig. 7-7. The data into the CPU are required to be on the bus *before* the trailing edge of ϕ_{11} occurs. Referenced to the trailing edge of ϕ_{22}, this allows only 1100 nsec for the data to be input to the CPU. By noting that the state out delay, t_{S1}, can be 1100 nsec in duration, we see that the use of state signal T3 to enable the tri-state buffers results in a possible conflict. Rather than examine many ways to resolve this conflict, we simply state the preferred way.

For simplicity, we assume that the READY line is always such that the CPU does not enter the WAIT state following T2. (The reader should convince himself that such an assumption is unnecessary.) A careful study of the 8008 CPU state transition diagram indicates that although many transitions are conditional, the state T2 is always followed by T3. As a consequence of this certainty we may *anticipate* the state T3 before we get a valid state signal from the state decoder. Thus we can prematurely *derive* the required T3 state signal in time to satisfy the "data in" timing requirements of the CPU. To rephrase this:

> *we note that the delayed state signal T3 that is needed to gate data into the CPU may occur too late. Since T3 always follows T2, we can anticipate T3 and design a special anticipation circuit that will derive the state signal in time.*

We conclude this chapter with the design of the T3 anticipation circuit.

By referring again to the CPU timing diagram of Fig. 7-7, we note, that, although the state-out-delay measured from the falling edge of ϕ_{22} can be as great as 1100 nsec, the SYNC out delay is only 700 nsec in the worst case. Thus, the positive going SYNC pulse will occur before the trailing edge of ϕ_{11} and can be used in conjunction with the derived T3 state signal to input data to the CPU. We now state our problem as:

> *design circuitry that will anticipate state T3 by making use of the fact that T3 always follows state T2. The anticipation circuit output, T3A, is to be ANDed with the SYNC signal to provide an INPUT DATA gate control function for the CPU.*

Consideration of the timing diagram has made it obvious that no combination of signals present at any one time will fulfil the requirements on the INPUT DATA control line. We must employ a flip-flop whose output can be set and reset at appropriate times. Since we wish to AND this output with the SYNC signal, we will require the output to be normally low, going high in anticipation of state T3.

The simplest choice of a flip-flop that can be set and reset is the R-S flip-flop. We desire the output Q to be normally low and to go high only in anticipation of state T3. Since this signal will essentially *replace* the T3 signal from the CPU, we also require that the output goes low prior to the actual end of state T3. This can be accomplished through the use of either T3·$\overline{\text{SYNC}}$ or T3·Φ_4. The relevant timing parameter is the hold time for data in, t_{IH}. The minimum hold time is specified to be greater than, or equal to, the SYNC out delay, t_{SD}. By noting that both t_{IH} and t_{SD} are measured relative to ϕ_2 clock phase, it can be seen that the $\overline{\text{SYNC}}$ signal can be used to drive the T3A output low during T3. The output is to be driven high in anticipation of T3, i.e., at the end of state T2. This is easily achieved with T2·Φ_4. The resultant circuit is shown in Fig. 7-32.

We note that since T2·T3 = 0, the indeterminate condition will never arise. We also note that regardless of the initial state of the Q output at turn-on, state T2 of the first execution cycle will force Q to go HIGH, and the circuit will run correctly from that point on.

It is instructive to compare this circuit with a D-type flip-flop implementation. The same timing scheme will be used; however, the T2·Φ_4 signal is now used to clock the hardwired "1" at the D input to the Q output. Comparison of

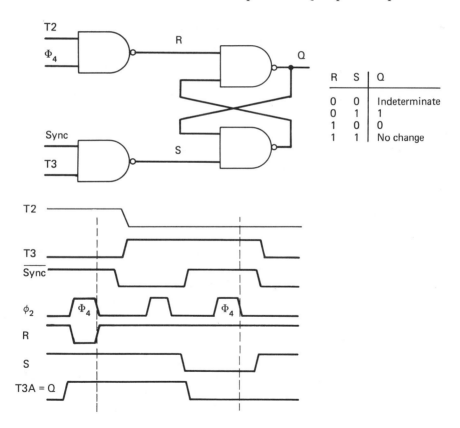

Figure 7-32   *R-S flip-flop T3A circuit and relevant timing diagram*

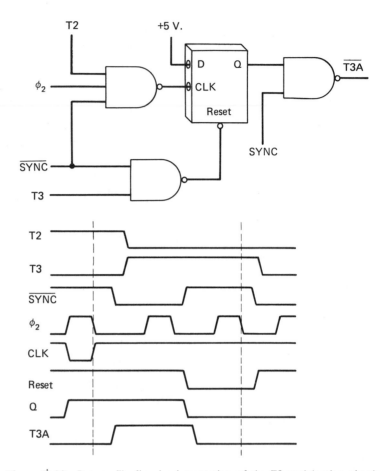

Figure 7-33 *D-type flip-flop implementation of the T3 anticipation circuit and associated timing diagram*

the timing diagrams indicates that the circuits are equivalent. The D-type implementation is shown in Fig. 7-33. The Q output is shown ANDed with the SYNC pulse to produce T3A, the T3 anticipation signal. This circuit is used in the Intel MCS-8 system that is based around the 8008 CPU.

SUMMARY

A stated goal of this chapter was to design the memory subsystem by using only word descriptions and logic symbols wherever possible. This approach is seen to be effective. However, the use of logic equations to simplify a specific circuit was desirable in one instance.

Another goal was to treat timing realistically via the design example. The detailed treatment included in this chapter is meant to emphasize the importance of this aspect of microprocessor systems design. Although the variety of both memory chips and microprocessor chips prevents a universal approach to this problem, the specific design illustrated here is very representative of problems that the reader will encounter.

Most memory interface problems will be much simpler than our treatment. The 8008 was pin-limited (18 pins) and required the design of external latching and READ/WRITE timing circuits. Later processors utilize 28-, 40-, and 64-pin packages and provide these signal pulses on pins, thus eliminating the need for such circuit design. It will, of course, still be necessary to perform the timing analysis to ensure that the memory timing and chip timing are compatible. In many cases, even this is unnecessary because the chip manufacturers will specify (or even design) memories that are compatible with their processors.

Despite the fact that the timing analysis illustrated herein will sometimes be unnecessary, the ability to perform such analysis and design is an absolute necessity for a systems designer. The need to generate READ/WRITE or other timing signals from the clock and CPU signals occurs in memory interface, I/O interface, and multiprocessor systems. The techniques developed in this chapter will apply to these and other design tasks.

8   the I/O subsystem

The concept of an information processor as a device that accepts binary information at an input port, performs a specified transformation on the information, and then presents the processed information at an output port is extremely general. As such it is applicable to the simplest logical processors, AND, NAND, NOR, and NOT gates, as well as to intermediate-level processors—exemplified by the MSI adders and arithmetic logic units—and also to the most complex monolithic devices—the central processor units. Since the actual transformation processes differ vastly for these devices, it is clear that the characteristics common to all information processors consist in the existence of input and output ports. These input and output ports normally define the boundaries between digital systems and subsystems. Generally the subsystems are not compatible in the sense that they may be directly connected to each other. This has been seen in Chapter 7 in the design of interface circuits between the CPU and the external RAM storage devices.

In an information-processing system, with many possible I/O channels connecting the processor to the outside world, maximum flexibility is obtained via the incorporation of an I/O subsystem that will act as a general interface to the processor. This allows a standard interface scheme to be used in each of the peripheral subsystems. The special requirements of the I/O device are then met in hardware on the device side of the interface, or in software on the CPU side. In general, a combination of these two are needed. The I/O subsystem serves as a buffer between the CPU and communicating devices. This is shown schematically in Fig. 8-1.

The *nonforced transfer process* between the CPU and external equipment unambiguously describes a process that must be executable by the I/O subsystem. This will serve as a starting point for design of such a system and may be stated as a design goal:

> *design circuitry that is capable of transmitting information from the CPU/MEM system to the $\overline{CPU/MEM}$ system.*

The existence of this process would seem to imply an instruction that could

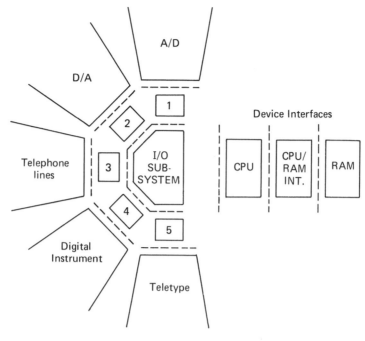

Figure 8-1

be used to initiate the process, and such is indeed the case. The format of the instruction is:

OUT | 01 | RR | MMM   1 | (output data lines) ⟵ (A)

The 5-bit Output Port Select field indicated by RRMMM is used to select one of several ports through which information can be channelled OUT of the I/O subsystem. The execution of the instruction is effected in two cycles: the PCI-Instruction fetch cycle and the PCC-I/O Command Execution cycle. The PCI cycle is identical to all other instruction fetch cycles in that the contents of the program counter are sent to the RAM address latches during T1 and T2, and the instruction is fetched from memory during T3. All of the multi-cycle instructions discussed in the last cycle have involved transfers to or from memory and have made use of the T1 and T2 states during each cycle to send low- and high-order addresses, respectively, to memory. The OUT(put) instruction does not address memory and, therefore, does not require a 14-bit address. The T1 and T2 states are, therefore, used in a different manner during an I/O cycle than during the execution of a memory reference instruction. In particular, the information to be output is placed on the data lines during T1 of the PCC cycle. This information consists of the contents of the accumulator and must have been loaded into the accumulator prior to the exceution of the output instruction. During the instruction fetch, the instruction proper is always loaded into the instruction register and into temporary register b. During T2 of the PCC cycle the contents of register b are sent out on the CPU data lines. Thus, either new circuitry must be designed for routing this data to the I/O subsystem, or else the existing circuitry must be modified. Since the RAM address latches are cycle independent (their operation depends only upon state and timing information, not on cycle codes), it may be seen that the data present on the bus at T1 and at T2 will be latched in the RAM address latches. The low-order latches will hold the data from the accumulator, and the high-order latch will hold the OUT instruction and (implicitly) the PCC cycle code. The cycles involved are:

Cycle	State	Process
	T1	PC_L sent to low-order RAM address latch.
PCI	T2	PC_H sent to high-order RAM address latch.
	T3	FETCH instruction from RAM to IR and reg. b.
	T1	Accumulator contents placed on data bus.
PCC	T2	Reg. b contents placed on data bus.
	T3	Idle state.

Execution of the OUT instruction results in the data and the port-select code being latched into the RAM address latches and made available for use by the I/O subsystem. It is at this point that the design of the I/O subsystem will begin. The contents of the low-order latch must be routed to the appropriate port by the information contained in the high-order latch, i.e., the port select code, RRMMM. A constraint on these bits prevents both of the two bits designated RR from being zero. Thus, one of 24 output ports can be selected. The system shown in Fig. 8-2 indicates the presence of buffers in parallel with the RAM memory system. The fact that these two systems are paralleled requires that some type of enable/disable mechanism be designed to select the appropriate system at any given time. Since most instructions executed by the processor are memory reference rather than I/O, it is to be expected that the output ports will normally be disabled. Each individual port will be selected by the presence of the PCC cycle code, a timing pulse, and the unique port code assigned to that port. A conceptual design of such a system is shown in Fig. 8-3.

The timing is fairly straightforward. The data from the accumulator is latched and waiting at T1, but the address of its destination is not available until T2 when RRMMM is latched. Thus, a timing signal derived from PCC and T3 will latch the data into the selected output port. This signal is ANDed with the decoded port select signal, as shown in Fig. 8-3.

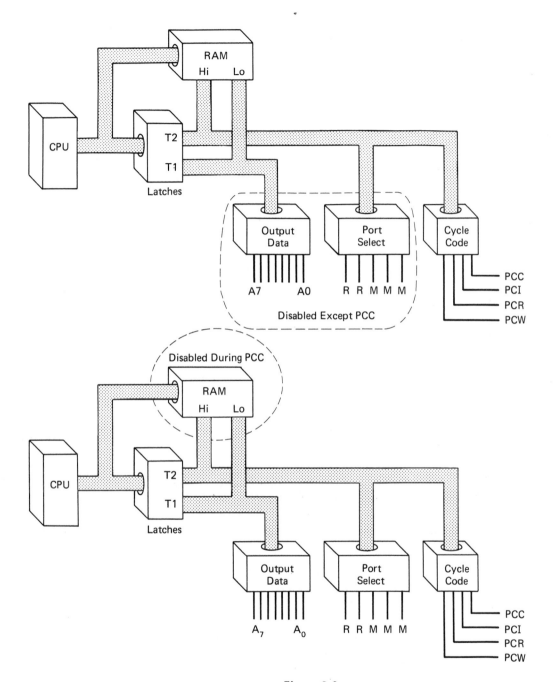

Figure 8-2

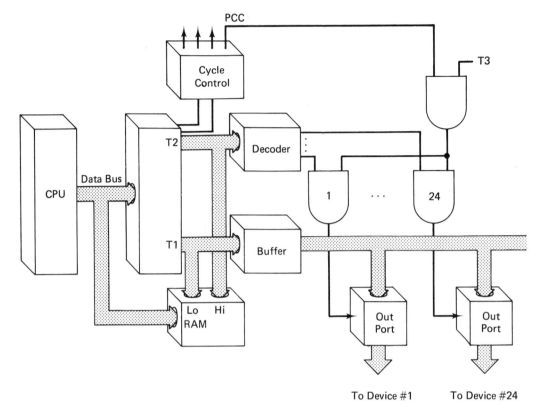

Figure 8-3

INPUT PORT DESIGN

A general-purpose information processor must have a means of inputting information into the system. The procedure may be selected either internal to or external to the processor, i.e., the transfer can be nonforced or forced. The instruction that will accomplish the transfer of data into the CPU is the INP (ut) instruction shown here:

INP | 01 | 00 | MMM | 1 | (A) ⟵ (input data lines)

The format of the input instruction is seen to differ from that of the output instruction only in bits D_5 and D_4. This accounts for the constraint imposed on those bits in the output instruction, $RR \neq 00$. In other aspects the two are similar. Both are one-byte two-cycle instructions that fetch the instruction during PCI and perform an I/O transfer during PCC. The input instruction also presents the data in the accummulator to the data bus during T1 of the PCC cycle where it is latched into the low-order address latch. The contents of the instruction register are also made available to external equipment during state T2 of the PCC cycle. During T3 of the INP execution the data from external devices is input to the CPU and temporarily stored in register *b*. During the T4 state the contents of the condition flip-flops are output on the data bus lines, DO, D1, D2, and D3. The signals on these lines are S, Z, P, and C, respectively. The T5 state is used to load the temporary register *b* contents into the accumulator. The input data are then available for use by the following instructions just as any other data would be. The input algorithm is:

Cycle	State	Process
	T1	PC_L sent to low-order RAM address latch.
PCI	T2	PC_H sent to high-order RAM address latch.
	T3	Fetch INP instruction into IR and reg. *b*.
	T1	Accumulator contents sent to data bus.
	T2	Register *b* contents to data bus and latched.
PCC	T3	Data from data bus input to temp. reg. *b*.
	T4	Condition flags SZPC output on D0, D1, D2, D3.
	T5	Contents of reg. *b* transferred to accumulator.

INPUT TIMING

Two alternative conditions are possible when the INP instruction is executed. The simplest case is that in which the data have already been latched into the input port by the external device and need only be placed on the data bus at the appropriate time. The other case is that in which the INP command initiates data taking in an external device. The device may then supply a $\overline{RDY}$ signal to the CPU to cause it to enter the WAIT state until the data are ready. Only the first situation will be treated in the following discussion.

The timing associated with data input to the CPU from an input port is identical to the timing of data input from RAM. The timing peculiarity that exists in the 8008, i.e., the requirement that data be input during T3 before the state signals indicate T3 to the data source, was handled in Chapter 7 by designing a T3-anticipation circuit (T3A). The T3A signal will be used to input data from input ports as well as from RAM. The actual input ports will receive two control signals; the first signal loads the input port latch with data from the device; the second signal, derived from PCC and T3A, places those data on the data bus where they are input to the CPU. A convenient choice for the input latch is the Signetics 8T10 tri-state latch shown in Fig. 8-4.

The timing that applies to this circuitry is shown in Fig. 8-4. The data are latched into the 8T10 by a clock pulse from the external device. The address of this device is sent to the RAM data latch at T2 and made available to the port select circuitry at the leading edge of the $T2 \cdot \overline{SYNC} \cdot \phi 2$ pulse. The T3A pulse is ANDed with the PCC signal to gate the data from the selected input

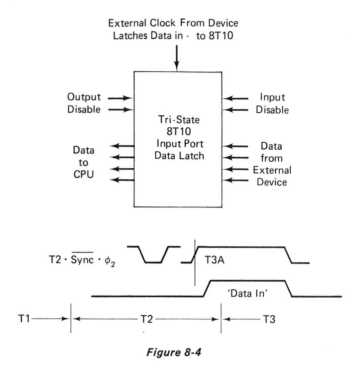

Figure 8-4

port onto the data bus. This is accomplished by enabling the tri-state output of the 8T10. The conceptual design of this circuitry is shown in Fig. 8-5.

The simplest possible INP instruction execution does not make use of the data in the accumulator at the beginning of the PCC cycle. The manner in which these data might be used is given in the following example. Assume that an 8-bit wide ROM has been loaded with a sine table for arguments ranging from zero to 90 degrees in one-half degree increments. These 180 values can be accessed by using an 8-bit address corresponding to the value of the argument. When the argument is applied to the address lines, the sine function is output on the data lines. This argument may be loaded into the accumulator prior to the fetch of the INP instruction. The execution of this instruction sends the accumulator contents out on the data bus at T1, and these contents are latched into the low-order address latch. This argument is applied to the address lines of the trigonometric ROM, as shown in Fig. 8-6. If a tri-state ROM is used, the output can connect directly to the data bus. The same pulse that is used to gate data from the selected input port is used to enable this tri-state output, and the data are then loaded into the accumulator. In the example, the input port is assumed to be selected by the code MMM = 010. Then the instruction *INP* 2 is equivalent to an instruction executing the algorithm that replaces the contents of the accumulator with the sine function of these contents, i.e., (A) ⟵ SIN(A).

A timing analysis indicates that either a fairly fast ROM must be used or

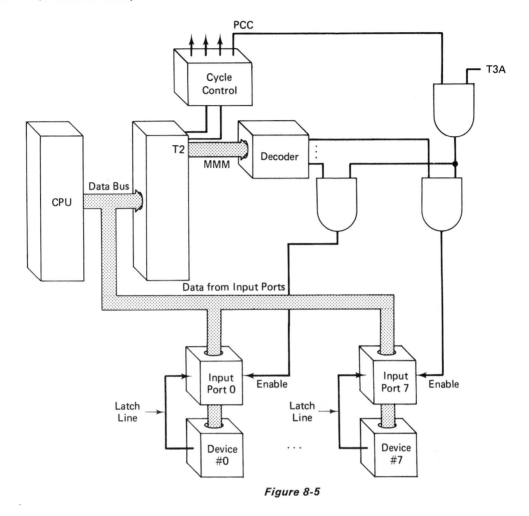

Figure 8-5

else a WAIT command must be generated to hold off the CPU until the function is ready to be input. In this example, the CPU instruction set has effectively been augmented by adding a dedicated hardware subsystem to the processor. The software analog of this process is found in a macro-instruction facility. The Intel software support provides this valuable tool, which will be discussed in the next chapter.

I/O SELECTION CIRCUITRY

The data input to the CPU will be either Memory data or I/O data. The circuitry designed in Chapter 7 is capable of inputting memory data during state T3, but must be disabled during the PCC I/O T3 input state. This can be stated

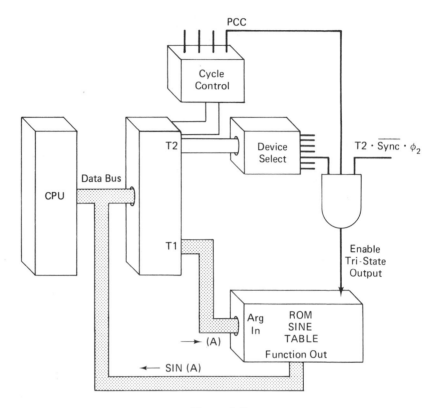

Figure 8-6

as a design goal:

> *design circuitry that will discriminate between Memory data and I/O data input to the CPU. At most, one input port should be enabled at any time.*

The I/O cycle code ($A_{14} = 1$, $A_{15} = 0$) does not distinguish between input and output commands. This may be done easily by using the "RR" bits (A_{12} and A_{13}). If RR = 00, the PCC cycle is an input data cycle. The use of a NOR gate to detect this condition can be combined with the cycle code and T3A timing, as shown in Fig. 8-7, to generate a signal capable of selecting the I/O input subsystem. This I/O INPUT signal is normally LOW and goes HIGH only when data is to be input to the CPU from input port MMM. The signal can, therefore, be used to gate the port select code, MMM, to a decoder. One possible implementation of this is shown in Fig. 8-8.

An alternate design will require that one of the input ports be dedicated to the Random Access Memory input. Although this would seem to cut down

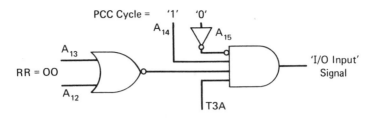

Figure 8-7

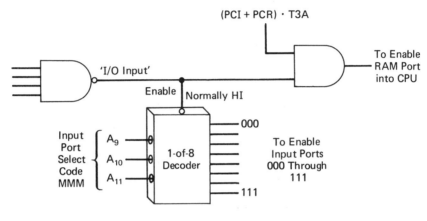

Figure 8-8

the number of input devices that may be interfaced to the processor, it will be seen later that this is not a real problem. The 000 port will be dedicated to the RAM and the I/O INPUT signal will be used to gate the MMM code into the decoder. The absence of the I/O INPUT signal should force the decoder output to 000, the RAM data port. A circuit that will accomplish this is shown in Fig. 8-9.

The 7421 Dual four-input AND gate used in the I/O INPUT circuit can also be used to generate an I/O OUTPUT signal, as shown in Fig. 8-10.

The output port select code will not be decoded in the I/O subsystem, but will be sent to each peripheral device along with the I/O OUTPUT ENABLE signal derived above. Thus, each output device must be able to decode the RRMMM code when commanded to do so by the port enable signal. Although a symmetrical system, in which eight input ports and eight output ports are handled in the same manner, could be implemented, the chosen design offers much greater flexibility. A system with only three output ports will require only three decoders, yet the system can be expanded easily to the full 24-port configuration simply by including the port select decoder with each added port. The decoder for output port with the device code "01101" is shown in Fig. 8-11.

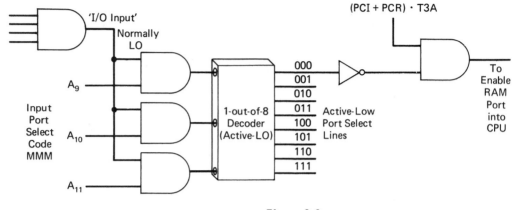

Figure 8-9

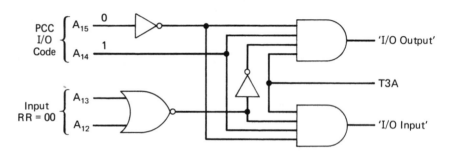

Figure 8-10

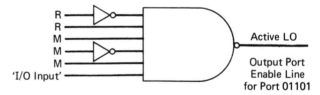

Figure 8-11

A preliminary design of the I/O subsystem is shown in Fig. 8-12. The dashed line indicates that the NAND decoders do not properly belong to the I/O subsystem. Each decoder is included as a part of the interface circuitry for a particular output device. This same system is shown again in Fig. 8-13. This figure shows explicitly the relationship between the I/O subsystem and the CPU/MEM system designed in Chapter 7. The circuit must be considered preliminary in the sense that no provision for forced I/O transfers of information to the CPU has been made. Such provisions may require slight modifications to the above subsystem. The design of this circuitry is considered in the next section.

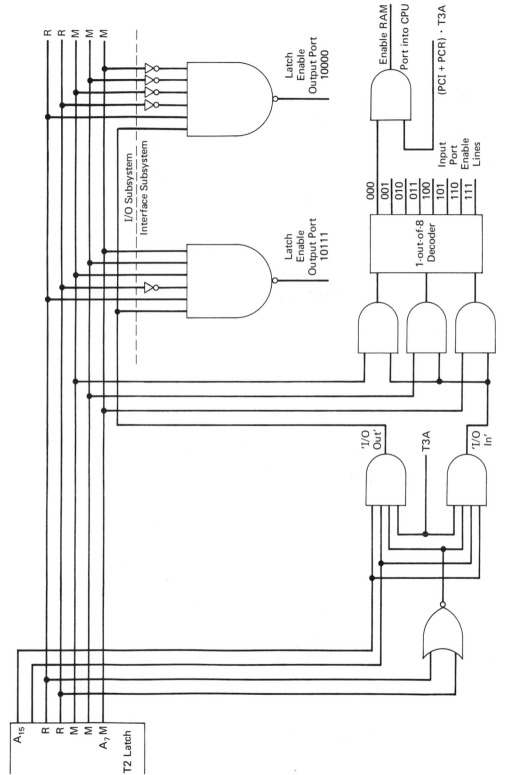

Figure 8-12

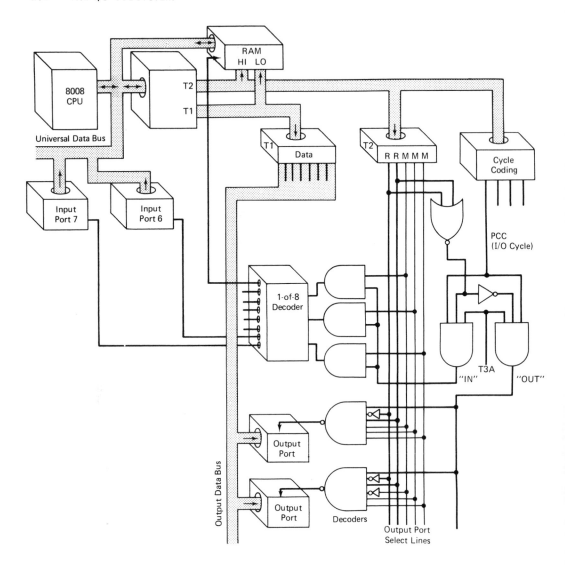

Figure 8-13

FORCED I/O TRANSFERS TO THE CPU

The circuitry shown in the preceding figures summarizes the design of the I/O subsystem that handles the normal, or nonforced, transfers of data between the CPU and external devices. These transfers occur under program control and, therefore, can deal only with generally predictable situations. Many real-world situations (power failure, human decisions, etc.) are inherently unpredictable. These constitute strong incentive to provide for forced entry of instructions into the CPU so that normal program flow can be overridden. Modern CPUs provide for such forced entry via the interrupt subsystem. A brief review of the Intel 8008 CPU interrupt capabilities precedes the discussion of the design of the interrupt subsystem.

One of the 8008 CPU input pins is labeled the INTERRUPT (INT) pin and allows the normal program flow to be altered by the application of a signal to this pin. During a normal instruction fetch, the opcode byte of each instruction is obtained by sending the low-order address bits to be latched at PCI·T1 and the high-order address bits and cycle coding bits at PCI·T2. The program counter is normally advanced and either additional bytes of instruction are fetched during succeeding PCR cycles or the fetched instruction is executed and the next instruction is fetched. The application of an active high INT signal to the INT pin alters this procedure. The INT signal informs the CPU that an instruction from an external source is ready for insertion into the CPU during the next instruction FETCH cycle. The CPU acknowledges the INT signal after completion of the current instruction execution. The procedure is:

> *normal Program flow occurs. This flow consists of a PCI instruction FETCH cycle followed by either*
>> *a PCR cycle to fetch succeeding bytes, or*
>> *a PCC or PCW cycle to finish current execution, or*
>> *a PCI cycle to fetch the next instruction.*

> *Assume that the INT is enabled* during *the current execution, i.e., during or after the PCI cycle. The current execution* will be completed *in normal fashion, and the program counter will be advanced for the next instruction FETCH (or the PC contents will be altered in the case of transfer of control instructions).*

> *Normal program flow would recycle through the first step above and continue PCI fetches and PC updates. This flow is altered by the INT signal, and the CPU acknowledges the INT during (and not until) the next PCI cycles as follows:*
>> *the state T1I replaces T1, PC_L sent to latches; state T2 occurs and PC_H is sent to latches; the Program Counter is* not *advanced; the Interrupt instruction may be jammed in during T3.*

Since the decoding of the first byte of the instruction occurs within the CPU instruction decoder, it is unnecessary to use multiple interrupts for a multi-byte interrupt instruction. The fetch of the succeeding bytes will occur naturally, i.e., T1I will be output during the following PCR cycles, replacing T1. The important points concerning the interrupt procedure are:

> *the instruction in progress when the interrupt signal arrives* always *finishes executing.*

At the end of the current execution, the program counter points to the next program instruction to be fetched in the normal program flow.

Although the contents of the PC are sent out during PCI-T1I and PCI-T2, no use is made of these contents and the PC is *not* advanced. The program counter is never advanced when T1I is output. T1I informs the interrupting device that an instruction can be jammed onto the data bus during T3 of the current PCI cycle. The ability to resume the normal program flow after the interrupting device has been serviced depends upon the instruction jammed in by this device. In order to save the current program counter contents, the instruction jammed into the CPU will be one that PUSHes the PC onto the stack, i.e., some type of CALL instruction.

The discussion of this instruction will be postponed and the actual mechanism by which the interrupt instruction can be jammed onto the data bus will now be considered. This mechanism must utilize the PCI-T1I interrupt acknowledgement signal. A design goal can be formulated.

Design circuitry that will utilize the T1I state signal to jam an Interrupt instruction onto the data bus and into the CPU.

The circuitry developed in Chapter 7 uses both the $\overline{T1}$ and the $\overline{T1I}$ signals to latch the data on the data bus into the low-order address latches. This circuit is redrawn in Fig. 8-14.

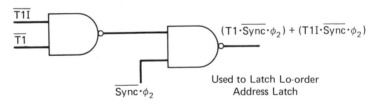

Figure 8-14

Since only one interrupt instruction is to be jammed into the CPU, it is necessary not only to generate the JAM signal from the T1I state signal but also to clear this signal. The more complete design goal can now be stated.

Design circuitry that will generate a JAM signal when T1I occurs and that will clear this signal at a later time.

Before a decision can be made concerning the best time to clear the JAM signal, it is necessary to understand more details about the effect of the interrupt signal on the CPU. The state transition diagram in Fig. 8-15 provides the necessary details. The WAIT state has been omitted since it is not relevant to this particular discussion.

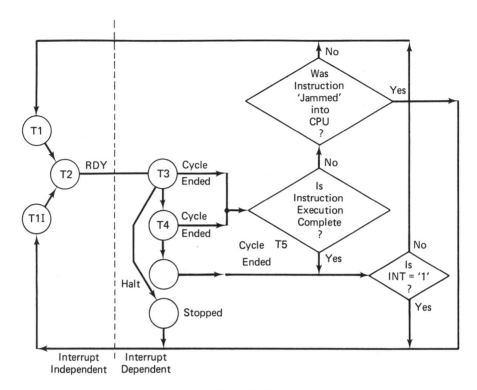

Figure 8-15

The states in Fig. 8-15 have been grouped into two categories that are separated symbolically by a dashed line. The states to the left of the line are Interrupt Independent, while those to the right are Interrupt Dependent. If a state will make a transition to the next state independently of the condition of the INT pin, it is placed on the left side of the line; otherwise, it is considered to be Interrupt Dependent. This classification is useful in determining the correct time to clear the INT line. From the diagram it can be seen that the INT line should be cleared, i.e., set INT = 0, to the left of the line. Once an interrupt has been recognized, the CPU will enter the T1I state as often as necessary until the JAMmed instruction has been fetched in its entirety, independently of the INT status. After completion of the fetch of this instruction, the CPU will enter the normal T1 state if the INT signal is clear. Enough detail has now been discussed to allow a final statement of the design goal.

> *Design circuitry that will generate a JAM signal when T1I occurs. Since T1I indicates that the INT has been recognized by the CPU, this JAM signal can also be used to clear the INT line. With the INT clear, the CPU will complete the fetch of the JAMmed instruction. Upon completion, the CPU will return to the T1 state. This state can*

then be used to remove the JAM signal before the next input to the CPU occurs at T3.

A JAM signal that must be set and reset and can last for several cycles must use a memory element or flip-flop. The simplest arrangement would be the use of the R-S flip-flop shown in Fig. 8-16; however, the existence of the T1 latching signal circuitry, developed in Chapter 7 and reproduced in Fig. 8-15, suggests another, more compatible approach. This latching signal can be used to clock a D-type flip-flop whose data input reflects the status of the CPU as regards interrupt acknowledgement. This circuit is shown in Fig. 8-17.

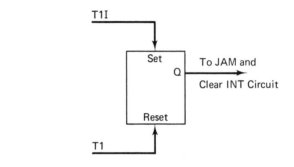

Figure 8-16

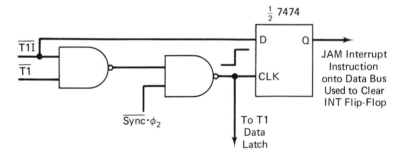

Figure 8-17

In Fig. 8-17 the $\overline{\text{T1I}}$ signal is normally HIGH; therefore, the Q output of the flip-flop will also normally be HIGH. When the INTERRUPT is acknowledged, the Q output goes LOW. This line can be used to jam the INTERRUPT instruction onto the data bus, and also to clear the INT flip-flop. Although this INT flip-flop has not been discussed, it will be considered necessary due to the transient nature of many interrupt requests. The INT flip-flop will record these requests and hold them on the INT pin until the CPU has issued the acknowledgement. This circuit will be developed later in this chapter.

The JAM line generated by the above circuit will go LOW at T1I; however, the CPU will not accept data until the T3 state. Therefore, the JAM line can be ANDed with T3A to guarantee that the "DATA IN" timing requirements of the CPU are satisfied.

Now that there is a signal that can be used to jam INTERRUPT instructions onto the data bus, it is necessary to decide the manner in which this signal will be utilized. One possible means of accomplishing this goal is suggested by the design of the I/O port select circuitry. One of the input ports was dedicated to the memory data port, and the select code for this port was forced by the I/O INPUT line in its OFF state. Thus, the JAM line can be used to force the selection of another input port that will be dedicated to the INTERRUPT instruction circuitry. This design goal can be stated.

> *Design circuitry that will allow the selection by the JAM signal of a special port designated the Interrupt Port. This circuitry should have no effect upon the circuitry already designed, except in the case in which an interrupt has occurred.*

The circuit shown in Fig. 8-18 accomplishes the stated objective as follows. The I/O INPUT line is normally LOW, forcing the NAND gate outputs HIGH. When the INP instruction causes this line to go HIGH, the input select code MMM is transmitted, but inverted. The normally HIGH JAM line holds open

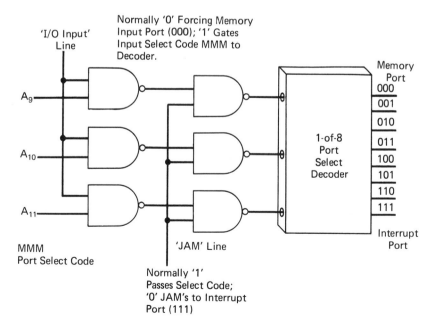

Figure 8-18

the second level of inverting gates, and the MMM code passes through to the port select decoder. When the JAM line goes LOW, these NAND gates are forced HIGH and the code 111 is forced into the decoder. This code selects the dedicated interrupt instruction port (111). The memory input port is still port (000), since the two levels of inversion have no effect upon this signal.

The circuit just described will sucessfully force the data bus into the INTERRUPT mode to accept the instruction to be jammed in. It is still necessary to complete the design of the INT flip-flop that is set by the external interrupt and cleared by the CPU acknowledgement of the interrupt. There are two timing constraints associated with this circuitry.

> *The system INTERRUPT signal (INT) must be synchronized with the leading edge of the ϕ_1 or the ϕ_2 clock and held for at least 200 nsec past the falling edge of ϕ_1.*

> *The INTERRUPT can be reset to "0" by decoding the T1I state signal at some time later than ϕ_{11}.*

The first criterion could be achieved easily via the use of a Texas Instruments 74120 Pulse Synchronizer, which was designed to synchronize asynchronous signals, such as interrupts, with a system clock. Since the signal will be stored in a flip-flop, it is easy enough to synchronize with the system clock by using a dual flip-flop. The design goal for this circuit can be formulated:

> *design circuitry that will capture the asynchronous interrupt signal from an external device, synchronize this signal to the system clock, ϕ_1, or ϕ_2, and apply it to the INT pin of the 8008 CPU. This interrupt flip-flop should be cleared by the decoded T1I state signal some time after ϕ_{11}.*

A dual D-type flip-flop can be used to implement this circuit. The first flip-flop can be set by the external device by simply using the interrupt request line as a clock and tying the D-input to $+5$ V. If the output is initially LOW, then any interrupt request will clock the "1" onto the output. This circuit is shown in Fig. 8-19. The output of this device can then be input to the synchronizing flip-flop that is clocked by the system clock. The output of this device will be presented to the INT pin of the CPU. This circuit is also shown in Fig. 8-19. All of the signals shown in this figure are self-explanatory except for the "CLEAR" line that has not yet been specified. It has been stated that the INT should not be removed from the INT pin until the CPU has acknowledged its presence via the T1I signal, and also that this should occur only after ϕ_{11}. The state transition diagram reproduced in this chapter indicates that this may occur anytime before T3; therefore, the use of T2 to clear the INTERRUPT satisfies all conditions: T1I$\cdot\phi_{11} <$ T2 $<$ T3. Since the INT line must not be cleared

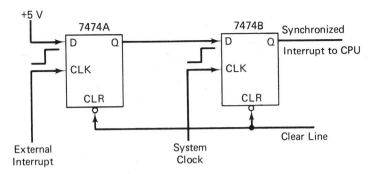

Figure 8-19

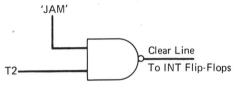

Figure 8-20

until it is acknowledged, the T2-clear line can be gated with the T1I·JAM signal as shown in Fig. 8-20. The timing circuitry discussed above is shown in Fig. 8-21.

THE RESTART INSTRUCTION

The RESTART instruction is a special 1-byte CALL instruction that obviates the design of the sequencing circuitry associated with a 3-byte CALL. It is a stack control instruction that can be inserted into the CPU during the PCI-INT cycle. The format of the RESTART instruction is:

RST | 00 | AAA | 101 | (Stack) ← (PC)
                          (PC) ← 000000 00AAA000

The AAA are address bits equal to any 3-bit binary number. The effect of this instruction is to store the program counter on the stack and jam the PC to address 000000 00AAA000; i.e., to any one of eight locations in the first 56 words of memory. These eight locations are called *trap cells*. Each trap cell serves as an entry point to the appropriate INTERRUPT service subroutine. These routines can use eight consecutive locations before writing into another trap cell. If the subroutine cannot be written with eight bytes, then a jump to another location in storage is normally made. The last instruction in any such

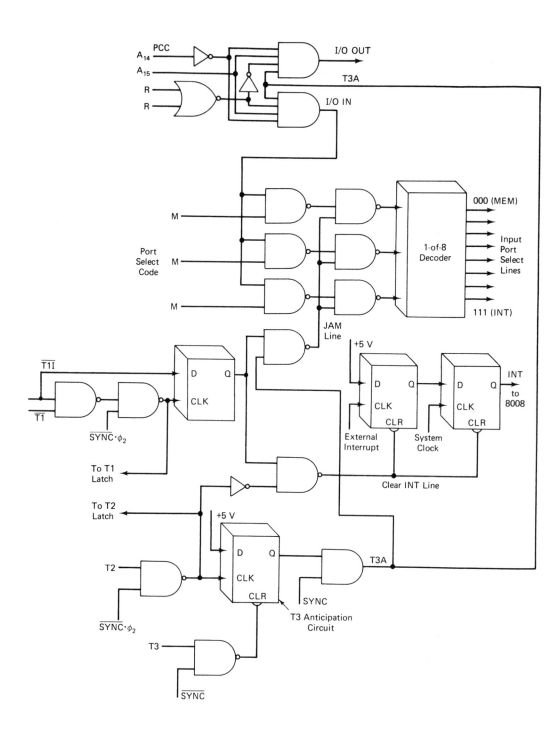

Figure 8-21

subroutine is always a RETURN instruction that POPs the stack, thus restoring the PC and allowing the execution of the program to continue from the point of interruption.

The trap cell address, AAA, must be supplied by the interrupting device. If there is more than one interrupting device, there is usually a hierarchical structure or priority associated with each device. The priority determination and addressing circuits will be treated in another chapter.

In many processors, the occurrence of an interrupt causes a subroutine to execute which then *polls* the external devices to determine which device requires service. Systems in which the address bits (AAA) are inserted via hardware are called *vectored* interrupt systems and have much faster response times than polled systems. The 8008 possesses a hardware vectored interrupt system. The use of this system will be treated in a later chapter.

THE CPU/$\overline{CPU}$ SYSTEM

The system designed by using the 8008 CPU has centered around the universal bus architecture. The primary consequence of such an architecture lies in the ability to "hang" devices on the bus at will. A flexible system that is easily expandable results from this design. There is no conceptual difference in a system with one output port and one with 24 output ports. The circuitry common to all ports has been designed as a part of the I/O subsystem. The circuitry unique to each port, i.e., the port select decoder and the latch and external latching signals, is then provided as needed.

The dedication of two of the eight input ports to MEM and INT inputs is of no real significance. Should more input ports be required, they can be hung on the universal bus and selected by several means. Either the accumulator contents sent out during T1 of an INP instruction can be used as a select code or a dedicated output port can select the input port. In either case, the conceptual expansion of the system is straightforward. Figure 8-22 attempts to emphasize the universal bus "backbone" of the system. The special-purpose circuitry, such as the T3 Anticipation circuit, has been deleted to minimize visual confusion. The reader may find it a worthwhile exercise to expand this figure via the inclusion of such circuits.

SUMMARY

Chapters 5, 6, 7, and 8 have treated the Intel 8008 in great detail for several reasons. The 8008 was the first 8-bit monolithic processor available and has strongly influenced most of the later CPUs on the market. A thorough understanding of the 8008 provides the most painless approach to the study of other 8-bit monolithic CPUs. An important consequence of the study of the first-generation CPU is the truer appreciation of the advances represented by the

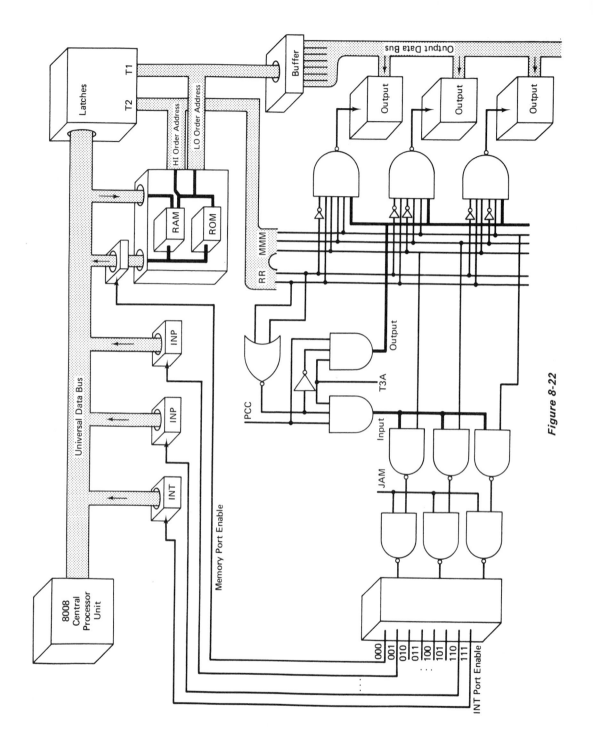

Figure 8-22

second-and third-generation CPUs. The 8008 also provides an excellent vehicle for teaching such concepts as status signals and multiplexed information transfer, and provides an ideal design base for realistic, nontrivial system design. In particular, the subsystem design offers excellent examples of the combination of *state* and *timing* information to develop control signals, a technique that is required in almost any digital design. The design of the interrupt structure introduces detailed hardware and timing concepts that will be expanded in Chapter 12.

The approach taken in the following chapters will retain the emphasis on subsystems or particular *structures*, but will range over many monolithic microprocessors. A general conceptual treatment of the various structures is used to lead into detailed examples of implementation of the structures.

PROBLEMS

1. Use a pair of Signetics 8263 3-channel × 4-bit multiplexors and a 2-bit counter (use J-K flip-flops) to jam ın a 3-byte CALL instruction in response to the interrupt acknowledgement TII.

2. Design a circuit to jam in a 3-byte CALL, using a 32 × 8 Programmable Read Only Memory (PROM) with tri-state outputs and a 2-bit counter that is clocked by TII.

3. Discuss the design of a system using the 8008 CPU that does not use the input-output instructions but views all I/O ports as memory locations. What costs are involved with this approach and when is it desirable to use such a scheme?

9 *languages and language translation*

INTRODUCTION: THE ORIGIN OF "SYMBOLS"

The most profound and least understood aspect of *symbol processors* is the hardware-software duality discussed in Chapter 1. The conceptual difficulty stems primarily from vagueness concerning the association of "symbols," or software quanta, with hardware quanta; i.e., real physical devices. The first section of this chapter attempts to clarify this topic by identifying the means by which symbols are "connected" to devices. The remainder of the chapter is devoted to an overview of language and language translation in terms of symbol replacement algorithms. The average reader is assumed to have some familiarity with programming languages and to possess some programming experience. Replacement algorithms are discussed and used as a vehicle for developing assemblers, MACRO-assemblers, and interpretive routines. Several aspects of MACRO-assemblers are handled in appendices A, B, and C. The concept of a machine and a meta-machine is presented and meta-instructions are treated as "binding directives" in this framework.

PHYSICAL QUANTA: DEVICES

The physical basis of microprocessor technology rests in the ability to alter, in a controllable fashion, the conductivity of certain materials to achieve "semiconductors" with properties intermediate between those of metallic conductors and dielectric materials. The semiconductor material is then endowed with geometric and topologic structure to form variable impedance channels or paths. The junction of three or more channels can be considered as shown in Fig. 9-1. An imaginary boundary enclosing the junction defines an element that may be characterized by the point-to-point impedance. The junction is designed so that the control of one impedance path affects the other paths. The use of one point as reference then allows the element to be considered as an "IN" (control) port and an "OUT" (controlled) port with all values referred to the "common" port.

The applications of these elements fall into two broad categories: analog and binary. Analog devices make use of the specific relations between input and

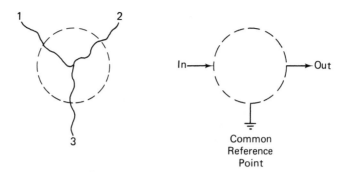

Figure 9-1

output and utilize a device equation of state. Binary devices depend only on the existence of two extremal conductance states, minimum and maximum, and the elements are operated to optimize the probability of being in one of the extreme states or the other with minimal time spent in transition.

META-PHYSICAL QUANTA: SYMBOLS

The all-important step necessary for the utilization of these physical elements in a symbol processor lies in *formal* definition, via TTL or any other specification, of one of these states as "ON" and the other "OFF." This allows the representation of an array of devices symbolically via the use of two symbols, usually "1" and "0." Strings of these symbols may be placed in one-to-one correspondence with the natural numbers, and thus the binary number system can be used to enumerate and symbolically represent the possible states of the array as shown in Fig. 9-2. The design of arrays has reinforced this interpretation in that the allowable transitions of the array are capable of being put in one-to-one correspondence with the Boolean logic and binary arithmetic relations

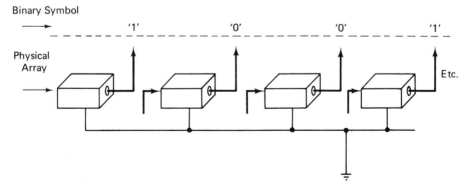

Figure 9-2

between the symbols; i.e., the arrays are designed to ADD, COUNT, AND, COMPARE, and so on.

It is a simple step from using binary symbols, whose elements are in one-to-one correspondence with the states of the elements of the arrry, to using a different number base, whose symbols bear no immediate relation to the states for which they stand. For example, the binary number "11111110" immediately describes the state of an 8-bit array, whereas the hexadecimal number base equivalent "FE" must be "translated" through some medium in order to relate it to the basic array state for which it stands.

The means of setting arrays to desired states range from very direct control via switches (one per bit) to very abstract control mechanisms. Most human/computer interfaces utilize a keyboard of some sort, and standardized keys and codes have evolved to maximize the ease of interface design. The American Standard Code for Information Interchange (ASCII) has been widely adopted and is used in this text. The ASCII code is shown here in tabular form for a few characters:

A	01000001
B	01000010
C	01000011
D	01000100
E	01000101
F	01000110
G	01000111

The reader should attempt to trace the steps by which the symbol "FE" in the mind of the programmer is converted via muscles, keyboard, and symbol replacement algorithms into the (hex) binary representation "11111110."

This conversion is a simple case of more general translation processes that will always reduce to a *series of transformations on sequences of symbols*. The ASCII-symbolized hex numbers are often used as a convenient method of manually entering binary coded state information into register arrays, either in the processor or its writable memory; i.e., of placing a (physical) array in a desired (symbolic) state via the ASCII keyboard. Similar techniques can be used to examine the state of an array and display the state symbolically by using an ASCII-coded print mechanism.

The above discussion treats the symbolic representation of binary '11111110' as hex-ASCII 'FE'. Rather than stop at this primitive level of representation, let us proceed to the final stage, the use of *Names*. The *Naming* process severs the connection between the name and its object; more specifically, the primitive connection is replaced by a symbolically functional connection.

To illustrate a symbolic name, we recall that the Intel 8008 CPU utilized the H-L register pair as a memory data pointer. The second-generation device, the 8080, possesses an extended instruction set that allows the H-L register pair to be loaded with a 16-bit number; the instruction

LXI H,435

will cause the H-L register pair to point to location 435 in memory. If location 435 is identified in a particular program with a data element, DATA, or a storage location, BUFFER, it is desirable to use names that make evident this identification. The actual physical CPU device requires binary terms; therefore, it is necessary to translate the decimal number 435 into its binary equivalent. It is possible to add another level of translation and replace "435" with the name "DATA" or "BUFFER" or any other appropriate ASCII term. Thus, the general instruction

LXI H,435

is replaced by

LXI H,BUFFER

and the instruction has thereby been placed in a *context*. It is fairly obvious that this requires some means of providing the context. Both direct (BUFFER EQUAL 435) and indirect (BUFFER: DS 10) means are available and are covered in a later section.

In the above example the number "435" was replaced with the name "BUFFER." Although the implications of this step may not be obvious, the replacement of specialized symbols (numbers) with generalized symbols (names) is probably the single most important step in the development of symbol processors. In fact, studies of brain-damaged individuals indicate that numbers and names are treated quite differently by the human brain!

ASSEMBLY LANGUAGE AND ASSEMBLERS

The facilities for translating one set of symbols into another normally include a set of tables or a data structure and a set of rules for using the tables, i.e., operating within the structure. Such operations can always be reduced to matrix operations. However, this perspective is currently of more interest from a theoretical viewpoint than an applied one. The program that effects the translation of assembly language into machine (binary) language is called the *Assembler* since it ordinarily breaks up an instruction into fields, separately translates each field, and assembles the binary fields or "pieces" of the instructions to create the complete instruction. Thus, for example, the instruction

MOV   D,C

would be broken into an operation code field,

MOV   01------

a destination field,

D   --010---

and a source field

C   -----001

and these fields assembled to give the machine equivalent of MOV D,C:

MOV D,C ⇒ $\boxed{01\ 010\ 001}$

where the INTEL 8080 register codes have been used

A	111
B	000
C	001
D	010
E	011
H	100
L	101
H-L	110

These codes are stored in tables to which the Assembler has access, as well as the codes for all of the possible opcodes, MOV, ADD, JMP, CALL, RET, etc. It is a straightforward if somewhat tedious procedure to analyze the separate fields (which must be formatted to some specifications) and translate each by replacing the alphameric symbol with its binary equivalent as determined by a table or a conversion routine. If the format is not followed, or if there is no corresponding table entry, then an error message can be issued.

For a given processor the names of the registers and those of the instructions are fixed, and the above procedure is readily applicable. However, the example in which LXI H, BUFFER was used to point to the location named BUFFER in RAM illustrates a case where it is impractical to write an Assembler with all possible symbols stored in tabular form. On the other hand, it is the freedom to use any names or symbols that we choose (exclusive of the defined registers and opcodes) that provides much of the vast power of computer software. The solution to this problem consists in designing the Assembler program to create its own symbol tables and to enter new symbols in these tables as they are encountered. The Assembler, of course, must be provided with the means to distinguish between new symbols and incorrect opcodes, etc., and this has been achieved classically via the addition of label fields in the format such that any symbol found in a label field is assigned to the symbol table. The move away from punched cards as storage and input/output media has resulted in a more "free-formatted" Assembler in which a label is marked with a special character, a colon (:) in the INTEL Assembler. Thus, any symbol followed by a colon is entered into the symbol table and the use of a colon in any other part of the instruction (exclusive of the comments field *that provides context* and therefore, a meta-field) is prohibited. Entries in the table must be unique, and use of two identical symbols as labels will result in a "multiply-defined" error message.

The process of assembly of the machine-language instructions normally is divided into two (or more) subprocesses or "passes." The first pass scans the program for labels and creates the symbol table. The second pass then uses this table and the other built-in tables to translate the assembly language into machine code.

"MACHINES" AND "META-MACHINES"—BINDING TIME

The word "machine" will be taken to refer to a functional entity, i.e., the hardware plus the software needed to perform a given function. A typical computer system will function as several different machines at different times; for example, our system can function first as a translating machine and later as a target machine. Most of the hardware will be common to both machines. The software will probably differ vastly.

The target machine is the one for which we write programs, i.e., compose instruction sequences to guide its operation. The translating machine also requires instructions to direct its operation, and since these instructions provide the "context" in which the target program is translated, they are called "meta-instructions." They are also often called "pseudo-instructions" because they do not generate executable code.

A Machine Hierarchy

If the basic hardware is identical between machines, then the distinction between a machine and a meta-machine is the same as between a program and a meta-program. Simply stated, this hierarchy is openended.

A program operates on data (voltages, hourly wages, Soc. Sec. #, etc.)

A meta-program operates on programs (translaters, linkers, loaders, etc.)

A meta-meta-program operates on meta-programs (operating systems)

A meta-meta-meta-program . . . etc.

Each meta-system provides a context within which its lower level(s) operates. It also provides a "binding" order for symbols that is implemented via meta-instructions.

Specific Meta-Instructions: "Binding Directives"

The types of meta-instructions associated with translating machines are described in this section. The first derives from the fact that the use of symbols as addresses, rather than numbers, usually implies that a program can be located anywhere in address space. Thus, it is necessary to bind these symbols to physical address space via an ORIGIN instruction that tells the translating machine the origin of a given sequence of code. The ORIGIN meta-instruction must specify an address that is interpreted by the Assembler to define the location in memory where the next instruction is stored. ORIGINs can be placed anywhere in a program to locate different program segments throughout memory. If no ORIGIN is used, the default starting location of zero is normally specified by the Assembler.

The target machine will normally continue to execute instructions until it comes to a HALT instruction. In similar fashion, the translating machine will normally continue translating until it comes to an END meta-instruction. This directive informs the Assembler that it has reached the end of the target program.

Binding Names to Numbers: The "Equate" Meta Instruction

Most names or labels used in a program provide access to a certain routine, i.e., specify the address of an instruction. This address is determined by the preceding ORIGIN meta-instruction and by the position of the instruction in the sequence. It is often desirable, however, to assign a number to a name that has nothing to do with memory locations or addresses. Thus a port number associated with a motor, a constant associated with a name, etc., can be bound via the use of the EQUATE meta-instruction:

```
MOTOR     EQU     5
ALPHA     EQU     137
```

The use of EQUATEs to bind names to numbers allows the ASSEMBLER to make entries into its symbol table that are valid throughout the assembly process. If conditional assembly is to be allowed, it is often desirable to bind new numbers to a given name at different places in the same program. The SET meta-instruction allows the Assembler to set a symbol equal to one value and later reset it to other values:

```
          .
          .
          .
COUNT     SET     1
          .
          .
```

```
        COUNT    SET    2
                  .
                  .
                  .
```

CONDITIONAL ASSEMBLY

The power of processor-based machines resides largely in the ability to make decisions; i.e., to conditionally execute certain sequences of code. This power can be extended to translating machines by providing *conditional translation* meta-instructions or conditional assembly directives. The IF/ENDIF pair of meta-instructions provides this capability. The IF directive is followed by an expression that the Assembler evaluates during the assembly process. The value of the expression is either zero or nonzero and is taken to be FALSE or TRUE, respectively. A TRUE result indicates that the sequence in question is to be evaluated, and the conditional assembly directive has no effect. Upon encountering a FALSE result, the Assembler scans the following program statements until the ENDIF is located and then assembly proceeds with the next instruction. The sequence of instructions bracketed by IF and ENDIF is not translated in this case. Thus, program segments can be inserted or deleted during the translation process, depending upon conditions expressed in the IF expression.

To demonstrate the use of some of these directives, we develop a routine that will convert binary numbers to ASCII format suitable for displaying on a teletype or CRT. The binary number is originally stored in a 2-byte buffer. The Assembler recognizes a directive that reserves a specified number of locations in memory to be used for data storage during program execution. The Define Storage (DS) directive, with an accompanying expression that specifies the amount of storage, can be used to create the binary number buffer via

```
    BINARYNUMBER:  DS 2
```

In similar fashion, a 10-byte decimal buffer can be created via

```
    DECIMALBUF:  DS 10
```

The Assembler binds the name DECIMALBUF to the address of the first byte of the decimal buffer. If the two specifications are in sequence,

```
    DECIMALBUF:     DS 10
    BINARYNUMBER:   DS 2
```

the Assembler will reserve ten bytes of storage for DECIMALBUF followed by two bytes for BINARYNUMBER.

The routine will utilize a table of negative integers that are powers of ten. The table will be stoppered with a constant that is an alternating bit pattern (unequal to any power of ten). This marker can be defined via the EQUATE meta-instruction

STOPPER   EQU   ØAAH

There will also be a table of ASCII digits used for forming the ASCII representation of the binary number. Constant bytes can be stored in memory via use of the Define Byte (DB) directive, and constant 16-bit words via the Define Word (DW) directive. Thus, the tables can be included in the program by writing

POWERTABLE: DW −10000, −1000, −100, −10, −1, STOPPER
DIGITABLE: DB '0','1','2','3','4'
             DB '5','6','7','8','9'

The assembler interprets as ASCII characters all symbols enclosed in single quotes. The assembler also possesses facilities for translating from the octal, decimal, or hexadecimal number system to the binary number system and thus will store the binary equivalents of the powers of ten in the power table as 16-bit numbers in twos complement form.

The use of tables often requires pointers that allow access to data in the table. These pointers can be defined and storage reserved for them via the binding directives

PTRDECBUF: DS 2
PTRPOWER: DS 2

A simple counting technique is used in which the number of powers of ten contained in a given term is determined by subtracting the largest power of ten from the binary number until underflow occurs. The count determined by this technique is then used as an index into the digit table and the ASCII digit is moved into the decimal buffer. The next largest power of ten is then divided into the remainder and the routine iterates until the stopper is reached in the power table. The ASCII representation in the decimal buffer is then terminated with an ASCII blank symbol defined by

BLANK   EQU   ' '

where the space-bar symbol is enclosed between quotes.

Although the following routine could be written with the Intel 8008 instruction set, it is simpler to use the extended instruction set of the 8080 microprocessor. The Intel 8080 instruction set facilitates buffer operations via the use of three different 16-bit memory data pointers, the B-C, D-E, and H-L register pairs. The H-L pair, or H-pointer, allows transfer of the contents of any scratchpad register to or from any memory register via the MOV *M,r* and MOV *r,M* instructions, respectively, where *M* designates the memory location whose address is contained in H and L. The B-pointer and the D-pointer work only with the Accumulator and can transfer its contents to or from memory via the instructions:

LoaD Accumulator through pointer   LDAX B
                                              LDAX D

and

STore Accumulator through pointer   STAX B
                                              STAX D

When multi-byte buffers of data are to be treated, it is often useful to "point" to one or more of the buffers, using the instructions

   LXI *pointer*, BUFFER

where *pointer* can be either B, D, or H (BC, DE or HL register pairs). Having pointed to the data buffer, it is then possible to transfer data bytes between the accumulator and memory, using the LDAX or STAX instructions for the B and D pointers (and the MOV *A,M* and MOV *M,A* for the H pointer as in the 8008). The pointers B, D, and H can be sequenced through the table via the 8080 16-bit increment instructions

   INX   *register-pair*

where the register pairs are B-C, D-E, H-L (and the stack pointers). Access to memory by using any of the pointers is essentially an indirect access. The 8080 also allows *direct* addressing of data bytes in memory via the 24-bit instructions

   LDA *address*   (LoaD Accumulator from address)
   STA *address*   (STore Accumulator at address)

These last two instructions are ideal for handling *named* data bytes. It is often useful to designate a byte of memory as a "flag" byte that serves as a status or mode indicator. For example, one byte of memory was reserved to hold a count via the specification

   COUNTER: DS 1

This byte can be accessed, and the count transferred to or from the accumulator, respectively, via the instructions

   LDA COUNTER

and

   STA COUNTER

The ability to access data by name is very convenient.

Note that we now possess the means to load either "static" or "dynamic" data into the 8080 accumulator. Constant data can be loaded via the

MVI A,DATA   A ← DATA

instruction that contains the data byte in a (normally) nonvarying instruction while data that vary during program execution can be loaded into the accumulator via

LDA DATA   A ← (DATA)

where parentheses, as usual, indicate "contents of." In the last case, the symbol DATA represents not the *actual data but its static component, i.e., its address in memory space.* In a similar fashion, it is possible to load constant 16-bit numbers into the H-L register pair via the previously introduced instructions

LXI H,DATAWORD   H-L ← DATAWORD

and to load variable data directly into the H-L pair via the direct load and store instructions

LHLD DATALOCATION
SHLD DATALOCATION   H-L ← (DATALOCATION)

These last two generally allow access of any 16-bit quantity *by name* but are particularly useful for saving pointers or markers into data buffers. (Note that, since the data bus and the memory registers are only eight bits wide, these instructions will involve two data access cycles and the bytes will be stored sequentially in memory.)

To illustrate the operation of these instructions, we consider decimal data and addresses:

```
MVI A,10        loads decimal #10 into the accumulator
LDA 10          loads the contents of location #10 into the accumulator
LXI H,2000      loads H-L with 2000 (points to 2000)
LHLD H,2000     loads H-L with the data stored at 2000 (and 2001)
```

These instructions can now be used as follows to initialize pointers required in the binary-to-decimal conversion routine:

```
BINTODEC:
INITIALIZE:
LXI H,DECBUF       ;point H-L to Decimal Buffer
SHLD PTRDECBUF  ;initialize pointer to DECBUF
LHLD BINARYNUMBER;   pick up the 16-bit number
PUSH H             ;save BINARY NUMBER on stack
LXI H,POWERTABLE;point to POWERTABLE
SHLD PTRPOWER      ;initialize POWER TABLE pointer
```

The PUSH H operation utilizes the STACK or FIFO buffer that is located in *external memory* in the 8080 (the 7 deep return address stack was *internal* to the 8008). By placing the stack externally to the CPU, several advantages are gained:

virtually unlimited nesting of subroutines is possible,

data as well as return addresses can be stored on the stack.

In particular, the instructions

```
PUSH  PSW        POP  PSW
PUSH  B          POP  B
PUSH  D          POP  D
PUSH  H          POP  H
```

allow 16 bits to be transferred between B-C, D-E, H-L, PSW, and the top of the stack. (PSW stands for *program status word,* defined as the accumulator and the 8080 flags.) The use of the stack for data storage is ideal for interrupt servicing as described in Chapter 12. Stacks are convenient for temporary storage of information and it is this feature that is utilized in the BINTODEC routine above in which the binary number to be converted is pushed onto the stack.

Having initialized the pointer to the power table, it is now possible to access the first power of ten from the table as follows:

```
GETPOWER:
MVI A,—1
STA COUNTER        ;initialize COUNTER
LHLD PTRPOWER
MOV A, M           ;pickup table entry
CPI STOPPER        ;end of table?
JZ EXITBINTODEC    ;if STOPPER was found
MOV E,M            ;retrieve high byte of power
INX H              ;point to low byte
MOV D,M            ;retrieve low byte of power
INX H              ;point to next power in table
SHLD PTRPOWER      ;update pointer into POWERTABLE
POP H              ;retrieve binary remainder
PUSH H             ;save on stack
```

The 16-bit binary representation of a negative power of ten is now stored in the D-E register pair. This power of ten will be repeatedly subtracted from the binary number to be converted (or the current remainder), and a counter maintained that records the number of iterations. This subtraction is performed in a subtract loop:

```
;
SUBTRACTLOOP:
INX SP             ;clear entry from top of stack
INX SP
PUSH H             ;save current remainder on stack
```

```
LDA  COUNTER        ;into ACCUMULATOR
INR  A              ;increment COUNT
STA  COUNTER        ;restore updated COUNT
DAD  D              ;add power of ten in D-E to H-L
MOV  A,H            ;move MSByte into ACCUMULATOR
ANI  0FFH           ;set FLAGS via ALU operation
JP SUBTRACTLOOP     ;LOOP until negative sign results
```

When the test of the sign bit indicates that underflow has occurred, the counter is used as an index into the ASCII digit table:

```
;
UNDERFLOW:
LXI  B,DIGITABLE    ;point B-C to first digit in table
LDA COUNTER         ;retrieve COUNT to be used as index
ADD  C              ;add index in A-REG to LSByte of B-C
JNC GETDIGIT        ;jump if no carry results
INR  B              ;increment MSByte of pointer if
                    ;carry occurred

;
GETDIGIT:
MOV  C,A
LDAX B              ;pickup ASCII digit from table
LHLD PTRDECBUF      ;point H-L to Decimal Buffer
MOV  M,A            ;store ASCII digit in Decimal Buffer
INX  H              ;kick up pointer
MVI  M,BLANK        ;mark end with BLANK
SHLD PTRDECBUF      ;update buffer marker
JMP GETPOWER
;
```

In the BINTODEC example, the Assembler replaces the names associated with various locations by numbers associated with various locations. It also replaces the names associated with various operations by the numbers representing the machine language opcode. In many respects, the translation process is simply equivalent to a symbol replacement process. From this perspective the question naturally arises as to the possibility of using new symbols for operations or sequences of operations.

MACRO-INSTRUCTIONS

The binary instructions that are fetched into the CPU from memory are divided into fields that specify the operation and the operand (unless the operand is implicit in the operation). The assembly language instruction set, therefore, specifies those basic operations that have been implemented in hardware. It is possible in theory to design hardware capable of performing any definable finite operation. If an instruction can be decomposed into orthogonal fields, i.e., into independent operations, then it is possible to perform the desired operation as a sequence of suboperations. A "complete" set of suboperations forms a basis in terms of which any finite operation can be expanded.

The instruction set of any microprocessor should form such a "complete" set, allowing any well-defined operation to be expressed in terms of this set. Actually almost all microprocessor instruction sets are "over-complete" in the sense that they consist of several complete sets whose intersections are unequal to their unions. If an operation is expanded in terms of a given basic set of instructions, i.e., assembly language instructions, it is possible to replace the sequence of operations by a symbol or name for the sequence. Programs can then be written in terms of the operations and later translated into sequences of the basic instructions. The new, often complex, instructions are termed *MACRO-Instructions* and an Assembler that will translate MACRO-Instructions is called a *MACRO-Assembler*. The following examples will use the Intel 8080 MACRO-Assembler.

A MACRO-facility allows the designer to program using problem-oriented instructions by providing a macro-definition capability that binds a user-defined symbol to a sequence of assembly language instructions. The definition phase utilizes the MACRO and ENDMacro meta-instructions as follows:

```
NAME          MACRO
              string
              of
              basic
              instructions
              ENDM
```

The use of problem-oriented instructions is to be preferred to machine-oriented instructions. Assembly languages are mnemonic replacements for machine language instructions, i.e., the basic operations within the CPU proper. These normally consist of data transfers, control transfers, and special operations, none of which normally bears much relation to the operations required by a particular application. For example, the basic MOV instructions, conditional JUMP instructions, etc., used in a program to calculate the square root of a given number are usually far removed from the conceptual operations needed to obtain the desired answer.

The process of scanning a buffer for a nonblank character exemplifies a basic problem-oriented instruction that must be implemented in machine-oriented instructions. Via the use of the MACRO-facility, it is possible to define a problem-oriented SCAN instruction:

```
SCAN      MACRO
LOOP:     INX H          ;move to next char
          MOV A,M        ;get next char
          CPI ' '        ;compare to blank
          JZ LOOP        ;repeat if blank, else proceed
          ENDM
```

It is now possible to use the instruction "SCAN" in writing a program. The macro-definition is read before the program proper and the MACRO-Assembler "learns" the new instructions. The very process of deciding which new instructions would be desirable requires the designer to perform an analysis primarily in terms of the problem to be solved. After the problem-oriented instruction set has been defined, it is a straightforward and usually relatively simple task to implement these MACROs in terms of the basic instruction set. As an added advantage, the process affords "portability" of software from one machine to another in the following sense: Analysis of the problem and decomposition into a set of basic procedures are normally the most difficult aspects of problem solution. Once this has been done, the basic procedures can be written in terms of different machine language (if a MACRO-facility is available for each language) with a minimum of added effort. Once the MACROs are defined, the program will run on the new machine.

PARAMETER PASSING

It is often desirable to define a functional MACRO, *POINT*, whose target may be specified upon each invocation. The process of binding arguments to a generalized functional procedure is termed *parameter passing*, and most MACRO-facilities provide this ability. Since the actual information will vary from invocation to invocation, it is necessary to provide a symbol or *place holder* to designate places where information will be provided. The symbols used are often called "dummy variables" since their only use is in the definition phase. In the expansion phases they are replaced by the actual variables.

The generalized POINT MACRO may be defined as follows:

```
POINT      MACRO      PTR,      TARGET
           LXI        PTR,      TARGET
           ENDM
```

The dummy variable, PTR, specifies the pointer register to be used and TARGET gives the location to be pointed to. Thus, the MACRO may be used in a program as follows:

```
          .
          .
          .
POINT H, DECBUF
          .
          .
          .
POINT D, TEMPBUFFER
          .
          .
          .
```

The MACRO-Assembler will replace the problem-oriented instructions by the defined machine-oriented string—in this case:

.

.

.

LXI H, DECBUF
.

.

.

LXI D, TEMPBUFFER
.

.

.

These instructions will then be assembled as usual.

ASSEMBLERS AND INTERPRETERS

The language translation accomplished via the Assembler is an intermediate stage between writing a program and running a program. In most cases, a file containing the source code is entered (from paper tape, magnetic medium, etc.) and an object file containing the assembled code is produced. The object file can be loaded into memory space and the program executed.

Interpretive translation is immediate in the sense that each instruction is translated as it is encountered by the interpreter. Although the run time of programs will generally be degraded in the interpretive mode, the program development effort is minimized. The programmer can immediately execute the program and determine from the response of the system whether or not it is functioning correctly. Program generation is essentially an adaptive process and is thus extremely sensitive to the response time of the system. From a systems perspective, we may view each command as an entry, E, that serves as a stimulus to excite the system ψ in a manner that is governed by the response function, H, of the system.

The formal process can be represented generally via eigenequations

$$H\psi \Leftarrow E\psi$$

where the eigenvalues are entries that drive the system. In the following sections we design a structure, ψ, that recognizes a set of commands, λ, and we will design the response function H_λ associated with each command. Our primary goal is to design a general structure that can be expanded via later addition of new commands and new responses without requiring any modification of the structure. We use MACROs to simplify the design of our interpreter. The level of complexity is determined by the following criteria. The system should be simple enough to treat in this chapter, yet complex enough to be useful. The key feature will be user-expandability.

A Simple Interpreter

The system will "boot up" in the command mode, in which the program prompts and waits for a keyboard entry. When a key is entered it is passed through a filter that recognizes eigenvalues of the system. The specification of the initial set of valid commands and the design of the eigenfilter provide a well-defined task with which we can begin. In view of the simplicity requirement, we use single (ASCII-)-character commands. These commands are input to the accumulator and compared with valid command characters via the Compare Immediate (CPI) instructions. The flow graph of this filter is shown in Fig. 9-3.

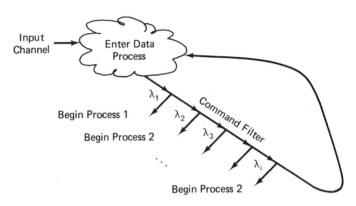

Figure 9-3

The filter can be implemented by using 8080 instructions and MACRO-instructions as follows:

```
ENTERDATA:
KEYINPUTPROCESS:
ISIT?    P1COMMAND
DO       COM1PROCESS
ISIT?    P2COMMAND
DO       COM2PROCESS
ISIT?    P3COMMAND
  .
  .
DO       COMnPROCESS
ELSE     ENTERDATA
```

Although we have formally designed a command filter, we do not yet have a set of valid commands. These commands will reflect the basic nature of the system and this must now be decided. In view of the requirements of both simplicity and usefulness, we will choose to implement an interpretive controller that will be designed to monitor and control simple processes. We thus need a set of measurement commands, computation commands, and control commands. Since a binary-to-decimal conversion routine has already been developed, we include it as a computation command. Another "computation" that is useful in control applications is a delay function that suspends operation for a specified period of time. Two extremely useful measurements consist of counting events and measuring voltages. The ability to set and reset switches provides a very powerful control mechanism. These functions are used to implement the basic command set:

MEASURE	·Count a specified number of events, then proceed
	·Convert analog voltage to binary representation
COMPUTE	·Convert binary representation to decimal representation
	·Count clock cycles to provide timed delay, then proceed
CONTROL	·Switch *ON* a specified control line
	·Switch *OFF* a specified control line
COMMUNICATE	·INPUT data from a console device
	·OUTPUT data to a console device

Although the two count functions are conceptually similar, they will be implemented as separate processes. This set can be augmented via the addition of other application-oriented commands. However, the basic set illustrates many of the features associated with control systems. Another class of commands, mode-switch commands, will complete our repertoire. The following section will discuss the modes of the interpreter.

Mode-Switches

The interpretive structure that we are designing will operate in three basic modes:

·COMMAND MODE

·PROGRAM MODE

·RUN MODE

In the command-mode the system tests the input channel for an entry that is then passed through the command filter. Those eigenvalues to which the system responds are recognized and executed immediately. The filter rejects all other entries.

In the program-mode the valid commands are not executed immediately but are, instead, used to compose a stored program that will consist of a sequence of valid commands linked in some fashion that can be executed at run-time.

In run-mode the interpreter executes the stored program sequence of commands. The mode of operation of the system is determined by a MODE-SWITCH that can be set by the user and tested by the system. Three switches, PROGRAM, EXIT, and RUN, allow the user to alter the mode of the system. A flag byte can be set by the mode switches and tested by a TESTMODE facility. The TESTMODE routine is called each time a valid command is recognized. If the system is in program mode, the command will be appended to the program buffer; otherwise the processing of the command will proceed immediately. The following routine will perform this test:

```
;-----------TEST MODE ROUTINE-----------
;
TESTMODE:
LDA        FLAG
ISIT?      INPROGRAMMODE
GOTO       APPENDTOPROGRAMBUFFER
RET        ;to process
;
```

Although many procedures exist for linking a sequence of commands, we will "store" our program by composing a sequence of CALLs to the various subroutines that execute the selected processes. While in the program mode, the system composes CALL instructions for each command as it is entered, stores the CALL in sequence in the program buffer, and then returns to wait for the next command. This continues until the E-switch is used to EXIT the program mode. This switch always restores the command mode of operation.

The R switch initializes pointers and enters the run mode at a specified location in the program buffer. If the R switch is set during the command mode, the system enters the run mode immediately. If it is set or entered while the system is in the P-mode, it is "stored" in sequence as a CALL RUN instruction. When it is encountered during execution, it causes a program loop to the beginning of the program sequence.

The list of valid commands is summarized below.

'P'–enter the program mode

'E'–exit P-mode, return to command mode

'R'–run program (from beginning)

'V'–read voltage (analog-to-digital subsystem)

'D'–delay for specified time perod

'N'–switch *on* specified control line

'F'–switch *off* specified control line

'C'–count specified # of events, then proceed

'W'–input 16-bit word from console

'T'–print (type) contents of decimal buffer on console

Sequential Processes and Parameter Passing

Several of the commands referenced "specified" numbers, for example, the count and delay and the switch routines. The specific numbers that serve as arguments to the functions can be derived in several ways. They can be programmed into the routine; they can be input from the console; or they can be passed from previous routines. Although all of these are of interest, we will examine in more detail a parameter-passing scheme. In particular, each process will be assumed to have access to an INBOX and also to an OUTBOX. In the simplest scheme these boxes will be the same, i.e., the input data will be picked up from the IN/OUTBOX, processed by the routine, and the result stored in the IN/OUTBOX to be used as input for the following process. The sequence of processes might look as in Fig. 9-4. This scheme suggests two additional commands: 'I' and 'O.' Data can be input from the console to the INBOX via the 'I' command and from the OUTBOX to the console via the 'O' command.

Process-Generation

The preceding sections have discussed the desired processes that the interpreter should be capable of executing and the commands associated with each. The remaining task consists of designing these functions into the system. The system has been designed to facilitate this procedure in that processes can be generated from assembly language subroutines by including a call to the TESTMODE routine as the first statement in each subroutine. The TESTMODE routine is used to determine whether the entry should be executed or appended to the program sequence in the program.

The interpreter that will be designed utilizes the name binding features of the Assembler for both operations (MACROs) and operands. The names have been made as descriptive as possible to aid in understanding the system. The following MACROs are used throughout the program:

```
;
;-----------MACRO DEFINITIONS-----------
;
POINT@   MACRO TARGET
         LXI H, TARGET
         ENDM
;
```

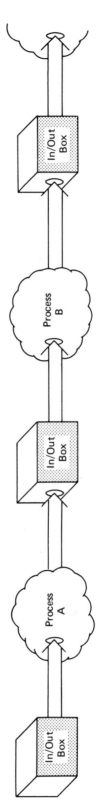

Figure 9-4

```
ECHO        MACRO
            MOV C,A
            CALL CNSOLEOUT
            ENDM
;
ISIT?       MACRO TARGETBYTE
            CPI TARGETBYTE       ;compare target byte to
            ENDM                     ACCUMULATOR
;
GOTO        MACRO TARGETADDRESS
            JZ TARGETADDRESS    ;JUMP if match occurred
            ENDM
;
DO          MACRO ROUTINE
            CZ ROUTINE           ;CALL if match occurred
            ENDM
;
STORE       MACRO
            MOV M,A ;move ACCUMULATOR into memory
            ENDM
;
LOAD        MACRO
            MOV A,M ;move memory into ACCUMULATOR
            ENDM
;
GET         MACRO CONTENTS
            LHLD CONTENTS        ;LOAD 16 bits into H-L
            ENDM
;
PUT         MACRO CONTENTS
            SHLD CONTENTS        ;store 16 bits
            ENDM
;
STEPOINTER MACRO
            INX H
            ENDM
```

The filter routine is presented below and shown in Fig. 9-5. The figure indicates the interpretive mode of operation utilizing the command filter and also the run-mode operation utilizing the stored program. The run-mode portion of Fig. 9-5 depicts a data fetch process executed by routine #j that has been called from the program buffer. Each routine can access the IN/OUTBOX or other common storage, and in addition can possess internal data structures as shown.

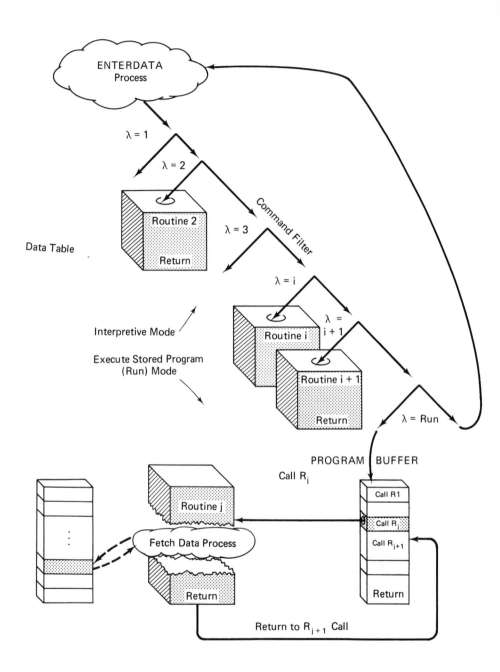

Figure 9-5

```
;-------ENTERDATA AND FILTER ROUTINES-------
;
ENTERDATA:
CALL KEYIN
;
FILTER:
ISIT?   PROGSYMBOL
DO      PROGRAMODE      ;store instructions in PROGRAMBUFFER
ISIT?   INTERPSYM
DO      PROGRAMODE      ;return to COMMAND mode
ISIT?   ONSYMBOL
DO      ONSWITCH        ;turn on SWITCH #N
ISIT?   OFFSYMBOL
DO      OFFSWITCH       ;turn off SWITCH #N
ISIT?   INPUTSYMBOL
DO      WORDINPUT       ;store 16-bit value in inbox
ISIT?   PRNTSYMBOL
DO      PRINTOUT        ;type contents of DEC BUFFER
ISIT?   WAITCOUNT
DO      DOCOUNT         ;count N events
ISIT?   DELAYSYMBOL
DO      DLAYSTATE       ;wait N time periods
ISIT?   BTODECSYM
DO      BINTODEC        ;BINARY to DECIMAL conversion
ISIT?   RUNSYMBOL
DO      RUNPROGRAM      ;execute stored program
CALL  CRLF
JMP     ENTERDATA
;
```

The EQU and ORG meta-instructions are used to bind names to the command characters and other items, and to bind the program to the memory space.

```
;
;--------NAME BINDING SECTION--------------------
;
BYTEINPUT       EQU 'I'
INPUTWORD       EQU 'W'
BYTEOUTPUT      EQU 'O'
VOLTSYMBOL      EQU 'V'
INTERPSYMB      EQU 'E'
PROGSYMBOL      EQU 'P'
RUNSYMBOL       EQU 'R'
DELAYSYMBOL     EQU 'D'
PRNTSYMBOL      EQU 'T'
ONSYMBOL        EQU 'N'
OFFSYMBOL       EQU 'F'
WAITCOUNTSYM EQU 'C'
BTODECSYMBOL EQU 'B'
```

```
STOPPER           EQU 0AAH
;
CALLCODE          EQU 0CDH
RETURN            EQU 0C9H
;
ASCIIMASK         EQU 07FH
BLANK             EQU ' '
;
CONSOLEIN         EQU 0F803H  ;location of
CNSOLEOUT         EQU 0F809H  ;I/O drivers
INRUNMODE         EQU 010H
INPROGMODE        EQU 020H
COMSYMB           EQU 030H
;
;------BIND PROGRAM TO PHYSICAL MEMORY------
;
ORG 3000H
;
;--------FLAG BYTE----------------------------------
;
FLAG:             DS 1
;
;---------COUNTER----------------------------------
;
COUNTER:          DS 1
;
;--------POINTERS----------------------------------
;
PTRPOWER:         DS 2
PTRDECBUF:        DS 2
PROGPTR:          DS 2
;
;-------BUFFERS----------------------------------
;
INBOX: OUTBOX:    DS 2
;
ENTRYBOX:         DS 1
DECIMALBUF:       DS 18
;
;-------DATA TABLES----------------------------------
;
POWERTABLE:       DW  -10000,-1000,-100,-10,-1,STOPPER
;
DIGITABLE:        DB '0','1','2','3','4'
                  DB '5','6','7','8','9'
;
```

Each of the modules or subroutines in the interpreter can be written as an assembly language program in the same fashion as the BINTODEC subroutine

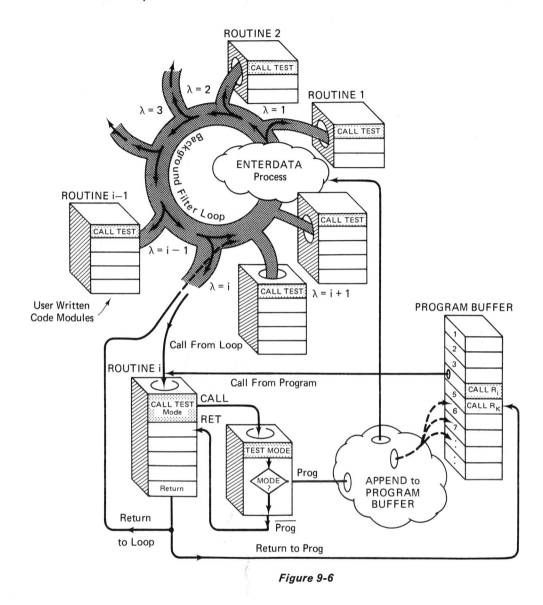

Figure 9-6

that is included here for completeness. Each of these routines must begin with the TESTMODE routine that branches to the "APPEND to BUFFER" if it is in the program mode (Fig. 9-6); otherwise, it returns to execute the process.

```
;
;-----------TEST MODE ROUTINE----------------------------
;
TESTMODE:
LDA     FLAG
```

```
ISIT?      INPROGRAMMODE
GOTO       APPENDTOPROGRAMBUFFER
RET                        ;to process
;
;--------'APPEND TO PROGRAM BUFFER'-ROUTINE-----------
;
APPENDTOPROGBUFFER:
MVI A,CALLCODE
GET PROGPTR
STORE
STEPOINTER
POP D                      ;pop top of stack into D-E
DCX D
DCX D
DCX D
MOV M,E                    ;store entry point in PROGRAM BUFFER
STEPOINTER
MOV M,D
STEPOINTER
MVI M,RETURN               ;mark end of program in buffer
PUT PROGPTR                ;back in place 'til next time
JMP ENTERDATA
;
;----BINARY TO DECIMAL CONVERSION ROUTINE------------
;
BINTODEC:
CALL TESTMODE
POINT@ DECIMALBUF
PUT PTRDECBUF              ;initialize pointer to DECBUF
GET INBOX                  ;pickup 16-bit value
PUSH H                     ;save BINARY NUMBER on stack
POINT@ POWERTABLE
PUT PTRPOWER               ;initialize POWER TABLE pointer
;
GETPOWER:
MVI A,-1
STA COUNTER
GET PTRPOWER
LOAD                       ;pickup table entry
CPI STOPPER                ;end of table?
GOTO EXITBINTODEC
MOV E,M                    ;retrieve high byte of power
STEPOINTER                 ;point to low byte
MOV D,M                    ;retrieve low byte of power
STEPOINTER                 ;point to next power in table
PUT PTRPOWER               ;update pointer into POWERTABLE
POP H                      ;retrieve binary remainder
PUSH H                     ;save on stack
;
```

```
SUBTRACTLOOP:
INX SP                      ;clear entry from top of stack
INX SP
PUSH H                      ;save current remainder on stack
LDA   COUNTER               ;into accumulator
INR A                       ;increment COUNT
STA COUNTER                 ;restore updated COUNT
DAD D                       ;add power of ten in D-E to H-L
MOV A,H                     ;move MSByte into ACCUMULATOR
ANI 0FFH                    ;set FLAGs via ALU operation
JP SUBTRACTLOOP             ;LOOP until negative sign results
;
UNDERFLOW:
LXI B,DIGITABLE             ;point to first digit in table
LDA   COUNT                 ;into ACC to be used as INDEX
ADD C                       ;add LSByte of B-C to INDEX
JNC GETDIGIT                ;get digit if no carry occurs
INR B                       ;increment MSByte of pointer if CARRY
;
GETDIGIT:
MOV C,A                     ;restore indexed LSByte of ptr.
LDAX B                      ;pickup ASCII digit from table
GET PTRDECBUF
STORE                       ;store   ASCII digit in DEC BUFFER
STEPOINTER
MVI M,BLANK
PUT PTRDECBUF               ;update pointer into DEC BUF
JMP GETPOWER
;
EXITBINTODEC:
POP D                       ;clear top of stack
RET
;
```

The entry of any of the mode-switch commands, 'P', 'E', or 'R,' occasions a branch to the following routines:

```
;-------MODE SWITCH ROUTINES----------------------------
;
PROGRAMODE:
MVI A, INPROGMODE
STA FLAG
CALL  INITIALIZEPOINTERS
JMP ENTERDATA
;
COMMANDMODE:
MVI A, COMSYMB
STA FLAG
JMP ENTERDATA
```

.
.
.
.

```
;---------INITIALIZE POINTER FOR PROGBUFFER-----------
;
INITIALIZEPOINTER:
POINT@ PROGBUFFER
PUT PROGPTR
RET
;
```

.
.
.

```
;--------STORED PROGRAM ENTRY POINT-------------------
;
RUNPROGRAM:
CALL TESTMODE        ;Allows 'R' to be used as LOOP instruction
MVI A, INRUNMODE   ;and stored in the program buffer.
STA FLAG
CALL INITIALIZEPOINTERS
;
;--------PROGRAM STORAGE BUFFER AREA-----------------
;
PROGBUFFER:  DS 200
;
;-----------------------------------------------------------
;
```

The user can add modules continually to this interpretive structure. Several are shown below. Note that the use of CALL TESTMODE is optional. Discuss the significance of this.

```
;--------PRINTOUT DECIMAL BUFFER----------------------
;
PRINTOUT:
CALL TESTMODE
POINT@ DECIMALBUFFER  ;print DECIMAL value
GETNEXT: LOAD         ;of BINARYNUMBER obtained from
ISIT? BLANK           ;A-TO-D conversion routine, BINTODEC,
RZ
ECHO                  ;or any other which loads
STEPOINTER            ;DECIMAL BUFFER.
JMP GETNEXT
;

;--------KEYBOARD INPUT ROUTINE-----------------------
;
```

```
        KEYIN:
        MVI A, '('
        ECHO ;on console device
        CALL CONSOLEIN
        ANI ASCIIMASK
        STA ENTRYBOX
        ECHO
        MVI A, ')'
        ECHO
        MVI A, '–'
        ECHO
        LDA ENTRYBOX
        RET ;return to calling routine
        ;


        ;--------SUBROUTINE ENTRY POINTS-----------------------
        ;
        DOCOUNT:
        ATODCONVERT:
        ONSWITCH:            ;the entry points listed here are dummy
        OFFSWITCH:           ;points. . . these and other routines would
        DLAYSTATE:           ;be written to access the required data
        ;USER-ROUTINE1:      ;and perform the desired actions before
        ;USER-ROUTINE2:      ;returning to the FILTER LOOP or the
        JMP ENTERDATA        ;stored PROGRAM sequence:
        ;
```

All routines can access INBOX for a relevant parameter. This number may be used in a variety of ways: as an index into a table, or an argument of a function or submode switch.

For example, an ANALOGTODIGITAL conversion routine can fetch a number to be used to select an analog information channel to serve as the source of an analog signal. Upon receiving this parameter, the routine then performs a READ operation on the selected channel and stores the result of the operation in IN/OUTBOX or the BINARYNUMBER buffer. Upon completion of this operation the system fetches the next command.

The code for the routines that drive I/O devices, such as ANALOG to DIGITAL converters, teletypes, CRTs, and other peripheral devices, is developed in Chapter 11 on I/O structures.

SUMMARY

Although many computer applications involve primarily arithmetic operations, they are by no means limited to such. In fact, the binary numbering system is only one of many ways of ordering the 2^m symbols formed by considering the permutations of *m*-indistinguishable two-state systems. The ability in a physical system to:

1. duplicate the state of one array in another array
2. compare the states of one array to another array
3. transform the state of an array via allowed transformations

provides us with the basic operations from which we abstract the properties in which we are interested. By abstracting the binary "state" of the array and neglecting the underlying physical media, we *invent* symbols, and the above operations allow us to

1. move a symbol from one location to another,
2. compare symbols to each other,
3. effect transformations on symbols.

The utility of the whole scheme derives from the fact that it is possible to partition, in some sense, most systems in which we are interested into subsystems and to assign a unique symbol to each subsystem.

The ability to design controllable systems capable of being driven into a large, but finite, number of distinct states allows a one-to-one correspondence to be set up between the natural numbers and the allowable states of the system. These numbers, expressed in any number base, can then be divided into fields that can be associated with operations and the targets of operations. The fields associated with the operations are called operators, or opcode fields; and those with the targets are called operands, or operand fields. The operands can often be put in correspondence with elements of an external system and the operators used to emulate transformations occurring in such systems. The success of this approach, even to the emulation of learning notworks, is having a most profound effect upon our world.

The ability to transform one operand into another provides for replacement of one symbol by another and thus forms the basis of language translation. The structure or syntax of the language specifies the allowable transformations as prescribed via the grammar, the collection of productions that formalize the replacement rules. This structure can be embedded in a machine or automata that *recognizes* allowable strings and behaves as a symbol filter. The meaning or semantics of the symbols that pass through the filter is then determined by a semantic routine that executes the appropriate replacement algorithm.

The discussion of replacement rules affords a natural introduction to the *data structures/procedure* equivalence principle, which states (without proof) that a desired functional relationship can be expressed either in an algorithmic or a tabular form. For example, the value of the sine function of an argument can be determined via a series expansion or other procedure *or* via a sine-table lookup. In the same sense, the translation of an opcode symbol into a machine code (binary) representation can be effected through the use of a transformation algorithm or from an opcode table. Throughout the remainder of this book it is assumed that any desired process can be implemented by using either the algorithmic or table-driven approach. Table-driven systems are just one step removed from matrix transformations, the most general formal approach to *any* systems description. As a practical criterion of design, note that, *as a general rule*, processes implemented via procedures require little memory space but appreciable execution time, whereas table lookup techniques minimize execution time but consume large amounts of storage space. Exceptions to this rule can be found.

The utility of the symbol replacement scheme has been attributed to the ability to partition systems into subsystems and to assign a unique symbol to each subsystem. The systems are interfaced or linked via the use of binding directives, either explicit or implicit. Explicit directives bind names to values or to physical locations in address space. Implicit binding directives are "built-in" procedures, such as those that assign sequential instructions to sequential storage locations or those that bind ASCII representations of numbers in various bases to binary representations. The art of computer programming consists largely in the skillful employment of these binding directives just as the art of processor design consists of interfacing the functional building blocks according to logical, electrical, and timing "binding directives" or interfacing rules.

PROBLEMS

1. The Intel 8080 and most other microprocessors utilize different assembly language instructions for each condition; i.e., JZ, JNZ, JP, JM, etc. Write a MACRO that will allow the user to specify a conditional jump by writing JUMPIF condition, target. Thus, JZ LOOP would become JUMPIF ZERO, LOOP. Do this for testing the zero, carry, parity, and sign flags, true and false. *Hint*: Set ZERO EQU ∅, NONZERO EQU 1, etc. and use conditional assembly in MACRO.

2. Give an example of a MACRO that both speeds up program execution and requires less memory space than an equivalent subroutine.

3. Write a MACRO that will append multi-character symbols to a symbol table.

4. Write a DO N ... MACRO and a CONTINUE-MACRO and discuss the problems associated with adding this type of 'DO LOOP' feature to an assembly language program.

5. Write DO N ... CONTINUE modules for the interpreter. Compare with Problem 4.

6. For what range of numbers will the BINTODEC routine work?

7. Are the binding operations discussed in this chapter related to the time-binding operation of General Semantics?

8. Most assemblers use only the first 5 or 6 characters in a symbol name. Discuss the implications of this for the following symbols:

    COUNT
    COUNTER

```
INITIALIZEPOINTER
INITIALIZE POINTERS
OUTROUTINEA
OUTROUTINEB
```

Note that this feature can be used to make code more easily readable.

9. Must the commands be input from a keyboard in the interpreter developed in this chapter? Discuss a multi-processor structure in which the interpretive structure is appended to a master processor.

10. Discuss the response of the system if the input channel is considered to consist of stimulus lines from a controlled process. If the input channel is continually sampled, what would be the effect of random inputs? Compare this structure with a programmed logic array (PLA).

11. Discuss the software interface between the interpretive system and a variety of console devices, each of which possesses a unique hardware/software/device interface.

12. Discuss the BASIC language developed at Dartmouth in terms of 1965 economics. In particular, relate features of BASIC to the fact that between 1967 and 1977 the density of RAM storage increased from 64 bits on a chip to 64,000 bits on a chip, while the cost of chips decreased and the access speeds increased.

10 *addressing structures*

The ability to access information organized in a random fashion implies a unique name or address associated with each datum. The incorporation of an addressing subsystem capable of fetching instructions from memory provides the primary distinction between microprocessors and previous integrated circuits, the latter requiring external address mechanisms to access instructions or provide control signals.

Consideration of addressing subsystems can be facilitated by treating as independent processes (1) the formation of an address, and (2) the presentation of this address to the target subsystem. Various presentation mechanisms in use with microprocessors are treated in the first part of this chapter.

ADDRESS PRESENTATION SUBSYSTEMS

A basic means of providing an address to a target subsystem has been discussed for the 8008 CPU. The need to transmit 14 bits of address over an 8-bit space channel was satisfied by creating two time channels, i.e., by multiplexing the pieces over the data bus and latching the address information from the bus at the proper time. This process was described earlier as "dis-membering" the address inside the CPU and "re-membering" it in external hardware for presentation to the target subsystem. The general scheme does not depend on the width of the word or the space channel involved; for example, two 4-bit processors, the Intel 4004 and the 4040, transmit 12-bit addresses over a 4-bit bus as three 4-bit "nibbles" of address—low, middle, and high.

Advances in packaging technology following the introduction of the first microprocessors resulted in a 40-pin package as the standard for second-generation microprocessors. The larger number of pins offers the possibility of using a separate address bus, and most microprocessors now employ separate address and data busses. The address bus is unidirectional out from the CPU, while data busses are bidirectional. Addresses fetched from memory will thus be multiples of the data width. The standard address width for 8-bit processors is 16 bits, which allows accessing any one of 64K target locations. Note that the choice of 14 address bits for the 8008 was primarily a consequence of the need to transmit

2 bits of cycle code along with the address. The economy associated with time-multiplexing has resulted in the retention of some aspects of this feature, even in 40-pin packaged microprocessors. Several semimultiplexed address presentation schemes, described below, provide a separate (latched) address bus on the microprocessor chip for the presentation of address bits, while other bits are placed on the bidirectional data bus and latched in the address-time channel prior to the flow of data occurring in the data-time channel. Since no data flow can occur until the target address has been set up, the data bus is available for the flow of other information during this period, and the addition of a cheap, off-chip latch to capture this information effectively increases the pin-count of the device. Processors employing such a scheme usually provide a latching signal that is available on a dedicated timing pin; it is necessary only to connect this timing signal directly to the latch WRITE line, no external decoding is required.

Examples of Multiplexed Machines

The fully multiplexed address subsystem employed in the Intel 8008 is shown in Fig. 10-1. All address information appears on the data bus at the beginning of each cycle and is latched for presentation to memory.

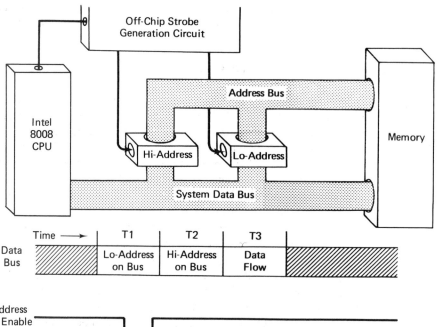

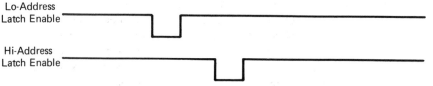

Figure 10-1

The timing signals are not available directly off the chip, and were derived in an earlier chapter. A straightforward extension of the use of the data bus for supplying address information occurs in the National Semiconductor PACE microprocessor. This device is a P-MOS monolithic microprocessor with a 16-bit address bus. The use of a separate 16-bit address bus along with the 16-bit data bus in a 40-pin package is too costly, and an off-chip address latch must be provided. The full 16-bit address appears on the data bus at the beginning of each cycle and must be latched at this time. The basic scheme is shown in Fig. 10-2. Either edge of the active LOW address strobe, that is available at

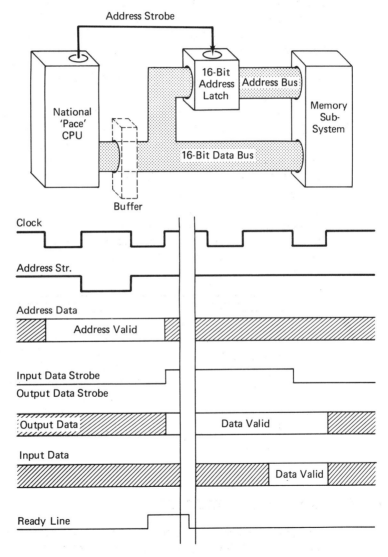

Figure 10-2

one of the 40 pins, can be used to latch the address at the proper time. The interpretation of the data appearing on the data bus is always time-dependent in multiplexed systems, and the different time slots are shown for the PACE microprocessor, relative to the system clock. All transactions consist of an address output interval followed by a data transfer interval. The presence of the address strobe timing pulse coming out of the processor reduces the design of this subsystem to the level, "connect point A to point B!"

Similar strobes are available for data flows to and from the addressed subsystem. The INPUT DATA STROBE (IDS) can be used to gate data from the target subsystem into the CPU. The data must be valid when the IDS goes LOW. Setup and hold times are indicated in Fig. 10-2 and specified in the PACE data sheets. The trailing edge of the OUTPUT DATA STROBE (ODS) can be used directly to latch data into the addressed target location. A separate ready line can extend the basic cycle for an integral number of clock cycles, thus giving the CPU the ability to WAIT for slow data sources.

The Intersil IM 6100 is a C-MOS 12-bit monolithic microprocessor with an architecture almost identical to that of the Digital Equipment Corporation PDP-8 minicomputer. The addressing circuitry is shown in Fig. 10-3 to be functionally identical to the PACE system described above. The 12 bits appear on the bus and are latched directly, using the address strobe labeled LXMAR (Load EXternal Memory Address Register). The memory select line used to enable the memory and the WRITE timing pulse used to write data into memory are also shown.

Other examples of multiplexed address presentation systems are given in the following sections. Several of these schemes are used in "paged" machines, and this concept will now be developed.

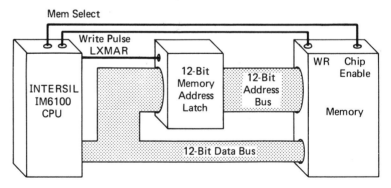

Figure 10-3

"PAGED" ADDRESSING STRUCTURES

Addressing structures of this form lend themselves well to "paged" address systems in the following sense: The number of bits of information for the description of any system determine the resolution, i.e., the size of the smallest element into which the system can be resolved. Thus, the high-order bits alone divide any memory system into gross elements called "pages." The increase in resolution accompanying the addition of low-order or "less significant"bits divides these pages into finer elements called *words*. The maximum resolution is into *bits* where the basic word size determines how many address bits are needed to acheive maximum resolution; for example, three address bits allow selection of any element of an 8-bit word.

Paged addressing schemes are provided as an economical means of achieving direct addressing, defined as the mode in which the address of the target location is contained *within* the instruction. The use of direct addressing removes the need to manipulate memory-data pointer registers and results in increased convenience. Hence, programmer efficiency also increases. The need to store (and retrieve) the full address with each memory reference instruction is obviated by fixing the high-order address bits in an appropriate latch and allowing these to remain unchanged for the duration of several instruction executions. Instructions that work on a given page then require only that the low-order bits that select the target *word* on the page be included for directly addressing this word.

The use of a paged address structure depends upon the internal architecture and cannot always be inferred from a study of the address presentation subsystem, as will become clear from a consideration of the next three systems. The MOSTEK MK 5065P is a P-MOS 8-bit microprocessor with paged addressing. As shown in the timing diagrams in Fig. 10-4, the 16-bit address is present at the beginning of each cycle: eight bits on the HIGH bus and eight bits on the LOW bus or DATA bus. The LOW-bus data are inverted in the output mode and should be latched into an inverting latch. The HIGH-bus data will be retained in the CPU as long as execution continues on the same page; however, the bus will go into a HIGH impedance mode after the trailing edge of the state strobe pulse; therefore, the HIGH-bus data must also be captured in a (non-inverting) latch for presentation to the memory subsystem. The strobe signals for latching the address data are generated by ANDing the active low MEMORY ACCESS COMMAND ($\overline{\text{MAC}}$) that is available from the CPU chip with the active low STATE STROBE pulse that is derived off-chip from the system clock. The subsystem and timing diagrams are shown in Fig. 10-4 for the 5065P. The 5056P uses paged mode addressing in that instructions stored in memory contain eight bits of opcode followed by eight bits of address. The address bits directly select one of 256 words on the same page as the instruction is located. The page can be changed by using indirect addressing that will be discussed later in this chapter.

Although the address presentation subsystem of the 5065P and that of the following microprocessor are very similar in appearance, the data flow and timing for the two systems differ considerably. (See Figs. 10-5 and 10-6.) The RCA COS/MAC is an 8-bit CMOS microprocessor with an 8-bit address bus and an 8-bit bidirectional data bus. The address is multiplexed over the address bus in two bytes, as shown in the address bus timing diagram. The HIGH address appears first and is latched into the page select latch, using the available timing

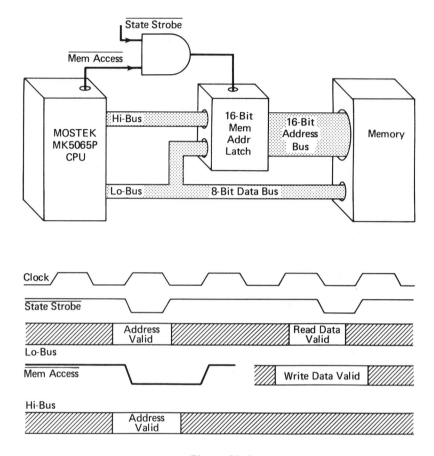

Figure 10-4

pulse T_A. This address then disappears and is replaced by the LOW-address byte that remains stable for the remainder of the cycle, thus obviating the need for an external LOW-address latch. The data then appears on the data bus and can be captured by using another directly available timing pulse T_B. The WRITE pulse, also available on the chip, may be used for writing data into memory.

The COS/MAC memory reference instructions are not paged; however, all transfer of control instructions, or branches, uses 8-bit displacement addresses and can be classified as paged mode addressing. The general addressing scheme for the COSMAC will be considered in a later chapter.

The Motorola M6800 N-MOS microprocessor utilizes paged mode addressing although there is no indication of this in the external addressing subsystem. This system consists of 16 address lines directly available from the 40-pin pack-

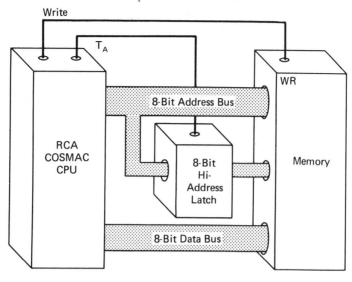

Figure 10-5

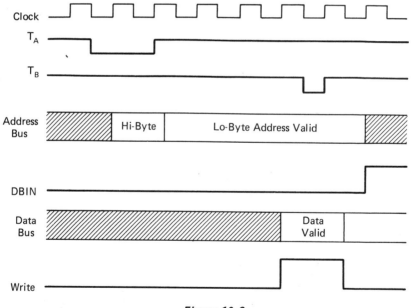

Figure 10-6

age. The interface to memory is straightforward, as shown in Figs. 10-7 and 10-8.

During ϕ_1, the address lines, R/W line and Valid Memory Address (VMA) line, are active, and during ϕ_2, data are transferred between the CPU and external subsystems. The READ cycle timing shown requires data input to the

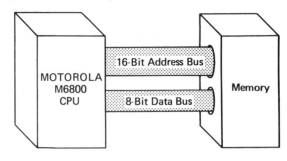

Figure 10-7

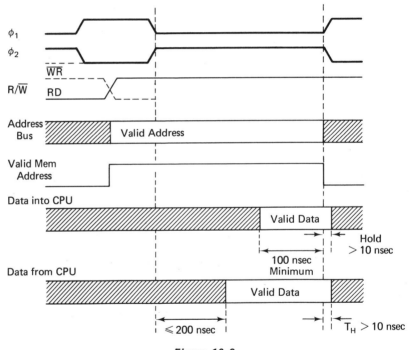

Figure 10-8

CPU to be valid 100 nsec prior to the trailing edge of ϕ_2 and held at least 10 nsec past this time. Data from the CPU appear within 200 nsec of the leading edge of ϕ_2 and remain valid for at least 10 nsec past the trailing edge of ϕ_2.

The 16 address lines coming from the chip do not visibly distinguish between high-order (page) bits and low-order (word) address bits. Internal circuitry, however, allows several modes in which 8 low-order address bits contained in the instruction can select any word on a 256-word page. The page location can be determined in a variety of ways, as indicated by appropriate bits in the instruction opcode. Various modes will be discussed later in this chapter.

DIRECT ADDRESSING

The source of the address bits supplied to memory is termed the Memory Address Register (MAR) and can be located within the CPU, external to the CPU, or a combination of the two. The simplest conceptual addressing scheme is direct addressing in which the location of the operand is contained in the instruction proper. The opcode specifies the operation to be performed, and the direct address specifies the location of the target, usually either a source or destination register. The address is normally fetched into the CPU along with the instruction, and in the most straightforward case is simply loaded into the

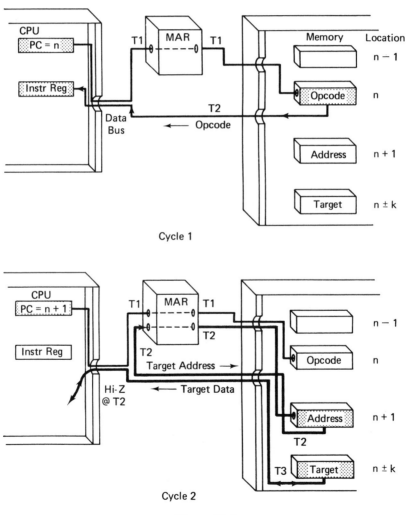

Figure 10-9

MAR. If the fetched address is to be modified in any fashion, this modification is performed in the CPU and the modified address is then loaded into the MAR.

An interesting and efficient approach to direct addressing is found in the General Instruments CP-1600. The CP-1600 has a 16-line data bus over which all addresses are multiplexed. The program counter is output at the beginning of each instruction fetch cycle, and the opcode is fetched into the CPU as shown in Fig. 10-9. The direct address is contained in the 2-byte word following the opcode, and this address is used to select the operand. The CP-1600 does no address modification and utilizes an external memory address register, thus eliminating any need to fetch the direct address into the CPU. Rather than simply inputting the 16-bit address on the address-fetch cycle and then outputting it on the following data-fetch (or data-store) cycle, the same result is achieved via the use of an (encoded) control signal ($BC_1 = 1/BC_2 = \phi/BDIR = \phi$). This state signal is used to latch the address data appearing on the data bus from memory into the memory address register, completely bypassing the CPU. The signal is activated during all instructions that specify direct addressing. The CP-1600 data bus is placed in the HIGH impedance state during this portion of the cycle.

During cycle 1, the program counter is used to fetch the opcode stored at location M in memory. This is decoded and determined to be a direct addressing instruction. PC + 1 is then sent to the MAR and the control lines are activated. The CPU data bus floats, the address contained in location M + 1 is placed on the memory data bus and latched into the MAR. This address is then used to address the target location.

The timing diagram for the CP-1600, shown in Fig. 10-10, relates the condition of the state signals (used to control the data bus flow) to the data bus and the clock. These three signal lines (BC1, BC2, BDIR) are exactly analogous to the 8008 state signals, and can be directly decoded, using a 1-of-8 decoder.

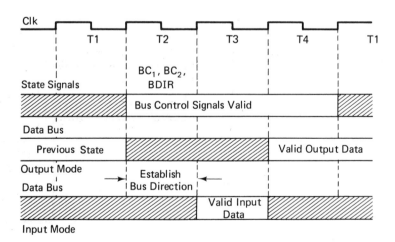

Figure 10-10

They are treated in Chapter 11 on I/O structures and in the section on Interrupt mechanisms. Also, like the 8008 (and most other processors), the CP-1600 possesses a READY line for extending data fetch cycles with slow memories or I/O. Unlike the 8008, the 1600 WAIT state stops the internal clocks and cannot be of indefinite duration because the dynamic CPU registers will lose data in 40 μsec.

SUBSYSTEM SELECTION

The Intel 8080 Addressing Structure

The memory subsystem has been divided into pages, words, and bits by increasing the resolution of the address. The same scheme can be applied to the entire system by specifying "higher-order" subsystem select bits. The two cycle code bits placed on the 8008 bus at time T_2 distinguished between READ, WRITE, and I/O subsystems. The use of this scheme has been retained in Intel's second-generation 8080 CPU in the form of status information placed on the data bus at the same time the address appears on the address bus. The (internally decoded) bits divide the total system into MEMORY, INPUT, OUTPUT, INTERRUPT, and STACK subsystems, as shown in Fig. 10-11. The inclusion of subsystems' select bits in the addressing mechanism expands the address space of the system. Shown in Fig. 10-12, for comparison, are the address spaces of the Intel 8080 and the Motorola 6800.

I/O ports are treated as memory locations in the Motorola 6800 and the National PACE in the sense that no special signals are generated to distinguish the I/O subsystem from the memory. There are, in fact, no input or output instructions in these processors, and the 16-bit address placed on the bus is decoded by memory and the I/O system to determine the appropriate target location. Any system with I/O instructions can be used in the memory-mapped

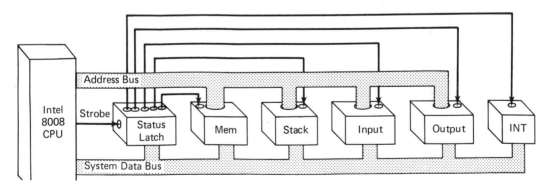

Figure 10-11

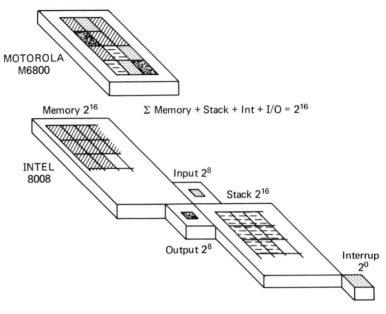

Figure 10-12

I/O mode simply by disregarding the I/O subsystem select signals and utilizing only the address appearing on the address bus at the beginning of each cycle. The Intel 8080 is shown in Fig. 10-13. Only the memory and the input system are shown for simplicity.

In the 8080 system there are three primary signals used by the CPU:

1. the subsystem select information (MEMRD, INPUT)

2. the target location information (ADDRESS)

3. the timing information (DBIN)

The operation of a data input to the CPU begins by placing the subsystem select *and* the target location information on the data and address busses, respectively. The address is automatically latched in the 8080, and the 8080 supplies a status strobe (SYNC) signal to latch the subsystem select bits into an external latch. This total address then selects the appropriate word in the appropriate subsystem. Following the address presentation to the system, the 8080 generates a timing signal, Data Bus IN (DBIN), that tells the selected subsystem to gate the data onto the data bus. (See Fig. 10-14.) It is the combination of the subsystem select bit and the timing signal that causes the appropriate system to leave the high-impedance mode and place the data on the bus. Note that the timing signal runs to all possible sources of data. Each source must have at least two enable lines, one for the timing pulse and another for the subsystem select line.

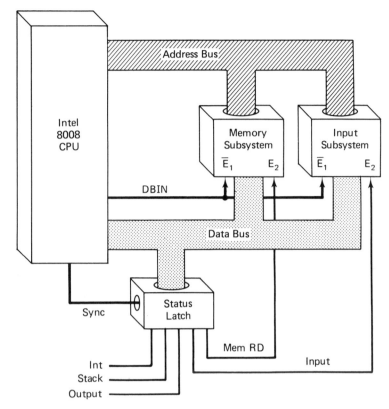

Figure 10-13

"Memory Mapped I/O"

The system described above employed the subsystem select lines that were provided by the CPU at the beginning of each cycle. An alternate scheme would utilize the address information appearing on the address bus at the beginning of each cycle. We treat the simplest case in which the memory subsystem contains less than 2^{15} words and, therefore, does not require the 16th address bit, A_{15}. This bit can then be used to choose between the memory and the input subsystem, as shown in Fig. 10-15.

Although the example shown used only one address line, A_{15}, for subsystem selection, the scheme can be expanded so that any number of address lines can be employed to select subsystems. In systems with very small memory space (and a correspondingly large number of unused address lines), this scheme is very feasible. For systems with large memory space, the use of this scheme requires external decoding of the address lines and is thus less practical. For large systems, the use of input and output instructions is to be preferred.

In addition to the simplicity of the memory-mapped I/O in small systems

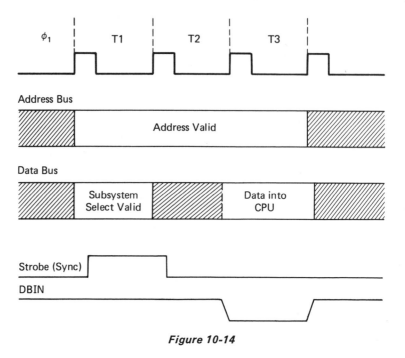

Figure 10-14

there are advantages to using memory reference instructions rather than I/O instructions. Generally, as in the 8008 and the 8080, the input instructions merely load the target data into the accumulator. Instructions that reference memory have much more flexible data-handling capabilities. Consider the following instructions, where it is assumed that the address stored in the memory data pointer (H-L) in the 8080 is that of an input port.

ADD	M	ADD the data from the input port to the accumulator
ANA	M	AND the data from the input port to the accumulator
ORA	M	OR the data from the input port to the accumulator
XRA	M	XOR the data from the input port to the accumulator
MOV	B,M	Load the data from the input port into the B register

These instructions are to be contrasted with the INPUT instruction that loads the data from the input port into the accumulator. Just as the presentation of memory addresses varied from processor to processor, the presentation of the subsystem select bits also varies. The Intel 8080 multiplexes these bits onto the address bus at the beginning of each cycle where they are latched and function as very high-order address bits. Some processors bring these select bits to separate pins on the package. The Intersil IM-6100 uses one pin for memory select (MEMSEL) and another for I/O device selection (DEVSEL) along with a couple of special-purpose selection lines (SWSEL) and (CPSEL). The RCA

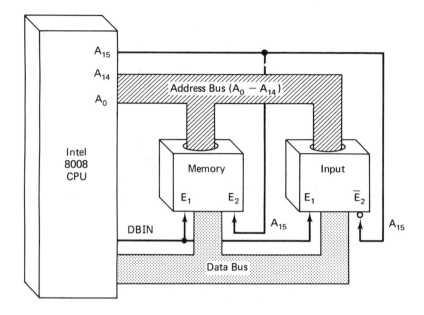

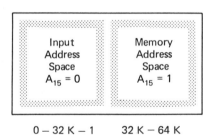

Figure 10-15

COSMAC utilizes two coded status lines similar to the 8008. These lines are decoded and used to select the various subsystems. Separate memory READ and memory WRITE lines are also employed and are available from the package. The MOSTEK 5065P uses a Memory Access Command (MAC) line and a Peripheral Exchange SYnchronization (PESY) line to distinguish between Memory and I/O. The detailed operation of these systems will be considered in a later chapter. The point to be noted here is that the subsystem select bits are conceptually equivalent to the addition of higher-order address bits, and the presentation mechanisms vary from multiplexing and latching these bits (INTEL 8080) to presentation of these bits in coded form (8008), presentation of the decoded bits (IM 1600), a combination of the above (COSMAC and 5065P), to the total absence of these bits and the inclusion of all possible target locations in the basic address space of the system as the M6800, PACE, and CP-1600 microprocessors. We also point out here that almost all microprocessors dedicate separate lines to selection and control of the interrupt subsystem. These systems will also be treated in a later chapter.

BUS PROTOCOL

The availability of low-power, inexpensive processing chips has resulted in increased activity in the field of multiprocessors and polyprocessors. Although there are many possible configurations in which processors can be connected, the connecting busses vary little from one configuration to another.

In uniprocessor systems, the processor is normally considered to be in full control of the bus, and peripheral devices request the use of the bus from the processor. Multi-and polyprocessor systems normally assume that the bus is busy and require each processor to generate a bus request signal and wait for an acknowledgment before proceeding. The P-MOS SC/MP microprocessor possesses a bus-oriented addressing structure. The P-MOS SC/MP, manufactured by National Semiconductor Corporation, has a 16-bit program counter and three 16-bit pointers, but only a 12-bit memory address register and on-chip address latch. In applications requiring more than 4K addressability, the address strobe can be used to latch the four high-order address bits $(A_{12}-A_{15})$ that are multiplexed over the 8-bit data bus during the first part of each cycle. The remaining four data bits are used for status flags in the fashion of the Intel 8080 status information. The scheme is illustrated in Fig. 10-16.

Each transfer of data to or from the CPU is termed a data I/O cycle. The CPU issues a bus request signal, as described in the DMA chapter and the final chapter, and maintains the address bus, data bus, and READ and WRITE

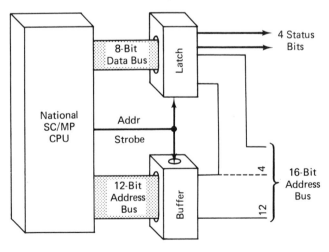

Figure 10-16

strobe lines in the high-impedance mode until the request is granted. The processor then places the address on the address bus, the four most significant address bits and the four status bits on the data bus, and activates the address strobe that can be used to clock external latches. The READ cycle timing is shown in Fig. 10-17. The WRITE cycle timing is similar.

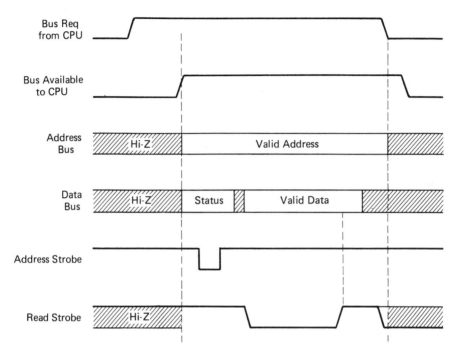

Figure 10-17

The four status bits appearing on the data bus are:

1. READ cycle flag
2. OPCODE FETCH flag
3. DELAY flag
4. HALT flag

The first two flags are similar to others that have been treated, and the last two flags are discussed in the SC/MP section of the I/O and Interrupt chapters.

The Toshiba TLCS-12 Bus Protocol

The Toshiba TLCS-12 is a 12-bit P-MOS microprocessor that features a completely asynchronous bus. The use of the bus is always in a "handshaking" mode, i.e., the CPU announces an event and waits for an acknowledgment from

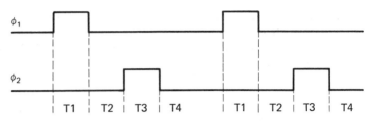

Figure 10-18

the appropriate device, either memory or I/O, before proceeding to the next state. The internal clock scheme is shown in Fig. 10-18.

During T_1 the results of the preceding cycle are latched into the internal registers. The microprogram branch control information is set up during T_2. The control word is fetched during T_3 and executed during T_4. If the cycle requires the use of the external bus, the clock is stopped in the T_4 phase. It is restarted by raising the ACKnowledge (ACK) line on the CPU chip. The external devices are informed of the bus status via two control lines, C_1 and C_2.

These lines rise to indicate that the address of an external device (memory or I/O) is available on the bus. The receiving device raises the ACK line to acknowledge receipt of the address. The CPU is then free to remove the address from the bus. The data flow between the CPU and the addressed location is also directed by C_1 and C_2. If C_2 drops while C_1 remains HIGH, the device is requested to place data on the bus to be input to the CPU. If C_1 drops while C_2 remains HIGH, the device is advised that the CPU has placed output data on the bus. In either of these situations, the change in the control line is keyed to the appropriate response from the acknowledge lines. The return of C_1 and C_2 to the LQW state signals the end of a data transfer and the device releases the bus. An example of this handshaking bus control is reproduced in Fig. 10-19.

The Harvard Architecture of the Rockwell PPS-8

The original memory scheme on the first computer built at Harvard, and called the Harvard architecture, employs separate memories for instructions and for data. The increased flexibility obtained by storing both types of information in a common store was first employed by von Neumann at Princeton and is termed the Princeton architecture. The microprocessors treated to this point have employed Princeton architecture; however, several microprocessors, including the Intel 4004 and the Rockwell PPS-8, possess a Harvard architecture.

The addressing schemes discussed above all present an address to a subsystem followed by a data flow between the CPU and the addressed subsystem. Some processors utilize the data bus for multiplexing part of the address, while others make no use of the data bus during this period. The Rockwell PPS-8 utilizes

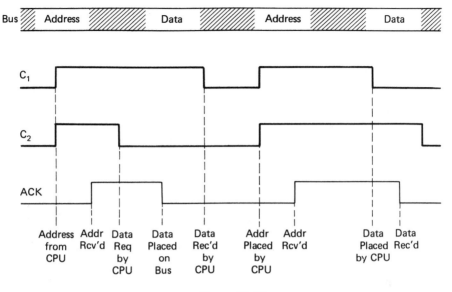

Figure 10-19

the address and data busses in an overlapping scheme based upon the separation of data and instructions. The instruction address appears on the address bus during T_2, and the instruction appears on the data bus during T_4. Also during T_4, the address of the target data location is placed on the address bus. During the next T_2 period, when the program counter is used to address the next instruction, the data bus is used for data flow between the CPU and the target location. The timing is shown in Fig. 10-20.

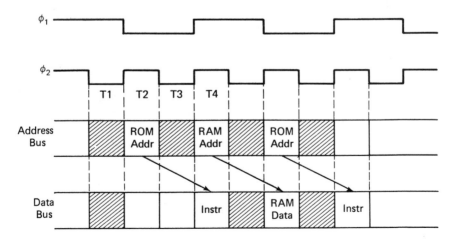

Figure 10-20

The Fairchild F-8 Addressing Structure

The addressing structures treated so far in this chapter have dealt primarily with the transfer of an address from the CPU to the target subsystem, usually the memory. Although many methods exist, they usually reduce to either a separate address bus or time multiplexing over another bus. The F-8 addressing structure is the first radical departure from these schemes. The F-8 utilizes a distributed architecture in which the addressing subsystem is separated from the CPU and physically located in the memory portion of the system. This has a number of consequences that influence the rest of the system design, both hardware and software.

If several *Program Storage Units* (PSU) are utilized with one CPU, each will contain its own addressing circuitry, making the F-8 impractical for large systems. In order to minimize the need for external RAM in small systems, the F-8 CPU includes 64 bytes of scratchpad memory in the chip itself. Thus, very small systems can be designed using only the CPU with 64 bytes of RAM and the PSU with 1000 bytes of ROM. The interconnections are shown in Fig. 10-21. By early 1977 both Fairchild and MOSTEK had produced a one-chip F-8 system, a microcomputer on a chip! The Fairchild version contained 1k ROM on the chip, while the MOSTEK version contained 2k ROM on one chip and sold for under $10 in large quantities. The number of transistors on one chip increased from 9500 for the two-chip F-8 to more than 18,000 for the one-chip version. The MOSTEK version operates with only +5 V.

In the 2-chip version, the five-line control bus is used to select addressing operations and other operations occurring with the PSU. The two timing

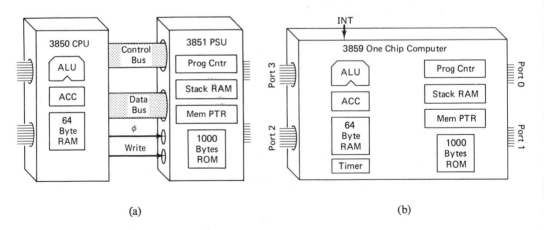

(a)   (b)

Figure 10-21

signals, ϕ and WRITE, synchronize the two chips. The 8-bit data bus carries instructions from ROM to the CPU and sends data to the address registers, I/O ports, or external RAM if used.

The control bus essentially replaces the 16 output lines necessary to send addresses to memory by five lines used to send addressing instructions to the local addressing subsystems. This immediately frees 11 pins on each chip, and these pins can then be used for other purposes. In the F-8 they are used for input/output ports as described in the chapter on I/O structures. This is consistent with optimal small systems design in that external decoders and latches are eliminated. The basic F-8 systems possess 32 I/O lines. In keeping with this minimal-parts-count goal, the devices work with a plug-in crystal or *RC* network, thereby eliminating the need for a clock chip.

The use of local addressing structures constrains the number of addressing modes, and the system operates in a fashion to minimize CPU/PSU address exchange. The address register can be loaded from dedicated bytes in the CPU register file and can be copied into these registers. The stack register serves as a one deep return address stack for interrupts or subroutine calls. This can be extended via software for multi-level calls, but such use is awkward and inefficient. The memory data pointer is used for memory reference instructions, similar to the H-L register in the Intel 8008. The F-8 pointer is auto-incrementing and, thus, eliminates the extra instruction often required for scanning a data field with such pointers.

ADDRESSING MODES

The addressing operation is the means by which a processor accesses a given register. This operation may be partitioned into address formation and address presentation operations. Preceding sections of this chapter have concentrated on address presentation mechanisms. The remainder of the chapter will consider address formation mechanisms, or addressing *modes*.

Associated with each operation of which an information processor is capable, there are generally two or more addresses: the address of the target data, or operand, and the address of the next operation to be performed. If the target data, or the result obtained by operating on this data, is to be moved from its source location, the address of the destination location must be specified. Any or all of these addresses can be implicit in the instruction and the hardware that executes the instruction. The address of the next operation is implicit in most processors. The operation specifications or instructions are stored in numerical sequence, and the instruction address register is then implemented in the form of a presetable counter. This *program counter* (PC) then traces out the locus of control of the program. If there are discontinuities in this sequence, the program counter can be preset or loaded with a new address. The address can be supplied by the instruction, as in a JUMP or CALL, or its location can be implicit as in a RETURN instruction in which the address of the next operation is located on top of a stack.

Immediate Addressing

The destination addresses are often implicit as seen in operations such as ADD (to accumulator) and PUSH (onto stack). An implicit addressing scheme that is sometimes considered a separate mode in itself is found in *immediate* data instructions. In this mode data are stored in the instruction stream and accessed by the program counter. This is often the most economical means of storage and retrieval of constant data such as numbers, ASCII characters, and masks. There is no need to provide explicit information about the location of the data. In essence, the data are fetched *with* the opcode. This occurs simultaneously in most 16-bit machines, and in consecutive fetches in many 8-bit CPUs. The economy of this scheme is shown in Fig. 10-22. Most instructions provide an address of, or pointer to, the operand. The immediate mode instruction supplies the operand itself, eliminating the pointer information.

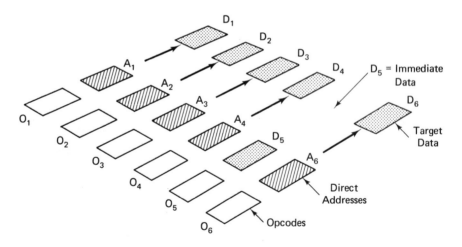

Figure 10-22

Direct Addressing and PC-Relative Addressing

The most primitive form of addressing is *direct* addressing in which the address of the target data is contained in each instruction, as shown above. If the address accompanying the opcode is capable of specifying *any possible* location in address space, it is called an *absolute* address. In most cases, this extreme range is not needed because the target data tend to be clustered. For clustered target locations, the address must range only over the cluster itself. Several addressing techniques have been devised for economically handling such data. These techniques can be made even more efficient by effort on the part of the designer to group the data.

Effort of this type falls under the general heading of "memory management." As a specific example of efficient memory management, consider sections of code with data grouped so that an operand is always within 128 locations of the operation specifying this data. Although the absolute address can contain 16 bits of address, the requirement in this case is only eight bits. Thus, by specifying the location of the operand *relative to that of the operation*, half of the absolute address can be eliminated. If this is a major addressing mode, the savings in memory required to hold operand addresses can be considerable. The scheme is illustrated in Fig. 10-23.

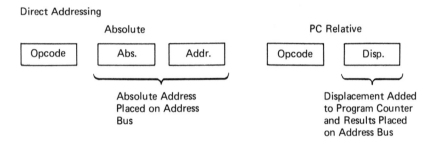

Figure 10-23

The program-counter relative addressing mode stores only the *difference* between the target location and the current operation location with each operation. This difference is then *added* to the program counter as a signed displacement, and the result is placed on the address bus and used to access the operand. Of all addressing modes in use, PC-relative addressing is probably the most effective at reducing memory costs and is often the simplest to implement. Note that the calculation of the relative displacement is performed by the assembler or language translator, and does not represent any additional effort on the part of the program designer. Many assemblers will flag out-of-bounds data so that they can be moved into reach of the economical mode. Otherwise, such data can be reached by either absolute addressing or some other addressing mode.

Base Page Addressing

Although much data can be located within reach of a given instruction, it is not at all uncommon to encounter programs with hundreds or thousands of instructions. In this case, instructions that can operate on the same operand can be located more than 512 locations apart, and it will be impossible to use relative addressing for *both* of the instructions. This occurs so often that another major addressing mode has been designed to access data efficiently from a variety of widely separated locations. This is achieved by directly addressing data stored in a segment of memory called a *page*. Pages are defined by holding high-order address bits constant and varying the low-order bits over all possible combinations. The high-order bits resolve memory into gross blocks called pages, and the low-order bits resolve each page into finer elements called words. The first page in memory is denoted by high-order address 00 . . . 0 and is called *page zero*. This is normally used as a place to store data that are accessed from many different locations. In 16-bit address space, the first page is usually the first 256 locations in memory. The ability to reach any word on this page with 8 bits of address is the basis for zero-page-mode addressing. An instruction that uses this mode contains only the 8-bit address. The memory address register is cleared, and this address is loaded into it. This technique is independent of the instruction location and, thus, allows *all* instructions in a program to access data from page zero with the economy of relative addressing.

Computed Addressing

The addressing methods discussed above allow access to a specified register that contains n bits of data. The basic word size ($n = 4, 8, 12, 16, . . .$) is the result of a number of compromises in which physical criteria assume an important role. Thus, machines are designed with basic word lengths that are often unrelated to the number of bits of information involved in specific applications. The inability of the hardware structure to handle data elements of certain lengths must be compensated by a software structure that will do so. This commonly occurring situation is usually resolved via the use of *register sequences* (hardware perspective) or *data fields* (software perspective). The addressing structure must then allow data in a given *field* to be accessed.

The addressing methods applied in this situation are generally classified as *computed* addressing techniques. The technique that is most often implemented in machines is that of *indexed* addressing. Operation on a field of data elements is preferably achieved via the use of a *field address* or *field name*, but must actually be achieved by operating on the basic n-bit data elements of which the field is composed. These elements can be individually accessed most effectively by using an *index* into the field, as shown in Fig. 10-24.

MULTI-FIELD INDICES

The routine that operates in the data field named FIELDNAME can use the indexed addressing mode in several ways. The index, or offset into the field, can be used to relate a data element with the corresponding element of another field. For example, a multi-byte number can be added to another multi-byte number, and the multi-byte result stored in a "result" field. In this procedure

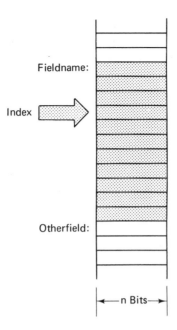

Figure 10-24

it is necessary that the fields be "aligned", i.e., byte three of the first argument should be added to byte three of the second argument, and the result stored in byte three of the sum. If each field name refers to the location of the first byte in the field, then the field names can be used with the index register to select the nth byte in each field.

Assume an instruction set that includes direct addressing operations: load accumulator (LDA), store accumulator (STA), and add to accumulator (ADD), all of which can refer to symbolic operands. The first byte of a multibyte addition can then be achieved by:

```
LDA          ARGUMENT 1
ADD          ARGUMENT 2
STA          RESULT
```

If these instructions can be used in the indexed addressing mode, each byte can be processed in the same manner as above. If the indexed mode is signified by the @ sign, then the following assembly language statements process the nth byte, where n is the contents of the index register:

```
LDA   @ ARGUMENT 1
ADD   @ ARGUMENT 2
STA   @ RESULT
```

The content of the index register is added to the direct operand address when @ specifies indexed addressing. It is this address that is placed in the memory address register and used to access the operand. The ability to specify any word in the data field via indexing is utilized in *scanning* the data fields by embedding the instruction sequence in a loop containing an "increment index register" instruction as follows.

```
.
.
.

STARTSCAN:
LDX ZERO              ; load zero into index register
CLR CARRY            ; clear the carry flag
SCAN:
LDA @ ARG 1          ; get byte
ADD @ ARG 2          ; add byte (with carry)
STA @ RESULT         ; store result byte
INX XREG             ; increment the index register
CPX LENGTH           ; compare length, in bytes, of field
                        to (XREG)
JMP (ZERO) TO SCAN   ; if finished, proceed, else scan
.                       next bytes.
.
.
.
```

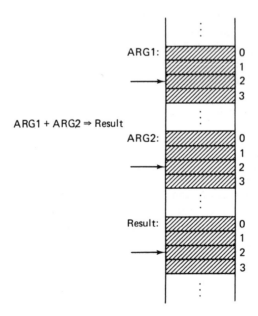

Figure 10-25

It is assumed that the ADD instruction is an "ADD with CARRY" that provides software carry propagation along a multi-byte numerical string. The bytes specified when $n = 2$ are shown in Fig. 10-25.

AUTO-INDICES

The above example illustrates a multi-field indexing operation in which the same index register contents are used to provide an offset into three different fields and then are incremented. Often only one field must be scanned and the index register incremented after each use. This can occur, for example, when an ASCII string is scanned for presentation to an I/O device. The increment operation can be combined with the use of the indexed addressing operation such that the index register contents increase by one each time the register is used. Such a register is said to be *auto-incrementing*. Auto-incrementing and auto-decrementing registers can be found in several microprocessors. The Intersil IM 6100 utilizes memory registers eight through fifteen for auto-increment operations. The Fairchild F-8 possesses an auto-increment/decrement register used for accessing data in a 64-byte scratchpad register file. The General Instruments CP-1600 possesses auto-increment addressing modes that will be described in a following section.

COMPUTED ADDRESSING; AN EXAMPLE

As an example of a "computed" address we consider an application utilizing an 80-character by 24-line cathode ray tube (CRT) display. If we wish to map each possible location in this two-dimensional (visual) array into a one-dimensional array (table) in memory space, it is necessary only to convert the ith character in the jth row (a_{ij}) into the $(80*j + i)$th element in the table (b_{80j+i}). This transformation is illustrated in Fig. 10-26.

The programmer can manipulate symbols in the memory "image" in terms of the visual image by transforming from one reference frame to the other. Although this can be accomplished with any complete instruction set, for simplicity we choose instructions from one of the first mini-/microprocessors, the Computer Automation ALPHA-LSI. The cell images will be stored in memory starting with line 1, character 1, and progressing through line 1, character 80; line 2, character 1; ... etc.

The displacement into the CELLSPACE can be obtained by calculating cell # = $(80*$line#$+$char#$)$. This can be readily achieved by using the ALPHA LSI multiply instruction that executes as follows.

The *multiply and add* (MPY) instruction multiplies the contents of the index register (X-REG) by the contents of the location addressed by the operand, and adds the contents of the accumulator (A-REG) to the product. The address

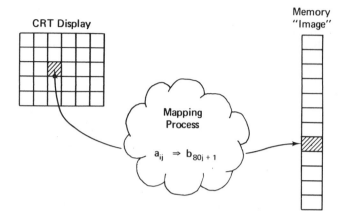

Figure 10-26

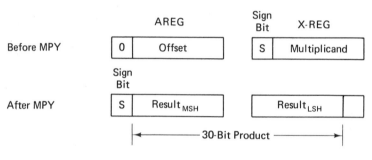

Figure 10-27

pointer can be direct or indirect and occupies the second word of the instruction in memory. The format for 16-bit registers is shown in Fig. 10-27.

The equation relating CELLSPACE address to line # and character # indicates that the character # may be loaded into the accumulator as an offset into the appropriate line and the number of lines placed in the XREG and multiplied by 80. This is easily achieved by

```
LDA CHAR #
LDX LINE  #
MPY EIGHTY
```

where EIGHTY has previously been equated to 80 via the appropriate meta-instruction. The product is displaced one bit to the left, but can be corrected by performing an arithmetic right shift on the index register. At this point the offset into the CELLSPACE table resides in the index register, and the indexed addressing mode can be used to retrieve the cell image from the table.

The ALPHA LSI, like the National PACE, has word and byte mode operations. In this example, the 16-bit word mode is used for computing the address, but the 8-bit mode is used for storing the image of each cell on the CRT screen. Thus, the accumulator is loaded with the *byte* (as specified by LDAB), using the contents of the index register (as specified by the modifier @) to point into the table that begins at the memory location named CELLSPACE. The complete code for this operation is:

```
        .
        .
        .

LDA  CHAR#          ; load character # as offset into line
LDX  LINE#          ; load line # as multiplicand
MPY  EIGHTY         ; multiply XREG by 80 and add AREG
ARX  1              ; shift index register (product) one bit right
LDAB @CELLSPACE     ; retrieve byte from CELLSPACE table
        .           ; using index register as pointer into table
        .
        .
        .
        .
        .
        .

CELLSPACE:          ; reserve 1920 bytes for cell images
DS 1920
        .
        .
        .
        .
        .
        .
        .
```

The above scheme allows the user to think and program in terms of lines and characters on the display screen, yet organize the memory map efficiently as sequential byte locations. An image in CELLSPACE can be updated by replacing the instruction

```
LOAD @ CELLSPACE
```

with the instructions

```
LDAB  NUCHAR
STAB  @CELLSPACE
```

that load the new character symbol into the accumulator and store it in the appropriate cell. The use of computed addresses often allows a transformation from a problem-oriented organization to a table-structured organization, and thereby enhances both programmer efficiency and memory management efficiency.

DATA-STRUCTURE/PROCEDURE EQUIVALENCE

An important concept in microprocessor systems design concerns the equivalence of procedures and data structures. These terms refer to the two major approaches to transformation processes and are most easily presented via the use of examples.

A procedure for calculating the value of the sine function of an argument, sin (x), is given by the series expansion;

$$\sin (x) = x - \frac{x^3}{3!} + \frac{x^5}{5!} - \frac{x^7}{7!} + \cdots$$

where the dots represent indefinite extension or "etc." This procedure can be structured so that each new term can be derived by one more iterations of the basic procedure, using the previous term as an input. Such procedures usually terminate when a "cut-off" point is reached, often based on the difference between successive results. The ability to iterate a relatively simple routine indefinitely by entering a loop with a conditional exit allows the determination of function values with arbitrary precision, using only a limited amount of storage space. The execution time, on the other hand, can be indefinitely long.

An alternate technique for obtaining the value of the sine function of a given argument consists in a "table look-up" method. In effect, the procedure has been executed in advance for a range of arguments and the results stored in tabular form. This technique eliminates the processing time required to obtain a given function value, but can require vast amounts of storage, depending upon the argument range and the accuracies required.

Although the sine function is chosen as a specific example to illustrate data-structure/procedural equivalence, these two approaches are universal and can be applied to any probiem. Most programs utilize procedures simply because time is cheaper than memory for most applications. When time constraints become critical, the addition of extra hardware or the conversion of procedural portions of the program into data structures should be considered by the designer. The two methods may be combined in some optimal fashion; for example, a table look-up or data structure can be augmented by an interpolation procedure. It is possible to go to the other extreme and replace *all* of the procedures with a "table-driven" system that corresponds to the application of a transformation matrix to the basic states of the system. This is seldom done in program-

mable processors, but represents an approach taken by using programmable
logic arrays. This treatment is beyond the scope of this text.

DATA STRUCTURES: INDIRECT AND MODIFIED INDIRECT ADDRESSING

The organization of data into tabular structures containing numerous entries
usually implies that a value needed at a certain point in a program is not known
at the time the program is written, but must be determined during program
execution. In this case, the address of the relevant data is unspecified and must
be *computed* during the execution of the program. In general, it is impractical
to modify the address bytes of an instruction, and impossible if the instructions
are in ROM. Thus, an intermediate or indirect addressing scheme must be
employed, as shown in Fig. 10-28.

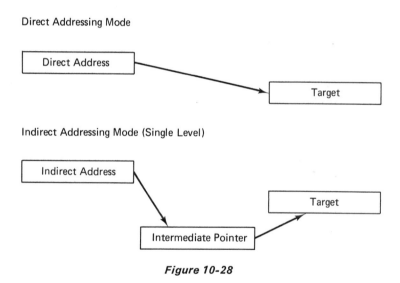

Direct Addressing Mode

Direct Address → Target

Indirect Addressing Mode (Single Level)

Indirect Address → Intermediate Pointer → Target

Figure 10-28

In this scheme, the address specified in the instruction is that of an intermediate location that will be loaded before use with the computed address of
the target data. During the execution of an instruction utilizing indirect addressing, the contents of the specified location are fetched into the memory address
register and used to access the target data. Note that the scheme can also be
used with control structures, i.e., the contents of the addressed location can be
fetched into the program counter and a transfer of control made to the instruction indicated by the intermediate pointer. This is usually termed *JUMP
INDIRECT*.

Although the illustration above shows only one intermediate location, it is possible to move indirectly through a series of such locations: Multi-level indirect addressing through an indefinite number of intermediate locations requires that a bit be dedicated to specify the end of this process. The MOSTEK MK 5065P microprocessor utilizes multi-level indirection. Many other microprocessors offer single-level indirect addressing modes, including the Signetics 2650, the Intersil IM 6100, the MOS Technology 650X processors, and the National PACE. The IM 6100 has only six bits of direct address and depends upon indirect addressing to reach operands that are out of the 6-bit range.

The use of *internal* pointers is technically indirect addressing; however, by convention, machines with *only* this indirect mode are said not to possess indirect addressing capability. The Intel 8080, RCA COSMAC, General Instruments CP-1600, Fairchild F-8, National SC/MP, and others possess such internal pointers.

The use of auto-incrementing pointers in the indirect mode occurs in the Intersil IM 6100 and the General Instruments CP-1600. The IM 6100 locations eight through fifteen are incremented by one and restored before being used to access the operand. This allows an indexing operation to be achieved through these eight pointers. Both auto-incrementing and auto-decrementing modes are available by using the CP-1600 internal memory pointers. These modes differ in that the incrementing registers are *post-increment*, while the decrementing pointers are *pre-decrement*. In addition to indexing operations, these provide the behavior necessary for maintaining a last-in-first-out buffer or stack.

Indirect Indexed Addressing

The two modes of computed addressing can be combined in one instruction. An intermediate register to provide an indirect path to target can be used with an index register whose contents are used to modify the target address, as shown in Fig. 10-29.

The indexing is used as described earlier in this chapter, i.e., indirection is generally employed whenever the user does not know the exact address during assembly time. This is often the case with general-purpose subroutines that operate on data that vary from one invocation to another. The two primary techniques of supplying data, or "passing parameters," to a subroutine consist of either (1) passing the data itself, via internal registers, stack storage, or other fixed locations, or (2) passing a *pointer* to the data. The second technique, that of using a pointer to the parameters, is readily achieved via the use of indirect addressing. This technique is especially valuable for handling parameters that vary in number from one call to the next. For example, a print routine to display messages should be able to handle variable-length messages. Prior to calling the routine, the user should load the intermediate register with a pointer to the

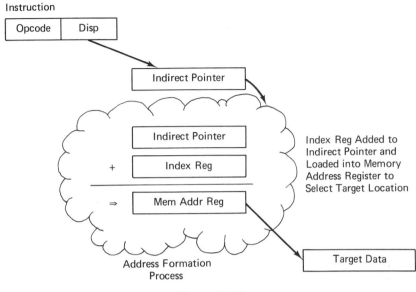

Figure 10-29

routine. Upon entry to the routine, the message bytes can be accessed by using indirection. The bytes can be accessed *in sequence* by using indirect indexed addressing. Auto-incrementing index registers are well suited to this mode of indirect addressing.

Indexed Indirect Addressing

Applications that utilize a data structure often contain a series of tables whose organization maintains a one-to-one correspondence between elements of two or more tables. The indexed indirect addressing mode is particularly well suited to such structures. The approach is useful when one of a number of arbitrarily located routines is to be selected as a response to an input. Such conditions occur in language translation, interrupt polling routines, and other application areas. The general scheme is outlined below.

A symbol is input from an input device or from a preceding software process. The symbol is to be used to determine program flow by selecting the control path. Although a procedural approach in the form of a generating polynomial, or some more exotic function, can be used to calculate the starting address of the appropriate routine, it is usually far simpler to use a data-structured approach in which a table of allowable inputs is scanned for a match. An index register can be incremented with each comparison so that the symbol that matches the input can be identified by its location in the sequence. Since the starting addresses of the various routines are usually unordered, an intermediate ordering is imposed via a sequential table of starting addresses that are put in one-to-one correspondence with the input symbol table. The index into the symbol table then serves also as an input into the *branch table* that contains the starting addresses. Thus, the use of a JUMP INDEXED, INDIRECT relative to the beginning of the branch table will transfer control to the appropriate routine. Both the procedural approach and the structural approach are illustrated in Fig. 10-30.

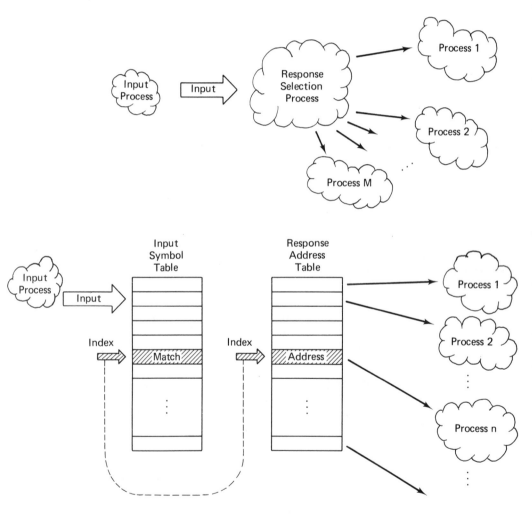

Figure 10-30

SUMMARY

Addressing mechanisms, both software address formation processes and hardware address presentation processes, while lacking glamour, provide the linkages that are basic to program structures consisting of discrete processes. The flow of control through a system is largely determined by the addressing mechanism and modes employed in the system. Although the topics treated throughout the rest of this book are presented in various ways, it is recommended that the reader attempt to frame these features in a generalized addressing context as a means of increasing coherence among the various structures.

11   I/O structures and techniques

Many processes require current information from, and interaction with, the "real world," i.e., the world external to the CPU/MEM system. An analog-to-digital converter can supply information concerning the voltage difference between two locations. A disc storage unit can return information associated with a key word that has been issued by the CPU. The maintenance and control of the information channels connecting the CPU to the external systems are accomplished via the Input/Output or I/O subsystems. Retrieval processes similar to those mentioned above often will require an access time of uncertain duration. Given no *a priori* assumptions about the information to be supplied to the CPU, there will be no way to distinguish random input data from the requested data. The source of information must, therefore, signal the CPU that the information is available. The CPU can either wait for this signal or can resume program execution following the request, with provision made for the signal to interrupt this execution when the information becomes available.

The general I/O structure associated with such processes is shown in Fig. 11-1.

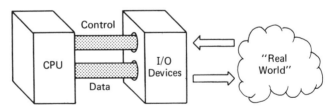

Figure 11-1

The control channel allows the CPU to request a transfer of data between the CPU and the selected device via the issuance of a command. The same channel allows the device to send status information to the CPU concerning the availability of requested resources. The data channel provides a data flow path between the CPU and the device.

An I/O Example: The Teletype™ Interface

An interface to a Teletype™ provides an example of several common I/O techniques. The teletype communicates asynchronously with the CPU, i.e., there is no common clock line connecting the CPU with the teletype. The use of teletypes for long-distance communication has led to serial transmission of information over one signal line rather than parallel transmission of *n*-bits by using *n*-lines.

ASYNCHRONOUS SERIAL COMMUNICATION

The desirability of minimizing the number of lines or space channels connecting teletypes has led to time multiplexing of the command channel and the data channel. The command to the teletype precedes the data flow and, therefore, allows the division of time into a command time-channel and a data time-channel, using only one signal line, as shown in Fig. 11-2.

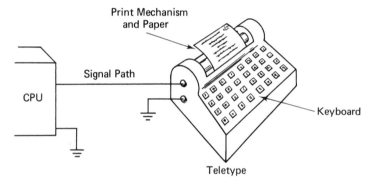

Figure 11-2

Timing and Framing

The signal path will normally be held **HIGH** and is continually monitored by the teletype. The CPU can issue a command to the teletype by pulling this line "low." This action announces to the teletype that a message is ready to be transmitted. The first bit of the message can also be LOW and, therefore, a means is needed to distinguish between the "start" command, which is transmitted as a LOW bit, and the first message bit, which can also be LOW. This is resolved via the use of the above-mentioned time-channels. Although there is no common clock in the system, there are two separate clocks—one in the CPU and one in the teletype—and these clocks are assumed to be calibrated but unsynchronized. The receipt of the LOW-going signal on the signal line starts the teletype clock, i.e., provides a synchronization signal. The clocks then provide a basic time interval (9.1 msec) that defines the command time-channel. The line is held down for 9.1 msec, and then the data time-channel begins. The line can be sampled again after this interval, and the first bit of data recovered. The data time-channel is subdivided into eight time slots, and the clocks are used to send and receive the serial data bit by bit. At the end of the data transmission the command time-channel is once more employed to close the transmission via the use of "stop-bits." These effectively bring the line HIGH so that the occurrence of a following "start" command can be detected, since the HIGH-to-LOW transition that initiates the sequence would not exist if the start command immediately followed a LOW data bit.

The serial I/O timing is shown in Fig. 11-3.

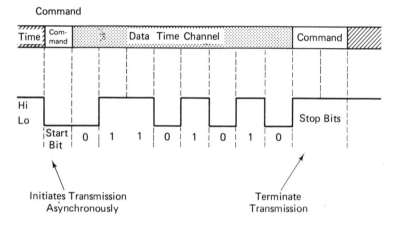

Figure 11-3

The advantages of standardization have led to the acceptance of the ASCII code (American Standard Code for Information Interchange) for communication with teletypes and many other devices. A portion of the code is shown here with its equivalent hexadecimal representation:

20	SP	30	0	40	@	50	P
21	!	31	1	41	A	51	Q
22	''	32	2	42	B	52	R
23	#	33	3	43	C	53	S
24	$	34	4	44	D	54	T
25	%	35	5	45	E	55	U
26	&	36	6	46	F	56	V
27	'	37	7	47	G	57	W

28	(	38	8	48	H	58	X
29	)	39	9	49	I	59	Y
2A	*	3A	:	4A	J	5A	Z
2B	+	3B	;	4B	K	5B	[
2C	'	3C	<	4C	L	5C	\
2D	–	3D	=	4D	M	5D	]
2E	.	3E	>	4E	N	5E	↑
2F	/	3F	?	4F	O	5F	←

The following example illustrates a serial I/O facility for teletype communications. Since the output data path is eight bits wide, we will use only one bit of an output port (say port 3, bit 0) and assume that a signal line runs from this location to the teletype. The flow graph for this process is shown in Fig. 11-4.

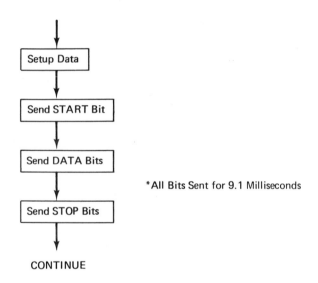

*All Bits Sent for 9.1 Milliseconds

Figure 11-4   *All bits sent for 9.1 msec*

A SOFTWARE DESIGN

We will partition the problem into a transmission segment and a timing segment. The process by which the 11 bits are sent will not change, only the bits will vary. This implies a loop, since a process should not be repeatedly encoded 11 times, and a counter that can be tested for exiting the loop. The Intel 8080 will be used for this example. Only one new instruction is used, STC, that sets (to 1) the carry bit. The data will be loaded into the A register (accumulator), and the B-register will be used to hold the count of 11. For convenience, the description of the rotate instructions is repeated in Fig. 11-5.

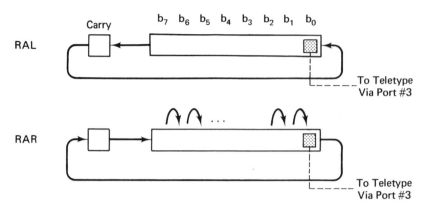

Figure 11-5

BEGIN:	MVI A, 'A'	; load ASCII 'A' into the accumulator
	MVI B, 11	; load the counter
	ORA A	; clear the carry bit
	RAL	; move carry ($=\phi$) into bit ϕ position
NEXTBIT:	OUT 3	; output bit ϕ of ACC to the teletype
	CALL DELAY	; delay for 9.1 msec
	RAR	; move next bit into bit ϕ position
	STC	; set the carry to '1'
	DCR B	; count down
	JNZ NEXTBIT	; send next bit until eleven sent

.
.
.
.
.
.

; continue

The program can be seen to generate a start bit by OR'ing the accumulator with itself. This bit-by-bit operation cannot produce a carry; therefore, the carry flag is reset to zero by this use of the ALU. The contents of A are unchanged (A OR A = A) and, therefore, the ASCII 'A' still resides in the ACCUMULA-TOR. The low carry bit is then rotated into the bit ϕ position and output to port 3. This drives the line connected to bit ϕ of port 3 low and signals to the teletype the start of a transmission. The CPU then delays 9.1 msec, rotates the first data bit into position, and repeats the above operation. The transmitted bits are rotated into the carry and set high to provide stop bits, since these are shifted into the high-order accumulator position with each RAR operation.

When 11 bits have been sent, the counter reaches zero and the loop is exited. Program execution continues from this point.

Software Delay Loops

In the teletype driver routine it is necessary to delay for 9.1 msec between bit transmission. The simplest means of providing exactly timed delays consists of loading a given number into a register and subtracting 1s from this number until zero is reached. The following code

```
                  .
                  .
                  .
                  .
            MVI  C, 250
LOOP:       DCR  C
            JNZ  LOOP
                  .
                  .
                  .
                  .
```

inserted in a program will load the C register with the number 250 and then proceed to execute the next two instructions 250 times before exiting the loop. By referring to the 8080 information manuals, we find (using a 2-MHz clock) that the decrement instruction executes in 2.5 μsec and the conditional jump instruction requires 5 μsec. Thus, one traversal of the loop takes 7.5 μsec and 250 loops will delay 1.875 msec before proceeding.

The longest delay, using register C, would loop 255 times, but this would still fall short of the desired 9.1-msec delay. Time-consuming statements can be included in the loop without affecting data. (Most processors provide NOP statements that literally execute no operation on data.) Several loops can be written in sequence and, thus, an additive delay achieved. This is impractical for larger delays; however, it suggests a solution. Repeated sequences can be encoded as loops; thus, the repeated delay loops can be written as one loop (Fig. 11-6) within a larger loop as follows:

```
      .
      .
      .
ENTEROUTLOOP:
MVI  D, 250
ENTERINLOOP:
MVI  C, 250
;
```

```
INLOOP:
DCR  C
EXITINLOOP:
JNZ INLOOP

;
DCR  D
EXITOUTLOOP:
JNZ  ENTERINLOOP
    .
    .
```

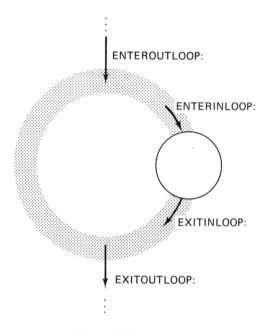

Figure 11-6

The above sequence is multiplicative rather than additive and results in a delay proportional to the number of times around the outer loop. This technique can be extended to any number of nested loops and readily provides large delays. The time resolution, however, is determined by the delay of the inner loop and cannot readily yield delays accurate to within a few tens of microseconds. If the large delays provided by nested delay loops are too gross, they may be followed by a single loop that adds a fine increment to the large delay. The 9.1-msec delay can be approximately achieved by using 200 in the inner loop counter and 6 in the outer loop counter. The delay routine would then be followed by a return statement to return to the calling program.

A HARDWARE DESIGN: UARTS

The hardware/software equivalence principle indicates that is would be possible to perform the above operations in hardware, and the almost universal requirement of teletype/computer interfaces indicates that a sufficient market exists to justify the development of special-purpose chips to perform this function. Several manufacturers produce such interface chips, which are generally referred to as UARTs (for Universal Asynchronous Receiver Transmitters) or USARTs if they include a synchronous operating mode. These devices accept parallel data, append start bits and parity bits, and transmit the data serially to a teletype or to another UART. In the receive mode they strip the start bits, check the parity bit, look for stop bits, and generate a "data received" signal that can be used to signal the processor. The term "universal" refers to the fact that UARTs can work with 5-, 6-, 7-, or 8-bit data, even or odd parity, 1, $1\frac{1}{2}$, or 2 stop bits, and several other optional modes. Most UARTs use a clock 16 or 64 times the frequency of the bit rate, thus dividing each bit time-slot into many subslots. This allows the UART to ignore false start bits caused by short duration noise pulses. The HIGH-to-LOW transition starts a counter that delays one-half of a bit time period and then samples the signal line. The transient noise pulse is assumed to have vanished; thus, if the signal line is still low, a valid start bit is assumed. The clock then recycles and counts a full bit period, reaching the middle of the first data bit time slot and sampling the signal line. This is repeated for the remainder of the bits. For simplicity, we now, repartition our system as follows: the CPU/device interface is considered to occur between the output port and the UART, i.e., the UART is considered part of the teletype, as in Fig. 11-7.

The accumulator data is then transmitted to the teletype merely by executing an OUTPUT instruction to the proper port. The cost associated with this is the UART and the extra seven lines. The primary benefit lies in the improved utilization of the CPU: it may now do useful, complex processing while the dedicated hardware performs the simple timing and shift operations and frames the data.

If there are many characters to be transmitted, the CPU timing must be matched to the teletype timing. Microprocessors can output from 10,000 to 100,000 characters per second, whereas teletypes can print only 10 characters per second. The CPU can output a byte and then enter a timeout loop; however, this defeats the purpose of the UART. Useful work can be done following a character output, and the CPU can periodically check to determine whether the teletype has completed printing the last character. Most external devices possess status lines that indicate whether the device is "busy" (i.e., responding to the last command) or "done." By monitoring the status line periodically, the processor

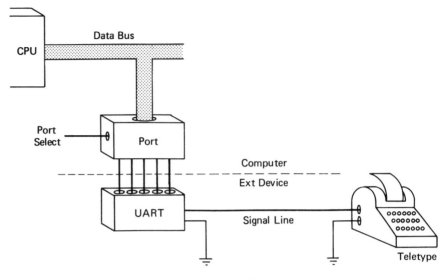

Figure 11-7

can accomplish useful work at its own rate and still drive the teletype at full speed. In the case of the UART, there is a "Buffer Empty" flag signalling the fact that the 8-bit data word deposited by the CPU has been dressed and serially shipped out to the receiving device. The buffer can then be loaded by the CPU with the next character to be transmitted.

Assume in the following that the "Buffer Empty" line is tied to bit 2 of input port 2 and that the CPU has finished processing and is simply waiting for the teletype to finish printing the last character before sending the next character.

A STATUS "FILTER": MASKS

The Intel 8080 code that will check the status bit is:

```
        .
        .
        .

LOOP:
INPUT 2        ; get status from port 2
ANDI  4        ; mask off other bits
JNZ LOOP       ; jump if not zero
        .
        .
        .
```

The first instruction loads the contents of port 2 into the accumulator,

$$\boxed{b_7 b_6 b_5 b_4 b_3 b_2 b_1 b_0}$$

and the second instruction performs a logical AND of the data in the accumulator with the number four:

The Accumulator	b_7	b_6	b_5	b_4	b_3	b_2	b_1	b_0
ANDed with	0	0	0	0	0	1	0	0
yields:	0	0	0	0	0	b_2	0	0

The AND is performed in the Arithmetic-Logic Unit and the result sets the condition flip-flops. It is seen that, depending upon the state of bit 2, the result is either zero or nonzero; thus, by checking the entire word via the zero flag, we can determine the state of bit 2. If the bit is set, the CPU proceeds to output the next character; otherwise, it loops back and tests the bit again.

The above routine illustrates a very common technique used to isolate and test individual bits in machines that do not possess bit-testing instructions. Use is made of an appropriate constant to filter out unwanted bits and pass only the bits of interest. The constant word is usually termed a *mask* and the process is termed a *masking* operation. Whereas the transmission of data from the CPU to the teletype could have been achieved via a known time delay, this is impractical in many cases. Assume that a "conversational" program has finished executing a command and has printed a "prompt" message asking the user to enter another command via the teletype. The user can respond in a second or an hour; thus, the use of a time delay is clearly inappropriate. The existence of a DATA READY status line that the CPU can monitor allows the CPU to wait in the above loop until the user enters data. The CPU then falls through the WAIT LOOP and inputs the data from the data port. In this example the information will then be processed to analyze the command.

Before proceeding to other topics, we illustrate another means of bit-testing. Let bit zero of input port three be the determinant in a wait loop. The following code will "fall through" the loop when bit zero goes high:

```
         .
         .
         .
LOOP:
IN  3        ; load the accumulator
RAR          ; shift bit zero into the carry
JNC LOOP     ; test the carry flag for one
         .
         .
         .
```

An example that uses the sign flip-flop is found in the problems at the end of this chapter. The use of masking techniques or any other bit isolation and test procedures is often required in machines that lack bit-testing instructions. In such machines there are usually numerous ways to accomplish this task, and any way that works is OK.

ORTHOGONAL OUTPUTS: IMAGES

The bit isolation techniques allow an 8-bit input port to be used for eight different independent devices so that the status bits can be individually tested. It is often desirable to drive eight independent lines from one output port so that a signal applied on one line has no effect upon the other seven lines. The port is loaded from the accumulator with eight bits at once, yet only the bit to the device that is being signalled should change. The seven other bits should be the same after the accumulator has been output as they were before, but this implies that the data in the accumulator be determined by the state of the output port. In the absence of feedback from the port itself, there must be a record, or *image*, of the port at all times, and the obvious place to maintain such a record is in an 8-bit memory register. This record is provided to maintain continuity of control, and the location of this record in memory will be given the name "IMAGE." The contents of IMAGE can be loaded into (stored from) the accumulator by using the direct addressing instruction LDA IMAGE (STA IMAGE). Assume in the following that bit 2 of output port 3 is to be cleared. In this example we do not care about the previous value of this bit. However, we do wish to preserve the previous value of the other bits. This can be accomplished via the instruction sequence:

```
        .
        .
        .
        .
        .

    LDA  IMAGE   ; retrieve record of port 3
    ANI  ФFBH    ; (11111011) AND (ACC)-filter out bit 2
    STA  IMAGE   ; store updated record
    OUT  3       ; clear bit 2, port #3
        .
        .
        .
        .
        .

    IMAGE:
    DS  1
```

.
.
.
.
.

The opcode DS is not a machine instruction, but is a directive to the Assembler program that directs it to define 1 byte of storage and to associate the name IMAGE with this location. The location should be chosen following a return or unconditional jump instruction, i.e., it should never be placed in the path of an executing sequence of instructions.

The above discussion has dealt with two common situations. The need to isolate one line of input signal from several simultaneously driven lines. The techniques described are general and do not depend upon a specific instruction set, but can be implemented with any general-purpose instruction set. The simplest implementation occurs, of course, in those sets that possess bit-set and reset instructions.

THE INTEL 8080 I/O STRUCTURE

Our execution of the nontrivial design of the 8008 I/O structure provides special motivation for the study of the first second-generation microprocessor, the Intel 8080. As described in the chapter on addressing structures, the 8080 sends eight status bits onto the data bus at the beginning of each cycle, during the time that the 16-bit address is placed on the address bus. These bits are latched by using processor-provided timing signals, and are present throughout the rest of the functional cycle for selection and control of subsystems. In particular, the INPUT and OUTPUT status bits are directly available for enabling the appropriate subsystem during input and output cycles. These signals are now decoded *in the processor* and only a latch is required for their use. In similar fashion, the generation of the READ and WRITE timing occurs in the CPU itself and these signals are available from two output pins on the 8080 package. The ease of interfacing the I/O subsystems to the CPU is illustrated in Fig. 11-8 for the input subsystem.

It can be seen from this diagram that there is no external decoding of timing or control lines required to read from either a selected memory location or input port. The address lines are usually decoded on the memory chip itself and by straightforward external decoders for the I/O ports. The system has been expanded to include 256 input ports and 256 output ports via the use of two byte instructions. The second byte contains an 8-bit device address. It is fetched into the CPU and placed (redundantly) on the address bus, on both the high address bits and the low. The special I/O timing found in the 8008 has dis-

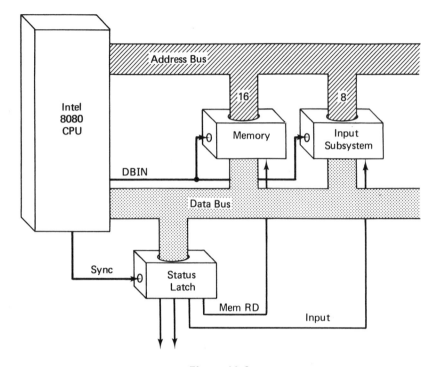

Figure 11-8

appeared and the 8080 I/O transfers occur with the same timing as do memory transfers. The 8080 timing is treated in later chapters.

If an INPUT instruction opcode has been fetched, the (incremented) program counter is sent to memory again during the following cycle, and the MEMRD status bit selects the memory subsystem. The INPUT status bit is LOW. These bits are used to pre-enable the data outputs of memory and the input subsystem for data presentation to the CPU.

The input timing signal Data-Bus-In (DBIN) finds the memory selected in the second cycle and the input system disabled by the LOW (OFF) input status bit. The port number stored as the second byte of the input instruction is then fetched from memory during T_3 and stored temporarily in the CPU. The final cycle is then entered by placing the input cycle status bits on the data bus. These bits de-select the memory subsystem and pre-enable the input subsystem. The DBIN timing signal then gates the selected input data onto the data bus, and the CPU loads this data into the accumulator.

The decoding performed in the CPU chip itself results in directly usable control signals from the 8080 and the status latch. The requirement that high-level clock drivers, synchronizing flip-flops on request lines, a status latch, and (usually) bidirectional buffers be used in most systems has led to the development of special-purpose support chips for the 8080. One chip, the 8224 clock driver, provides a 12-V-swing clock pulse compatible with the 8080 and a synchronizing latch for the READY line that is used with slow memories, and one for the RESET line that is used to reinitialize the processor by clearing the program counter and forcing a jump to location zero. A status strobe for strobing the status latch is available from the 8224.

Another support chip, the 8228 Bus Controller, provides buffering for the 8080 data bus and also contains a latch for capturing the status bits at the beginning of each cycle. These bits are then combined with the DBIN, $\overline{\text{WR}}$, and HOLDAK signals from the CPU to provide MEM-RD, MEM-WR, I/O-RD, and I/O-WR timed selection signals for controlling the data bus. The HOLDAK is used to float the data bus as described in the DMA chapter, and the INTA status line from the 8228 is used as described in the Interrupt chapter.

The scheme shown in Fig. 11-9 is typical of second-generation processors in which a maximum of decoding is performed inside the chip or in "support" chips and all control signals are available from this nucleus. The support chips connect directly to the CPU with no intermediate buffers or gatings.

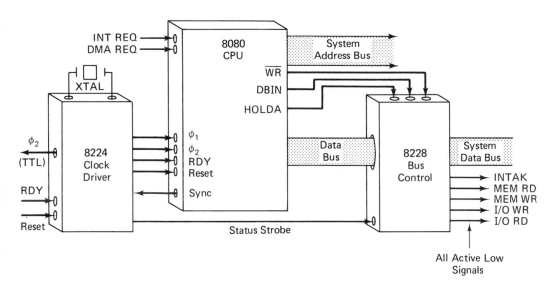

Figure 11-9

The design of the 8080 and 8224/8228 support chips obviously minimizes the amount of design necessary for I/O interfacing and also minimizes the number of components required. In 1977 Intel introduced two new computers that extended this trend to the limit: the 8048 monolithic microcomputer and the 8085 CPU and family of parts. Figure 11-10 illustrates this trend by plotting the number of components in an "average" system against time. This curve has resulted from increased integration of such devices as the Intel 8355 Read Only Memory/I/O chip (also shown in Fig. 11-10) which provides 2048

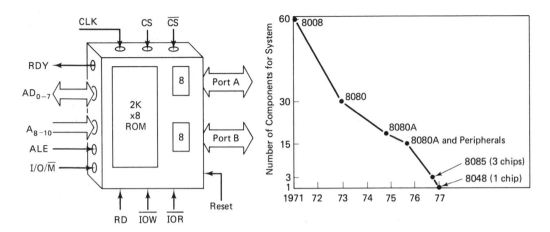

Figure 11-10   (*Courtesy Intel Corporation*)

8-bit bytes of instructions and includes two 8-bit I/O ports which can be programmed to serve as input lines or output lines. All of the control signals involved in its use interface directly to the chip. An ultraviolet erasable PROM version, the 8755, is also available.

Third-Generation 8080s: The Zilog Z-80 and Intel 8085

The overwhelming dominance of the 8080 in the microprocessor marketplace from 1973 to 1977 established it as the "Model T" of the industry and resulted in a "second sourcing" of the 8080 by at least four companies. In such a situation there is incentive to maintain continuity by designing "upward compatible" systems that will run programs designed for the earlier machine but that possess extended instruction sets and other improved features. Two such systems are the Z-80 introduced by Zilog and the 8085 from Intel. Both of these machines develop all control signals *on the chip* itself.

Perhaps the most interesting feature of the Intel 8085 CPU is its return to an 8008-like multiplexed address and data bus. The hi-byte of the 16-bit address is available on the chip, while the lo-byte appears on the data bus at the beginning of each cycle. An Address Latch Enable (ALE) line is provided to directly latch the lo-address into any 8-bit latch. In order to minimize parts count and maximize pin utilization, most of the peripheral component parts provide an on-chip address latch to accept the lo-address byte. This is illustrated in Fig. 11-11 via the Intel 8155 ROM. This device contains 256 bytes of static RAM and also provides the on-chip address latch, on 6-bit and two 8-bit I/O ports which can be programmed either as input lines or output lines, and one 14-bit programmable interval timer which can operate with an external clock. The

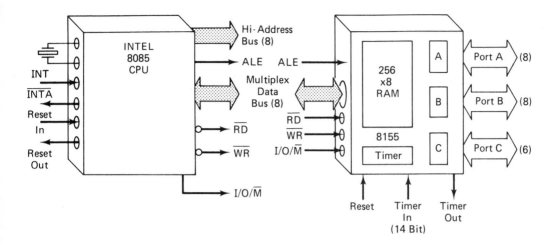

Figure 11-11

reader should estimate the number of medium-scale integrated components necessary to design an equivalent circuit with the 8008. Note that the 8085 and *all* of its support chips are 5-V only devices, thereby minimizing power supply costs. A further advance associated with integrated families of devices is that inter-chip timing relations are designed to be compatible, thereby relieving the designer of a considerable amount of work. The Z-80 is built by using an N-channel, ion-implanted, silicon gate MOS process. It requires only a single

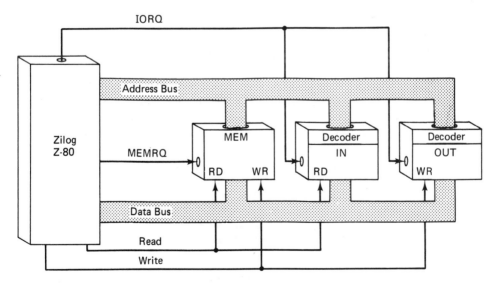

Figure 11-12

phase TTL clock and is completely TTL compatible. The internal register file has been doubled, using a technique described in Chapter 14, and the instruction set of 158 instructions includes all of the 78 instructions of the Intel 8080.

A diagram of the device is shown in Fig. 11-12. The I/O timing shown in Fig. 11-13 is straightforward. The port address appears on the address bus during T1 and remains throughout the I/O cycle. An extra WAIT state is inserted automatically to allow the I/O device to decode its address and activate the WAIT line if a longer wait is required. The $\overline{IORQ}/\overline{RD}/\overline{WR}$ lines are combined, since the timing of these signals is essentially the same.

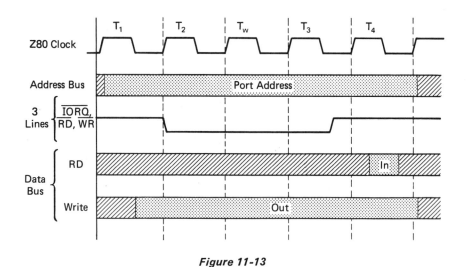

Figure 11-13

SERIAL I/O FACILITIES: THE SIGNETICS 2650

The Signetics 2650 processor possesses a program status register containing condition codes, status bits, internal stack status, a sense bit, and a flag bit (Fig. 11-14). The last two bits are directly connected to the outside world via pins on the CPU chip and are useful for serial I/O interface design. The *SENSE* bit can be tested under program control and thus provides a built-in status-testing facility. The *FLAG* bit can be set or reset under program control and thus may be used for serial transmission.

The instructions that affect these bits are:

Preset Program Status, Masked
Clear Program Status, Masked

and

Test Program Status, Masked
Load and Store Program Status

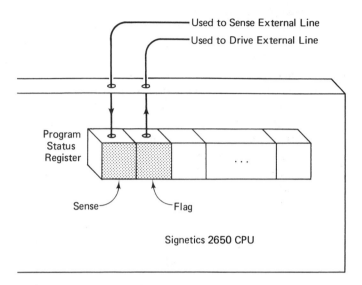

Figure 11-14

They are immediate-mode instructions whose second byte contains the mask used to specify the particular bits selected. The use of these instructions with conditional branches and time-delay loops provides the basic facilities necessary for serial asynchronous communication of the type described in the preceding section. The use of serial off-the-chip I/O channels for simplified interfacing is becoming an almost standard feature with microprocessors and will be mentioned again in the following sections.

The 2650 parallel I/O structure utilizes a MEM-I/O pin that specifies to the external circuitry whether the CPU is executing a memory reference or an I/O instruction cycle. The address bus is interpreted according to the state of this pin. The full 15 bits of address lines are utilized in the memory reference mode. During I/O cycles, the two most significant bits of the address bus are used for mode control.

The Memory-I/O pin distinguishes between the CPU-MEMory operations and the CPU-I/O operations. When this pin is high, the 15 address lines contain memory address information. When it is low, bits A_{13} and A_{14} contain mode information.

Non-Extended I/O

The 2650 CPU provides several 1-byte I/O instructions that allow data transfer between a specified internal register and an external device. No device address information is provided per se. Bit A_{13} is used to specify whether the data is DATA or CONTROL information. The CONTROL information can be utilized by the designer in any fashion. In the very simplest scheme, the DATA/CONTROL (D/$\bar{\text{C}}$) bit serves as a 1-bit address to select the I/O device. During the non-extended I/O operations, the address bus is unused. The use of data and control I/O instructions fits the general I/O structure developed earlier in this chapter. The control channel consisted, in an earlier example, of the command output channel and the status input channel. The generalized control channel provides for these modes; WRITE CONTROL (WRTC) can be used to send commands to the I/O devices. READ CONTROL (REDC) may be used to test status or receive device commands. The general structure is symmetrical. The I/O instructions operate in either mode as selected by the programmer and reflected by address line A_{13}. The instructions are shown in Fig. 11-15. The register field, *r*, specifies the source or destination for a write or read instruction, respectively.

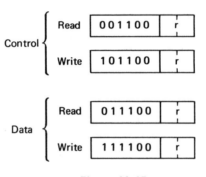

Figure 11-15

Extended I/O

The 2650 possesses 2-byte I/O instructions that provide eight bits of device address in a manner very similar to the Intel 8080 CPU. During execution of these instructions, the second byte is fetched from memory and placed on the eight low-order address lines. The MEM-$\overline{\text{I/O}}$ signal line enables the I/O system. Bit A_{14} specifies Extended or Non-Extended (E/$\overline{\text{NE}}$) mode. If this bit is set, the I/O system can use the data appearing on the LOW address bus. These data are normally interpreted as a device address. The I/O control signals are readily decoded, as shown in Fig. 11-16.

A variation on this circuitry is obtained by using a mode-decoder as shown in Fig. 11-17. The decoder is enabled by the active LOW M/$\overline{\text{I/O}}$ signal. When this signal is HIGH, the two HIGH address lines supply memory address information and the READ/WRITE line controls the bidirectional buffer. The decoded control signals are used to select the appropriate channels. The WRITE command lines are used to select, and the WRITE PULSE (WRP) is used for

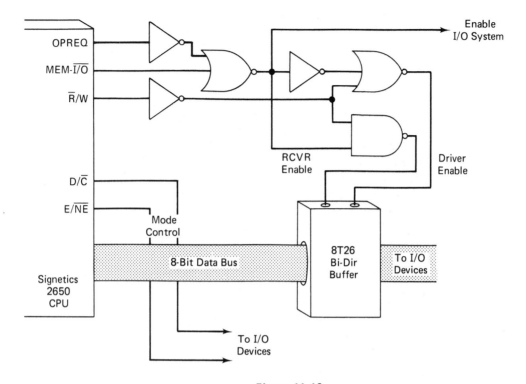

Figure 11-16

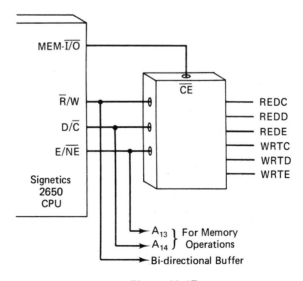

Figure 11-17

write timing. All operations are synchronized via a master control signal, OPREQ, that is discussed in the following section.

2650 Timing

The 2650 announces all external operations with an Operation Request Line (OPREQ). This line indicates that signals on other control lines are valid and can be used by external devices. OPREQ initiates external operations and remains active until the receipt of the active LOW Operation Acknowledge ($\overline{\text{OPACK}}$) from the device. If the $\overline{\text{OPACK}}$ is not forthcoming, the processor delays executing an integral number of clock cycles, in the fashion of the Intel 8008 and 8080 WAIT state. The control lines are unchanged during this time. If the $\overline{\text{OPACK}}$ is active at least 100 nsec prior to the trailing edge of T_2, the CPU will not WAIT, but will proceed to the next cycle.

The $\overline{\text{OPACK}}$ must be returned within 600 nsec of OPREQ; however, the data will be accepted by the CPU up to 1000 nsec after OPREQ is issued. If external devices will always return data within 1 μsec of OPREQ, the $\overline{\text{OPACK}}$ line can be tied LOW and the CPU will run at its maximum rate. The 2650 timing diagram shown in Fig. 11-18 illustrates the DATA-IN timing. The DATA-OUT or WRITE timing is similar, but is not shown. Note that, since the address and control lines will not change during the active OPREQ period, it is often unnecessary to latch these before using them. If OPREQ is

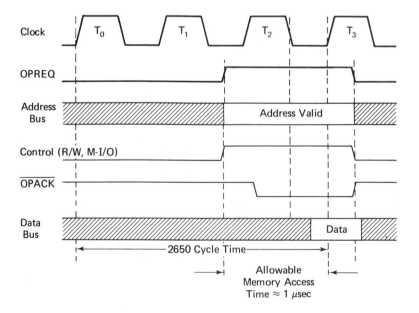

Figure 11-18

used as a chip select (CS) line, the address and control lines serving the chip will remain stable as long as the chip is enabled.

THE INTERSIL IM 6100 I/O STRUCTURE

Timing and Subsystem Selection

The IM 6100 is a 12-bit microprocessor with the architecture and instruction set of the PDP-8/E minicomputer. The I/O structure was designed to minimize the circuitry necessary to interface to peripherals. Four decoded control lines are output from the chip, and four control lines from external devices are input directly to the chip. Three timing lines are also available from the package. One of the timing lines, T_A, indicates input transfers to the CPU, while time pulse T_B signals output transfers from the CPU. The third pulse T_C is used with the subsystem select lines to specify READ or WRITE operations. The first two timing signals are shown in Fig. 11-19 with the data bus. The system clock is not shown.

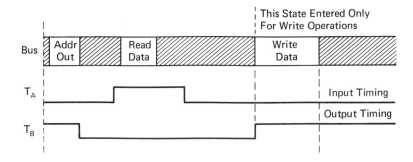

Figure 11-19

All data flow occurs over the system bus. The four control lines from the chip are subsystem select lines that have been compared to decoded high address bits. These lines are listed here with their functions:

1. MEMSEL-   select memory for data transfer
2. DEVSEL-   select device for I/O transfer
3. SWSEL-   select switches (used with special instruction)
4. CPSEL-   select control panel subsystem.

The SWSEL control line is placed in the active state via the receipt of an OR Switch Register (OSR) instruction. It is used to gate onto the system bus the contents of a 12-bit switch register that is ORed with the contents of the

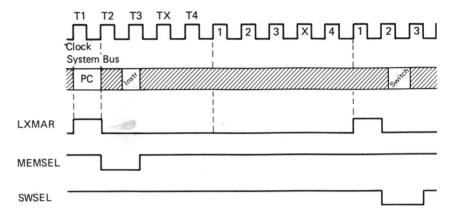

Figure 11-20

accumulator. The execution of OSR requires three cycles, as shown in Fig. 11-20. The address is placed on the system bus and latched by the Load External Memory Address Register (LXMAR) line. The selected instruction is input to the CPU during T_2. Internal operations occur during T_4, T_x and T_5. Another cycle occurs with no active control, and the third cycle uses the SWSEL line to gate the switches into the accumulator (via the ALU).

The presence of the SWSEL line as a separate control line simplifies the task of reading switches under software control. The line can be used to enable the tri-state output of the switch register directly. These bits can then be tested to determine the direction of program execution. The output control lines and their associated subsystems are shown in Fig. 11-21. The input control lines are shown at the bottom of the CPU.

The output control lines are identical in function to the status bits latched from the 8080 bus at the beginning of each cycle. They select the subsystem that will transact business with the CPU during the cycle. The 8080 used 8 data lines and 16 address lines and was forced to multiplex these "highest" address bits over the data bus. The IM 6100 multiplexes the memory and I/O addresses over the data bus and, consequently, has enough pins to bring the high address or subsystem select lines directly from the chip. (Note that the 8080 DMA GRANT (HOLDA) line is available as a separate pin.)

The input control lines have few analogies among the other microprocessors. During I/O transfers, these lines allow external devices to control instruction execution through these lines. They are, in effect, a "window" into the instruction decoding and control unit that is opened during the execution of an I/O Transfer (IOT) instruction, allowing the selected device to control data flow *within* the CPU.

The skip line is not unique but functions as the FLAG line in the Mostek 5065P. The active state of this control line causes the next instruction in sequence

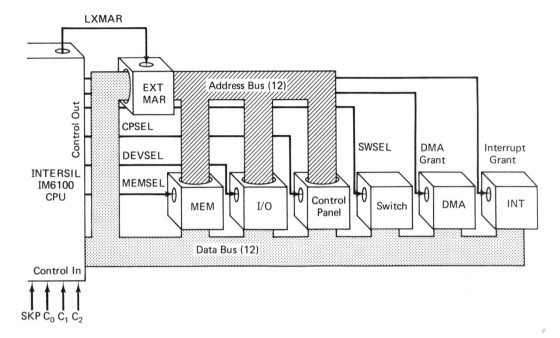

Figure 11-21

to be skipped and, thus, is well adapted to checking the status of external devices. The other three control lines (C_0, C_1, C_2) affect the disposition of I/O data *within* the CPU.

Two possible settings relate to output transfers from the CPU. When $(C_0, C_1, C_2) = (1, 1, 1)$, the contents of the accumulator are output to the system data bus and made available to the selected I/O device. The setting $(0, 1, 1)$ transmits the accumulator contents; however, the accumulator is then cleared prior to the next instruction fetch cycle.

The input instructions are more flexible and more interesting. The data to be input to the CPU appears on the data bus in response to the DEVSEL and timing signals. The effect of the control bits C_0, C_1, C_2 for an input cycle are described in a following section.

THE I/O TRANSFER INSTRUCTION

The opcode for the I/O Transfer instruction is of a standard format. Three bits specify the class as IOT, and the remaining nine bits specify the device address and control word. Six bits are allocated to device address and three to device control. With this scheme, up to 64 I/O devices can be selected. The

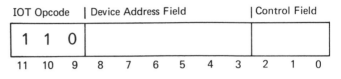

Figure 11-22

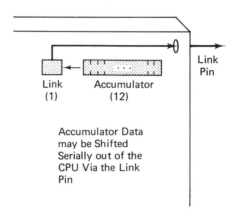

Figure 11-23

format is shown in Fig. 11-22. In addition to these described control lines, the contents of the internal LINK flip-flop are available at the LINK pin on the CPU chip (Fig. 11-23). Although the pin can be used for control of external devices, it is more common to employ this feature for serial communication. The ability to set or clear the LINK under program control, combined with the ability to link the accumulator and the LINK for shifting data, makes this ideal as a parallel-to-serial converter.

IM 6100 I/O EXAMPLE

An analog-to-digital converter can be configured to deliver a digital measure of the difference between two potentials, as shown in Fig. 11-24. It is assumed that the microprocessor must respond rapidly to this measure; by "rapidly" we mean with little time available for computations. Two cases will be examined. The first assumes a linear response and, therefore, minimal computation based on the value input to the accumulator.

Note that there are no input instructions as opposed to output instructions. The I/O Transfer (IOT) instruction presents a 6-bit device address capable of selecting one of up to 64 devices, and the selected device then responds by

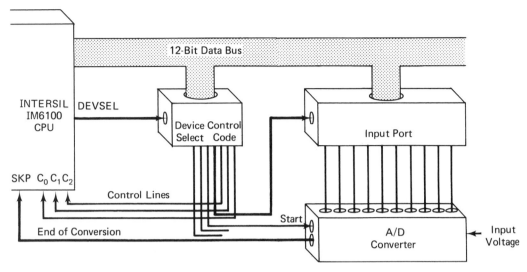

Figure 11-24

placing control signals on the input line C_0, C_1, C_2 and SKIP. The possible options are described in this table:

Control functions associated with C_0, C_1, C_2:

C_0	C_1	C_2	
1	1	1	OUTPUT ACCUMULATOR TO DEVICE
0	1	1	OUTPUT AC AND THEN CLEAR AC.
1	0	1	INPUT DATA FROM DEVICE; *OR* WITH ACC
0	0	1	INPUT FROM DEVICE; *LOAD* INTO ACC.
*	1	0	INPUT FROM DEVICE; *ADD* TO PROGRAM COUNTER
			This effects a *RELATIVE* JUMP.
*	0	0	INPUT FROM DEVICE; *LOAD* INTO PROGRAM COUNTER
			This effects an *ABSOLUTE* JUMP.

The system in Fig. 11-24 has been designed for simplicity and utilizes the IOT control bits (9–11) to supply the signals C_0, C_1, C_2. The IOT instruction is latched into the IOT latch via the DEVSELect line and is used to control the process. Six bits are used to select the device; in this case, the A/D converter and three control bits are used to select the mode. In our example, the control bits are fed back to the control lines C_0, C_1, C_2 and control the mode of CPU execution. These bits are set to (001) and cause the data to be loaded into the accumulator. It is assumed that the A/D converter requires several CPU cycles to complete its conversion and that the A/D status will be available on the end-of-conversion

(EOC) line that is set to "1" at the start-of-conversion, indicating "BUSY," and is reset to "0" at the end-of-conversion, signaling "DONE." This line will be connected to the SKIP line into the CPU and will determine whether the instruction following the IOT is to be executed or skipped. The next instruction will be a JMP-1 that repeats the input and execution loops in this fashion until the EOC line drops. This causes the next instruction to be skipped and execution proceeds with the value of the potential difference now in the accumulator. A simple linear calculation can be made and the output response determined.

The second case to be treated assumes a nonlinear response to the measured potential difference and further assumes insufficient time to calculate the response function. The system shown in Fig. 11-25 is designed to use a data structural approach to the nonlinear response problem. Here it is assumed that the response can be tabulated prior to operation, and the program can be designed accordingly. The IOT instruction is latched by the DEVSEL line, and the device code provides a START signal to the A/D converter. The command field supplies the control bit 010 to the control lines C_0, C_1, C_2, thereby causing a relative jump to occur. The N-highest-order bits from the A/D converter are used to divide the potential difference into 2^n regions, to each of which corresponds a pre-computed response. The n-bits are offset by m-bits, effectively multiplying each n-bit number by 2^m. The program control will then transfer to location $(PC) + V * 2^m$, where V represents the n highest bits from the A/D converter. The SKIP line in this case relates to the instruction that follows the relative jump. Although this could be handled in software, the system shown

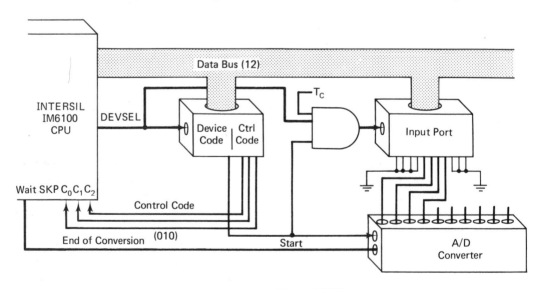

Figure 11-25

utilizes the WAIT line to extend the IOTA cycle an integral number of clock periods until the end-of-conversion line goes true. When this occurs the measure of potential difference effectively offsets the program counter, and the program sequence at the target location yields the proper (non linear) response. The timing is shown in Fig. 11-26.

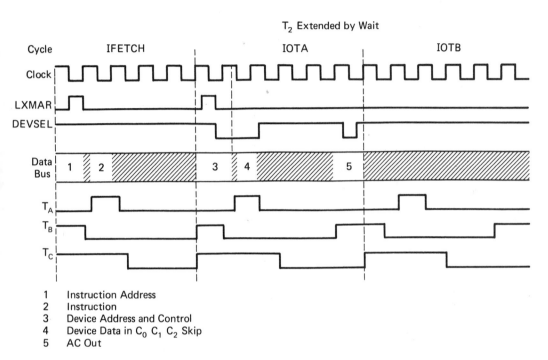

1   Instruction Address
2   Instruction
3   Device Address and Control
4   Device Data in C_0 C_1 C_2 Skip
5   AC Out

Figure 11-26 *(a) Instruction address; (b) Instruction; (c) Device address and control; (d) Device data in C_0, C_1, C_2, SKIP; (e) AC OUT*

As a final example, we use the device address to select the A/D subsystem and use the control field to select an analog multiplexer channel. There are a large number of such devices available, and we rather arbitrarily choose the Fairchild 34051 C/MOS 8-channel analog multiplexer/demultipluxer to use with the CMOS IM 6100 CPU. The system is shown in Fig. 11-27.

In this system one of eight unknown voltages is input to the A/D converter that is started via the appropriate device select field. The device address must also select and enable circuitry that will supply the proper C_0, C_1, C_2 code to the CPU. The design of this circuitry is left to the reader, as is the use of the end-of-conversion signal. For simplicity, the device select lines are shown directly driving the appropriate inputs. In most cases they would be binary encoded, and a decoder would be used to drive these inputs.

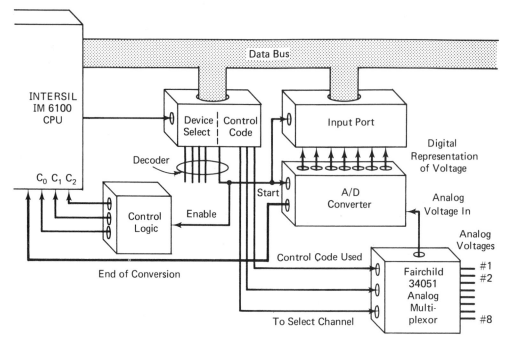

Figure 11-27

MOSTEK MK 5065P I/O STRUCTURE

The MK 5065P utilizes a 4-bit "free field" I/O instruction in which the least significant 4 bits of the opcode are ignored by the instruction decoder. These bits are made available to I/O devices by placing them on the LBUS along with two mode bits in the opcode. The format of the I/O instructions is shown in Fig. 11-28.

There are four I/O instructions, two input and two output. The contents of the accumulator are sent out during the execution of any of the four instructions, appearing on the HBUS at the same time the two mode bits and the free field bits appear on the LBUS. The timing is shown in Fig. 11-29.

The three input timing signals are derived from the system clock. Upon receipt of an I/O opcode (01xx xxxx) the CPU generates the Peripheral Exchange Sync (PESY) timing pulse that is used in conjunction with the STATE STROBE timing signal to sequence the events occurring in the I/O instruction execution. During the output instructions, the contents of the accumulator provide the primary data, i.e., the data from the CPU to the output device. During input instructions, these data are secondary and can be used in any manner compatible with the design of the I/O system. The primary data from the input device are loaded into the accumulator, while the data output from the

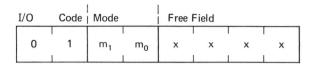

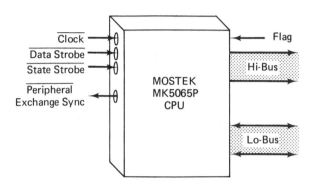

Figure 11-28

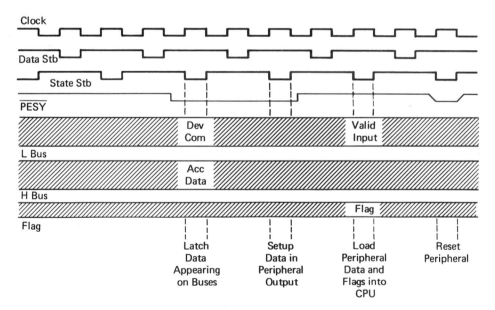

Figure 11-29

accumulator can provide either address or control information. These data amount to an additional eight "free field" bits and offer extreme flexibility to the system designer.

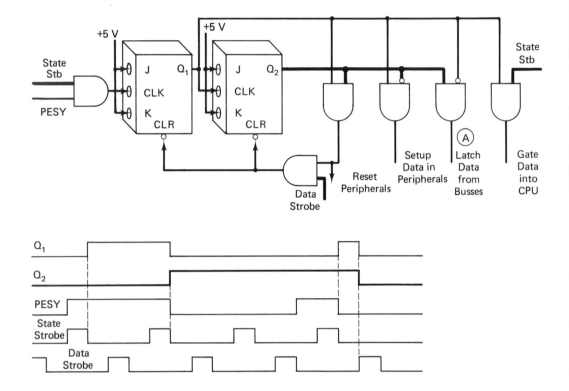

Figure 11-30

The output timing sequence can be decoded by using the two-stage counter shown in Fig. 11-30.

Skip Mode I/O

There are two types of 5065P I/O instructions. The first consists of unconditional input and output instructions that execute and are followed by the next instruction in sequence. The second type performs the I/O execution and tests the flag bit via a LINK flip-flop in the CPU to determine whether to skip the next (two-byte) instruction or not, allowing program execution to be keyed to external devices. The status bit from the device can be wired to the flag pin on the CPU, or it can be channeled through a multiplexer. The system in Fig. 11-31 illustrates the use of the "free field" I/O instruction and the flag-testing mode of execution. The four "free" bits allow the designer to build simple systems and "customize" his control signals through the use of these four bits that are part of the I/O instruction but are ignored by the instruction decoder and merely placed on the LBUS at the beginning of the I/O cycle. In this elementary scheme,

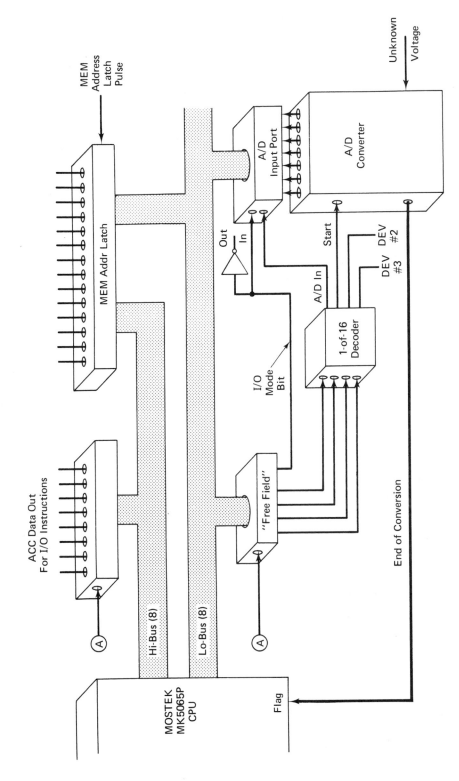

Figure 11-31

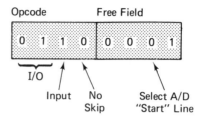

Figure 11-32

the I/O mode bit is used to enable the INPUT subsystem by activating one of the two enable pins on each input port. The other pin on the selected input port is enabled by the appropriate line out of the one-of-sixteen decoder. The four free field bits are used to drive the 16-line decoder. In Fig. 11-32 the input instructions can be used to "start" the analog-to-digital converter by selecting line 1 out of the decoder (which is tied to the start pin of the A/D). This instruction is then followed by the Input And Skip (IAS) instruction (Fig. 11-33) that clears the "start" line and enables the A/D input port, thereby gating data into the accumulator. The A/D converter can require a number of CPU cycles to complete the conversion and the input data will be meaningless until this time. Therefore, the instruction following the IAS instruction should branch back and execute the IAS instruction again. This will continue until the A/D converter activates the end-of-conversion line that sets the flag, causing the next instruction to be skipped. The data in the accumulator should represent the value of the unknown voltage, and the program execution resumes with this information.

The program segment that will effect this action is:

```
        .
        .
        .

START:
INP 1               ; start A/D conversion
LOOP:
INSKIP φ            ; select A/D input port
JMP LOOP            ; repeat until flag set
Continue
        .
        .
        .
        .
        .
        .
```

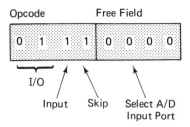

Figure 11-33

NATIONAL PACE I/O STRUCTURE

The National PACE microprocessor is a P-MOS device with a 16-bit wide data bus used for all parallel communications with external devices, including memory. The 16-bit address space is available for memory or I/O devices, and address assignment is left to the user. The machine possesses no input or output instructions per se, but utilizes any external reference instruction for either memory or I/O. All transactions consist of an address output on the bus followed by a data flow between the CPU and the target location. The latching signals and the timing diagram are described in the section on address presentation subsystems. In addition to the bus communication with peripherals, the PACE provides several general-purpose input and output pins that greatly simplify I/O interface design (Fig. 11-34). These pins are best discussed in terms of the internal architecture, the relevant aspects of which are described next.

The internal jump condition multiplexer is used with the branch on condition (BOC) instruction that selects one of 16 possible conditions to be tested. Thirteen of these conditions are pre-assigned and allow testing of the status register (SIGN, CARRY, OVERFLOW, etc.) in the normal fashion. The BOC instruction format is shown in Fig. 11-35.

The four condition code bits are used to select which of the 16 possible conditions is to be tested. The selected bit is tested and, if true, the 8-bit (signed) displacement is added to the program counter to effect a PC-relative jump or branch. The inclusion of a "free field" in the condition space adds considerable flexibility to I/O design. The three JUMP CONDITION bits, labelled JC_{13}, JC_{14}, and JC_{15}, are connected to external pins and, thus, allow testing of conditions existing external to the chip. This feature is found in the Intel 4040 (TEST PIN), the MOSTEK 5065P (FLAG PIN), the MOS-TECHNOLOGY 6501/2 (SETOV), and the Intersil IM 6100 (SKP PIN), and is extended in the PACE to three pins with a 256-word branch condition rather than a single-instruction skip-on condition. The condition field is shown in Fig. 11-36. The continue bit is dedicated to use with the HALT state and is not considered a free field.

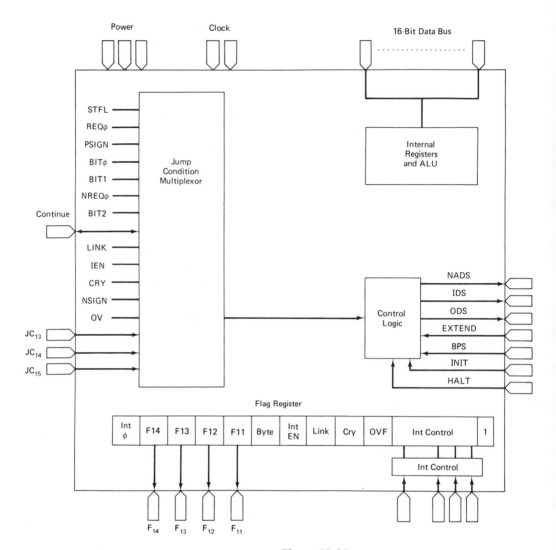

Figure 11-34

Although the condition bits are shown in Fig. 11-36 in register format, the actual bit locations are assigned to the 16 inputs to the JUMP CONDITION MULTIPLEXER. The free inputs come directly from the pins, and the status conditions are input from a separate status or flag register. The 16-bit register is similar to the more conventional status words; however, it has also been enhanced via the inclusion of a "free field" that provides another linkage between software and external hardware. The flag register or PROGRAM STATUS WORD can be read from, or written into, under program control. The register

Opcode	Condition Code	Displacement
0 1 0 0		

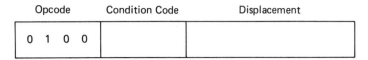

Figure 11-35

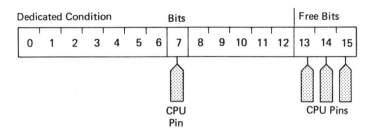

Figure 11-36

is extremely general purpose and includes the usual status bits (carry, overflow, sign, link) as well as mode information (byte or word) and interrupt mask bits in addition to the four undedicated flags (Fll through F14). These flags are available on four separate pins and provide four 1-bit-wide I/O channels to the external world.

The combination of these 1-bit output channels with the three 1-bit input channels to the JUMP multiplexer offers one of the most powerful serial I/O facilities found on any microprocessor. Their power derives from the fact that these 1-bit channels are accessible by both software and external hardware and, thus, provide a direct link between the operating processor and the outside world with *no* external registers, latches, or timing required. (Note that the low-power P-MOS lines *do* require buffers to increase the drive capability.)

The flag register can be pushed or pulled from the internal stack and can be stored in the internal register file by using a Copy Flags to Register (CFR) instruction, and loaded from the register file with a Copy Register to Flags (CRF) instruction. In addition, two special instructions take into account the I/O nature of the free flags and allow operations upon individual bits in the FLAG register. The flag manipulation instruction format is shown in Fig. 11-37.

Opcode	Flag Code	Mode	Unused Bits
0 0 1 1	f l a g	m	— — — — — — —

Figure 11-37

The bit specified by the flag code is effected according to the setting of the MODE bit. If this bit is one, the set flag (SFLG) operation sets the specified bit to logical·one. When the mode bit is zero, the pulse flag (PFLG) operation first sets the bit to one and then resets it, providing either a clearflag function if the flag was already set or a pulse on the appropriate line if the flag was initially reset.

In order to transmit a character to the teletype by using the serial line connected to the flag pin designated TTYOUT, the character is loaded into $AC\phi$, and the following routine is called:

```
CHAROUT:    PFLG TTYOUT        ;send start bit
            LOADI AC1,9        ;SET ACz to count of 9
TIMEOUT:    CALL DELAY
            ROR AC0, 1,1       ;shift AC0 into LINK flag
            AISZ AC1,−1        ;add −1 to AC1, skip if zero
            JMP TESTBIT
            JMP SENDSTOP
TESTBIT:    BOC LINK, SET HI
SET. LO:    PFLG TTYOUT
            JMP TIMEOUT
SET. HI:    SFLG TTYOUT
            JMP TIMEOUT
SENDSTOP:   SFLG TTYOUT
            CALL DELAY
            CALL DELAY
            RETURN
TIME:       · WORD 375
TIMER:      · WORD 0
DELAY:      LOAD AC2,  TIME
            STORE AC2,  TIMER
LOOP:       DSZ TIMER
            JMP LOOP           ;24 μsecond loop
            RETURN
```

The off-the-chip I/O facilities provided by the PACE can be used in a variety of ways. The system shown in Fig. 11-38 utilizes an active LOW 1-of-16 decoder to bring the line selected by the flag register to a low state. Three keys are positioned so that each can make contact with a different sense line, and the three sense lines are connected with the JUMP CONDITION inputs JC_{13} to JC_{15}. The keyboard is scanned by selecting the first output line and checking each of three keys associated with that line. The next line is then selected and its three keys checked, and so on.

The PACE microprocessor contains so much circuitry that insufficient room remains in the chip for output drivers, and the outputs must, therefore, be buffered. The outputs are designed to drive current sense amplifiers; however, they may be interfaced to voltage-driven CMOS or LPTTL devices via the use of switched pull-down resistors, as shown in Fig. 11-39. The resistors are

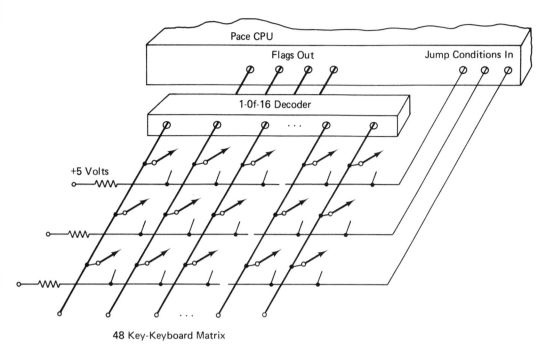

Figure 11-38

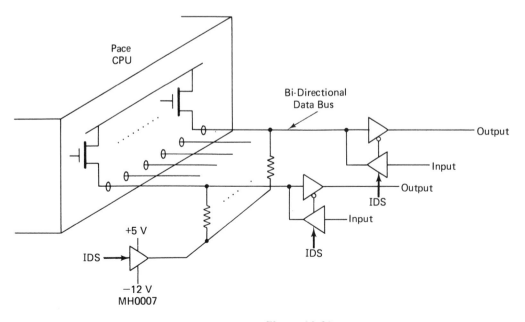

Figure 11-39

switched from -12 volts to $+5$ volts by the Input Data Strobe (IDS) so that an adequate logic "1" will be available to the PACE in the input mode. This scheme is inherently slower than the use of sense amplifiers that maintain constant voltage. The voltage swings with the switched system require time to charge the capacitive load on the data bus. Most of the PACE input lines provide on-chip pull-up resistors so that they can be driven directly by TTL signals.

MOTOROLA 6800 AND MOS TECHNOLOGY 650X I/O STRUCTURES

The 6800 and 650X I/O structures resemble the PACE system in that they both lack I/O instructions and depend instead upon memory-mapped I/O. This scheme simply allots certain locations to I/O devices and addresses these I/O registers in the same manner that memory registers are addressed. Some external decoding of the address lines is required in large systems. In small systems that use only lower-order address lines, the high-order address lines can be used to distingush between memory and I/O as described in the discussion of memory-mapped addressing in the chapter on addressing structures. This technique is most efficiently employed then in small systems with "free" address

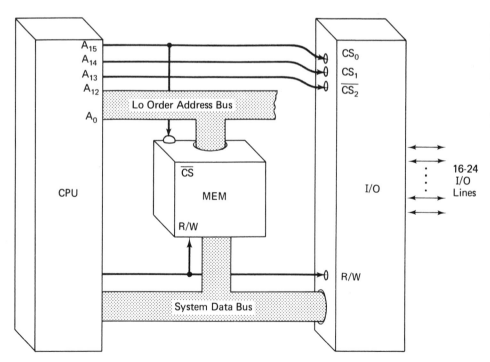

Figure 11-40

lines, and both Motorola and MOS Technology, Inc., have designed I/O support chips to operate by using these lines. The evolution of peripheral chips will be covered briefly in the final chapter. For our present purposes it is sufficient to state that, in their simplest mode of operation, these chips behave as latches and buffers that interface the data bus to the outside world and can be enabled by several lines that are usually tied directly to the high-order address lines in small systems. The devices are written into by means of the same WRITE line that controls memory and read from just as is a memory location. The electrical characteristics and chip timing match the processor they are designed to complement, and any special control signals are usually available directly from the processor chip. The interface to the CPUs is shown in Fig. 11-40.

650X Serial I/O

The 6501 is pin compatible with the Motorola 6800. One of the pins that is not connected on the 6800 has been used to provide an input channel into the CPU. This is achieved by setting the overflow bit in the program status register in the manner described for earlier processors possessing "testable" pins. The status register can be loaded into the accumulator and tested by using the 650X BIT instruction that consists of one byte of opcode followed by a mask byte.

COSMAC I/O STRUCTURE

The RCA COSMAC uses a "free field" instruction format in conjunction with four output pins to obtain a powerful control structure; it also provides four input pins for testing external flags via conditional branch instructions. This general I/O structure has been discussed in sufficient detail that a minimal treatment is appropriate here. The COS MAC instructions are all eight bits and are executed in a two-cycle fetch/execute sequence. The opcode is four bits wide, and the remaining four bits vary in their interpretation. The bits either (1) specify a memory address register, (2) specify an ALU operation, or (3) provide the "free field" bits for the I/O instruction. The instruction format is shown in Fig. 11-41, and the I/O timing diagram is shown in Fig. 11-42.

The bottom timing pulse is generated by ANDing the inverted timing pulse B signal with the I/O signal decoded from the two state code lines. The state

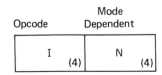

Figure 11-41

Internal Timing Intervals

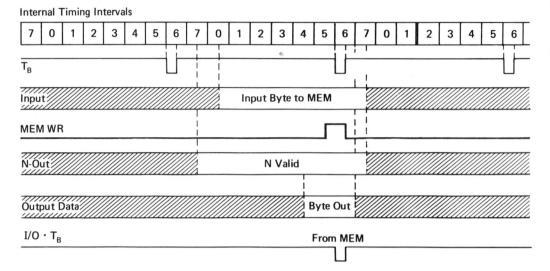

Figure 11-42

information appears on these two lines (SC_0, SC_1) in the middle of internal timing interval #7 and defines the CPU mode as:

1. I/O execution,
2. Interrupt acknowledge,
3. DMA processing, or
4. None of the above.

The following example utilizes the control field N appearing on the N-pins and the $I/O \cdot \overline{T}_B$ timing pulse. The control field is used to select 1-of-8 latches and to provide the data input to the latch. The timing signal is used for the Latch enable signal that writes the data into the latch. An MSI chip (discussed in Chapter 4) that is appropriate for this system is the 9334 8-bit addressable latch. Fairchild also makes the device in C/MOS as the 34099, which is shown in Fig. 11-43 with the RCA C/MOS CPU. It should be pointed out that only three of the N-bits are actually "free," i.e., ignored by the CPU. The MSB, bit three, is interpreted by the CPU as in Fig. 11-44.

The COSMAC differs from most microprocessors in that I/O data flows between the selected device and memory rather than between device and CPU. The target register in memory is specified by the contents of an index register. This flow occurs at the same time that the N-bits are presented externally and should be planned for; the index register should point to an unused memory location. This precaution arises from the necessity to use all four N-lines to control the addressable latch. An inefficient design that uses only the three

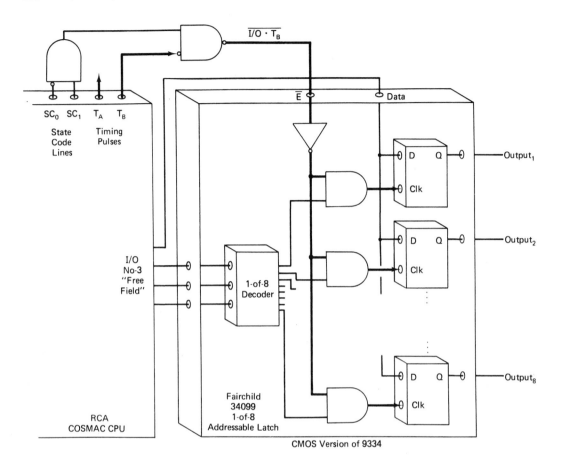

$\overline{I/O} \cdot T_B$

$\overline{E}$

Data

SC_0 SC_1 T_A T_B

State
Code
Lines

Timing
Pulses

Output₁

Output₂

I/O
No-3
"Free
Field"

1-of-8
Decoder

Output₈

D Q

Clk

D Q

Clk

D Q

Clk

Fairchild
34099
1-of-8
Addressable Latch

RCA
COSMAC CPU

CMOS Version of 9334

Figure 11-43

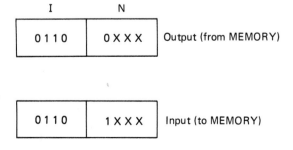

I	N	
0 1 1 0	0 X X X	Output (from MEMORY)

| 0 1 1 0 | 1 X X X | Input (to MEMORY) |

Figure 11-44

"free" bits would employ half of a 34723 dual 4-bit addressable latch. In this case, the output command 6/Oxxx could be used with no effect upon memory.

The COSMAC input instruction executes as follows. The selected device places data on the system data bus in response to the I/O control signals, the index register supplies an address to memory, and the WRITE pulse (MWR) stores the data in the addressed memory register. The output instruction uses the same enable signal $(I/O \cdot \overline{T}_B)$ as shown above to latch the data from memory into the selected I/O device.

The four external flags can be tested via conditional branch instructions. The byte following the opcode is used for program counter-relative branching if the flag is true; otherwise, the following instruction is executed.

GENERAL INSTRUMENT CP-1600 I/O STRUCTURE

The CP-1600 utilizes a 16-bit wide data bus over which all addresses and data words are bussed. The CPU utilizes memory-mapped I/O and, therefore, possesses neither input nor output instructions. Communication with external devices, including memory, is channelled by three control lines, BUS CONTROL 1 (BC1), BUS CONTROL 2 (BC2), and BUS DIRECTION (BDIR). The use of these signals to latch direct address data from memory into the memory address register was described in the section on address presentation mechanisms. During I/O operation, three of the eight combinations of primary interest are:

BUS TO ADDRESS-REGISTER	used to load data on bus into external register for addressing memory or I/O device
DATA WRITE STROBE	used as a write enable for the addressed memory or I/O device
DATA TO BUS	used to gate data from memory or any peripheral device onto the bus for input to the CPU

Several of the remaining codes are used in conjunction with the interrupt system and will be treated later.

Test External Conditions

The CP-1600, like the PACE, is able to test both internal and external conditions via the use of Branch-on-Condition instructions. The CP-1600 possesses a number of specific instructions that test internal status and a Branch-on-External Condition (BEXT) that selects 1 of 16 external conditions to be tested. Since this is too many conditions to enter the CPU on individual lines, the Jump Condition Multiplexer has been moved outside the CPU and is driven by four coded channel select lines. The output of the multiplexer is input to the CPU via the External Branch Condition in pin. The BEXT instruction format is shown in Fig. 11-45. Although the CP-1600 possesses

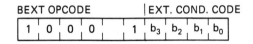

Figure 11-45

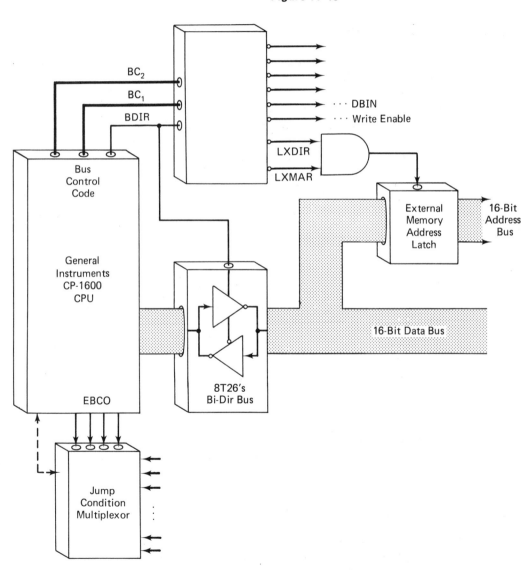

Figure 11-46

internal 16-bit data paths and registers, the instruction decoder is only 10 bits wide. The six bits accompanying the opcode in a 16-bit memory are unused. The displacement address is in the second word and can usefully be 16 bits wide.

The four least significant bits of the BEXT instruction are buffered and presented to the External Branch Condition Out lines (EBCO 1-4). The selected input is tested, and a branch occurs if the condition is true. The basic circuitry necessary to decode the status and channel information is shown in Fig. 11-46.

FAIRCHILD F-8 I/O STRUCTURE

The F-8 basic system provides a two-chip microprocessor with 32 bidirectional I/O lines. This is achieved via the distributed addressing architecture described in the chapter on addressing structures. The 16-bit address circuitry is located in the Program Storage Unit (PSU) and in the other memory subsystems. Thus, there is no need to send 16 bits of address from CPU to memory with each execution. The 16 lines normally used for address bus on both the CPU *and* on the memory chips have been deleted and the free pin space used for I/O. The lines are divided into four 8-bit I/O ports, two on the CPU and two on the PSU, as shown in Fig. 11-47.

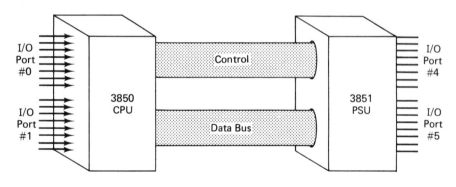

Figure 11-47

The I/O port numbers are not always numbered consecutively due to the presence of dedicated ports or registers inside of the chips which have fixed addresses.

The F-8 Philosophy of Design

The F-8 system based on a two-chip 3850/51 processor provides an accumulator, 64 bytes of RAM, 1000 bytes of ROM instruction store, and 32 bidirectional I/O lines. The system is very compact and will work with an RC clock and a +5- and +12-V power supply. The separation of processing and addressing circuitry has resulted in extremely small die size and, consequently, high yields. The cost of a system is proportional to the yield, and these factors all point toward high-volume, low-cost applications in basically simple systems. Although the F-8 can be expanded to larger systems, it is designed for applications that require minimal hardware and software. In support of this philosophy, over half of the instructions are 1-byte long, thus conserving limited memory space. The use of an auto-incrementing memory data pointer allows the scan and manipulation of a data field with 1-byte opcodes requiring no address information. In order to provide the capability for expansion, the F-8 set includes 2-byte I/O instructions that address up to 256 I/O ports. Since, many applications will possess less than 16 I/O ports, however, 1-byte (short) I/O instructions are included, which use four of the eight instruction bits to select the port. These operations cause data flow between the accumulator and the specified I/O port. The format of these instructions is shown in Fig. 11-48.

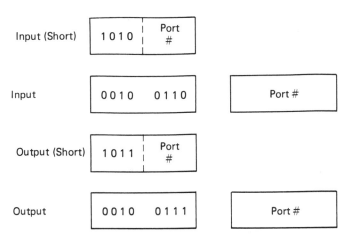

Figure 11-48

The effect of output instructions is to latch the contents of the accumulator into the selected output port. The input ports are not latched, and the effect of the input instruction is to copy the instantaneous data at the input port into the accumulator. The I/O lines are bidirectional and interface to TTL as shown in Fig. 11-49.

As can be seen from the diagram, it is necessary that the bit latched in the output port be zero if a given line is to be used as an input line. Thus it is possible to use several lines of one port as input by latching zeros into the appropriate output bits and using the remaining lines as output lines. This can be implemented by using the "image" technique described earlier, masking the accumulator contents to filter out the appropriate bits before each output operation. During an input instruction execution all eight bits will be loaded into the

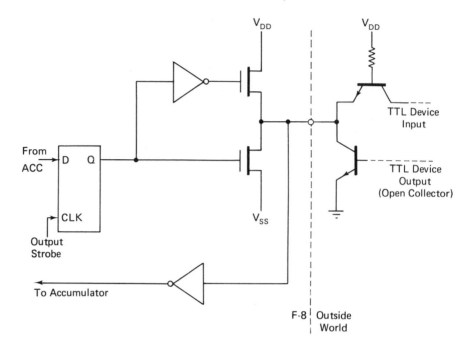

Figure 11-49

accumulator, but only those dedicated to input lines will have meaningful information. Note that it is even possible, using the I/O scheme, to treat an unused I/O port as a register, loading the data from the accumulator and reading it into the accumulator via an input instruction.

F-8 I/O Timing

The timing relationships for the F-8 CPU I/O (short) instructions are shown in Fig. 11-50. The timing for data that are input or output from the CPU on the data bus is not shown. The timing is dependent upon the source of data, i.e., data in the accumulator reach the data bus more rapidly than data from the 64-byte scratchpad file. Input timing varies slightly as a function of the data path and destination within the CPU.

The F-8 Interval Timer

In a large number of microprocessor applications it is necessary to provide a measure of time. The microprocessor clock is usually very precise and allows quite accurate timing to within the resolution of the shortest instruction execution time. Large time intervals can be provided via nested "countdown" loops as

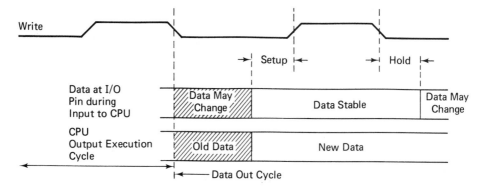

Figure 11-50

described in the teletype example. The highly sophisticated and complex processor is merely emulating a counter in this case. With medium-scale integrated technology, it is often cheaper to count in software than to implement a hardware timer, even though the processor can do no useful work while counting. As the large-scale integration progresses, simple processing tasks that recur frequently are implemented in LSI hardware.

The first processor to integrate an interval timer into the basic architecture was the Fairchild F-8. Each 3851 PSU contains an integral timer that is addressed as an output port and is capable of generating a signal to notify the CPU that a specified time interval has elapsed. The discussion of the interrupt mechanism will be postponed to the interrupt chapter; however, one of the ports in the PSU contains a control register that allows the timer to be enabled or inhibited. The other dedicated timer register is loaded via an output instruction with the number of cycles to be counted by the timer. Using a 2 MHz clock, the F-8 timer can generate delays from 15.5 μsec to 3.950 msec. During these intervals the CPU can be executing *any* program and yet, when the specified interval elapses, the processor will switch to the program that is necessary for the critically timed process. In essence, the CPU sets an alarm clock and then forgets about the timed process until the alarm goes off.

F-8 I/O Summary

The distributed architecture of the F-8 system replaces the normal address bus, data bus, and elementary control bus connecting the CPU to "nonintelligent" support chips with a data bus and expanded control bus structure linking the CPU with a set of more complex or "intelligent" support chips. The local maintenance of addresses favors the use of integral I/O ports. Although it is possible to design an external I/O system, it is not desirable and is seldom necessary. The number of I/O ports needed in a system is usually related to the program size, and, thus, as more ROM chips are included in a system, the number of I/O lines increases proportionately.

NATIONAL SC/MP I/O

The SC/MP microprocessor uses memory-mapped I/O for parallel byte I/O transfers and, therefore, possesses no I/O instructions or control lines per se; however, the device also possesses a serial I/O structure and instructions relating to this operation. The 8-bit extension register (E-reg) provides a serial I/O register, as shown in Fig. 11-51.

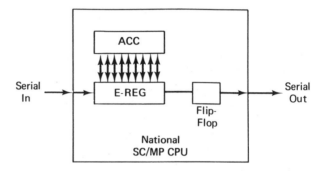

Figure 11-51

The execution of a Serial I/O (SIO) instruction causes the serial input to be sampled and a 1-bit right shift to be performed. The right-most bit of the E-reg is clocked into the serial out flip-flop and made available to external devices. In addition to the shift in/out operation, the E-reg can perform parallel operations with the accumulator. The E-reg contents can be ADDed (bin or dec), ANDed, ORed, XORed, COPYed into, or EXCHANGED with the contents of the accumulator. During the parallel operations, the serial input is not sensed, nor is the serial output affected.

I/O Address Modification

A unique feature of the serial I/O register is its ability to use the E-register contents as an address displacement. The normal address modification procedure utilizes the second byte of an I/O-MEM-reference instruction as a signed displacement that is added to the specified 16-bit address pointer register. The usual "seven bits plus sign" format allows −128 to +127 displacements by treating 00000000 as a positive zero displacement and treating 10000000 as −128 rather than negative zero. In the SC/MP, this last value (80 Hex) causes the contents of the E register to be used as the displacement. This operation is particularly well suited to branch table operation, as discussed in the section on data structures and as illustrated in the second IM 6100 A/D example.

Programmable Pulses

The SC/MP possesses a status bit that is set by the execution of a DELAY instruction and reset by the fetch of the next opcode. The DELAY instruction is a 2-byte instruction, the second byte of which is combined with the accumulator to produce a 16-bit count specifying the length of the delay. The delay status bit (D-flag) is set during the fetch of the second byte of the instruction. Programmable delays, ranging from 6 μsec to over a quarter of a second, are available by using this feature. The D-flag returns low when the next opcode is fetched from memory.

The timing is shown in Fig. 11-52. Note that the fetch of the next opcode can be further delayed in DMA or multi-processor configurations in which the processor can relinquish control of the system.

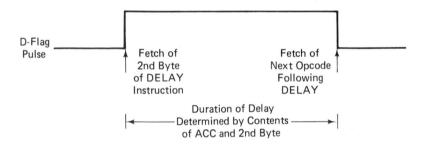

Figure 11-52

ROCKWELL PPS-8 I/O

The Rockwell system utilizes the Harvard architecture described in the addressing chapter. The I/O timing diagram is shown in Fig. 11-53. The WRITE command line that deposits data in RAM during T_2 is used to enable the I/O system during T_4. The PPS-8 RAMs are always in the READ mode unless inhibited by the "read inhibit" command line. This line is used to disable the RAM during T_2, following a valid WRITE command during T_4.

The I/O instructions consist of two bytes, an opcode byte followed by a device command byte. The receipt of the opcode byte during T_4 sets up the CPU for the fetch of the device command byte.

The program counter appears on the address bus during T_2, and the second byte is fetched during the following T_4. It is at this time that the WRITE line

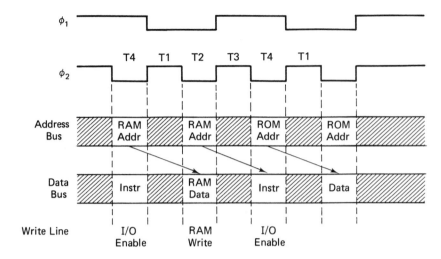

Figure 11-53

is used to enable the I/O system. The format of the device command byte is:

7	6	5	4	3	2	1	0
DEVICE ADDRESS				I/O	COMMAND		

Bit three of the second byte indicates to the CPU, and also to the selected device, whether the data flow is a READ or WRITE operation. In either case, the RAM is inhibited during the T_2 period, following the appearance of the device command byte, and the data bus is used for data flow between the CPU and the selected device. Up to 15 devices can be selected and presented with one of eight commands. The sixteenth code (all zeroes) is used as an "all call" command in conjunction with the interrupt system. The use of this command will be described in the section on the PPS-8 interrupt structure. The PPS-8 also has an I/O instruction that was included for operation with PPS-4 peripheral chips. The format is almost identical with the byte transfer I/O instruction described above; however, rather than a unidirectional flow, a bidirectional transfer of four bits occurs. The upper half of the accumulator is sent to the I/O device, and the lower half of the accumulator is loaded from the I/O device.

THE INTEL 8048/8748 I/O STRUCTURE

The device that seems destined to become even more popular than the Intel 8080 is the Intel 8048 single-chip computer introduced at the beginning of 1977. Designed especially for I/O oriented applications, the chip can use 27 of its 40 pins for I/O! In addition to this remarkable number of I/O lines, the 8048/8748 possesses a very powerful set of I/O oriented instructions.

Containing 1K bytes of PROM (8748) or ROM (8048) for instructions and 64 bytes of RAM for data, status, and pointers, the device can be used in a free-standing mode with no external ROM or RAM. In this case the data bus functions as an I/O port to achieve the full 27-line capability. If the device is used with external memory and I/O, the bus becomes a bidirectional port with synchronous strobes. The bus lines are active only during a transfer of information; they are latched only if single-chip operation is desired. See Fig. 11-54.

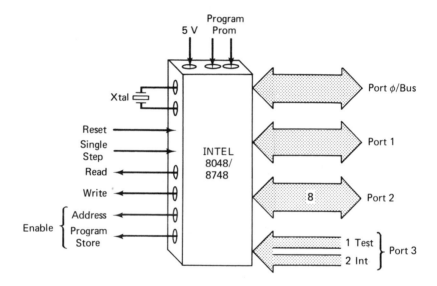

Figure 11-54

The I/O instructions address all of the ports on the 8048 as well as four extra ports in an 8243 I/O expander (support) chip. The BUS and Ports 1 and 2 are on chip and Ports 4, 5, 6, 7 on the 8243 can be read and written. A unique feature allows the BUS and Ports 1 and 2 to be ANDed and ORed with the second byte of ANL and ORL instructions, while Ports 4, 5, 6, and 7 can be ANDed and ORed with the low-order 4 bits of the accumulator. The third I/O port consists of three special-purpose pins that can be tested directly under program control and one of which may be used for interrupt.

The basic timing of the 8048 I/O or data read cycles is shown in Fig. 11-55a and the timing for the I/O write in Fig. 11-55b.

The 8048 MOVX instructions transfer both accumulator data and register file data to and from I/O port ϕ.

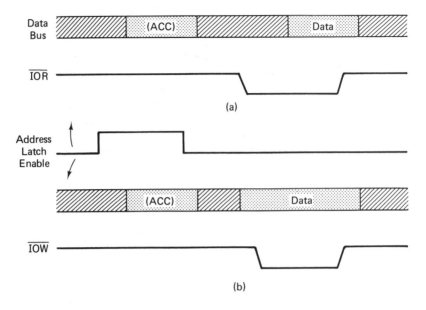

Figure 11-55

MOVX @Rj,A	places the contents of register *j* on the bus at ALE time and writes the contents of the accumulator onto the bus at $\overline{WR}$ strobe time.
MOVX A,@Rj	places the contents of register *j* on the bus at ALE time and reads the bus contents into the accumulator at $\overline{RD}$ strobe time.

The *OUTL port*, *ACC* instructions *latch* the contents of the accumulator into the selected port while the ANL and *ORL port*, # *data* are used to AND and OR the immediate data contained in the second byte of the instruction with data already latched into the port. These allow resetting and setting, respectively, of individual bits with no effect on neighboring bits. The bus can be read into the accumulator via the *INS A,BUS* instruction. This instruction produces a strobe that is useful for peripheral I/O chips of the type covered in Chapter 14.

The 8048 I/O features treated in this section have been presented in the "free-standing" mode of operation in which the device operates with no external memory or I/O. The flexibility that has been designed into the 8048 I/O structure allows the device to operate in many different modes and in different configurations.

However the last 8048 I/O feature that we will treat is the "quasi-bidirectional" that allows buffered outputs and also allows external input. When a particular output pin is set by writing a "1" to that bit, the pin can serve as a true high level latched output pin. However, *it can function simultaneously as a pullup register on an input*. This is achieved in the following fashion. (See Fig. 11-56.)

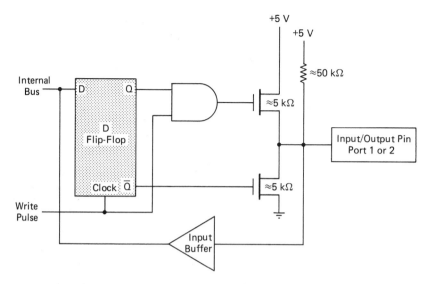

Figure 11-56

When the bit is driven LOW, the pulldown device (≈ 5 k) sinks an external TTL load. When it is driven HIGH, the (≈ 50 kΩ) pullup device supplies a large current to allow a fast data transfer into capacitive loads. However, a short time later (less than one instruction cycle) this device is shut off and the small pullup (≈ 5 k) maintains the '1' level indefinitely. In order to read data from this pin, the input device needs only to be capable of overriding the small sustaining current supplied by the ≈ 50 kΩ device.

I/O SUMMARY

This chapter has been concerned with *programmed data transfers*, i.e., those transfers of data in and out of the system that are effected via the I/O instructions as part of a program sequence, in contrast with interrupt- or event-driven transfers that are treated in the next chapter.

I/O Protocol—"Handshaking"

The transfer of data from a source to a destination normally requires two channels: a control channel and a data channel. The control channel is used to initiate the transfer and to close the transaction. For example, the data source can signal "data available" on the control channel. The normal handshaking protocol requires that the destination device acknowledge the receipt of the data by placing a "data received" signal on the control channel.

Alternately, the destination can issue a "data request" on the control channel.

When the data are placed in the data channel, the source will acknowledge with a "data available" signal on the control channel.

"Status" Lines

Programmed data transfers are asynchronous data transfers with synchronization accomplished via a control channel that can be implemented in time or space. Serial, one-line channels employ control time slots, whereas parallel transfers normally dedicate separate lines for control. Programmed data transfers usually imply that CPU time is more important than device time, i.e., the device can wait until the CPU is ready to service it. Since many mechanical devices require extremely long operation times (by CPU time standards), they are often commanded (via the control channel) to perform a specific function and to signal (usually via a separate line in the control channel) their readiness for a data transfer. The CPU will often proceed with other program execution and later return to sample the device status via this "status line." This periodic sampling will continue until the status line indicates READY, and the transfer of data then occurs under program control.

Polling Status and Isolation of Status Bits

In systems with a number of peripheral subsystems, the CPU can sample several devices by testing the individual status lines in sequence. This is known as "polling" the status lines. Since most input ports are at least eight bits wide, it is inefficient to use one port per status line, and several status lines can then be tested at a single input port. There must then exist some means of isolating the desired status bit from the rest. This is achieved via bit-testing instructions in some processors. However, not all processors possess such instructions. The logical AND instructions, common to most processors, can be used to "mask off" the undesired bits and then test the entire word (which will be zero or nonzero, depending upon the desired status bit).

A similar technique for isolating output bits requires the use of feedback or a record in memory that is usually called an "image" of the port.

Response to Status Bits

The general response to status bits is quite simple: proceed if status indicates READY; else, wait for READY. This is usually accomplished via masking and testing the word with a conditional jump. Some processors use an integral status "sense" line that is automatically tested during the execution of I/O instructions, causing the next sequential instructions to be skipped if the sense line indicates READY. Otherwise, the next instruction will repeat the operation. Sense lines of this type can also be used for serial I/O transfer directly into the CPU, in which case the next instruction will transfer control to the routine that handles a "LOW" bit. In polling situations, the CPU will not hang up in a WAIT loop for one device, but scans all of the status lines, responding only if a line is READY.

Data Transfers

Once the appropriate DATA AVAILABLE signals have been posted, the data transfer can occur over the data channel. This transfer could occur directly between the registers in the CPU and the device; for example, from an A/D converter directly into the accumulator or from the accumulator directly into a device register. Although this is often done, the use of latches or buffers in the data channel is probably more common. The "double-buffered" data transfer allows a number of buffers to be loaded in sequence and then transferred in parallel. This is desirable in many control situations. For example, two D/A converters can control the position of a CRT curser. Although the data bus might require that an 8-bit X-co ordinate be followed by an 8-bit Y-co ordinate, the X-Y display should change from the current point to the next point in one operation. This can be achieved by first transferring the X-data to the X-channel buffer and the Y-data to the Y-channel buffer, and then loading the two D/A converters simultaneously with the information that is now available in parallel at the two buffers.

Time Delays

In many situations, the peripheral device will operate at a known rate, and we desire to synchronize the CPU to the device during the transfer period. This requires a control signal to initiate the transfer and a timing capability within the CPU. The most universal means of achieving known timing delays is via the countdown loop method. The execution time of a certain loop is computed, then the loop is executed repeatedly until the desired time has elapsed, at which point the loop is exited. This technique is also used widely for generating output pulses of specified duration. The use of crystal-controlled clocks allows precise timing with this method. The primary disadvantage of the delay loop is simply that the CPU is dedicated to this task. Interval timers that can be set and then ignored until they signal allow the CPU to perform other duties during the delay period. These timers can be tested via status bits, but ordinarily they utilize interrupt systems described in the next chapter.

Special I/O Features

The inclusion of sense lines in a CPU provides a flexible I/O structure that is easily interfaced to external devices. In CPUs with several sense lines, they can serve as the receiving end of the control channel (the data bus will be the data channel in this case). The ability to send control signals is provided in a number of ways. "Free field" I/O instructions provide control bits in the instruction that are ignored by the instruction decoder. In the most flexible case, these control bits are directly available off the chip. A variation of this method utilizes two types of I/O instructions: control and data, and a C/$\bar{D}$ pin to enable the appropriate channel. An extremely flexible I/O structure is found in the Intersil IM 6100 that allows external devices to execute control functions normally reserved for the instruction decoding and control circuitry. As the prices of processors decline and it becomes more and more practical to use a processor to control a simple system, the desirability of directly connecting the CPU to the controlled system increases. This will result in an increasing variety of flexible I/O structures, all of which will be consistent with the principles of programmed data transfer that have been illustrated in this chapter.

PROBLEMS

1. Generate a 2-second delay in software accurate to within 50 microseconds.

2. Write a routine to detect a start bit and then receive the serial transmission from a teletype occurring on line ϕ of input port 2.

3. Discuss the use of the Ready line on the 8008 to detect an end-of-conversion signal from a slow analog-to-digital converter.

4. Assume two different wait loops can be written to test a particular bit. One occupies less memory space and the other requires less execution time. Which is probably "best" and why?

5. Assume a process must wait until bit 2 and bit 5 of port 3 are simultaneously HIGH. Write a program that will wait until this event occurs.

6. Write a routine that will drive a teletype tied to (port ϕ, bit ϕ) without affecting any of the other bits of port ϕ.

7. Is the use of a UART always desirable? Describe a case in which a software teletype driver is preferable.

8. In the 8008 and the 8080 the sign flag consists of a D-type flip-flop whose input is connected to bit 7 of the ALU output. Use this fact to write a wait loop to test bit 7 of input port 5.

9. Describe the modification to the nonlinear response routine using the Intersil IM 6100 in the case where the A/D end-of-conversion line is tied to the SKIP control input instead of the WAIT line. (The SKIP line takes effect after the transfer-of-control effected by $(C_0 \, C_1 \, C_2) = (010)$ during the IOT instruction execution.)

10. Design the control logic needed to drive the IM 6100 control line ($C_0 \, C_1 \, C_2$) in the example that used the control field of the IOT instruction to select an analog multiplexer channel. Use the end-of-conversion signal from the A/D to control the input timing.

11. Compare the use of the 8080 I/O instructions for inputting a 12-bit A-to-D results with the use of the LHLD in a memory-mapped I/O mode.

12 interrupt structures

A very large percentage of microprocessor systems are employed in control applications, i.e., situations in which the CPU controls a process in the "real" world by analyzing information concerning the behavior of the process.

Information is a measure of "surprise," and in many systems this equates as much to "when" as to "how much." To find out "when" an event occurs, it is possible to input and test status bits that are set by its occurrence. For a number of systems this may require almost continuous sampling, while only a relatively few samples return much information. The machine can do no useful work while sampling and, thus, is inefficiently utilized. By allowing the events of interest to signal for the machine's "attention," the efficiency can be vastly improved. Thus, interrupt structures allow "event-driven" systems in which the concept of temporal continuity has little relevance.

The ability to respond "instantly" to events allows processors to be shared by one or more processes if a means can be found to handle "simultaneous" events, i.e., those events occurring within one basic system cycle—normally the current instruction cycle. The usual means of handling simultaneous "interrupt requests" is by embedding the "concurrent" processes within a priority structure.

PRIORITY REQUEST STRUCTURES

The priority structure can be implemented in hardware and/or software. An interrupt structure that has been employed in many large processors and several micro processors is based on the "daisy chain" shown in Fig. 12-1. Here the highest priority is assigned to the left most device, $\#\phi$. If this device places an interrupt request on line IN_ϕ, the OUT_ϕ line will both signal the CPU that a request is present and disable all the lower priority devices "downstream." If the request had come instead from device 1, the IN_1 signal would disable device 2 and the rest downstream, but would leave device 0 free to interrupt. This feature, by which higher priority devices can interrupt lower priority devices, but lower priority devices cannot interrupt higher, is common to most

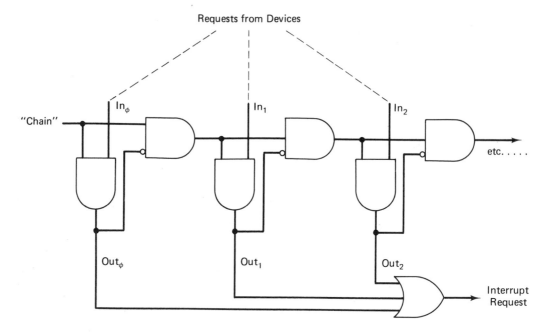

Figure 12-1

interrupt structures. The highest priority is often allotted to a RESET line that initializes all internal flags and clears the accumulator and the link.

There are often other dedicated interrupt request lines on a processor. Several machines possess a "power-fail" interrupt, which is useful in environments where the power supply may fail. This line is utilized with a voltage sensor that detects a drop in the supply voltage and calls a save-state routine which saves the state of the machine in a nonvolatile media. Some machines provide "console" interrupt request lines to allow the operator the highest priority access to the CPU, normally for examining and/or modifying register contents. Many systems utilize a clock that provides a time base and a counter, or counters that provide interrupts after specified (elapsed time) delays. These are often given high priorities. Interval timers (counters) that provide this function are implemented as LSI chips (Intel 8253), or are integrated into the CPU as in the Fairchild F-8.

The "mechanical" response times associated with many peripheral devices usually are so much greater than processor times that such devices do not need "instant" service and their requests are, therefore, assigned lower priorities. The assignment of priorities to these and other devices is always made by the systems designer. The priority structure is highly application dependent, and no "preferred" structure exists.

The varieties of interrupt structures presented in this chapter have all been designed with one goal in mind: to share one CPU efficiently between several "concurrent" processes. This will be accomplished via this procedure:

1. save state of current process;

2. identify device requesting service;

3. transfer control of CPU to this device;

4. upon completion of service, restore state; and

5. transfer control of CPU back to interrupted process.

Although minor variations exist in implementation of these steps, they are always executed. The scheme is shown diagrammatically in Fig. 12-2.

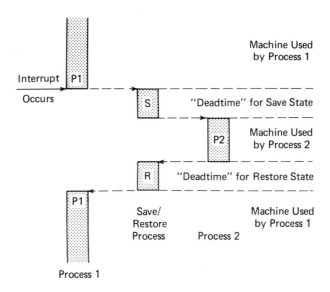

Figure 12-2

CALL (SAVE STATE)/RETURN (RE-STORE STATE)

The elementary process that is crucial to an interrupt structure is the CALL/ RETURN transfer-of-control process. The subroutine is a sequence of code that is executed upon the invocation of its name and that returns control to the calling sequence upon completing its execution. An interrupt process can be thought of as an unexpected or surprise subroutine call. In a program, the invocation is accomplished by inserting a call instruction at a known position in the instruction sequence. During interrupt processes, the invocation will occur at unknown positions in the control sequence. Thus, provision must be made for saving the return address in a known location for later retrieval. Mathematics can be described as a "replacement" process in which the replacements are made under control of the mathematician. Interrupt systems are those in which the replacement of a given control sequence by another can be made upon request from any external system. The complete control sequence is composed of a set of elementary sequences, or control strings, that can be edited by real-world systems to adapt to local conditions.

A Single-Level Interrupt

As a simple example, we consider adapting the microprocessor to communication with a teletype so that communication occurs at the rate determined by the teletype without any "waiting" on the part of the CPU. This can be accomplished in the transmit mode by using the "Buffer Empty" signal from the UART. If the UART has been configured to operate at teletype speed, then its buffer can be loaded by the processor with a character that will be framed and transmitted serially bit by bit. After writing the character into the buffer, the CPU continues operations with memory data or other I/O devices until the "Buffer Empty" signal interrupts to announce that the last character has been transmitted and the teletype would like the next one. The CPU then goes to the message buffer, finds the next character to be transmitted, loads it into the empty buffer, and returns to the interrupted process.

The circuitry designed for the 8008 included an interrupt port that was selected when the CPU acknowledged an interrupt request. We wish to concentrate more on function than on circuit details, so we utilize the simpler 8080 CPU that provides the timing pulses and subsystem select signals as described earlier. This system is reproduced in Fig. 12-3.

In the following, we assume that an INTERRUPT request signal has become active during the execution of an instruction fetched from memory at location one hundred. The program counter has been adjusted to point to the next instruction, and the current instruction completes its execution. The instruction can be one to five cycles in length, where each cycle consists of these states:

> T1 place address on address bus, status on data bus
> T2 sample RDY, HOLD, HALTAK. (increment PC if used in T1)
> (TWAIT) optional; entered if $\overline{RDY}$ during T2
> T3 DBIN or $\overline{WR}$ timing signals for data flow to/from CPU
> T4 $\Big\}$ optional; if needed for internal processing.
> T5

The completion of each instruction execution is followed by the FETCH cycle that brings in the next instruction. If, prior to the fetch, the interrupt system is enabled and an interrupt request has been presented to the system, the following events occur:

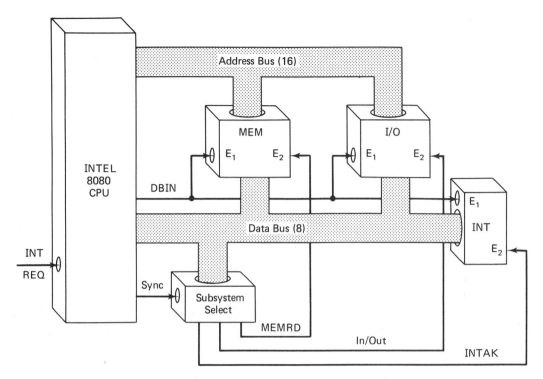

Figure 12-3

An internal interrupt flip-flop is set by the presence of an interrupt request. This flip-flop is used to:

1. disable the interrupt system,
2. set the INTA status bit,
3. reset the MEMRead status bit,
4. inhibit the store of the incremented program counter.

The sequence is shown in Fig. 12-4.

The timing diagram illustrates that the trailing edge of ϕ_2 is used to set the internal INT flip-flop, Ⓐ, if the request is present for the specified setup time. The output of this flip-flop then gates a reset pulse to the INTE flip-flop at the next ϕ_2 rise time, Ⓑ, thus disabling the system for further interrupts. Not shown, during T2, is an internal pulse that inhibits the store of the incremented program counter. The INTA status bit must then be employed *by the designer* to remove the (acknowledged) interrupt request, Ⓒ. Finally, this same status bit must be used to select a subsystem that will supply a call to be jammed onto the system data bus.

The INTA status bit is used as shown in Fig. 12-3 to select the interrupt subsystem. All of the subsystems hung on the system data bus are tri-state and

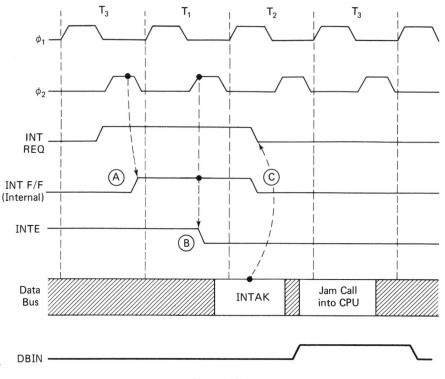

Figure 12-4

must be enabled by two signals to exit the high-impedance mode. The timing signal, DBIN, runs to all systems in parallel, announcing that the CPU expects data to be gated onto the bus and into the CPU. The status bits, INPUT, OUT-PUT, MEMREAD, INTAK, etc., are used to activate the other tri-state enable line on the selected subsystem.

The result of this design is that the CPU, as it finishes executing one instruction, places the program counter contents on the address bus to point to the next instruction in memory. The MEMREAD status bit, which has been reset by the internal interrupt flip-flop, is now used to de-select memory by keeping it in the HIGH-Z mode, thereby holding the instructions selected by the program counter off the data bus. Instead, the INTAK status bit enables (one-half) the interrupt port, and the DBIN timing signal gates the instruction onto the data bus. This system must supply a CALL instruction that will be loaded into the instruction register and executed. Of course, the CPU does not "know" what we have done with INTAK. It merely enters a state expecting an instruction on the data bus and treats whatever it finds as the proper instruction.

The program counter at this time still points to the instruction that was selected but was not accessed from memory. Thus, the return address saved by the CALL instruction will cause control to return to this point at the completion of the CALLed sequence. This is effected by PUSHing the program counter onto the top of the stack. The RETURN instruction POPs the top of the stack back into the program counter, and the interrupted program picks up where it left off.

We now investigate ways by which the CALL instruction can be furnished.

The system developed in this section is functionally equivalent to the 8008 interrupt scheme developed in Chapter 8. The standard CALL instruction used with these processors consists of an 8-bit opcode followed by two bytes of address. These three bytes are normally fetched via the program counter; however, the program counter does not affect the interrupt port. Thus, sequencing of the three bytes must be accomplished at the port. A special 1-byte CALL is provided to relieve the designer of this chore. The 8080 TRAP format is

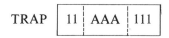

where the three bits denoted by AAA are address bits. The effect of the TRAP instruction is to:

- save the current Program Counter on the top of the stack
- load the address of the TRAP-CELL AAA (0000000000AAA000) into the Program Counter.

Control is transferred to the trap cells, 0, 8, 16, 24, . . . , 56, depending upon the value of AAA. (NOTE: TRAP is called RESTART in Inter manuals.)

Single-Level Interrupt Hardware

The interrupt scheme employing the simplest hardware would consist of a hardwared tri-state buffer whose inputs were tied to $+5$ volts. When the combination of INTAK and DBIN removes the outputs from the HIGH impedance state, the TRAP 7 instruction is inserted onto the data bus and into the CPU instruction register. This instruction calls the routine located at location $7 \times 8 = 56$, i.e., TRAP CELL 7. This routine services the requesting device and returns control to the interrupted program.

A synchronous communication with a Teletype™ has been described in terms of Programmed I/O in which status bits are monitored by the CPU. The signals that carry status information can be used to interrupt the CPU. For example, if the request originated at the "Buffer Empty" signal line from the UART, the CPU would service the TTY by finding the next character in the message buffer, loading it into the UART buffer, and returning to the interrupted program execution.

Saving the State Vector

It will probably be necessary to use a memory data pointer to obtain the next character and it will normally be necessary to use the accumulator to output to the UART. If the contents of these registers are destroyed, there will be no way to resume the execution of the interrupted sequence from the interrupted state. Thus, in addition to saving the program counter, it is necessary to save the state of the machine—at least those portions that will be altered by the interrupt service routine. It follows that the first thing to be done upon entry to the service routine is the storage of the state vector, and the last act before returning to the interrupted control sequence is the re-storing of the state vector. This first-in-last-out is the same Last-In-First-Out structure that distinguished the LIFO buffer or stack; therefore, the state of the machine should be saved on the stack.

In the 8008 the stack was internal to the CPU and was accessible only to the program counter. The inability to store the state of the machine in the stack was one of the weakest aspects of the design. This fault was corrected in the 8080 by designing only the stack pointer into the CPU and placing the stack proper in external RAM. The stack pointer (SP) is 16 bits wide and can reach any word in 64K of RAM. This RAM can be the main memory, of which a part is dedicated to use for the system stack. Or by using the stack subsystem select bit that appears during T1 of every stack operation cycle, the stack can be in a separate RAM. The stack can be pointed to any location, XYZ, via the use of the immediate load instructions

LXI   SP, XYZ

The ability to store the system state in 16 bit parcels is provided via the

PUSH reg. pair

instruction that operates with the B-C, D-E, H-L register pairs or the accumulator and the flags that are referred to jointly as the Program Status Word (PSW).

Let us assume that a microprocessor system is monitoring a process, say, taking experimental data, and is required to report certain threshold crossings and the times at which they occur. Assume also that other measurements must be made every few milliseconds. The program that tests for threshold crossings will have access to a buffer in which the value of the variable and the times of the crossing are stored. After storing this information, the processor enables the interrupt system, transmits the first character, and then returns to scan the other instruments. The first character is sent to the teletype serially and the "Buffer Empty" signal interrupts the scan and calls a routine of this sort:

TTY SERVICE: *SAVE STATE*
                PUSH PSW
                PUSH H

```
     FETCH NEXTCHAR
           LHLD NEXTCHAR
           MOV A, M
     TEST ENDMSG
           CPI '*'               ; '*' used to terminate
           JZ ENDMSG             ; message in buffer
     TYPE TTY
           MOV C, A
           CALL CO
     MOVEUP NEXTCHAR
           INX H
           SHLD NEXTCHAR
     RESTORESTATE
           POP H
           POP PSW
           EI
           RETURN
```

The routine saves the contents of the registers that will be used in the routine by pushing them onto the stack in external RAM. The memory data pointer is loaded with the contents of the register named NEXTCHAR that is always left pointing to the next character in the message buffer. Then the memory data pointer (H-L) is used to move the character into the accumulator. The character is tested by comparing it with the terminator character, in this case the asterisk, and if a match results, the message is terminated and control transfers to the ENDMSG routine. Otherwise, the character is loaded into the empty UART buffer, the NEXTCHAR pointer is adjusted, the machine state vector is restored, and the interrupted program resumes execution.

The ENDMSG routine should leave a note in an agreed upon location that the processor will check before writing a new message into the message buffer.

Increase in Efficiency Due to Use of Interrupt

The above routine requires approximately 75 μsec per character versus the 100,000 μsec required by the 10 char/sec teletype to receive the character. Thus, CPU efficiency is vastly increased by the use of the interrupt system, and the CPU can continue making measurements and processing data while the UART sends characters to the teletype.

MULTI-DEVICE, SINGLE-LEVEL INTERRUPT HARDWARE

The same scheme that applied to the teletype can work with other devices as well. There can be successive approximation analog-to-digital converters or integrating digital voltmeters that require from several microseconds up to 10 sec to obtain binary representations of analog voltages. These and other devices can be allowed to interrupt the CPU when they have data available, using an END-of-CONVERSION signal line, or its equivalent.

The existence of two or more interrupting devices complicates the system somewhat, but does not alter the basic scheme. In the following, it is assumed that a teletype (TTY) subsystem will interrupt with a "Buffer Empty" signal and A/D converter will interrupt with an END-OF-CONVERSION signal. The signals will be ORed and connected to the Interrupt pin on the 8080. They will also run to separate lines of an input port, say, port 2. Figure 12-5 illustrates the ORed status lines, the connection to the status port ($\#2$), the A/D data input port ($\#3$), and the Teletype output port (0).

Although the interrupt port and INTAK are shown explicitly in Fig. 12-5, this interrupt mechanism has been implemented in the 8228 bus control chip. The status is latched inside of the 8228; therefore, the INTAK signal is readily available. The INTAK is run to an external pin for use by the interrupt system; however, the chip is designed so that the application of 12 V to this pin will cause the data bus to be pulled high (by Zener diodes) when the INTAK status bit becomes active. This results in 11111111, i.e., TRAP 7, being inserted into the CPU in response to the interrupt acknowledgment. Thus, the 8080 can be operated in a POLLed interrupt mode with no extra hardware.

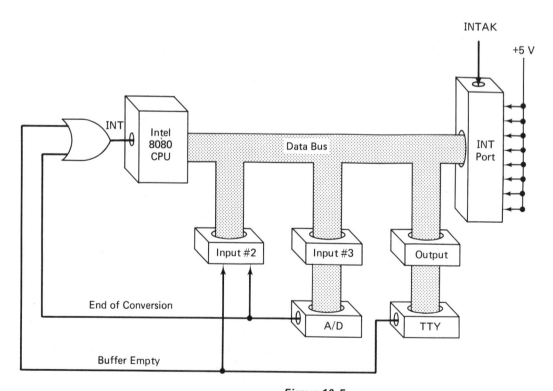

Figure 12-5

MULTI-DEVICE, SINGLE-LEVEL INTERRUPT SOFTWARE

Polling Routines

When either device interrupts the processor, the TRAP 7 (11111111) instruction is read from the INTERRUPT port. This instruction saves the program counter contents on the stack and transfers control to location 56. It is assumed that the A/D status is available at port 2, line 1, and the TTY (UART Buffer Empty) status at port 2, line 2. The routine that POLLs these status lines will begin at location 56:

```
56:   POLLDEVICES:     SAVE PSW
                       PUSH PSW
                POLL A/DSERVICE
                       INPUT STATUS
                       ANI 1      ; mask for A/D
                       JNZ  A/DSERVICE
                POLL TTY SERVICE
                       INPUT STATUS
                       ANI 2   ; mask for TTY
                       JNZ  TTYSERVICE
                ERRORPOINT
                       JMP ERRORROUTINE
                         .
                         .
                         .
                         .
```

If the END-OF-CONVERSION line was HIGH, the result of ANI 1 will be nonzero, and the routine will branch to the A/DSERVICE routine. This routine will save any additional registers on the stack, if necessary, and process the A/D data. Upon concluding this process, the routines will restore the CPU state vector, enable the interrupt system, and return to the interrupted sequence of instructions.

Similarly, the TTYSERVICE routine must save state, process the TTY, restore state, and return. Any additional devices will be handled in the same way.

Polled Priority Interrupt Summary

The type of system just described is called a POLLed Interrupt System. All interrupt requests trap to a common location, and a routine that POLLs status bits determines the source of the interrupt request. If the interrupting devices can be arranged in a hierarchical order, then the highest priority device will be polled first, the next highest will be polled second, and so on. Thus, if two devices request service at once, the higher priority will be encountered first in the poll and it will receive service first. Note that the system shown above does not provide a means of clearing the interrupt request. This is left as a problem for the reader. It will be treated later in another system.

VECTORED PRIORITY INTERRUPT CONTROL

Although the simplest interrupt scheme jammed only one instruction (TRAP 7) onto the data bus, the CPU is designed for up to eight interrupt instructions, TRAP ϕ through TRAP 7. The use of hardware to encode these instructions for up to eight separate devices will speed up interrupt servicing by eliminating the need to POLL the devices. In addition, standard hardware is available for conflict resolution. (See Fig. 12-6.)

If two devices simultaneously request service, a priority encoder will pass only the higher priority request. The Fairchild 9318, presented in Chapter 4, accepts up to eight inputs and generates a 3-bit binary code that indicates the highest priority line active at any time. A second-generation priority encoder and interrupt control unit, the Intel 8214, has additional features that are useful in interrupt situations. The three encoded outputs can drive the AAA lines in the TRAP instructions and can also be compared against three bits stored in an on-chip latch.

The latch that sets the interrupt threshold is called the Current Status Latch. It is loaded under program control via an output instruction. The decoded address line is ANDed with the WRITE pulse, and the product is applied to the ENABLE CURRENT STATUS line. The inputs to the latch are tied to the data bus, and at T3 of the output cycle the accumulator contents are placed on the data bus and latched into the Current Status Latch. The enable line also clocks a D-flip-flop whose output enables an AND gate input and also enables the priority encoder latch so that the output of the encoder appears on the AAA outputs. If the inputs are active, the "request activity" signal also enables the gate. The priority code is compared against the interrupt threshold, and if it is above the threshold, the comparator provides the final active input to the AND gate whose output serves as the input to the Interrupt Request Latch. This latch is clocked by the 8080 system clock. The output is inverted and provides an active LOW interrupt request to signal the 8080 that an interrupt is pending. The line is also fed back to the 8214 Interrupt Disable Latch and used to set the output HIGH. This output disables the AND gate, blocking further interrupt requests, and latches the priority code so that it will not change while AAA is read by the CPU. The output of the AND gate goes LOW, and the next system clock pulse returns the Interrupt Request Latch output to its original state. The occurrence of an interrupt above the threshold effects three actions.

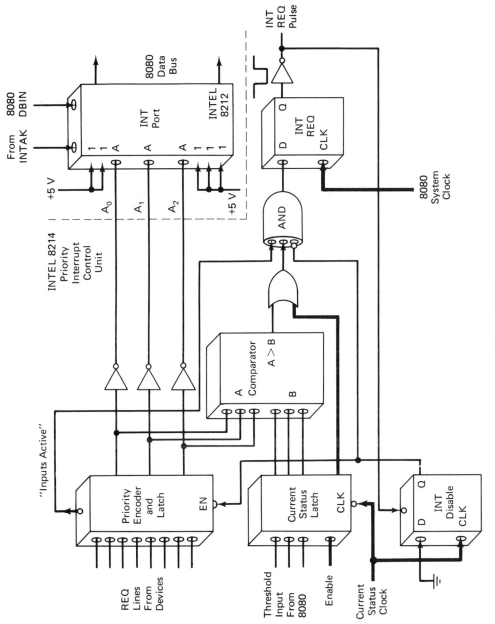

Figure 12-6

1. It generates a pulse on the 8214 Interrupt Request Line.

2. It latches the code of the requesting device onto the AAA lines.

3. It disables the AND gate, blocking further requests and effectively disabling the 8214.

The Interrupt Request pulse from the 8214 lasts only one system clock period ($\approx$500 nsec), whereas the 8080 Interrupt Request should remain until cleared by the 8080 INTAK status bit. This can be accomplished by setting an S/R flip-flop with the 8214 pulse and resetting the INTREQ flip-flop with the 8080 INTAK.

As discussed earlier, the 8080 completes the current instruction execution before sensing the INTREQ line. It then issues the INTAK status bit at the beginning of the next opcode fetch cycle. This is used to gate the TRAP instruction from the Interrupt port into the instruction register where it causes a branch to a service subroutine beginning at TRAP CELL $A_0A_1A_2$ location 0...$A_0A_1A_2$ in memory. The current program counter is automatically stacked, thus providing a return address for returning to the interrupted routine. INTAK also clears the INTREQ line.

VECTORed Interrupts

Each device (000 thru 111) can have a unique address associated with its service routine, and the hardware just described automatically provides a 1-byte call instruction that causes transfer of control to this address. An interrupt system in which the hardware supplies a separate address for each interrupting device is called a VECTORed interrupt structure as opposed to the POLLed structure in which all devices trap to the *same* address, and device identification and conflict resolution are accomplished in software. VECTORed interrupt systems provide the fastest possible interrupt servicing, because no time is wasted polling status bits.

Since the highest priority requests override all others, there must be a means of individually removing each request as it is serviced, so that lower priority requests can be seen. The lower requests must, therefore, remain active until their time comes. The 8214 Priority Interrupt Control Unit does not possess individual latches or clear lines; therefore, it is necessary to precede the inputs with eight flip-flops that possess individual set and reset lines, as shown in Fig. 12-7. The latches are set by the request from the appropriate device and cleared under software control by the service routine for the device. There are several lines associated with the 8214 that are not shown. These are for "cascading" several 8214s if more than eight interrupting devices require vectoring. Since the 8080 handles only eight levels of VECTORed interrupt, these lines have been omitted for simplicity. There is also a comparator override line that is shown

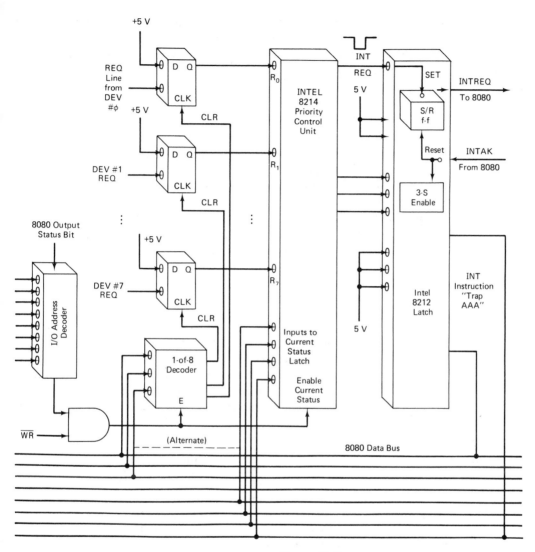

Figure 12-7

in the 8214 diagram. This line is ORed with the comparator output so the device zero can generate requests when the threshold is completely open.

The 1-of-8 decoder allows the use of three bits for clearing the individual request latches. This can be accomplished at the same time that the threshold is set, and the decoder is then enabled by the same decoded I/O address as is used for selecting the current status latch. The WRITE pulse ($\overline{WR}$) is ANDed with this select line to enable the devices as the data appear on the data bus from the accumulator. Although the diagram shows positive true inputs, the 1-of-8 decoder has active LOW outputs and the request inputs to the 8214 are also active LOW. In most cases the threshold will be set to the number of the highest priority device, active, and the inputs to the 1-of-8 decoder can be derived from the same lines that serve as input to the Current Status Latch, as indicated by dotted lines in Fig. 12-7.

Summary

The individual request lines from the devices clock their appropriate flip-flops, causing the output to become active and remain active until cleared via the interrupt service software, as described in the next section. The interrupt request pulse from the 8214 sets the flip-flop in the 8212 latch that generates an Interrupt Request to the 8080. The CPU finishes the current execution and then issues the INTAK that clears the request and enables the 8212 tri-state outputs. The TRAP instruction from the 8212 then causes a return address to be pushed onto the stack and tranfers control to the selected TRAP CELL. The software that completes the interrupt processing is described in the next section.

SOFTWARE INTERRUPT PROCESSING

In the following exposition, it is assumed that devices 3 and 5 interrupt almost simultaneously and that device 2 and then device 7 interrupt, during the service routine. Although this example is more complex than some, it illustrates all of the major features of interest. Its study is recommended therefore. We will build up the sequence successively from an initial main program execution:

		PROGRAM EXECUTION
DEVICES 3	INTREQ	(INTERRUPT
AND 5	$\longrightarrow$	SYSTEM
INTERRUPT		ENABLED)
"SIMULTANEOUSLY"		

The lines from device 3 and device 5 clock the appropriate flip-flops, and the "REQUEST ACTIVITY" line becomes active. We assume that the comparator override is active and the binary code "5" from the encoder causes a high input to appear at the Interrupt Request flip-flop D-input. The next system clock pulse causes an interrupt request to be presented to the 8080 CPU. This same signal also latches the "5" into the priority latch and disables the gate following the comparator, thereby preventing further interrupts.

The CPU will finish the current execution and then, at the beginning of the following FETCH cycle, the INTAK status line will go high (and MEMRD will go low), causing the instruction to be fetched from the Interrupt Instruction Port instead of from memory. This port uses the output of the Priority Control Unit to compose a "TRAP 5" instruction that causes the (unincremented) program counter to be saved as a return address on top of the stack in the RAM and loads the program counter with 0. . .0101000. Thus, the next instruction is fetched from TRAP CELL 5 (location 40) in memory. (See Fig. 12-8.) This location contains a JUMP to FIVE-SERVICE, which is the routine we now develop.

The service routine for device 5 performs the following tasks.

1. Push PSW, B, D, H onto the stack. The CPU state vector is saved for later return to the interrupted program execution.

2. Save the current status "IMAGE" by pushing it onto the stack.

3. Updata the "IMAGE" in memory.

4. Load the current status latch with 5, thereby enabling the 8214 Priority Control Unit, and clearing device 5 flag.

5. Enable the 8080 Interrupt system via execution of EI.

6. Begin servicing device 5.

Assume that at this point device 2 issues a request. Since the threshold is set at 5, this request will not generate an interrupt but will remain present as

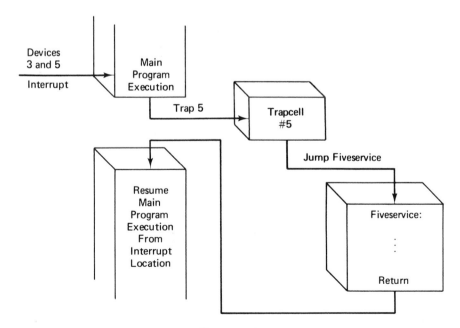

Figure 12-8

the device 2 flag. The 5 service routine continues executing. During its execution, device 7 issues an interrupt request. This code is above the threshold, and the 8214 PICU generates an interrupt to the 8080 CPU, latches #7 into AAA, and disables itself until enabled by the 8080. The hardware causes a TRAP 7 instruction to be composed and jammed into the CPU.

The location of the next instruction to be executed in FIVE-SERVICE is stored on the stack, and TRAP CELL 7 is entered. TRAP CELL 7 contains a JUMP SEVEN-SERVICE instruction, and control transfers to this routine. The 8080 state vector (accumulator, flags, and register file) is pushed onto the stack, and the current "IMAGE" is also stored there. The Current Status Latch is updated, and the "IMAGE" is updated in memory. The device 7 flag is cleared when the current status is updated and the 8214 is re-enabled. The 8080 is re-enabled via an EI instruction, and device 7 is serviced. Upon completion of the device service, the 8080 is disabled via the DI instruction, and the "LAST STATUS" is POPped into the accumulator and restored to the current status latch, resetting the threshold to 5. Device 6 is assumed inactive; therefore, no INTREQ is generated by the 8214. The 8080 state vector is restored from the stack, the 8080 interrupt system is enabled, and a RETURN instruction is executed. (The system is enabled on the second instruction FETCH cycle following EI to prevent wild stack growth in a dense interrupt environment.) The return address stored on the stack is jammed into the program counter, and control returns to the interrupted FIVE-SERVICE routine.

Upon its completion, the CPU interrupt system is again disabled, the state vector restored from the stack, the IMAGE or "LAST STATUS" is POPped and loaded into the current status latch. The initial status was "ALL" (i.e., the comparator override bit was set); therefore, the device 3 flag that is still set causes the PICU to generate an interrupt request and a vector to TRAP CELL 3. The FIVE-SERVICE ends with an EI and a RETURN to the interrupted program. The enabled 8080 interrupt system responds immediately to the pending request and enters TRAP CELL 3.

From this point, the THREE-SERVICE routine behaves exactly as the FIVE- and SEVEN-SERVICE routines. If no higher devices interrupt, THREE-SERVICE completes, returns to MAIN, and finally device 2 flag gains entry to the TWO-SERVICE routine via TRAP CELL 2.

The just procedure described is summarized now for a general device #N interrupt process.

1. Store JUMP TO N-SERVICE in TRAP CELL N.

2. Jam TRAP N instruction into CPU via INTAK.

N-SERVICE:

1. Push CPU state vector onto stack.

2. Get "IMAGE" of status and save as "LAST STATUS" on the stack. Update "IMAGE" in memory.

    3. Load current status latch with N, clearing device N flag and re-enabling the 8214 Priority Interrupt Control Unit with threshold set to N.

    4. Enable the 8080 interrupt system via execution of EI.

    5. Service device N.

    6. Disable 8080 interrupts (DI).

    7. Reset threshold to "LAST STATUS" and update IMAGE in memory.

    8. Re-store CPU state vector from stack.

    9. Enable 8080 INT system (EI).

  10. Return to interrupted location.

  11. Honor highest pending interrupt, or proceed with interrupted routine if no interrupts are pending.

8080 Interrupt Summary

The Intel 8080 interrupt system has been described in detail in order to present the hardware and software concepts associated with such systems. The concepts include POLLed versus VECTORed systems, priority determination and conflict resolution, priority thresholds, stacked state vectors, individually CLEARable device flags, and service routines. With minor variations, almost all interrupt systems will utilize these concepts. The remainder of this chapter will treat such variations as currently exist in microprocessors.

THE MOTOROLA 6800 INTERRUPT STRUCTURE

In normal usage the 6800 CPU uses a POLLed interrupt structure. An interrupt pin on the device is used to inform the CPU of a request for service. The current instruction execution is completed, and then the interrupt process begins. (If the request occurs during the last cycle of the current instruction, the process is held off for one more instruction execution.) The register complement of the 6800 is reproduced in Fig. 12-9.

The 6800 state vector consists of the contents of the condition flags, both accumulators, the index register, and the program counter. The occurrence of an interrupt request when the system is enabled causes the state vector to be stored on the stack automatically, as shown in Fig. 12-10. The 16-bit program counter and index register are stacked as two bytes, and the 8-bit accumulators and condition codes are stacked on top of these. The machine is thus "clean" and ready for the service routine.

Since the return address has been stored, there is no need to input a CALL instruction; however, there must be a transfer of control from the interrupted sequence to the service routine. Instead of obtaining the transfer address from the external world, the CPU utilizes a pointer that has been stored in RAM at

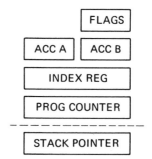

Figure 12-9

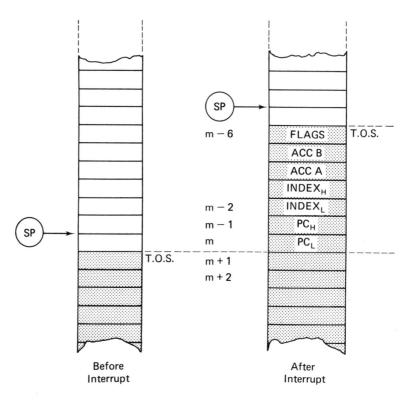

Figure 12-10

a special location. This pointer is loaded into the program counter, and the next instruction is fetched from the location pointed to. This process is independent of the origin of the interrupt and, therefore, cannot vector to a different location for each device, but must POLL status bits to determine which device needs service. As is usually the case, the interrupt system is disabled by the Interrupt and can be re-enabled only by software command. The status of the interrupt system is indicated by one of the condition code bits that can be set or reset individually, or changed when the condition codes register is loaded from an accumulator.

SPECIAL INSTRUCTIONS

The automatic stacking of the entire state vector (i.e., including the program counter) is initiated by the hardware INTERRUPT signal that can occur at any time. Unstacking must be done at the end of the service routine and is, therefore, initiated via software. The Return from Interrupt (RTI) instruction differs from the Return (RET) instruction that is used to return from a subroutine call. RTI restores the entire state vector, whereas RET restores only the program counter.

Two other special instructions transfer the state vector to the stack. Soft-Ware Interrupt (SWI) pushes the state into the stack and loads a pointer into the program counter in the same fashion as the hardware interrupt. After the status is saved, the interrupt bit is set, i.e., the system is disabled. The WAit for Interrupt (WAI) stacks the state vector, but does *not* inhibit the interrupt system. The CPU suspends execution and waits for the interrupt line to become active. The pre-stacked state allows immediate response to a request. When a request occurs, the system is disabled, and the pointer is loaded into the PC for transfer of control to the service routine. The service routine can re-enable the interrupt system if higher priority devices are to be allowed to interrupt current service. If not, the system is re-enabled at the end of current service when the RTI restores the state vector (which must have had the Interrupt mask bit inactive).

DESIGN OF A VECTORED SYSTEM

The pointer to the polling routine is stored at locations FFF8 and FFF9. When the interrupt cycle is entered, these addresses are sent to memory and the contents of these addresses are jammed into the Program Counter. If, instead of polling, we wish to vector immediately to the service routine, the address jammed into the PC must reflect the origin of the interrupt request in some fashion. This requires several pointers and a means of selecting between them. A selection mechanism is shown in Fig. 12-11. In this scheme the locations FFF 0 through FFFF are dedicated to the interrupt system. The address space is:

$$\ldots . . b_5 b_4 \quad b_3 b_2 b_1 \quad b_0$$

| 11... | ....1 1 | X X X | b_0 |

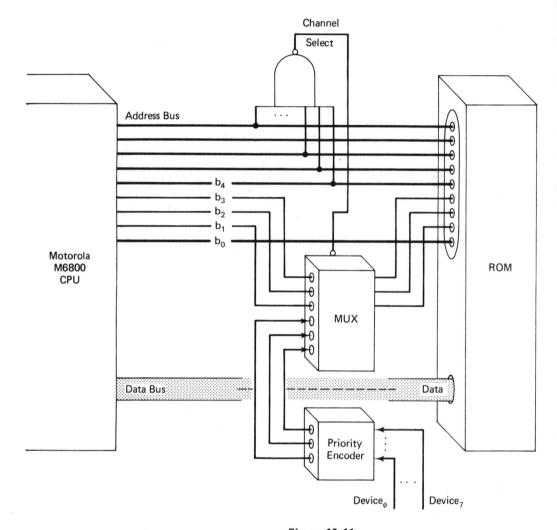

Figure 12-11

The high address bits, from b_4 to the most significant bit, are ANDed and used to control a multiplexer that is placed in the address bus. The multiplexer has two channels, each three bits wide, and normally is set to pass the address from the 6800 CPU. When the high bits are all 1s, as will occur when the interrupt cycle begins, the multiplexer is switched to the interrupt channel and bits $(b_1b_2b_3)$ are replaced by $(b_1'b_2'b_3')$, which are provided via the eight-level priority encoder. Thus, when the CPU places address FFF8 on the address bus, the ROM "sees" address

$$....11111(\#)0$$

followed by

$$....11111(\#)1$$

that replaces FFF9. The octal number, ($\#$), is provided by the priority encoder. If device 2 requests an interrupt, the pointer to its service routine will be stored at locations FFF4 and FFF5. The program counter will be loaded sequentially from these locations. The address map for such a system is shown in Fig. 12-12.

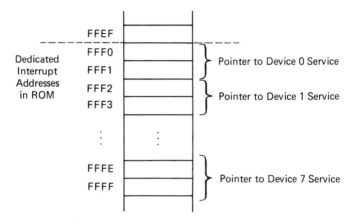

Figure 12-12

The program counter will be placed on the address bus to fetch the first instruction from the service routine. By definition, this must be an address other than FFF___ ; therefore, the multiplexer is switched back to the normal mode.

"SPECIAL-PURPOSE" INTERRUPTS

There are three other pointers, stored in high memory, that are usually dedicated to specific processes. A NONMASKABLE INTERRUPT (NMI) pin is available for extremely high priority events that should never be locked out of service. Most processors assign highest priority to power-fail sensors. Processors operate so rapidly that they are able to execute a number of instructions between the time that a power failure has been sensed and the time that the voltage drops below the operating level for the CPU. Thus, it is possible to provide nonvolatile storage for saving the state vector as well as other relevant information, and thereby to allow system recovery when power returns. When the return of power is sensed, a signal can be applied to the RESET pin. This pin allows program execution to begin at a known starting location. In the 8080 the program counter is cleared, and the next instruction is fetched from location ϕ when the RESET pin is activated. In the 6800, RESET causes address FFFE and FFFF, the highest in memory, to select the pointer that is jammed into the PC. The routine selected can be either the power-fail-restart sequence or simply a power-on initialization sequence. In addition, this line is often used to recover from system crashes or hangups that are unrelated to power failures. Due to normal assignment of the RESET pin to initialization sequences, the state vector is not stacked for this interrupt; however, the interrupt system is disabled.

The pointers associated with the INTERRUPT REQUEST line, the NON-MASKABLE INTERRUPT line, the RESET line, and the SOFTWARE INTERRUPT process are stored in the high memory locations shown in Fig. 12-13.

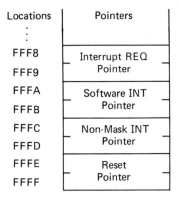

Locations	Pointers
⋮	
FFF8	Interrupt REQ Pointer
FFF9	
FFFA	Software INT Pointer
FFFB	
FFFC	Non-Mask INT Pointer
FFFD	
FFFE	Reset Pointer
FFFF	

Figure 12-13

These locations are permanently assigned to these processes and should be considered in any hardware priority scheme. Note that the fetch of any of these pointers would activate the multiplexer in the hardware priority scheme described in this section.

MOS TECHNOLOGY 650X INTERRUPT STRUCTURE

The MOS Technology family of microprocessors offers several variations on the basic Motorola 6800 interrupt structure. They are all polled machines, using interrupt vectors in high memory. The majority of the machines possess both INTERRUPT REQUEST for I/O devices and the NONMASKABLE INTERRUPT for power-fail or highest priority interruption. Several of the CPUs that are packaged with 28 pins sacrifice the NMI for some other function. The 6503 retains the NMI function, while the 6504 replaces it with an extra address line, A_{12}, and the 6505 has a READY line in its place. All of the 40-pin versions offer the NMI function. The automatic save/restore interrupt response has been dropped. The program counter and status register are saved automatically, but the accumulator must be pushed onto the stack, and the index registers transferred to the accumulator and then pushed onto the stack.

The 650X series machines replace the SOFTWARE INTERRUPT (SWI) of the 6800 with a BREAK (BRK) command. There is no separate vector for this command; instead, a "break bit" has been added to the Program Status Register, as shown in Fig. 12-14.

Sign	Over Flow	Future Expand	Break Bit	Decimal Mode	Int Disable	Zero Flag	Carry Flag

Figure 12-14

The Program Status Register is always stored on the stack by an interrupt and so allows the break bit to be tested to determine the source of the interrupt, i.e., hardware or software. If the break bit is set HIGH, the interrupt source was the BRK command. The break bit is not set or reset by any instructions and is thus dedicated to this function. The bit can be tested after the save routine is executed in the interrupt service routine:

```
POP  A                      ; load status into accumulator
PUSH A                      ; restore onto stack
ANDI 10H                    ; isolate the break bit
BRANCH ZERO BRKPOINT        ; branch to breakpoint
      .
      .                     ; else proceed with interrupt
      .
```

Breaks are most useful in debugging programs. If the user is unsure about certain sections of code, the BRK can be placed at strategic locations causing a branch to a debugging routine that will normally display the location and contents of selected registers and then return control to the user. This general method is often implemented in processors and provides one of the more powerful tools for debugging a system.

SIGNETICS 2650 INTERRUPT STRUCTURE

The Signetics 2650 CPU provides a single-level VECTORed INTERRUPT system. An interrupt request will be honored after the current execution is completed. The system is disabled, and a special branch instruction is inserted into the instruction register. The ZBSR causes a branch to a subroutine (thus saving a return address) relative to byte zero on page zero. This instruction uses a second byte that is treated as a signed displacement with indirect addressing possible. The format is shown in Fig. 12-A.

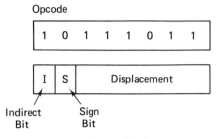

Figure 12-A

The 6-bit displacement allows any location within 64 bytes of location zero to be accessed. Negative displacements wrap around the high end of the 8K zero page. The ability to specify indirect addressing provides a means of reaching any location in the 32K memory space. After the ZBSR instruction has been inserted by the CPU, the INTAK and OPREQ signals are issued.

The OPREQ informs external devices that a new operation is beginning and that all CPU signal lines are valid, as explained in the 2650 I/O discussion. The INTAK is used to insert the second (address) byte of the ZBSR instruction into the CPU. Thus, the interrupting device can supply the address vector to the service subroutine. The current program counter contents are stored on an internal eight-deep return stack similar to that of the Intel 8008. This stack is not available for storing the CPU state vector. The INTERRUPT INHIBIT bit in the program status word can be reset under software control during the execution of the service routine or by executing a RETURN-and-ENABLE instruction at the end of the routine. The INTAK signal should be used to clear the INTREQ signal. The interrupt timing is shown in Fig. 12-15.

A system is shown in Fig. 12-16 for providing branch addresses upon the occurrence of an interrupt request. The scheme is similar to the 8080 addressing mechanism except that the full 8 bits are address information rather than an

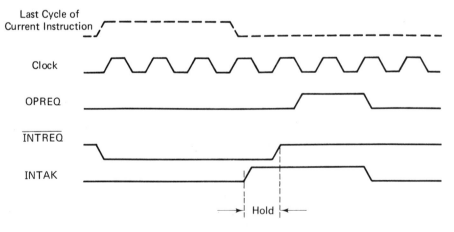

Figure 12-15

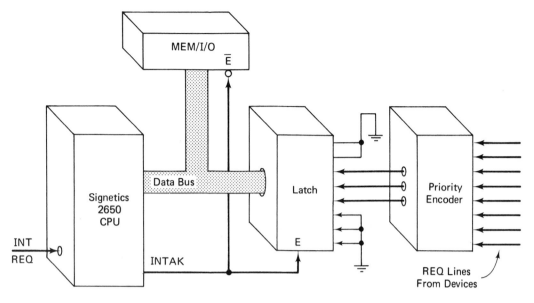

Figure 12-16

instruction to be fetched. The use of the priority encoder guarantees that the highest priority device, as determined by a rigid priority structure, will gain entry to its service routine at any time.

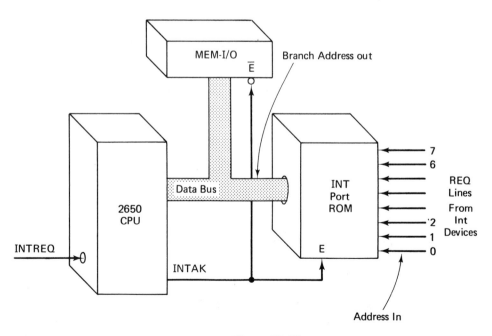

Figure 12-17

A more flexible priority structure is obtained by utilizing a ROM for storage of interrupt branch addresses. Such a system is shown in Fig. 12-17. The request lines from as many as eight devices provide the address of the word in ROM, and this word provides the branch address to the CPU.

This scheme allows a variable priority structure that is dependent upon the devices requesting service at any particular time. The highest priority device at one time cannot be highest at another. Consider three devices, say those represented by request lines 1, 2, and 3. Any of these can become active, providing eight possible combinations. The accompanying table lists the possible branch addresses.

Active Devices 3 2 1	Address to ROM	Branch Address from ROM	Service Routine Selected
0 0 0	. . . .	. . . . .	
0 0 1	0 0 1 0	0 0 1 0 0	A
0 1 0	0 1 0 0	0 1 0 0 0	B
1 0 0	1 0 0 0	1 0 0 0 0	C
0 1 1	0 1 1 0	0 1 0 0 0	B
1 0 1	1 0 1 0	1 0 0 0 0	C
1 1 0	1 1 0 0	1 1 0 0 0	C'
1 1 1	1 1 1 0	0 1 0 0 0	B

The table shows three service routines, A, B, and C, dedicated to devices 1, 2, and 3, respectively. In some cases, device 3 has highest priority, followed by devices 2 and 1. When devices 3 and 1 interrupt at the same time, routine 3 is selected, corresponding to device 3. When devices 2 and 1 interrupt simultaneously, execution branches to routine B. However, if device 3 becomes active at the same time device 2 is active, a special routine, C, is entered. Thus, servicing of devices is contextual, i.e., the service of a given device varies according to the other devices active at the time. In similar fashion the priority assignment can be made contextual as indicated by the branch to routine B, rather than C, when *all* devices are active. This contextual assignment can be extended to any combination of devices. Note also that a ROM with 2^N 8-bit words can be used to service N devices where N may be greater than eight. Some of the 2^N combinations of active devices will be forced to branch to a common location; however, this is quite normal and is not a shortcoming.

Summary of Signetics 2650 Interrupt

The interrupt mechanism of the 2650 forces the execution of a branch to subroutine relative to location zero instruction and uses an address vector jammed into the CPU. The INTAK signal is used to activate the subsystem that supplies the address vector. The use of the relative indirect addressing mode allows access to service routines located at any addressable memory location. The inability to stack the state vector in external RAM effectively limits the interrupt system to a single-level interrupt, as does the very limited depth of the return address stack inside the CPU. The use of the firmware contextual contention resolution subsystem complements the single-level CPU capability and provides a flexible interrupt system.

THE GENERAL INSTRUMENT CP-1600 INTERRUPT STRUCTURE

The CP-1600, like the 2650 just discussed, acknowledges an interrupt at the end of the instruction currently being executed and jams a self-identifying vector appearing on the data bus into the program counter. There are two standard interrupt levels: the nonmaskable, high-priority channel used for power-fail or similar interrupts, and the maskable interrupt that is normally used with interrupting I/O devices. Two decoded state signals are used to control the interrupt process: INTAK enables the priority resolution subsystems and signals the beginning of the interrupt sequence. The Interrupt Address to Bus signal (IAB) is used to gate the interrupt vector onto the 16-bit data bus. This address is loaded into the program counter and causes a transfer of control to the interrupt service routine after the current program counter has been PUSHed onto the stack.

THE NATIONAL PACE INTERRUPT SYSTEM

Most microprocessors currently available possess only rudimentary priority determinations on the chip and require external priority resolution circuitry if several devices are to be vectored to their service routines. The PACE microprocessor was the first to offer a six-level priority interrupt structure on the chip itself. The treatment of the PACE I/O structure discussed a 16-bit status register that is accessible by several instructions, including bit SET/RESET instructions. Four of these bits were available off the chip via four pins that provide a flexible output channel. Five of the status bits are used as mask bits for the interrupt system. Individual bit manipulation instructions allow any of these five interrupt request lines to be separately enabled or disabled and provide one of the most flexible interrupt structures available. In addition, a Master Interrupt Enable (IEN) is provided for all five lower priority levels. The highest priority interrupt request (IRϕ) is dedicated to power-fail service normally or to control panel service. The next highest request is dedicated to stack maintenance as follows:

The PACE contains a 10-deep push-down stack that is used for subroutine calls, interrupts, and temporary data storage. If the stack should approach an overflow condition, the stack interrupt request becomes active; a service routine then transfers the stack contents to external memory and returns to the current

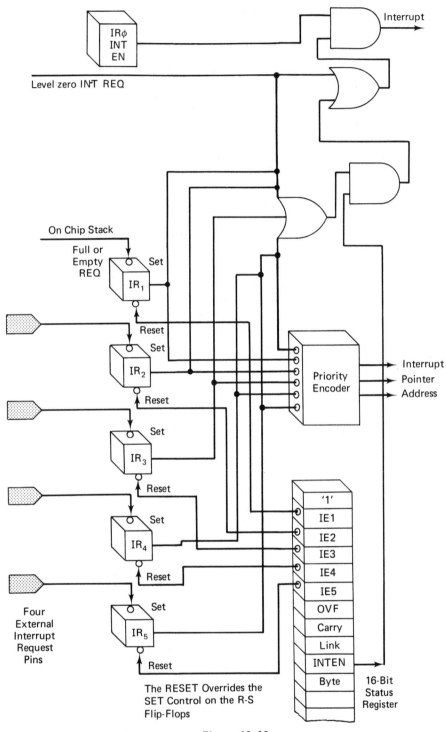

Figure 12-18

routine. The stack interrupt is also generated when the stack becomes empty. This request is generated internally. The four lowest request lines are for servicing external devices and are available via four pins, as shown in Fig. 12-18.

The operation of the PACE interupt system is conventional. A negative TRUE on any line that lasts longer than one system clock period will cause the interrupt sequence to be entered at the conclusion of the current instruction execution. The current program counter is stacked, and a pointer is loaded into the program counter. The pointers are stored in locations 2 through 7 and are selected by the output of the priority encoder. The system is disabled by setting the Master Interrupt Enable bit LOW. If the system is enabled by setting this bit with the Pulse Flag instruction, the CPU delays one instruction execution to allow a return to the interrupted program. The Return From Interrupt (RTI) instruction resets the Interrupt Enable bit and entails no delay. Since the individual latches for each request line are on the PACE chip, the line being serviced can be cleared and re-enabled by pulsing the appropriate bit in the status register.

If the Master Interrupt Enable line is FALSE, the individual R/S latches will "remember" which lines have requested service and, upon re-enabling the system, the highest of these will be vectored to its service routine. If higher priority devices are to be allowed to interrupt the current service routine, the master bit is set TRUE and the current level and lower bits are disabled. Unless external latches are provided, these disabled lines will not "remember" transient requests for service.

The generation of a Zero-Level Interrupt is achieved via the use of the NHALT and CONTINUE pins on the PACE. These pins are bidirectional control lines and work in several modes. The CONTIN line is driven low at the end of the current instruction to acknowledge an interrupt, i.e., INTAK. The NHALT line is used as the nonmaskable interrupt line, the programmed HALT acknowledgment (HLTAK) output line, and as a HOLD request line for DMA-type applications. The timing and sequence of control signals vary for the different modes. Only the HOLD mode timing is treated, and its discussion occurs in the DMA chapter.

The nonmaskable interrupt lines are often used for power-fail-auto-restart in applications that are used in the "field." For development systems these lines are often dedicated to control panel interrupts. Since they can never be disabled by software, the operator always maintains control of the machine.

THE RCA COSMAC INTERRUPT STRUCTURE

The COSMAC interrupt structure is well integrated into its unconventional architecture. The addressing structure of the COSMAC utilizes a 16-register pointer array, only three of which are active at any given time: a program counter, a memory data pointer, and an index register. These are selected by three 4-bit meta-pointers, as shown in Fig. 12-19.

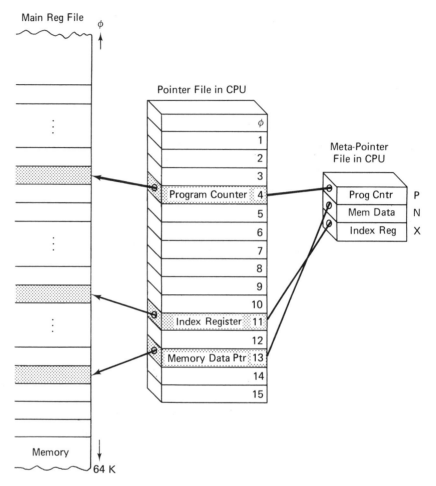

Figure 12-19

From Fig. 12-19 it is obvious that the state vectors need not be saved in external registers, as is usually the case, but can simply be left "in place" while the machine utilizes another set of state registers. It is necessary then only to store the "Meta-State" vector, i.e., $(\mathbf{P}, \mathbf{X}, \mathbf{N})$. The meta-state vector is re-stored upon return to the interrupted state. This is accomplished on a one-level interrupt basis via the use of the temporary storage register, T, shown in Fig. 12-20.

Several of the processors that have been discussed, automatically store the program counter upon acknowledging an interrupt and jam the address of an interrupt trap cell into the PC. The corresponding process in COSMAC stores the current meta-state vector $(\mathbf{P}, \mathbf{X})$ in register, $T = (T_p T_x)$, and forces the meta-state to $(1, 2)$, i.e., register 1 becomes the new program counter and register 2 the new index pointer. The interrupt system is disabled automatically,

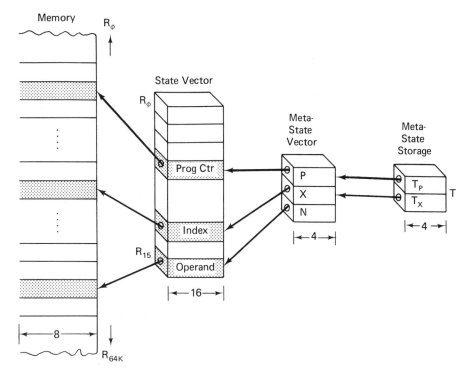

Figure 12-20

and the service routine accessed by register 1 begins execution. Multi-level interrupts are made possible via an instruction that stores register T in the memory location pointed to by R(X). Thus, prior to enabling the interrupt system, the program must load register 1 with the pointer to the service routine and register 2 with the pointer to the SAVE-meta-state storage location.

The SAVE-state instruction stores the contents of the T register at the location in memory addressed by the index register, i.e.,

$$T \longrightarrow M(R\ (\mathbf{X}))$$

where $\mathbf{X} = 2$ following an interrupt. There are two RE-STORE-state instructions for returning to the interrupted sequence. The RETURN instruction restores $\mathbf{P}$ and $\mathbf{X}$, increments R ($\mathbf{X}$), and enables the interrupt system by setting the Interrupt Enable bit to 1:

$$M\ (R\ (\mathbf{X})\ ) \longrightarrow \mathbf{X}, \mathbf{P}$$
$$R\ (\mathbf{X}) +1 \qquad , 1 \longrightarrow IE$$

while the DISABLE instruction effects the same transfer but disables the interrupt by clearing the Interrupt Enable bit. The execution of the IDLE instruction causes the CPU to wait for an Interrupt or DMA request. As described in the section on COSMAC I/O, the instruction format always contain a 4-bit instruction field, *I*, and a 4-bit operand field, **N**. Two of the *I*-field opcodes allow the **P** and **X** register to be loaded immediately with the N-value appearing on the operand field, thus allowing either program counter or index register to be changed at any point in a program.

The COSMAC interrupt response is internal and requires no externally supplied vector. The coded state control lines SC_ϕ and SC_1 provide an INTAK signal that can be utilized to remove the INTREQ. Although extra hardware may be added for multiple interrupting devices, the system is designed to operate in POLLed mode with very little external hardware required to support this operation. Since no vector is inserted into the CPU, the interrupt timing is extremely simple, requiring only that the INTREQ be present prior to the $\bar{T}_B$ transition during the execute cycle in order to be recognized.

THE INTERSIL IM 6100 INTERRUPT STRUCTURE

The IM 6100 responds to interrupt requests—if the system is enabled with no higher requests pending—by completing the current execution, storing the program counter in memory location zero, and executing the instruction stored at location one. Upon completion of the interrupt service, the processor can return to the interrupted sequence by jumping indirectly through location zero. The Interrupt Enable flip-flop is cleared, disabling the system, at the time the interrupt request is acknowledged. Thus, in most respects, the IM 6100 interrupt structure is a very conventional POLLed system. External priority resolution hardware and a software-implemented return address stack can be added to allow multi-level nested interrupts.

The I/O Interrupt for servicing I/O devices has the lowest priority of the several possible interrupting signals, as shown in Fig. 12-21. These lines are sampled during T1 of the last cycle of an instruction execution.

The INTERRUPT timing for the IM 6100 is shown in Fig. 12-22. The request line must be low by T1 of the current execution cycle. If this condition is met, the INTAK becomes active at the end of this cycle and an INTERRUPT cycle is entered. The system is disabled at this time. During the INT cycle, address zero is placed on the data bus and loaded into the memory address register via LXMAR ①. The data read into the CPU ② is ignored, and the contents of the program counter are written into location zero ③. The CPU then enters a FETCH cycle. Address one is loaded into the MAR ④, and the instruction stored at one is fetched ⑤ and executed during the following cycle.

The I/O Transfer (IOT) instructions for the IM 6100 have been described in detail in the chapter on I/O structures. The 6-bit device address allows up to

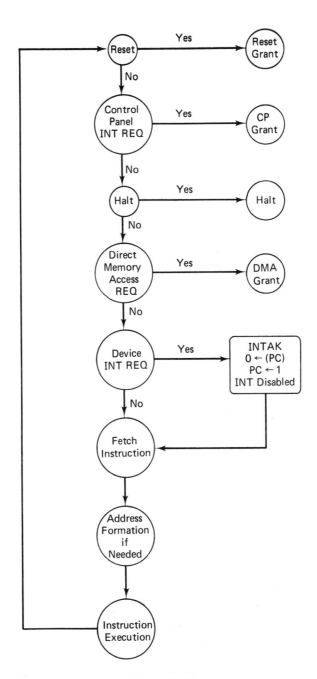

Figure 12-21

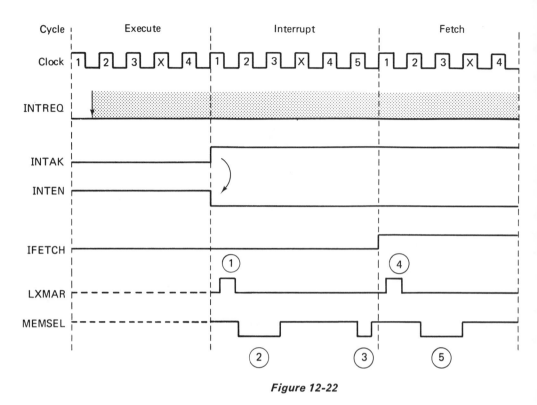

Figure 12-22

64 peripheral devices to be selected. The IM 6100 interrupt system has been assigned device address zero, and the IOT instructions to device zero are used to control the interrupt system:

IOT Opcode			Address of Interrupt System						Control Field
1	1	0	0	0	0	0	0	0	Control

Figure 12-B

Via the use of the three control bits, $(C_0C_1C_2)$, the interrupt system can be enabled (001) or disabled (010). The next instruction in sequence can be skipped if an interrupt request is present (011) and the system is disabled, or if the interrupt system is enabled (000). The last instruction disables the system. These instructions are used to manipulate flag bits. Control word (100) loads accumulator bits ϕ, 2, and 4 with status information:

bit ϕ—Link bit
bit 2—INT REQ line
bit 4—INT Enable flip-flop

Control word (101) restores the link bit from AC (ϕ) and enables the interrupt system after the next instruction execution. Control word (111) clears the AC and link bit and disables the interrupt system.

IM 6100 Control-Mode Interrupt

In addition to the I/O Interrupt system, the IM 6100 possesses a control-mode interrupt system. Although this is customarily implemented for a control panel that can display and alter register contents, it is ideal for multiprocessor applications. This interrupt request takes precedence over the INTERRUPT, DMA, and HALT request lines. It is acknowledged by CPSELect that forces MEM-SELect inactive and transfers control to control memory. The current PC is stored at location zero, and the next instruction is fetched from high memory. The usual configuration then consists of control RAM in low memory and control ROM in high memory. These memories will be selected by the CPSEL line.

The control panel interrupt timing is shown in Fig. 12-23. Address zero is loaded into the external memory address register, ①, and the data read is ignored, ②. The program counter is then written into location zero, ③, during

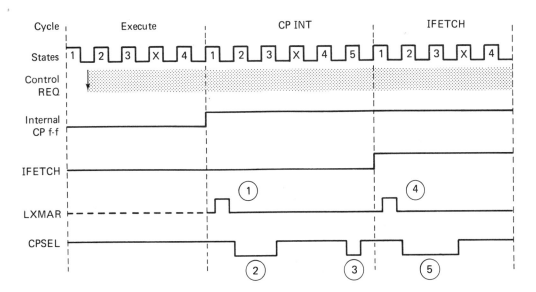

Figure 12-23

the write state. The following FETCH cycle sends out the high memory address, FFFH, to control memory, ④, and fetches the first instruction of the control routine, ⑤.

In order to gain access to noncontrol memory locations, the use of indirect addressing causes the MEMSEL to become active during the data fetch cycle. Thus, the control memory provides the effective address, but the main memory is accessed for the data transfer. Timing is shown in Fig. 12-24. The instruction is fetched from control stores ① and ②, and the effective address in control store ③ is accessed for the operand address ④ which is then used ⑤, to read ⑥, or write ⑦, data into the main memory. The control routine is exited by executing an Enable Interrupt IOT $(6001)_8$ instruction followed by an indirect jump through location zero in the control memory that contains the return address.

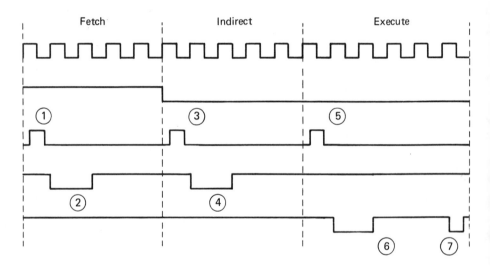

Figure 12-24

Reset and Halt

The highest request priority is alloted the RESET line that initializes all of the internal flags and clears the accumulator and the link. Third in the priority request structure is the RUN/HALT line, which can stop the machine, and which can be pulsed to single step through a program execution, a common debugging technique.

NATIONAL SC/MP INTERRUPT STRUCTURE

The National SC/MP microprocessor possesses two *sense lines,* lines A and B, which can be tested under program control. Sense line A operates in this fashion when the Interrupt system is disabled and functions as an INTREQ line when the system is enabled. The interrupt response of the SC/MP consists in disabling the system and swapping the contents of memory pointer #3 (which has been previously loaded with the address of the service routine) with memory pointer #0 (which serves as the program counter). The basic system does *not* provide an INTAK signal; however, one of the status bits appearing on the data bus with each address cycle may be used to generate a software INTAK upon entry into the service routine.

If the HALT status bit has been set by a HALT instruction, latched by the address strobe, and applied to the SC/MP CONTINUE pin, the CPU enters a wait for interrupt (WAI) state. Upon receipt of the INTERRUPT, the first address cycle resets the HALT status bits, and this signal can then function as a hardware INTAK. The SC/MP provides the usual one-instruction delay following the execution of the ENABLE INT instruction to allow a return to the interrupted routine.

THE ROCKWELL PPS-8 INTERRUPT STRUCTURE

The Rockwell PPS-8 utilizes a three-level interrupt scheme with the highest priority normally given to power-fail interrupts. The next level is usually assigned to a real time clock, and the third and lowest priority is dedicated to I/O device interrupts. These three interrupts utilize pointers in low memory. The occurrence of an interrupt request on any of the three lines causes a Branch to Subroutine to be executed by using the appropriate pointer. The system is disabled when the CPU recognizes the request. If the request occurs on the I/O interrupt line, the CPU issues an INTAK signal. This signal is utilized by the interrupting device as described in the following section. The PPS-8 family of devices include a number of support chips with an integrated interrupt structure known as a "daisy chain."

"Daisy Chain" Interrupt Structure

A structure that can be utilized by machines lacking hardware vectored interrupt circuitry is shown in Fig. 12-25. The circuitry associated with each device utilizes "priority in" and "priority out" signals with the leftmost (highest priority) signal a binary one. This signal is used to gate the request from the device into interrupt flag and address generation circuitry associated with each device. If the priority-in is HIGH, the device request sets a request flag and enables the device address circuitry. The request flag is ORed with other device flags to generate an interrupt request to the CPU. It is inverted and ANDed with the priority-in signal to produce a priority-out signal. This signal then becomes the priority-in for the next device in the chain. An examination of Fig. 12-25 shows that the request from a given device "breaks the chain" and inhibits all lower priority devices, preventing them from requesting service. The INTAK from the CPU enables all of the device address circuits; however, only the

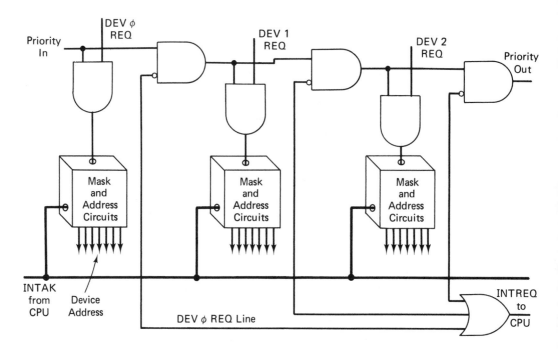

Figure 12-25

highest priority active device (above the break in the chain) will supply its address to the CPU. This address is then used to vector to the service routine.

The PPS-8 utilizes a daisy chain with a slightly different mode of operation. Each device has an Acknowledge Input (ACKI) and an Acknowledge Output (ACKO). These are chained with the ACKO of each device fed to the ACKI of the next lower priority device. The ACKI of the highest priority device is supplied by the interrupt acknowledge line from the CPU. The interrupting device request lines are ORed and used with the I/O interrupt request pin to initiate an interrupt cycle. The CPU responds by transmitting a *pulse* on the INTAK line. The pulse has a one-cycle duration and propagates down the chain at the rate of one device per cycle. When the pulse encounters the highest priority active device, the chain is broken and propagation ceases. While the pulse is traversing the chain, the CPU is performing the branch to the POLLing subroutine. The interrupting devices are interfaced via special PPS-8 support chips that provide the priority propagation chain described above and that respond to an "all call" command sent out by the CPU.

Just as device address zero was dedicated for use with the interrupt system in the Intersil IM 6100, address zero is also a dedicated interrupt address in the PPS-8. The CPU executes an input instruction from device zero, and all of the devices are interrogated at once. The interrupting device that has received the acknowledge pulse then places its own address on the data bus. The device also clears its request flag, thus removing its interrupt request from the CPU. Other lower priority device requests can still be present, but the PPS-8 must be re-enabled via software in order to respond to these. The "all call" command originates in the polling routine, and this routine then uses the supplied device address to branch to the appropriate service routine. This service is ended by a Return From Interrupt (RTI) instruction that re-enables the interrupt system and responds to pending interrupts or resumes execution of the interrupted sequence.

THE FAIRCHILD F-8 INTERRUPT STRUCTURE

The F-8 microprocessor architecture is unconventional in that the program counter, memory data pointer, and a stack register are external to the CPU. The F-8 has been optimized for small systems and uses memory elements that contain these address registers. These elements also contain interrupt circuitry similar to the PPS-8 support chips in that each chip can receive requests from external devices and pass the request to the CPU. The outputs are ORed together, and a priority chain is established as described in the last sections and shown in Fig. 12-26.

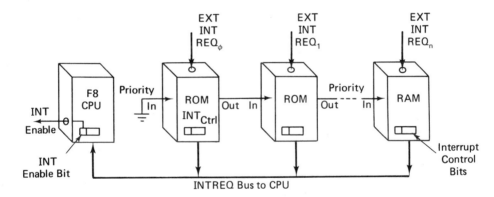

Figure 12-26

The Read Only Memory (ROM) chips contain both priority-in and priority-out control lines, whereas the (interface chip for) read-write memory contains only a priority-in channel and must be at the low-priority end of ·the chain therefore. As shown at the high end, the inputs are active LOW. The operation of this chain is straightforward. The occurrence of a device interrupt request at any chip breaks the chain, thus inhibiting all lower priority requests and signaling to the CPU via the interrupt request bus that a request is present.

Also shown in Fig. 12-26 are two local interrupt control bits per memor·' chip. Each memory chip contains an interval timer that can be preset to cov·'

a specified number of clock cycles and, upon reaching this count, generate an interrupt request to the CPU. One of the interrupt control bits specifies whether the local interrupt system is to be enabled or disabled, and the other selects between the timer and the external interrupts:

Select Bit	Interrupt Enable Bit	
0	0	no interrupt
0	1	Ext interrupt enabled
1	0	no interrupt
1	1	Timer interrupt enabled

The control bits can be set or reset under program control via an output instruction. The CPU interrupt mask bit in the CPU W register is set under program control and automatically cleared at the beginning of the interrupt sequence. In addition to the two control bits, each local interrupt control circuit has a 16-bit interrupt address vector. This vector may be accessed via I/O instructions as two bytes of address. Bit seven of the vector is not under program control but specifies whether the interrupt is internal or external as determined by the local interrupt control bits. The address vectors in the ROM chips are mask options and are not programmable. When the CPU acknowledges the interrupt request, the requesting local interrupt circuit transmits the address vector as two bytes over the data bus. All of the address control circuits utilize this to vector to the service routine. The current program counter is loaded into the stack register, and the current stack register contents are lost.

F-8 Interrupt Example

The minimum F-8 system consisting of a CPU and a ROM with 1K-byte of instructions can use up to 32 input lines (without multiplexing). A Fairchild application note describes a basic polled system that uses eight input ports. The basic scheme is shown in Fig. 12-27. Using negative-TRUE Interrupt lines to take advantage of the availability of eight-input AND gates (negative-TRUE OR), the request lines are ORed to generate an interrupt to the CPU and each line is run to a separate input line. The POLLing routine then scans the eight status lines to identify the source of the interrupt.

F-8 Interrupt Summary

As described elsewhere, the F-8 has been optimized for operation in a minimum package configuration. The physical separation of the ALU and register file from the addressing circuitry, connected by a data bus and control bus,

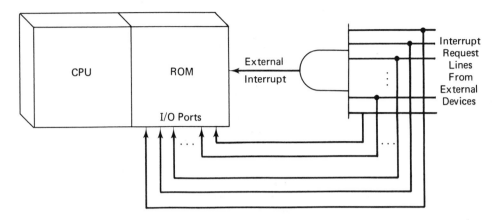

Figure 12-27

suggests that the interrupt applications should be kept at an elementary level. The presence of interrupting hardware interval timers provides the ability to do timing in an interrupt environment that would be almost impossible via the use of (interrupted) wait loops.

THE MOSTEK 5065P INTERRUPT STRUCTURE

The 5065P utilizes the classical one-accumulator architecture. With no internal register file, every instruction that transfers data must reference memory. When flip-flops were built from vacuum tubes it was considered too costly to have an internal or scratchpad register file. As the cost of integrated electronics dropped, scratchpad registers were added to speed up many operations since data already in the machine could be moved without sending an address to memory. The 5065P uses this architecture, not because of the expense of a register file, but because of the space required by such a file. With no file there is room for three one-accumulator machines. This architecture provides an efficient approach to the "change state" process initiated by interrupt requests.

The SAVESTATE process cleans the machine out and presents a clean machine to the interrupting process. The bookkeeping needed to save and restore the state vector is dead time in that no useful work is done. The whole system is designed to share one machine between two or more processes. If there were two or more machines available, it would not be necessary to save state; we could simply switch machines (assuming that the power supply and front panel, etc. will support only one active machine at a time). In this case there would be almost no dead time associated with the switch. This is the approach that is taken in the MOSTEK MK 5065P. The architecture is shown in Fig. 12-28.

The three machines are labeled level 1, 2, and 3. Only one level is operational at any time, and this level has access to an auxiliary link bit, an arithmetic logic

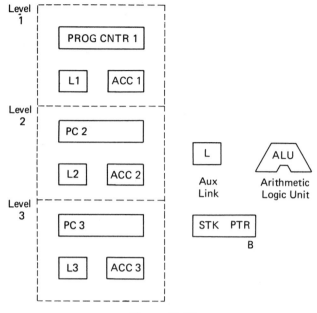

Figure 12-28

unit, and an 8-bit stack pointer for saving subroutine return addresses. The instructions utilize page-mode addressing with multi-level indirect addressing possible.

Level Switching

As with most interrupt systems, control can be effected in the 5065P via either hardware or software. The active level may be changed by executing either a LEVEL DOWN or a LEVEL UP instruction that causes control to be transferred either to the next lower or higher level machine, respectively. LEVEL DOWN has no effect if executed at level 3, and LEVEL UP is ineffective at level 1. Hardware control of the operating level is available via the two interrupt pins, INT 1 and INT 2. Normal operation wil! utilize the level 3 machine. If the system is enabled and INT 2 become active, control is transferred to level 2. If the machine is on either level 2 or level 3 and INT 1 becomes active, control is transferred to level 1. Two status pins, LEV 1 and LEV 2, are used to indicate the active operating level as given here:

Lev 1	Lev 2	
0	0	Level 3
0	1	Level 2
1	0	Level 1

The switch from one level to another requires no save-state or re-store-state overhead since the abandoned machine state is left in place and can be returned to directly.

The triple-level architecture modifies slightly some of the features of other conventional pins or instructions. For example, the RESET pin not only forces to a known location, but in this machine forces to a known level, level 1. The software control of the interrupt enable status also reflects the multi-level structure. Two modifier bits are present in the instructions, one for each interrupt that is to be enabled or disabled. Both may be enabled or disabled at once, or they may be individually controlled.

Finally, there is a LEVEL-DOWN-AND-CALL-SUBROUTINE instruction that allows control to be transferred to a known location on a lower level. The use of the simple LEVEL DOWN transfers control to the program counter of the next lower level, wherever it may be pointing.

THE TEXAS INSTRUMENTS 9900 CPU

The first third-generation microprocessor, the TI9900, possesses an architecture well suited to context switching, i.e., to interrupt processing. The 9900 is a memory-to-memory machine with no internal register file. All data operations fetch the data from memory, operate within the CPU, and store the result in memory. Thus there is no need to save and restore register file contents, as in other machines. The three working registers—PC, status, and workspace pointer—must be saved, of course, and later restored. In some aspects this resembles the RCA COSMAC "meta-state" storage.

Workspace pointer selects the first of 32 contiguous memory locations that function as the scratchpad or workspace. The classical scratchpad register file existed because internal register-register transfers occurred much faster than memory-memory transfers. Since N-MOS memories are available with speeds below 100 nsec, the memory-memory transfers can occur as rapidly as internal transfers. In applications that require numerous context switches, this architecture should be more efficient due to the lack of need to save and restore the register file. The 9900 can switch context in three store cycles and three fetch cycles.

The 9900 Interrupt Structure

The 9900 combines features of the National PACE and the Intel 8214 to produce a simple but powerful interrupt structure, as shown in Fig. 12-29. Four bits in the status register provide a threshold corresponding to the current active level. When an interrupt request occurs, the four interrupt control lines $(IC_\phi - IC_3)$ are compared to the threshold. If they are greater than or equal to the threshold, an interrupt occurs and the threshold is updated. Otherwise,

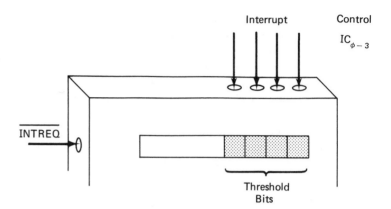

Figure 12-29

no interrupt takes place. The 16-level interrupt structure is vectored through locations in low memory (0 – 3C). The processor fetches the new program counter and workspace pointer from these locations, and then the previous state vectors (**WP, PC, ST**) are stored in registers 13, 14, and 15 of the new (32-register) workspace.

The state transition diagram is shown in Fig. 12-30. Two special lines, RESET and LOAD, jam to special locations in memory. Two special instructions, XOP and BLWP, inhibit interrupt acknowledgment as shown. All other instruction executions are followed by an INTREQ test to determine whether a request has occurred during the execution. If it has, and if the interrupt system is enabled, the interrupt control bits are compared to the threshold mask in the status register. Valid interrupts then switch context and reset the status mask to the interrupting level minus one.

ZILOG Z-80 INTERRUPT STRUCTURE

The "super-8080" designed by Zilog possesses an interrupt structure that combines several features treated in this chapter. The interrupt request line is tested at the end of each instruction execution. If a request is present, a special M1 cycle (instruction fetch cycle) is generated in which the M1 line becomes active and the I/O Request line becomes active (replacing the normally active MEMRQ line). These signals indicate to the I/O device that it is time to place an 8-bit vector on the data bus. Two wait states are automatically inserted so that a ripple priority interrupt scheme can be implemented easily.

In addition to the interrupt level just described, there is another Non-Maskable Interrupt (NMI) that has a higher priority and is always enabled. An interrupt on the NMI line automatically vectors to location 0066H.

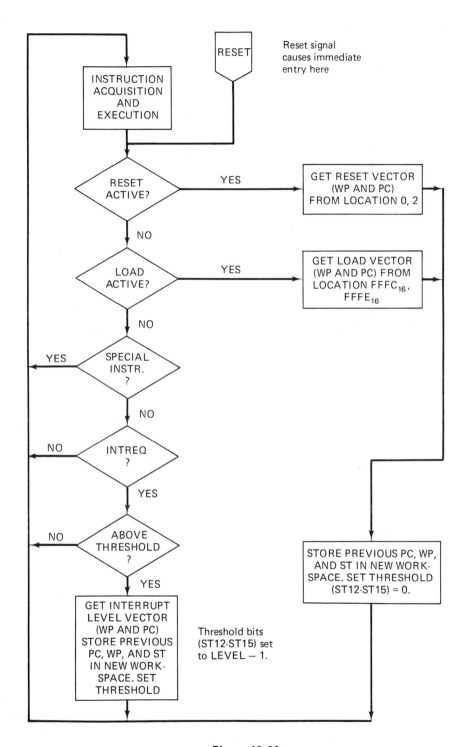

Figure 12-30

INTEL 8048 INTERRUPT STRUCTURE

An interrupt on the 8048 interrupt line vectors to location 3 in the program store. The 12-bit return address and the 4-bit program status word (PSW) are saved in an internal pushdown stack. This stack and two banks of eight working registers are implemented in the 64-byte on-chip RAM file. By including a bank switching instruction at the beginning of the interrupt service routine, the initial bank is restored automatically, as is the status of the interrupted program.

The interrupt line is one of three special lines that comprise "port 3." If the interrupt is disabled, the line can be tested as an input line. There is no automatic interrupt acknowledge generated. However, individual bit set operations, possible with on-chip output lines, allow simple software generation of an ACKNOWLEDGE in the service routine.

An extremely nice feature is an on-chip timer that provides an interrupt vector (if enabled) to instruction address 7. This timer can also be used in a count mode as an event counter that calls instruction 7 when a specified number of events have been detected.

SUMMARY

In many systems, a microprocessor must respond to events that occur relatively infrequently. If response time is unimportant, the processor may sample status lines periodically and, upon finding that an event has occurred, call the appropriate subroutine. If the processor must respond immediately, it is usually more efficient to allow the event to call its own subroutine. This can be achieved via the interrupt systems described in this chapter.

Response to Interrupt Requests

Requests can be presented to a processor at arbitrary times. The processor normally finishes executing the current instruction and then executes a subroutine call. This can be accomplished in several ways. A CALL instruction can be jammed into the CPU from an external device, or the CPU can be "hardwired" with an integral CALL capability. The location of the service subroutine may be fixed or may be supplied by an external device. For processors that provide a fixed address, it is still possible to modify the address between the CPU and memory.

External devices that provide CALL instruction and/or addresses are enabled by an INTerrupt ACKnowledge signal supplied by the CPU. The CPU normally issues this signal and disables its own request line, thereby responding to the current request and inhibiting further interrupts.

Priority Service

The asynchronous nature of interrupts allows the "simultaneous" (i.e., within the current execution cycle) occurrence of two or more interrupt requests. In order to resolve simultaneous requests, a priority structure is implemented, with each requesting device assigned a unique priority level. Thus, contention between two or more devices is always resolved in favor of the highest priority device.

Priority Determination

Priority can be established in either hardware or software. As usual, the hardware solution provides "instantaneous" (parallel) vectoring of control to the proper location. The software solution consists of sequential POLLing of device request flags, beginning with the highest priority device.

The Pecking Order

The unpredictable feature of INTERRUPTs that allows two to occur simultaneously also allows a low-priority request to occur during the servicing of a high-priority request. Although automatic shutdown of the interrupt system upon acknowledgment of any request prevents the lower-priority requests from interrupting higher-priority service routines, it also locks out even higher-priority requests. Since high priority usually implies a need for rapid response, it is often unacceptable to leave the interrupt system disabled throughout any but the highest priority service routine. If the interrupt system is to be enabled during a service routine, it is necessary to establish a pecking order that will allow higher requests to interrupt but will lock out lower requests.

There are several standard solutions to this problem. The most general solution is to mask out, or selectively disable, certain interrupts at the beginning of each service routine. This actually allows the dynamic reassignment of priorities in a contextual fashion. A less general, but usually sufficient, approach is to establish a threshold at the current highest active request level, inhibiting all requests below the threshold. This can be done with a comparator, as described for the Intel 8214, or it can be accomplished via some form of daisy chain.

Interrupt Service Housekeeping

Most systems require several housekeeping tasks to be performed in addition to the actual device service. Although they vary from machine to machine, these usually include:

1. saving state vector
2. setting threshold

3. clear interrupt request

4. enable interrupt system

5. ⟨service device⟩

6. disable interrupt system

7. reset threshold

8. re-store state vector

9. re-enable interrupt system

10. return to interrupted program

These functions can be implemented in hardware or software. The hardware approach to these requirements results in some unusual structures. For example, the RCA COSMAC (1800) saves the meta-state vector, while the Mostek 5065P saves the whole machine by switching to another.

Purpose of Interrupts

Regardless of the manner in which an interrupt system is implemented, all interrupt systems have one purpose in common: to increase the efficiency or utilization of the CPU. This is achieved by sharing the CPU between competing concurrent processes that have been ranked by the designer. The "dead time" associated with state transitions reduces efficiency somewhat, but the use of INTERRUPTs generally provides the most efficient, cost-effective technique for handling concurrent processes.

PROBLEMS

1. The BRK command is used in the 650X series microprocessors for debugging purposes. What command will allow the same function to be performed in the 6800 CPU? In the 8080 CPU? Describe a utility program that will allow the user to set breakpoints, examine and modify registers, clean up breakpoints, and proceed.

2. Use the TRAP instruction and a dedicated TRAPCELL in the Intel 8080 to implement a "breakpoint" routine or control program that should be capable of introducing breakpoints that cause execution of the program to cease and control to transfer to the breakpoint routine, which displays the location and any desired register contents, "cleans up" the breakpoints by restoring the original code, and then returns control to the user. Assume the existence of the 16-bit ADD instruction that adds the contents of the stack pointer to the H-L register pair. Make up simple MACROs as needed.

3. Describe the modifications necessary to the above, using the MOS Technology 650X BRK instruction.

4. Design circuitry that will propagate the INTAK pulses, one device per clock cycle, as required by the PPS-8 interrupt structure. (Note that this circuitry is actually implemented in each chip and need not be added externally.)

5. Draw a flow graph that describes a multi-level priority interrupt service structure. The structure should be implementation independent; i.e., it does not matter whether the state vector is stored automatically or via instructions, or whether priority is determined via a polled or vectored method.

6. Design a "watchdog" timer that will interrupt any process that executes for any length of time beyond a specified maximum interval.

7. Assume that the supply voltage will drop from 5 volts to $1/e$ of this value in 25 msec. Assume that 200 μsec are needed to store the state of the machine in a nonvolatile medium. The machine can be expected to operate only above 4.5 volts. To what threshold voltage should a power-fail sensor be set?

8. Discuss the hardware/software associated with a "live" keyboard, i.e., one that is not locked out during processing.

13 direct memory access; structures and techniques

The development of processor systems in the preceding chapters has concentrated upon the *symbol processing* capabilities inherent in these structures. An extremely general view of these processes can be summarized as:

1. load symbols into memory,
2. process symbols,
3. obtain processed symbols from memory.

The first and third steps have been implemented by using the processor I/O structure in a variety of ways; however, all of the techniques reduce to these steps.

1. Transfer the symbol from the source into a processor register.
2. Transfer the symbol from the processor register to the destination.

A distinction can be drawn between two types of data transfers, the transfer of an element of data *that is being processed* and the transfer of a block of data that has been processed or will be processed. It is to this second class, or block transfers, that this chapter is addressed.

Some general observations can be made concerning data *transfers through the CPU*. First, the processor itself is a complex, high-technology device that contains far more capability than required for such transfers and is, therefore, extremely underutilized while transferring blocks of data. Second, the time required to move data into the processor and then out of the processor is dead time that slows down the data transfer rate. If the machine must adjust pointers, maintain counters, and check status bits for each transfer, the rate diminishes even more. In most processors, the steps required to complete the transfer of one element of a block of data require from 20 μsec to 100 μsec and will, therefore, handle maximum data rata rates from 10 kilo-bytes/sec to 50 kilo-bytes/sec. If a typical memory element is assumed to possess 1-μsec cycle time, the memory is capable of 1 mega-byte/sec transfer rates. There are many real processes that provide data at these rates. High-speed analog-to-digital converters can operate in the MHz range. Transfers of data to or from a disc can easily exceed 10 kilo-bytes/sec. In a number of instances, it is not practical to slow down the external process to CPU block transfer rates. In these cases, the CPU must be bypassed and the memory directly accessed, as shown in Fig. 13-1.

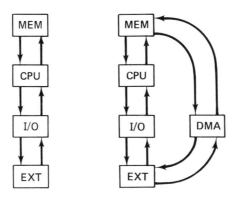

Figure 13-1

Although the idealized diagram in Fig. 13-1 shows a separate channel into memory, the structures used in microprocessor systems usually provide only one channel divided into address, data, and control buses. Thus, it is necessary to *share* this channel with the CPU, as shown in Fig. 13-2. This scheme requires that either the CPU *or* the DMA controller can be using the memory at any given time, and the other system must be electrically disconnected. The ability to electrically "disconnect" a subsystem from a system is provided by tri-state outputs, as described earlier. Thus, a CPU that will support a DMA subsystem should be able to send its address bus, data bus, and control bus into the high

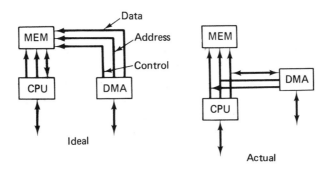

Figure 13-2

impedance mode, and also to suspend operations with memory while the direct memory access is occurring.

The remainder of this chapter will treat specific DMA facilities available with the monolithic microprocessors. The requirements of the DMA subsystem will also be treated and several DMA support chips will be presented.

THE INTEL 8080 DMA STRUCTURE

As a brief review and as a means of placing the DMA timing in context, the DMA mode will be compared with the WAIT and INTERRUPT modes of operation for the 8080. These modes are all requested by external circuits, and each provides an acknowledge signal, as shown in Fig. 13-3.

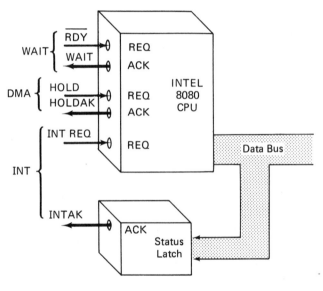

Figure 13-3

From an analysis of the *purpose* of each of these modes it is possible to deduce the appropriate timing for each mode. First, however, a review of the instruction timing for the 8080 is presented. Each instruction execution consists of up to five *functional cycles* that involve a transfer of information between the CPU and some external subsystems: memory, stack, input, output, or interrupt. The status bits available at the beginning of each cycle describe the function to be performed. Each cycle, in turn, consists of three to five basic *functional states*, such as present address, sample request lines, transfer data, process internal data. The sequence is shown in Fig. 13-4, which illustrates a normal mode, 2-cycle instruction execution. Each of the special modes, WAIT, INTERRUPT, HOLD, must be inserted in this sequence and each has an appropriate insertion point.

Cycle m m ⩽ 5	Cycle 1				Cycle 2			Cycle 1	
State L	T1 ADDR	T2 SMPL	T3 DATA	T4 PROC	T1 ADDR	T2 SMPL	T3 DATA	T1 ADDR	etc. . . .
INSTR n − 1	INSTRUCTION n							INSTR n + 1	

Figure 13-4

Entry into the Wait Mode

The purpose of the WAIT mode is accomodation of the processor to slow data sources (or sinks). The processor presents a target address during the first state of each cycle, and a transfer of data between the CPU and the target location occurs during the third state of the cycle. The time from address presentation to data transfer depends upon the system clock rate, and the target location must either respond in this time or the CPU must WAIT for the target response. Thus, it is appropriate to enter the WAIT mode of operation between the address presentation state and the data transfer state. The decision to enter this mode is made during the SAMPLE state that follows the address presentation state. If the mode is to be entered, the CPU inserts a WAIT state (Fig. 13-5) between the sample state and the data transfer state and activates the WAIT acknowledge signal.

Note that the processor "idles" until the WAITREQ line indicates the data are ready, and then resumes normal operation on the next ϕ_1 clock cycle.

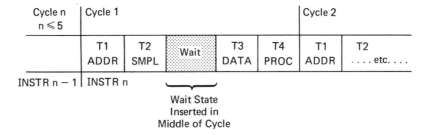

Cycle n n ⩽ 5	Cycle 1					Cycle 2	
	T1 ADDR	T2 SMPL	Wait	T3 DATA	T4 PROC	T1 ADDR	T2 . . . . etc. . . .
INSTR n − 1	INSTR n						

Wait State
Inserted in
Middle of Cycle

Figure 13-5

Entry into the Hold Mode

The purpose of the HOLD mode is to allow direct access to memory by external subsystems. The processor must float its busses and thereby allow the requesting device to access memory. The 8080 CPU samples the HOLD request line during the sample state following the address presentation state. If a request is pending, the CPU will detect it and set an internal HOLD request flip-flop. It is clearly undesirable to break the CPU/MEM connection prior to the data flow state as this would require, at the very least, that the CPU be able to later present the same address to memory. Rather, the CPU completes the data transaction with the addressed target and *then* releases the busses. If there is an internal processing state in the current cycle, the HOLD mode can be entered since such processing does not utilize any of the busses. Thus, the HOLD mode and internal processing states can overlap. Once the internal processing has finished, the CPU normally enters the address presentation state for the following cycle; however, the address and data busses have been relinquished to the requesting device; therefore, the CPU must again "idle" until the device releases the memory and drops the request. The appropriate time to enter the HOLD mode is, then, *following* the current data flow state but *prior to* the next address presentation state, as shown in Fig. 13-6. When HOLD request is released, the CPU begins the next cycle and places the address on the address bus.

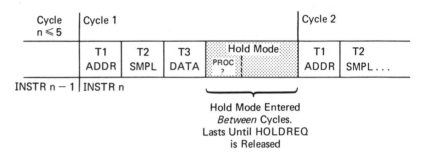

Figure 13-6

Entry into the Interrupt Mode

The WAIT mode and the HOLD mode both cause the CPU to "idle" while their respective request lines are active. This is to be contrasted with the INTERRUPT mode that is used to share the processor between two or more devices. As covered in the last chapter, it is always necessary to save the state of the interrupted machine because the use of the processor by the interrupting device will change the machine state with possible disastrous consequences upon return to the interrupted sequence. Since it is impossible for the monolithic processors discussed to return to the *middle* of an instruction execution, it is necessary that processors be interrupted only at the end of an instruction execution, as shown in Fig. 13-7.

To summarize the discussion so far:

1. WAIT between address presentation and data flow, i.e., in middle of cycle;

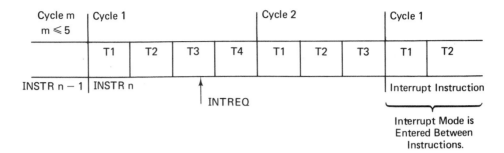

Figure 13-7

2. HOLD between data flow and *next* address presentation, i.e., between cycles;

3. INTERRUPT after current execution is complete, i.e., between instruction executions.

Note that during one instruction execution the CPU can WAIT, then HOLD, then enter the INTERRUPT mode upon completion of the execution.

The possible state transitions described above are shown on the 8080 state transition diagram in Fig. 13-8. Although the diagram clearly illustrates most of the possible transitions, there is some uncertainty concerning a HOLD request pending during T_3, T_4, and T_5. To understand the processor behavior in this situation, it is better to refer to the timing diagram shown in Fig. 13-9. Since READ and WRITE timing differ, it is necessary to consider each separately.

During an arbitrary cycle M_n, the HOLD request line becomes active during state T_1. As shown above, the WAIT request is also active. The address appears during T_1 and the processor enters state T_2 where it samples the WAIT request line. Upon finding the $\overline{RDY}$ condition, the CPU proceeds to the WAIT state and remains in this state, sampling the WAITREQ line at the trailing edge of each ϕ_2 pulse until the line indicates READY. When data is READY, Ⓐ, the CPU detects this at the ϕ_2 trailing edge, and also detects the HOLD request that is pending, Ⓑ. It then sets an internal HOLD flip-flop, Ⓒ, that is used to set the HOLDAK signal at the leading edge of the next ϕ clock pulse, Ⓓ. Note that the CPU began reading data from the bus at time, Ⓑ, and will complete this read at the leading edge of ϕ_2 during T_3. At this point, Ⓔ, the address and data busses will enter the high-impedance mode, and the requesting device can use these to gain access to memory.

Note also that T_4 and T_5, which do not appear in all cycles, can be entered while the busses are floating. The active-LOW WRITE control line does not float; therefore, it must be ORed with the DMA WRITE control line in order to give complete control of memory to the DMA device. After completion of

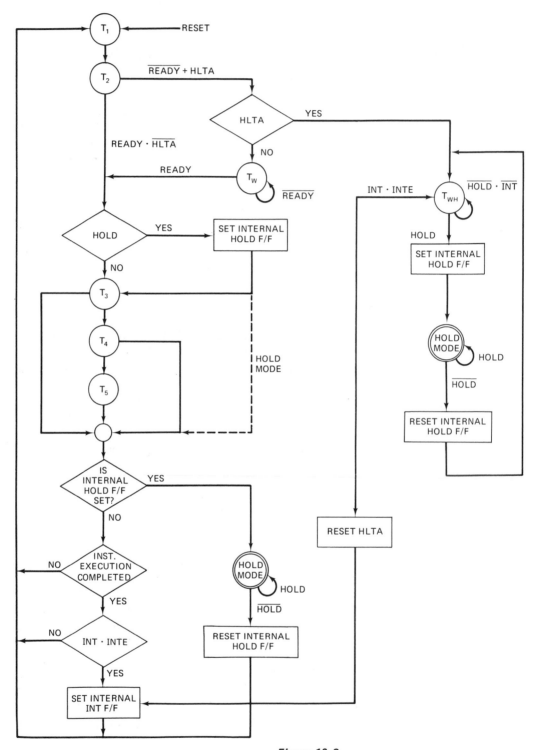

Figure 13-8

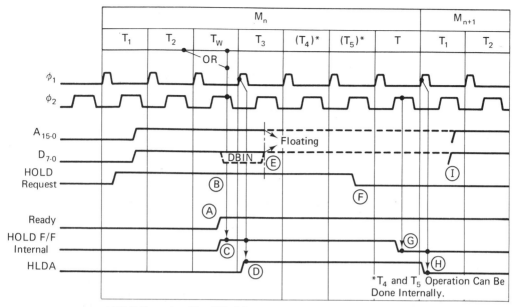

HOLD Operation (Read Mode)

Figure 13-9

the current cycle (M_n), the processor enters the idle HOLD state, (T), until the HOLD request line is released, Ⓕ. This is detected at the rising edge of ϕ_2 and the internal HOLD flip-flop is reset, Ⓖ. The processor then enters the next cycle (M_{n+1}) and drops the HOLDAK at the leading edge of ϕ_2, Ⓗ. The busses come out of the high-impedance mode at the rising edge of ϕ_2, and the address and status appear on the busses.

From this description it can be seen that the timing diagrams give detailed information about a given operation, while the state transition diagrams present an overall behavioral perspective. Both the "forest" view and the "tree" view are necessary for proper understanding of the device. The appearance of the HOLDAK *before* the busses float is quite unconventional. Normally, the acknowledge signal indicates to its target that an action has *already* occurred. The 8080 HOLDAK should be synchronized with the ϕ_2 clock pulse to achieve this normal interpretation. For comparative purposes, the READ and WRITE timing for the 8080 are shown in Fig. 13-10, although the two can never occur in the same cycle.

The READ state can be followed by either T_4 or T_1 of the next cycle (ignoring HOLDs), while the WRITE state is always followed by T_1 of the next cycle since the CPU never performs internal processing after sending data out. From the above it can be seen that the entry to the high-impedance state during ϕ_2 of T_3, as occurred in the READ mode, will occur in the middle of the WRITE

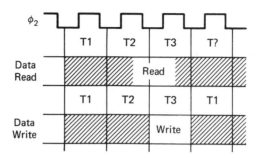

Figure 13-10

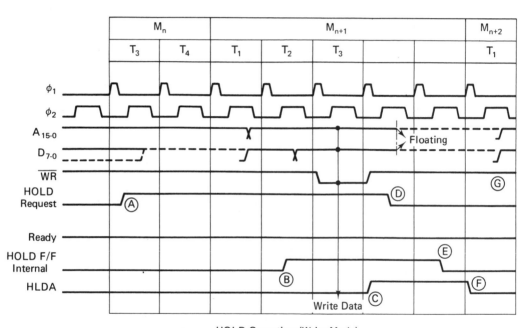

HOLD Operation (Write Mode)

Figure 13-11

state. The entry to the HOLD mode must then be delayed, as shown in the timing diagram in Fig. 13-11.

In this diagram the HOLD request occurs following the T_2 sample state of cycle M_n, Ⓐ. It is ignored and the processor finishes cycle M_n and begins M_{n+1}. Since the request line is active when sampled during T_2, the internal HOLD flip-flop is set, Ⓑ, and the processor enters the WRITE state, T_3, The internal flip-flop prevents the normal entry into the T_1 state of the following cycle and is used instead to set the HOLDAK signal on the rising edge of ϕ_1, Ⓒ. The busses begin floating at the leading edge of the following ϕ_2 clock pulse. The processor remains in the HOLD state, as shown in the state transition diagram, as long as the request is held. When the HOLD request line is dropped, Ⓓ, it is detected on the next rising ϕ_2 clock pulse, and the internal HOLD flip-flop is reset, Ⓔ. The HOLDAK is then removed at ϕ_1 of the next state, Ⓕ, that initiates the M_{n+2} cycle, and the busses come out of the high-impedance mode with ϕ_2, and the address and status appear.

The internal flip-flops function as a "string around a finger" to remind the processor either to inhibit certain modes or to enter other modes at appropriate times. Their outputs are normally used as gating signals on the clock lines or data lines of other flip-flops. The inclusion of this information in the timing diagrams aids in understanding the relation between externally unrelated signals. For example, the state transition diagram shows that the processor can be interrupted from a HALT mode (if enabled), or forced into a HOLD mode from a HALT mode. The presence of a pending INTERRUPT inhibits the HOLD mode and the presence of a pending HOLD inhibits the INTERRUPT. The inhibiting agents are the internal INTERRUPT and HOLD flip-flops. The reader will find it instructive to trace this relation through the diagram in Fig. 13-12. Examination of the HOLD timing diagrams and the INTERRUPT timing diagrams show the normal, noninhibited action.

The timing diagrams allow the designer to understand the exact sequence of

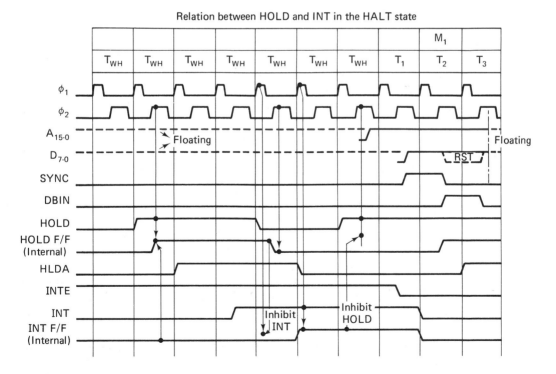

Figure 13-12

operations necessary to interface the CPU to a DMA subsystem (or memory subsystem, or interrupt subsystems, etc.). They are idealized and do not include any delays that are introduced by capacitive loading effects. In general, a timing analysis of the DMA/MEMORY interface *and* of the DMA/CPU interface must be performed.

THE INTEL DMA SUPPORT CHIP

Although the above timing detail has been presented as illustrative of the general approach to DMA design, the Intel 8080 family includes circuitry that relieves the designer of many headaches. The extension of LSI technology out from the CPU and into a growing family of support chips for each processor is beyond the scope of this volume. The UART discussed earlier hints at this trend and it seems appropriate in this chapter to introduce another such chip.

Referring to the 8008 design, the reader may remember the effort required simply to provide a WRITE signal to memory. When the CPU relinquishes memory to another device, it is then necessary for that device to supply the *addresses* to memory, the *data* to memory, and the *read* or *write* control signals to memory as well as to keep track of the number of records transferred, in addition to satisfying the timing requirements of both memory and the CPU. This, obviously, is a major design task and the application of LSI technology to this area is enough to warm a designer's heart.

The Intel 8257 DMA Controller shown in Fig. 13-13 provides all of the functions listed in the preceding paragraph! It is an N-MOS device operated from a 5-volt supply that can handle four different DMA devices on a priority basis and can be cascaded easily to handle even more channels.

As indicated in the figure, there are eight address lines (A_0–A_7) and eight data lines (D_0–D_7) available from the DMA chip. The data lines are input to an 8212 8-bit latch that functions as an external memory address register for the 8257. The 8212 output combined with A_0 through A_7 provide 16 address lines. These 16 outputs are normally in the high-impedance mode and are enabled only when the 8080 address lines are floating. The four bus control signals— memory-read and -write and I/O-read and -write—are also normally floating. The address enable line from the DMA chip that enables the 8212 latch outputs is also used to disable the 8228 system bus controller (described in the I/O chapter). When the 8228 lines float, the DMA bus control lines take control of the system, and the data bus is available to the requesting device.

The diagram in Fig. 13-14 illustrates the bus layout for the system described above. The dotted lines across the three busses are labeled *tri-state switch* as they represent the place where the busses are effectively switched between the 8080 and the DMA controller when the CPU relinquishes control of the system. In order to develop the operation of this system, we consider a specific example. Assume that a floppy disc has been commanded by the 8080 to move to a certain track and sector. The 8080 continues processing while the slow mechan-

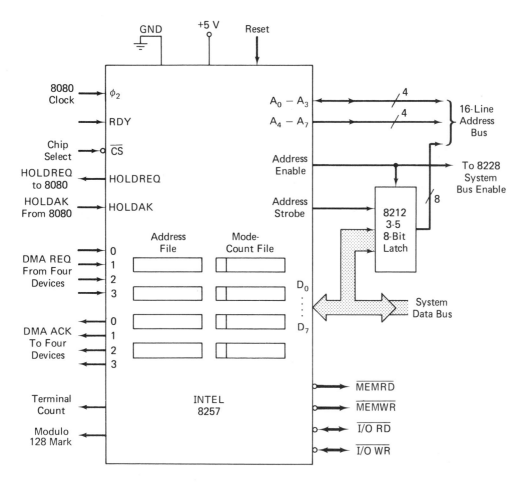

Figure 13-13

ical operation takes place. When the disc is on track and sector, the disc controller sends a signal to inform the processor. If the data from the disc are to be loaded into memory, the DMA controller can take over and dump the block directly into memory. The disc will be assigned DMA 0 and the "disc ready" signal will be used to activate the 8257 DMAREQ 0 input. There are four such inputs and the DMA controller contains prioritizing circuitry to resolve simultaneous request. Assuming that the disc request is the highest priority active line, the controller sends a HOLD request to the 8080. The CPU detects this request during the following sample state, completes the READ or WRITE, and issues a HOLDAK to the controller. The controller, in turn, issues a DMA acknowledge to the disc. The disc is now prepared to place data on the data bus for transfer to the memory; however, the memory address and timing must be supplied by the controller that is clocked by the 8080 ϕ_2 clock phase.

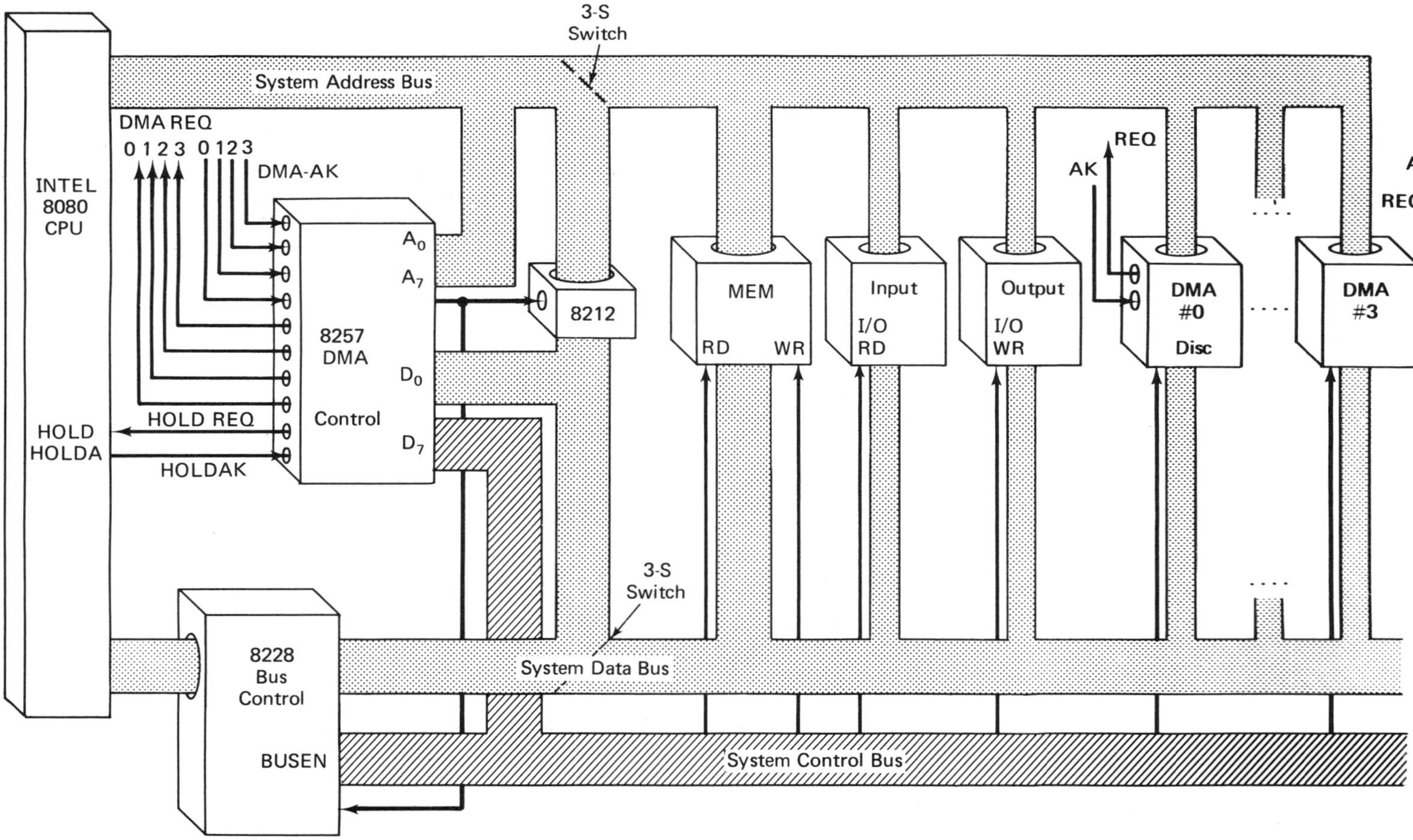
3-S
Switch
System Address Bus
DMA REQ
0 1 2 3 0 1 2 3
DMA-AK
INTEL
8080
CPU
HOLD
HOLDA
HOLD REQ
HOLDAK
A_0
A_7
8257
DMA
Control
D_0
D_7
8212
MEM
RD
WR
Input
I/O
RD
Output
I/O
WR
AK
REQ
DMA
#0
Disc
DMA
#3
AK
REQ
3-S
Switch
System Data Bus
8228
Bus
Control
BUSEN
System Control Bus

Figure 13-14

DMA Controller Operation

The 8257 controller diagram in Fig. 13-13 shows eight 16-bit registers inside the chip. The four on the left are labeled "Address File" with one register corresponding to each requesting DMA device. Assume that register zero has been loaded with a 16-bit address (we'll see *how* later) specifying the start of the destination file in memory that is to be loaded with data from the disc. This address must be presented to memory to select the location where the first disc record is to be stored. The timing diagram in Fig. 13-15 illustrates the sequence of operation for the first DMA cycle. Upon receiving the DMAREQ, the 8257 controller enters state S0 in which it issues a HOLDREQ to the 8080 and then waits for the HOLDAK.

The 8080 cycle, both READ and WRITE mode, is shown at the top of the

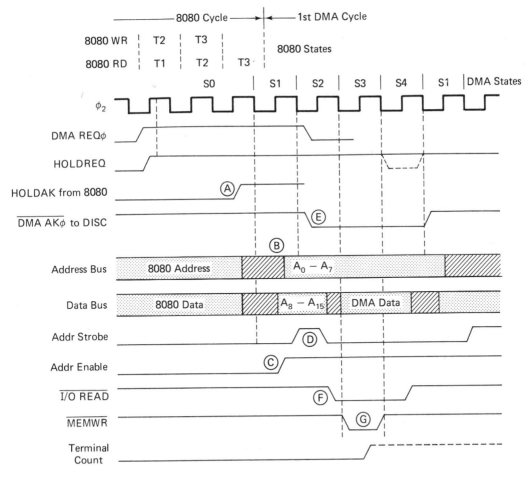

Figure 13-15

diagram. The 8080 states begin with the ϕ_1 clock pulse, which is not shown. Upon completion of the current data transfer, the 8080 issues the HOLDAK with the rising edge of the ϕ_1 clock pulse, Ⓐ. This is detected by the DMA controller that uses its priority logic to determine the highest priority active device and select its address register. With the rising edge of ϕ_2 following the last 8080 transfer state, the controller gates the lower byte of the selected address register onto the address lines A_0-A_7, Ⓑ, and at the same time gates the upper byte onto the data bus D_0-D_7. This occurs during the first state, S_1, of the DMA controller operation. The Address Enable line, Ⓒ, enables the 8212 outputs and disables the 8228 System Bus Controller, sending the 8080 system data bus and control bus into the high impedance mode.

During the second DMA state, S_2, the Address Strobe pulse, Ⓓ, latches the upper address byte into the 8212. By the end of this state the DMA chip is supplying 16 address bits to memory, and the data and control busses are floating. At the beginning of state S_2, the DMA AK_ϕ line, Ⓔ, informs device zero (the disc) that the 8257 controller is operating. The I/O READ signal becomes active, Ⓕ, near the end of the state and attempts to read data from the DMA devices onto the data bus. Only the disc that was selected by DMA AK_ϕ responds and places the first record on the data bus.

The memory is now presented with a 16-bit address from the 8257 and a byte of data from the disc. The memory WRITE pulse, Ⓖ, causes this record to be stored into the target location during controller state S_3. The actions taken during state S_4 can vary, depending upon several conditions. If the final record has been transferred, as indicated by the terminal count, or if the DMA controller is in rotating priority mode, the disc request vanishes and control passes to the next highest priority device or returns to the 8080.

Several possible modes of operation will now be described. Two major modes are known as "cycle-stealing" and "burst" DMA transfers. The first mode transfers one record at a time, between CPU cycles, while the second consists of a block transfer that locks out the CPU until the transfer is complete. The 8257 can operate in either of these modes. In the cycle-stealing mode, the controller can rotate priority so that after each transfer the current device moves to the bottom of the priority list. The next in line then transfers one byte and moves to the bottom. If rotating priority is not selected and the DMAREQ is ORed with the 8257 HOLDREQ, locking out the 8080, the transfer continues until the block has been dumped. In this mode the 8257 can perform consecutive DMA cycles every four clock periods.

Address Maintenance and Counting

If data records are to be stored in successive memory locations every four (or more) clock cycles, it is obvious that the DMA controller should provide address incrementation and, of course, it does so. There must also be some means of determining the end of a block transfer and this is provided by the record length registers shown in Fig. 13-13 as the MODE-COUNT register file on the right. These are four 16-bit registers, one per channel, that use 14 bits to contain a count (up to 16,384) of the number of records to be transferred. Thus, each time a record is transferred, the address register is incremented and the count register is decremented. When the count reaches zero, the Terminal Count (TC) line becomes active, informing the disc or other device that all records have been transferred and the HOLDREQ can be released.

Mode Control Bits

The two high-order bits of each 16-bit MODE-COUNT register are used to specify the mode of DMA transfer: READ, WRITE, or VERIFY. The WRITE DMA cycle has been described above, in which the I/O READ signal places the data from the disc (I/O device) onto the data bus and the MEMWR pulse then causes the data to be written into memory. Had the problem specified transferring a block of data *from memory to the disc*, then a READ DMA cycle would have been selected by setting the mode control bits to READ mode. In this case, the MEMRD signal would place the data from the addressed memory register onto the data bus and then an I/O WRITE pulse would write it into the disc (interface) register for transfer onto the disc storage media. In the VERIFY mode, in which two files of data are compared against each other, none of the control lines is active. Note that provision has been made for asynchronous device operation by providing a WAITREQ or $\overline{\text{READY}}$ line that functions in the same fashion as the 8080 READY lines. If the slow device does not have the data, it signals with a $\overline{\text{RDY}}$ and the 8257 enters a WAIT state until the READY signal is true. This feature greatly expands the usefulness of the chip.

Mode Control of the DMA Controller

The variety of operating modes possible with the 8257 DMA controller are selectable by the 8080 CPU. This is accomplished by the use of two meta-modes, MASTER and SLAVE. In the MASTER mode, the 8257 is in control of the system, as described in the preceding sections. In the SLAVE mode, the 8080 "sets up" the 8257 by specifying the addresses, counts, and modes of operation that will be used by the 8257 in the MASTER mode. The MASTER mode is entered when the 8257 receives the HOLDAK from the 8080. The SLAVE mode is selected when the Chip Select ($\overline{\text{CS}}$) line is active and HOLDAK is inactive. A third, nonoperating mode is selected at all other times.

For the following discussion, the DMA controller should be thought of as a number of I/O ports. The CPU will address these ports by specifying the port number, and then transfer data between the accumulator and the selected port.

I/O addresses appearing on the 8080 address bus can be decoded and used to activate the chip select line as well as specify the target register within the chip. The $\overline{CS}$ enables the I/O READ and I/O WRITE lines that are shown as bidirectional on the 8257 diagram. The four low-order address lines A_0–A_3 are also bidirectional and are used (in the SLAVE mode) to select the target register. The I/O WRITE is used in this mode to load the registers from the data bus, and the I/O READ is used to read the registers onto the data bus and into the CPU. The A_3 address bit is used to select between Program Commands that load the 16-bit registers and Mode Command or Status Read Command that is described next.

Program Command

When an output instruction from the CPU results in the $\overline{CS}$, I/O-WRITE, and bit $\overline{A}_3$ being activated, the accumulator data will be stored in one of the DMA controller registers. Address bits A_1 and A_2 select one of the four DMA channels, and bit A_0 selects either the address register or the Mode-Count register associated with this channel. Since these registers are 14 bits wide, and only 8 bits are output from the accumulator, it is necessary to load these registers by using two output operations.

To this end, there is a First/Last flip-flop in the 8257 that toggles at the completion of every Program Command to determine whether the lower or upper register byte is to be loaded. Thus, the order of loading is important and register operations should come in pairs. Via the use of the Program Command mode, the CPU can specify starting address, record length, and mode of operation for each of the four channels and can dynamically alter these specifications during the course of a program. Thus, the disc-DMA channel can be used at one point in the program to load a given block from memory to disc, and later transfer another block from the disc into another register file, etc.

Mode Set and Status Read commands

In addition to the 16-bit registers described above, there is a 6-bit mode set register and a 4-bit status register in the 8257, both of which are accessible by the CPU. These are selected by $\overline{CS}$ and A_3, and the I/O WRITE or I/O READ, respectively. Bits A_0–A_2 must be held low, i.e., $\overline{A}_0, \overline{A}_1, \overline{A}_2$. The mode set register bits are shown in Fig. 13-16. There is an individual enable bit for each of the four direct access channels. The fifth bit is used to select the "Rotate Priority" mode if desired. The sixth bit is used to "Extend" the WRITE pulses, i.e., to activate the WRITE lines earlier than shown in the diagram.

The status READ register contains 1 bit for each channel that indicates whether the channel has reached terminal count. These bits can be read into

Figure 13-16

the accumulator by executing an input instruction that will result in $\overline{CS} \cdot I/O$ READ $\cdot A_3 \cdot \bar{A}_2 \cdot \bar{A}_1 \cdot \bar{A}_0$ applied to the DMA chip. These bits are polled if the terminal count is used to interrupt the 8080. They identify the source of the interrupt and inform the CPU that the block transfer is complete.

ROCKWELL PPS-8 DMA STRUCTURE

One of the first microprocessors to be supported by a DMA controller was the Rockwell PPS-8. The diagram of the 10817 DMA chip is shown in Fig. 13-17. The DMA chip is a 17-volt P-MOS device, as is the Rockwell CPU. The CPU possesses a DMA-REQ/AK channel that is driven by the 10817 REQ and provides the DMA-AK. There is an address strap that can be tied HIGH or LOW, providing a 1-bit address for the chip, and thereby allowing two such chips to be used in one system and addressed separately.

Each DMA chip contains eight direct memory channels consisting of a Request/Terminal-Count line from/to the I/O device, and an Address register and Record Length register for each device. When the DMA-AK from the PPS-8 indicates that it is HOLDing with its busses floating, the appropriate address register is placed on the system Address bus and the I/O device either

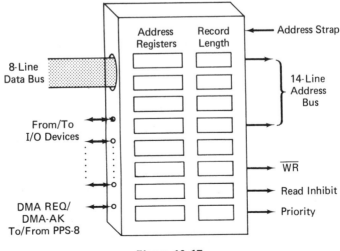

Figure 13-17

drives or receives the data on the data bus. The device DMAREQ lines are prioritized to resolve simultaneous requests. If direct access is established over one channel and a higher priority device DMA request occurs, access switches to the higher priority channel at the next cycle. The Address register for this channel begins incrementing, as does the Record Length register. When the record length register reaches zero the CPU resumes normal operation. Only the power-fail INTERRUPT, the highest priority Interrupt line, can break into a DMA transfer before it is complete. If the DMA-requesting device drops its request line, the transfer is terminated. The end-of-block or terminal count also generates a CPU interrupt if the CPU is enabled.

The 10817 address and record length registers are loaded via the use of the Load DMA (LDMA) instruction where the device address specifies the DMA channel and register to be loaded with data from the accumulator. The READ DMA (RDMA) input instruction causes the accumulator to be loaded with the contents of the selected record length register. This may be used in POLLing routine entered via the end-of-block interrupt.

RCA COSMAC DMA STRUCTURE

The COSMAC architecture provides for one "cycle-stealing" direct access channel within the program itself. Two request lines, DMA IN and DMA OUT, inform the CPU that an external device is requesting direct access to memory. The processor finishes executing the current (two-cycle) instruction and uses the 16-bit register R(0) to provide the next address to memory. The requesting device drives or receives data over the data bus and the R(0) is incremented. Control then returns to the current program counter that is unaltered during this process. The address in R(0) is easily loaded under program control during initialization or at any other time. If DMA is used in the COSMAC system, register R(0) must be dedicated to this function. R(1) and R(2) are dedicated to the Interrupt system if such is desired, as explained in the section on COSMAC interrupts. Since the processor is not used during the DMA cycle, except to provide the address, there is no need to save the the state or meta-state as required for interrupts.

The COSMAC I/O structure utilizes program-controlled direct memory access. The execution of an I/O OUTPUT instruction ($I = 6$, $N = 0xxx$) is signaled by the state lines ($SC_0 = 0$, $SC_1 = 1$) and the most significant bit of N, as shown in the diagram in Fig. 13-18. These signals can be combined and used to gate the output timing pulse, T_B, to the clock line of a C-MOS 74C173 latch. The memory read timing causes the memory data addressed by the index register to appear on the data bus, and the output timing latches these data into the output latch. The output timing is shown in Fig. 13-19.

The COSMAC cycle that fetches an output instruction is followed by a cycle during which the current index register, R(X), is placed on the address bus.

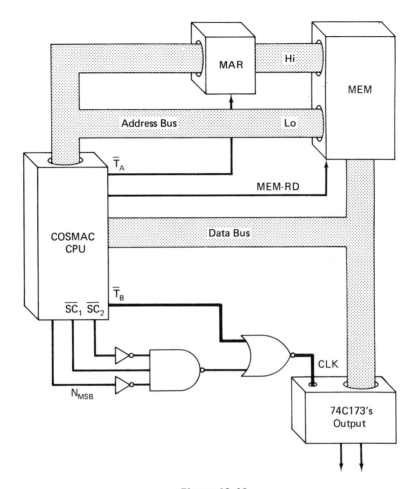

Figure 13-18

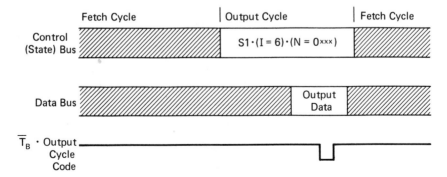

Figure 13-19

Memory data goes directly to the output latch, *completely bypassing the CPU.* The control lines used to output the data are set to the proper levels by the instruction. Similar circuitry can be used to gate the data to the DMA requesting device. The decoded state lines for state two, the DMA state, can be used to gate the output timing pulse in response to DMA-OUT request activity. The DMA-OUT process effectively executes externally initiated output cycles in the same sense that interrupt processes execute externally initiated subroutine calls. This is illustrated by the COSMAC architecture more vividly than by any other microprocessor architecture. The circuitry is shown in Fig. 13-20. The DMA-OUT request line is sampled between the leading edge of $\bar{T}_B$ and that of $\bar{T}_A$ during an execution cycle.

Note that the DMA subsystem must provide a record length counter to terminate transfers. The COSMAC input instruction utilizes $\bar{T}_B$, the decoded state lines, and the most significant bit of N to gate data onto the bus, and the memory WRITE pulse loads these data into memory. The DMA-IN request utilizes the decoded "state two" lines and $\bar{T}_B$ to enable the output of the DMA port, and

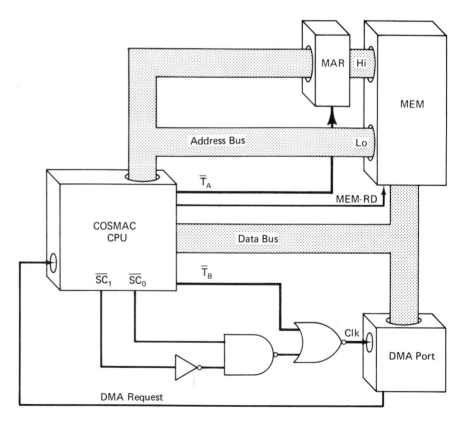

Figure 13-20

the processor supplies the memory WRITE control to memory. Thus, the DMA-IN process also functions as an externally initiated input instruction in the COSMAC system. The use of state two and $\overline{T}_B$ to enable both DMA-IN and DMA-OUT ports assumes that the DMA subsystem selects the appropriate port. The single "OUT" port is shown for simplicity.

Concurrent DMA and INTERRUPT requests are resolved in favor of the DMA.

THE INTERSIL IM 6100 DMA STRUCTURE

The IM 6100 accepts a DMA request from a device, completes the current execution, and enters a DMA cycle. The data bus is sent into the high impedance mode and the DMA-AK line becomes active. The CPU "idles" with only the timing signals T_A, T_B, and T_C active. The acknowledge should be used to reset the DMA request line, as shown in Fig. 13-21. After one DMA cycle, the CPU enters the next instruction fetch cycle.

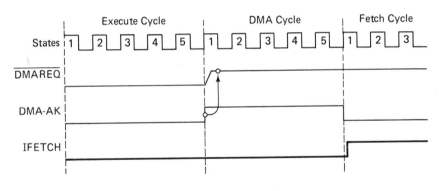

Figure 13-21

The IM 6100 DMA request takes priority over pending I/O interrupt requests. The CPU provides only the timing pulses, and the requesting device must provide the address to memory, the WRITE signal, and the data as well as a means of counting records transferred.

MOSTEK MK 5065P DMA

The 5065P uses the WAIT line to request direct memory access. The active low "DMA" pin on the processor serves as the DMA-AK. The processor "idles" as long as the WAIT line is active. The control of transfers is the responsibility of the DMA subsystem.

SIGNETICS 2650 DMA

The PAUSE pin stops the 2650 processor at the end of the current instruction execution. The RUN/$\overline{\text{WAIT}}$ line is used as the acknowledgment. Control of the tri-state address bus and data bus is provided by the ADRENable and $\overline{\text{DBUSEN}}$able lines, respectively. Provision of Addresses, WRITE control signals, and Record counts is the responsibility of the DMA subsystem requesting memory access.

THE MOTOROLA M6800 DMA STRUCTURE

The 6800 HALT line serves as a DMAREQ signal. Activity on this line causes all tri-state lines to go into the high impedance state, including the address bus, data bus, and R/W control line, and the open collector, valid memory address (VMA) line goes HIGH. The Bus Available (BA) line serves as the DMA-AK signal, or HOLDAK, and can be used to activate the DMA subsystem. The ϕ_2 system clock is used to synchronize the DMA data.

The DMA subsystem must provide a VMA signal to enable the RAMs for transfers and an R/W signal to establish the direction of data flow. The timing is shown in the diagram in Fig. 13-22. The DMAREQ line is clocked with the rising edge of ϕ_1. The CPU then completes the last cycle of the current instruc-

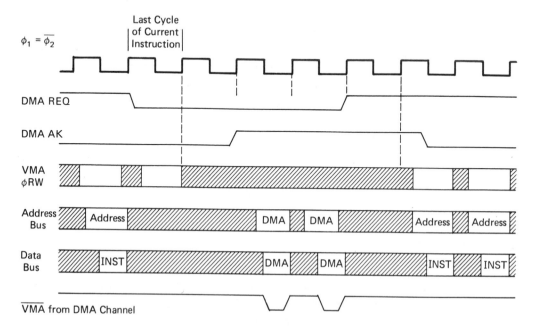

Figure 13-22

tion and brings the VMA line LOW during the first 300 nsec of the next cycle. This prevents the memories from responding to invalid addresses as the Address and R/W line goes into the high impedance state.

The Bus Available or DMA-AK then enables the DMA subsystem that provides all necessary signals, including the VMA line control that enables the RAM. The system operates in this mode as long as the DMAREQ is active. When this request is removed, the CPU executes one cycle and drops the DMA-AK. The system then resumes normal operation.

Block Transfer vs. Cycle Stealing

The DMA described above, which uses the HALT line as the DMAREQ, requires from two to 13 machine cycles, at 1 μsec/cycle, to access memory. Once access to memory is established, the channel is held open as long as the DMAREQ is active, thus allowing block transfers of data of arbitrary length.

An alternate technique that gains immediate, but limited duration, access to memory utilizes the Tri-State Control (TSC) line. This line causes the address bus and the R/W signal to go into the high impedance state and causes VMA to go LOW. The TSC line requires that the ϕ_1 clock be held HIGH and the ϕ_2 clock LOW during, and for one cycle following, the period that TSC is active. The use of dynamic registers inside of the processor requires refreshing every 4.5 μsec, and this effectively constrains the use of TSC to 3.0 μsec.

The above technique literally "stops the clock" and sends the busses into the high impedance state. The processor execution "freezes" and the DMA system "steals" a cycle. This can occur at *any* cycle, even in the middle of a long instruction execution; thus, the maximum delay associated with this technique is one cycle, i.e., a DMA device will never have to wait more than 1 μsec to access memory. On the other hand, the requirement that the clock be stopped for no more than 4.5 μsec limits the DMA transfers to two bytes per transfer.

THE FAIRCHILD F-8 DMA STRUCTURE

The F-8 DMA system is designed to work with dynamic memories and takes full advantage of the speed differential between N-MOS dynamic RAMs and N-MOS microprocessors. The 3852 interface between the 3850 CPU and dynamic memory performs two functions: (1) It contains the distributed addressing elements and circuitry necessary to decode the control bus, thereby maintaining a 16-bit program counter, data pointer, and stack register. (2) It decodes the control bus to determine when memory is idle and utilizes this information to dynamically refresh memory without slowing down the CPU. It is the last feature that is relevant to DMA. The memory is normally refreshed either every four or eight cycles, and there are idle memory cycles while the CPU is not accessing RAM that represent "free time." The free time can be used for direct access to memory without *any* degradation in system performance. The memory interface chip informs the DMA subsystem of free time by setting the memory idle (MEMIDLE) line HIGH. The system is illustrated in Fig. 13-23.

The 3852 memory interface chip contains a control register that can be loaded by the CPU to control the mode of operation. Bit zero is set to inhibit DMA transfers and reset to enable DMA. This is achieved via control of the MEM IDLE line that signals the DMA chip. Bit one is set to refresh memory or to inhibit memory refresh. If in refresh mode, bit two selects between using every fourth or every eighth slot for memory refresh. Each machine cycle in the F-8 system is divided into a CPU FETCH cycle and a second memory access cycle.

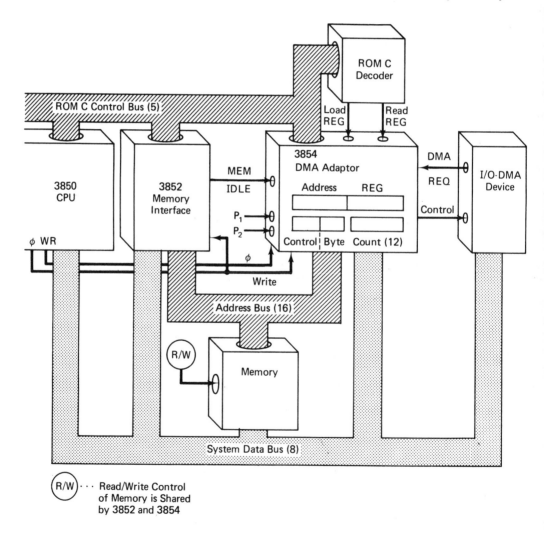

Figure 13-23 *READ/WRITE control of memory is shared by 3852 and 3854.*

The second cycle can be used for either refreshing memory or for DMA transfers.

The Fairchild 3854 Direct Memory Access chip is used to control the system during DMA slots. The 3854 does *not* cause the CPU to HOLD; it uses the (fast access) memory during periods when the (slower) CPU is performing internal operations. Its operation is completely invisible to the CPU. The CPU controls DMA operations by setting the control bits in the memory interface described above and by loading registers in the DMA chip. There are four 8-bit registers in the DMA chip that are handled as I/O ports. Two of the registers are used for supplying addresses to memory, and the other two are divided between control and record length.

The control register is 4 bits wide, two of which are available as outputs on external pins, and the byte count register is 12 bits wide. Selection of these registers is achieved via two pins, P1 and P2, on the 3854 package. Two other pins, LOAD REG and READ REG, determine whether the selected register is to be loaded from or into the F-8 accumulator, respectively. These signals are derived by decoding the control bus from the F-8 CPU, as shown in the preceding diagram. The registers are loaded with the CPU WRITE pulse.

The two control bits that are available on output pins are ENABLE and DIRECTION. The CPU enables the DMA chip by setting the bit in the control register. The setting of the DIRECTION bit determines whether the DMA device will write into memory or read from memory. This bit is ANDed internally with the transfer (XFER) signal to produce the data write slot (DWS) signal that is active whenever DMA is writing into memory. The XFER signal is HIGH during all DMA transfer time slots.

THE NATIONAL SC/MP DMA STRUCTURE

The SC/MP microprocessor control structure readily accomodates DMA operations. The bidirectional bus request (BUSREQ) line is used by the CPU to sense DMA requests before entering an I/O cycle and, if none is present, to issue its own bus request, which can be used to inhibit other requesting devices. If the BUSREQ line is HIGH, the SC/MP senses this and postpones its own request, keeping the address bus, data bus, read and write strobes in the HIGH impedance mode. The detailed treatment of the timing and bus control logic will be presented in the next chapter in terms of a multi-processor control structure.

SUMMARY

The transfer of data between memory and the "real world" often occurs via programmed data transfer through the CPU-I/O system. Direct memory channels bypass this bottleneck and increase system throughout. DMA controllers, although integrally connected to the CPU, are properly associated with the memory subsystem and alter the basic nature of this subsystem. The "passive" memory becomes, via the addition of direct access channel controllers, an *active* subsystem with enhanced importance.

In some systems, the active memory is viewed as *the* major subsystem. The further development of DMA controllers will almost certainly lend support to this perspective. It is probable that these devices will become more "intelligent" and will assume some of the functions of the CPU; i.e., future direct access channels will probably incorporate special-purpose *information processing* capability. In place of a general-purpose processor, they will provide *preprocessing* of data in a manner somewhat resembling the operation of a *filter* in analog systems. These channels will possibly execute data compression algorithms, removing the redundancy inherent in much data before storage, and reconstructing the data upon retrieval. The reconstructed data can then be transferred to cache memories for local processing.

The evolution of direct access channels (and thereby *active* memories) is just beginning and the trends are not yet apparent. However, development in this area is likely to be rapid. The "burst" and "cycle-stealing" techniques discussed in this chapter will probably endure. The addition of elastic first-in-first-out (FIFO) buffers, followed by specialized processing functions, will produce intelligent access channels. The continued development of hierarchal memory systems and intelligent memory channels should lead to an architecture characterized as an intelligent memory system.

14 *microprocessor architectural themes*

Previous chapters have covered individual structures in detail and developed contexts in which these structures operate. This chapter attempts to move to the next level in the hierarchy and treat architectural strategies or themes that are developing. The two primary themes of bundled versus orthogonal structures are explored and used to predict future microprocessor developments.

MULTI-OPERATING LEVEL ARCHITECTURE

The desirability of sharing processors between two or more processes led to the interrupt structures discussed in Chapter 12. Considerable attention was given to the save state/re-store state mechanisms commonly employed to interface the two or more operating systems. It was also noted that several structures have been designed to optimize this interface in terms of minimal time in transition and to minimize instruction executions required to effect the transition. As an example, the Motorola 6800 microprocessors automatically stack the state vector upon receipt of an interrupt request and disable the system (functionally disconnecting the two processes in a manner somewhat analogous to the tri-state high impedance isolation techniques used to "electrically disconnect" passive subsystems while an active subsystem is accessed by the CPU), and restore the state vector and enable the interrupt system upon execution of the return-from-interrupt (RTI) instruction. This automatic response minimizes the "change-state" time requirements and the instructions required to do so.

An alternate approach to the multi-process system can be seen in the Intel 4040, Signetics 2650, MOSTEK 5065P, RCA COSMAC, and other microprocessors. These multi-level architectures approach the problem of optimizing state transitions by minimizing or eliminating the save and re-store state vector operations. This is achieved via redundant structures which can be treated as orthogonal states in the sense that transformations on any state vector are independent of transformations on the other state vectors. This being the case, it is unnecessary to save or re-store such state vectors, and optimal state transitions are achieved by leaving each state vector "in place" and simply switching to another independent state or operating level.

The most extreme development of this multi-level architecture is found in the 5065P tri-level machine produced by MOSTEK. This machine, consisting of an accumulator, link bit, and program counter, provides a highly orthogonal structure. Linkage between these levels is achieved via an auxiliary link register that is always projected into the operating level. An idealized illustration of this system is shown in Fig. 14-1.

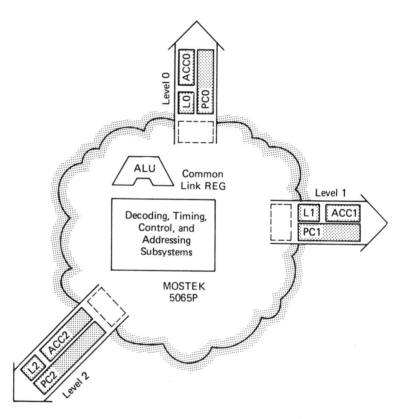

Figure 14-1

Each of the three operating levels possesses software extensions into memory. The degree of orthogonality of such extensions varies greatly. In general, a high degree of independence is desirable in such systems. If the systems have access to common registers, a well-defined access structure is required, whose treatment is beyond the scope of this volume.

The transition between operating levels in a multi-level system is usually possible under both hardware and software control, i.e., transitions can be either generated from within a software process or imposed on the system from without.

ORTHOGONAL "WORKING FILES"

A multi-level evolution of the Intel 8008 is seen in the Signetics 2650 illustrated in Fig. 14-2. The same basic register architecture is embedded in a different control structure to achieve a radically different total system architecture.

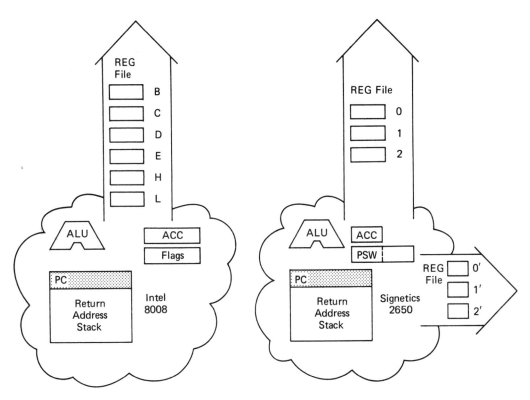

Figure 14-2

The register file in the Intel 8008 consists of six 8-bit registers designed for scratchpad operations. The same six registers are treated as two 3-register files in the Signetics 2650. Only one of these files is accessible by instructions at any given time. A register select bit in the program status word selects the active file at any given time. This bit can be tested, loaded, stored, set, or reset under program control. The accumulator is always active and available for transfer to or from registers in the active "bank."

Orthogonality Facilitates System Expansion

The use of orthogonal structures has been seen to provide optimal state switching for concurrent processing in an interrupt environment. There are additional advantages, as illustrated in the evolution of the Intel 4004 microprocessor. This 4-bit machine, which uses 8-bit instructions and 12-bit addresses, was the first truly general-purpose processor available as a standard part. The device was introduced in early 1971 with a well-designed integrated chip set

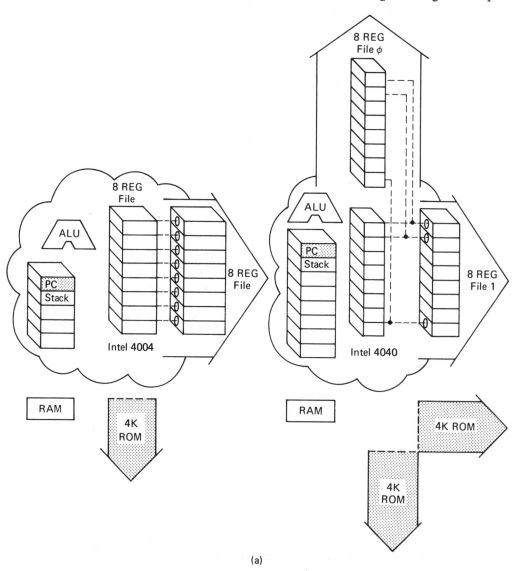

(a)

Figure 14-3(a)

that included multiplexers, demultiplexers, and I/O ports on both RAM and ROM chips. A calculator influence is discernable in some of the instructions and in the partitioning of the memory; however, the instruction set is general purpose and is powerful. The 4004 posesses an ALU, accumulator, program counter and three-deep integral return address stack, and a 16-register file that also functions as eight register pairs. The Harvard architecture can address 4K bytes of instruction store.

The second-generation Intel 4040 is upward compatible with the 4004 in the sense that programs that execute on the 4004 will also execute on the 4040. The 4040 has been expanded via extension of the return address stack from three to seven deep, and an interrupt facility, lacking on the 4004, has been added. Program store has been expanded from 4K to 8K, and the register file has been lengthened from 16 to 24. This has been accomplished within the constraints of the 4004 instruction format via the addition of new bank switching instructions that effectively perform a "rotation" of the orthogonal structure. The two systems are schematically represented in Fig. 14-3.

Sixteen of the 4040 scratchpad registers will be active at any given time, and these registers function in the same fashion as the 4004 register file, i.e., either as registers or as register pairs. The registers are normally used for data storage, and the register pairs normally function as indirect pointers. There is no neces-

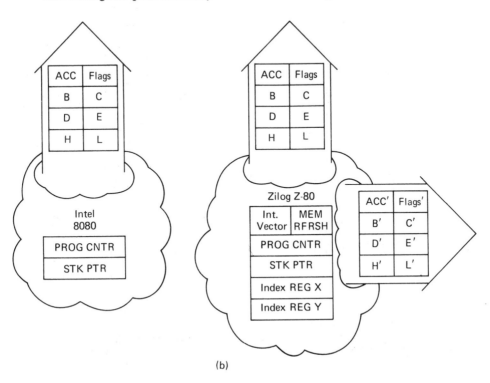

(b)

Figure 14-3(b)

sary connection between the orthogonality of the internal files and that of the two ROM banks. Either or both of these orthogonal systems can be utilized in interrupt processing. When only one level of interrupt is implemented, the "save state" instructions are replaced by "switch register file" instructions, and one file is dedicated to the interrupt process while the other is used at all other times.

The ability to extend internal workspace, yet retain compatiblity with an existing instruction set, has been exploited by Zilog in its Z-80. This device, with 158 instructions (including all of the original 78 8080 instructions), possesses a dual register bank as shown in Fig. 14-3b.

The Z-80 possesses both bank switching instructions and a bank "swap" instruction that exchanges the contents of B, C, D, E, H, and L with B', C', D', E', H', and L'.

VARIABLE DIMENSIONALITY: THE RCA COSMAC

The structure of the COSMAC provides extreme flexibility and allows operation in a broad range of system configurations, ranging from one-dimensional to eight-dimensional. The 16-register file is highly symmetrical and consists

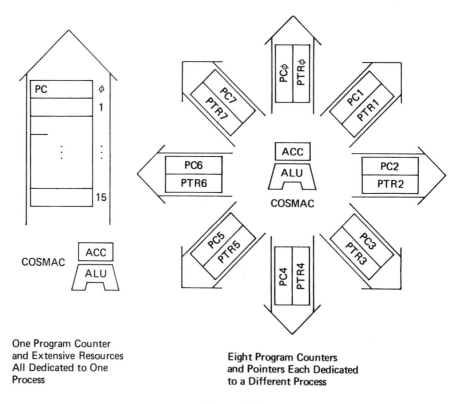

One Program Counter
and Extensive Resources
All Dedicated to One
Process

Eight Program Counters
and Pointers Each Dedicated
to a Different Process

Figure 14-4

of 16-bit general-purpose registers that can be used as program counters, memory data pointers, or for working storage. The assignment of register function is made under software control, except as described in the Interrupt and DMA chapters in which the first three registers can be dedicated to these functions. This flexibility is represented in Fig. 14-4. Typical applications of the COSMAC would utilize intermediate configurations between these two extremes.

SYSTEM ARCHITECTURES; BUNDLED VS. ORTHOGONAL

The concept of orthogonality or mutual independence applies to major subsystems as well as to the operating levels discussed above, and represents one of the major approaches to microprocessor systems design. The Intel 8080 best represents this design approach and has for this reason been used for detailed treatment of various subsystems throughout the book. The orthogonal subsystem architecture separates every major function into "eigenvector"-like functions that can be scaled with no effect on neighboring eigenvectors. For example, the addition of RAM, ROM, Interrupt levels, Interval timers, I/O ports, etc. has minimal, if any, cross correlation. This can best be seen by comparison with a "bundled" architecture like that of the Fairchild F-8 in which the addition of ROM automatically results in the addition of I/O ports, an interval timer, and another interrupt port. The basic systems are shown in Fig. 14-5.

The characteristics have been emphasized in this illustration. A bundled system can always be made more orthogonal by "grafting on" special-purpose hardware, although the basic architecture may make this somewhat awkward. Similarly, an orthogonal architecture can be made less so via the inclusion of multi-purpose chips, such as those available from MOS Technology containing RAM, ROM, timer, interrupt control, and I/O ports bundled together into one system.

HARDWARE/SOFTWARE ORTHOGONAL EXTENSIONS

A unique technique of orthogonal expansion has been employed in the Texas Instruments 9900 third-generation processor. The inclusion of an Extended Operation (XOP) instruction allows the designer to add 16 "custom" instructions which may be executed either in special-purpose hardware or interpreted by software. When an XOP instruction is executed, the instruction may be detected by a hardware module and control transferred to the module. An example of such might be a floating point processor. If there is no response from the module, the processor traps to one of 16 trap cells located in low memory.

The XOP instruction format is shown in Fig. 14-6. The four bits in the operation select code field are used to specify one of 16 extended operations. If hard-

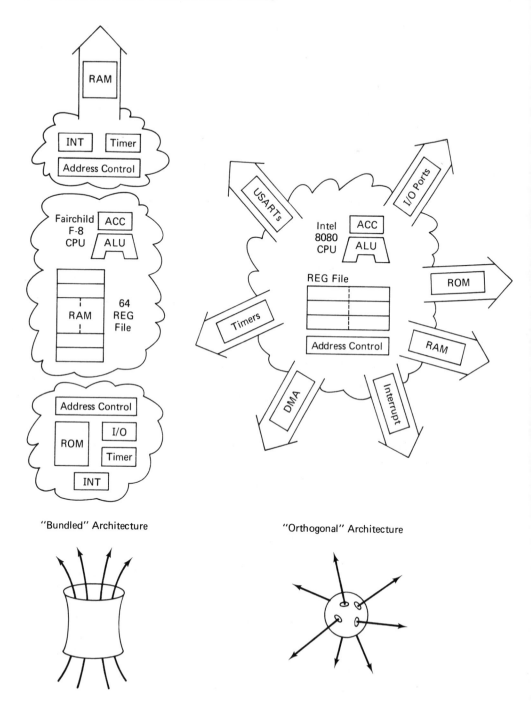

"Bundled" Architecture

"Orthogonal" Architecture

Figure 14-5 (a) "Bundled" architecture; (b) "Orthogonal" architecture

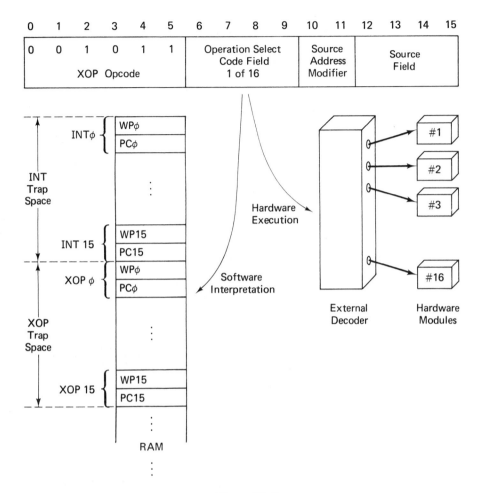

0	1	2	3	4	5	6	7	8	9	10	11	12	13	14	15
0	0	1	0	1	1	Operation Select Code Field 1 of 16				Source Address Modifier		Source Field			
		XOP Opcode													

Figure 14-6

ware modules are present, these bits are decoded (in external hardware) and used to select the appropriate module. If the XOP is to be interpreted in software, these bits are used to select the transfer vector in the XOP trap space that consists of 32 contiguous locations immediately following the interrupt trap space. Both options are shown diagramatically in Fig. 14-6. Only one of these would be implemented in any given system.

The trap vector points to the new workspace area for the extended operation. The current state (PC, WP, ST) is stored in the new workspace registers, WR13, 14, and 15, PC and WP are loaded from the trap cell. The XOP status bit ST6 is set in the status register, and the source address is calculated from S and T_s and stored in workspace register 11. The subroutine can then access this data and execute the special operation. The result should be the same for two systems,

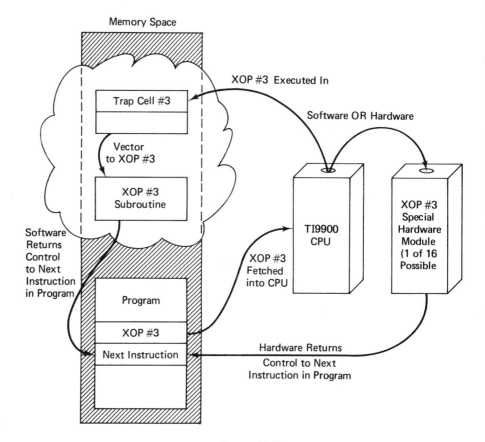

Figure 14-7

one of which possesses special hardware and the other special software. Both options are shown in Fig. 14-7.

MAJOR DIRECTIONS

The direction of microprocessor-related development is determined largely by two factors: user needs and production economics. The first factor is ideally met by custom design tailored to each problem. This customization can be achieved in two ways. The availability of simple, highly orthogonal pieces allows any user to design a custom system that is best suited for the intended application The medium-scale integrated (MSI) components treated in the first chapters of this book provide such an orthogonal family. Such systems, if thoughtfully designed, offer easy expansion capabilities at relatively low cost. Disadvantages of such systems generally relate to parts count. The large number of pieces require more board area, consume more power, and are less reliable due to the higher number of connections between devices. The need to design, build, test, stock, and distribute many different parts at *relatively* low volume means that the economics of mass production are not fully realized.

Custom LSI

An alternate approach consists in designing custom LSI devices that will tailor one-chip systems or subsystems to meet each user's requirements. Although fully automated design techiques may eventually establish this approach as the only viable one, the semiautomated techniques are not economically competitive with the orthogonal scheme discussed in the second section of this chapter. low-volume LSI components are expensive to design, test, and produce—in most cases, prohibitively so.

Programmable LSI

The "middle way" taken by LSI designers is clearly established as the economically feasible approach for semiautomated design technology. The hardware/software blend is extended into the pieces to such an extent that it is becoming exceedingly difficult to say just where software ends and hardware begins. The perspective in which software is viewed as "on-the-spot rewiring" is fully exploited to optimize all of the factors required for custom designs, resulting in

1. single package-low power, small space requirements, high reliability;
2. universal design-one-time design costs and testing amortized over mass production and distribution;
3. tens or hundreds of user-selected configurations thus allowing low-cost custom system design.

Special-Purpose Processors

The universality of microprocessors as system-building blocks, deriving essentially from their design as general-purpose symbol processors, has been treated in this book. In order to utilize such free-form or unstructured systems in conjunction with a host of specific control and communications applications, it becomes necessary to *formalize* certain control and communication tasks. In the same sense that formalization via TTL and other specifications led directly to well-defined *symbols* and, hence, to symbol processors, the formal specification of control and communications processes leads directly to well-defined *tasks* and, hence, to special-purpose processors.

TASKS AND MODES

Although it is relatively easy to define a set of *tasks* that occur almost universally, it is much more difficult to define a universal *mode* or method of accomplishing these tasks. For this reason, the special-purpose processors that have been designed for given tasks operate in a variety of modes so that they will be as universally applicable as possible. It is through control of the *operating mode* that system designers customize these processors. This control is effected through mode-control instructions sent to the special-task processor by the CPU. The number of special processors exceed the number of CPUs, and their complete treatment would constitute a volume in itself; however, we will present a brief treatment with examples that will illustrate the principles involved.

Mode Control of Task Processors

The almost universal requirement of mode control has been generally solved via the inclusion in each Task Processing Unit (TPU) of a mode control register that is loaded from the CPU with an appropriate control word. In effect, the mode control register in the TPU corresponds to the instruction register in the CPU. The control word is decoded and sets up the data paths and internal operations in the task processor.

Since almost every task involves the transfer or transformation of data, there is also a data register in the TPU; in fact, most such processors provide *two* registers, one for data out (*from* the CPU) and one for data in (*to* the CPU). From earlier chapters, it is clear that most tasks can proceed through a variety of operational *states* and, therefore, the presence of TPU status information is usually required.

The generalized picture of a special task processor is illustrated in Fig. 14-8.

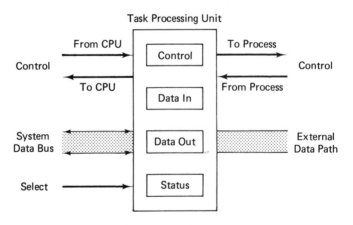

Figure 14-8 *Task processing unit*

Note that, from the perspective of the CPU, each of the task processor registers is an I/O port. (For CPUs with memory-mapped I/O, each task processor register is simply a point in address space.) For example, to output a control word to the task processor, the CPU moves the control word into the accumulator and then executes an OUTPUT (or WRITE) instruction to the proper port. The port address appearing on the address bus must (1) select the task processor and (2) select the control register in the task processor.

THE INTEL 8255 PROGRAMMABLE PERIPHERAL INTERFACE UNIT

A task common to all processors is that of interfacing to peripheral equipment. The asynchronous nature of this interface usually involves "handshaking" signals, i.e., requests and acknowledgments. These operations can be implemented easily and inexpensively in LSI I/O-port devices and provide one of the basic modes of operation for such ports. Since the number of input ports and the number of output ports vary from one application to another, a universal I/O port would allow trade-offs in this variable. For processors that lack bit-set/reset instructions, it is desirable to provide the ability to drive individual lines, thereby relieving the CPU of maintaining an image of the output port.

The Intel 8255 Programmable Peripheral Interface Unit (PPIU) provides 24 I/O lines that can be operated in several basic modes. The first, MODE 0, is the basic Input/Output mode in which the 24 I/O lines can be selected as three 8-bit ports, A, B, and C, each of which can be specified to operate either as an output or as an input port. All of the output lines are latched, but not all provide

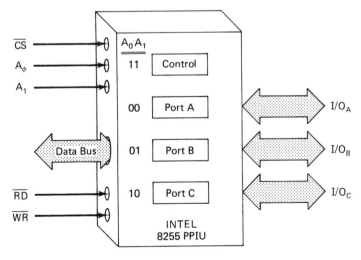

Figure 14-9

latched input capability. Some inputs are buffered lines that sense the condition of the input signal line. The three ports are shown in Fig. 14-9.

The most significant bit selects the bit-set/reset mode, and the least four bits specify which line is to be set or reset. Three bits are unused. (See Fig. 14-10.) If the most significant bit is HIGH, the control word selects the mode for the three ports. The following example will treat port A as a strobed input port and port B as a strobed output port. Port C will furnish the control signals. The 8255 PPIU can be operated in approximately 100 different configurations, and the following example is meant to show typical applications only. Many details have been omitted in the interest of simplicity.

The portion of the control word that causes port A to operate in the strobed input mode is shown in Fig. 14-11. In this configuration the ith line of Port C,

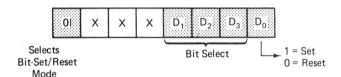

Figure 14-10

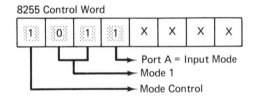

Figure 14-11

designated PC_i, is used for control purposes; for example, PC_4 provides an input strobe that must be provided by the external data source and is used to latch data into the input port. The acknowledge signal, Input Buffer Full (IBF), appears on PC_3 and is set by the falling edge of the strobe. It is reset automatically by the rising edge of the READ control line when the CPU reads the data from the input latch. In addition to the acknowledgment sent to the peripheral device, there is a status line which can be sampled by the CPU or used to interrupt the CPU to inform it that data have been latched into the 8255 input port A. If enabled, the interrupt request appears on PC_2, clocked by the trailing edge of the input strobe and reset by the leading edge of the read control line. The interrupt request can be inhibited via the bit-set/reset command by clearing PC_4, which serves as a mask bit in this mode. The timing diagram and circuit schematic are shown in Fig. 14-12 and Fig. 14-13.

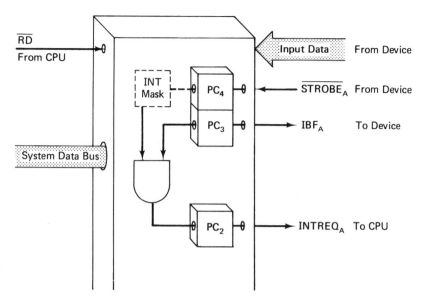

Figure 14-12

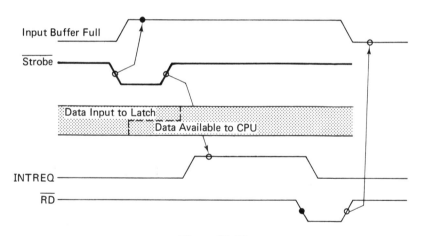

Figure 14-13

To output to the 8255, the CPU executes an output command to a specified port, and it is the responsibility of the system designer to ensure that the address lines and output signal are used to enable the chip select ($\overline{CS}$) line and provide the register select bits, A_0 and A_1. These allow selection of the control register or one of the three I/O ports. The WRITE control then causes the data on the data bus to be loaded into the selected register. In the input mode, the read control gates the input port data onto the bus. The second mode, MODE

1, provides Strobed Input/Output for handshake operation with peripheral devices. The A and B ports provide I/O lines, while port C may be used either for I/O or control lines. The third mode, which is MODE 2, configurates port A as an 8-bit bidirectional I/O bus, and uses five lines from port C as the control and the other three for I/O. Ports A and B can operate in different modes, with port C divided as required for the A and B control functions. When port C is used in this fashion, each bit of C can be set or reset by using the control word shown in Fig. 14-10.

The use of port B for strobed output to a peripheral device is very similar to the above. The strobe, appearing on PC_1, originates when the CPU writes the data into latch B and informs the device that data are available. The device acknowledges the receipt of data by strobing PC_2. If enabled, this acknowledgment generates a HIGH output on PC_ϕ, which may be used to interrupt the CPU for more output data. The INTerrupt REQuest line is enabled or disabled by the bit-set/reset of PC_2. The control word and schematic are shown in Fig. 14-14. The timing is not shown.

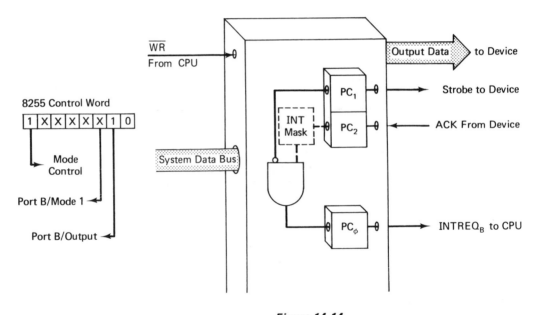

Figure 14-14

PROGRAMMABLE I/O SUMMARY

Several of the basic modes and configurations of the Intel 8255 peripheral interface TPU have been described. The configurations are representative of approximately 100 possible with this device, and this device is representative of a score of similar devices available from other manufacturers. All such devices have in common:

- their selection as I/O ports (or memory locations)
- their control via CPU-loading of a control register
- specialized intelligence dedicated to common I/O tasks.

These devices represent integrated hardware/software building blocks that provide the most powerful and, at the same time, most economical devices possible with semiautomated production. The use of a device that can be custom programmed assumes an initialization routine that is executed at system start-up and selects the configuration for the particular system. It should be noted that such devices can be dynamically reconfigured during system operation, although this feature is seldom required in typical systems.

SERIAL I/O TPUs; THE INTEL 8251

The common requirement of serial I/O can be met by another dedicated Task Processing Unit (TPU), the Intel 8251 Universal Synchronous, Asynchronous, Receiver/Transmitter (USART), which is also representative of a great number of similar devices. The asynchronous mode of transmission utilizing framing start- and stop-bits has been described in the I/O chapter and a software implementation presented. The following brief discussion of the hardware implementation of this task is presented primarily to show the similarity of many of the operational features of TPUs by comparison with the parallel I/O TPU just described, and to present the use of the status register.

The "universal" in USART refers to the ability to operate in many basic modes. These are enumerated without explanation.

- Operation with 5-, 6-, 7-, or 8-bit characters
- Clock rates 1, 16, 64 times the Baud rate
- Operation with 1, $1\frac{1}{2}$, or 2 stop bits
- Baud rates of DC to 9.6K Baud in the asynchronous mode or DC to 56K Baud in the synchronous mode
- Internal or external character synchronization in the sync mode.

These modes are selected via the control register, which is loaded by the CPU in the usual fashion. The device is shown in Fig. 14-15 in simplified form.

8251 Operation

The basic task of the 8251 TPU consists in accepting parallel data from the CPU, appending a start bit, a parity bit, and stop bits, and transmitting the framed character serially at a rate determined by the transmitter clock input.

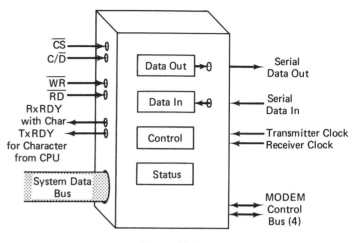

Figure 14-15

At the same time, the receiver section can be receiving a framed word, stripping the start and stop bits, checking the parity, and signaling to the CPU via the status/interrupt line that a character has been received. The input rate is determined by the receiver input clock line. The *modem* control bus can be interfaced directly to standard *modulator/dem*odulators that convert binary TTL signals to a binary frequency scheme for transmission over telephone lines. The modem control bus signals are reflected in the status register, which can be read by the CPU. In addition to these, the status register contains bits that announce

- parity error detected on received word;
- framing error (ASYNC only), indicating that the stop bit was not detected; and
- overrun error, which indicates that the CPU did not read a received character before it was written over by another received character.

8251 Mode Control

The CPU controls the operating mode of the 8251 by writing into the control register. The TPU expects a mode instruction, followed by SYNC characters (if in the SYNC mode), followed by a command instruction. All of these are addressed to the single control register, and the 8251 interprets each according to the sequence in which it is received.

Referring to the TPU schematic diagram in Fig. 14-15, it can be seen that there are two *control* registers, CONTROL and STATUS, and two *data* registers, INPUT and OUTPUT. The selection of these registers is achieved via the

CONTROL/$\overline{\text{DATA}}$ (C/$\overline{\text{D}}$) pin on the 8251. Each of these classes contains a register that is loaded by the CPU (control or output) and one that is read by the CPU (status or input) and, therefore, selection of the appropriate register in either class is uniquely determined by the READ and WRITE control lines. The selection bits are shown in this table:

C/$\overline{D}$	$\overline{RD}$	$\overline{WR}$	Register Selected
1	0	1	status word
1	1	0	control word
0	0	1	input data
0	1	0	output data

GENERAL TPU MODE CONTROL

In order to emphasize the pervasiveness of the mode control scheme described above, we recall that the Signetics 2650 microprocessor provides both special instructions and a $\overline{\text{CONTROL/DATA}}$ pin available from the CPU for interfacing to TPUs. These instructions were described in the I/O chapter and should be reviewed with the results of the preceding sections in mind. In the interests of simplicity, primarily to avoid decoding address lines, the 2650 is shown in Fig. 14-16 with the 8251 TPU as its *sole* means of I/O communications. In this simplest configuration, the 8251 chip select is activated by the MEMORY-I/O control line directly available from the CPU, the 8251 C/$\overline{\text{D}}$ line is controlled by the (inverted) C/$\overline{\text{D}}$ line from the CPU, and the 8251 INTERRUPT lines are run directly to the CPU INTerrupt REQuest pin.

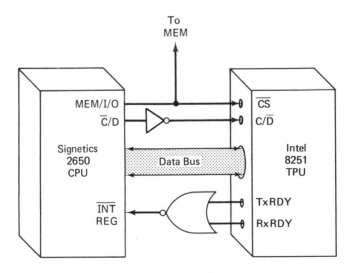

Figure 14-16

TPU SUMMARY

The special task processors already described in this book, for handling DMA, Interrupt Priority and conflict resolution, parallel I/O, and serial I/O, are typical examples of orthogonal TPUs. Other TPUs, including programmable interval timers, Synchronous Data Link Control (SDLC) chips, cyclic redundancy checkers, hardware floating point and special function chips, magnetic cassette and floppy disc control chips, and others, are increasing the dimensions of orthogonality and extending the power of the designer. This trend will certainly increase and should tend in the direction of special-purpose unified task processors that provide all of the required CPU functions on the TPU chip itself. The other direction is toward the totally bundled unified general-purpose processor that will provide the universal building block.

The Ultimate TPU

A crucial step in the development of Task Processing Units has been that of programmability. Early TPUs were "nonintelligent" units that were programmed by the CPU, as exemplified by the 8257 DMA controller. Although TPUs generally operate under the control of a CPU, a natural evolution has occurred which serves to erase the distinction between the general-purpose TPU and the general-purpose CPU. With the introduction of the Intel 8748/8048 single-device microcomputer, this distinction has almost vanished.

The 8048 is a 5-volt only device that includes on *one* monolithic chip:

- 8-bit CPU–70 instruction set (21 conditional jumps)
- 1K × 8 PROM program memory with direct addressing to 4K
- 64 × 8 RAM memory
  —contains 8-deep PC stack (can be used for data storage)
  —dual 8-register banks for working files
  —external expansion to 256 × 8 directly addressable pages
- clock and oscillator—*RC* or crystal controlled
- power-on clear—extend timing capacitor required
- 27 TTL-compatible I/O lines
- 5 control lines for external I/O and memory
- Interrupts
  —external interrupt—vector to location 3
  —interval timer/event counter—vector to location 7 upon overflow.
- logical AND and OR directly with I/O ports and conditional branching on test lines

The 8048 is a 5-V N-MOS processor with a 2.5 μsec cycle time and binary and BCD arithmetic capabilities. It offers many unique features, some of which have been covered in the I/O chapter. The 8748 possesses a 1K ultraviolet erasable PROM on the chip, while the 8048 uses ROM for mass-production economy. The architecture is shown in Fig. 14–17.

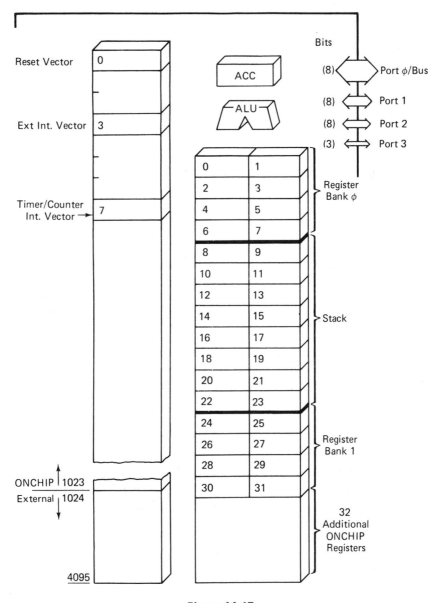

Figure 14-17

The chip is available in two versions: the 8048-1 that is a microcomputer serving as a main processor in a system, and the 8048-2 that serves as an intelligent, programmable peripheral controller and TPU and that can be used to implement distributed intelligence systems.

MULTI-PROCESSOR CONTROL STRUCTURE

One of the first microprocessors to possess a multi-processor-oriented control structure was the National Semiconductor SC/MP. In this, the BUSREQ line is bidirectional and is designed to be shared by all devices that are capable of controlling the system busses. As described in Chapter 13, the DMA chapter, the SC/MP senses this line prior to issuing a request. If the line is HIGH, the request is not issued, and the SC/MP busses remain in the high impedance mode. If the BUSREQ line is not HIGH, the SC/MP issues a WAITREQ on its ENABLE OUT line. This signal is normally connected to the ENABLE IN or RDY pin of a device that is downstream in a daisy chain. The multi-processor system is illustrated in Fig. 14-18.

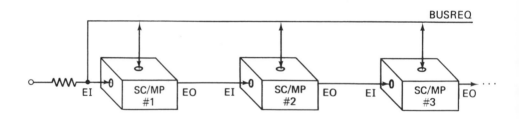

EI = Enable In
EO = Enable Out

Figure 14-18

If SC/MP #n is not requesting control of the bus, its ENABLE OUT line is equal to its ENABLE IN line. Thus, the RDY or WAIT signal is transmitted down the chain. When a particular processor, SC/MP #k, desires control of the BUS, it transmits a WAIT REQ down the chain, thus breaking the daisy chain at this location. This request is presented as long as the CPU requests control of the bus. The CPU then drives the BUSREQ line HIGH, which pulls the left-most ENABLE IN line to the RDY state, and the RDY propagates down the line from the left. The processor idles until the RDY signal is received. Since any upstream device desiring service will have sensed the BUSREQ line, there are two possible cases.

1. The upstream device sensed a HIGH BUSREQ line and did not issue a WAIT command, but entered the blocked state. The RDY signal

then propagates down to SC/MP #k and it enters the *active* state, gaining control of the bus.

2. The upstream device sensed the BUSREQ line "simultaneously" with SC/MP #k and, finding it LOW, issued a WAIT command, then also pulled the BUSREQ line HIGH. The upstream WAIT command propagates down to SC/MP #k and causes it to enter the blocked state. The left-most ENABLE IN line is pulled to RDY, and this signal propagates to the left-most SC/MP requesting the bus. *This* processor then gains control of the bus while SC/MP #k waits.

The timing is shown in Fig. 14-19.

The SC/MP cycles are designed so that the CPU cannot execute two successive bus request cycles, thereby preventing deadlock in a two-processor system. There is always *at least one* open cycle, as shown in Fig. 14-20, enabling another CPU to grab the bus.

An exception does exist for two special instructions that do not possess open cycles. These are instructions that access a particular memory register, increment

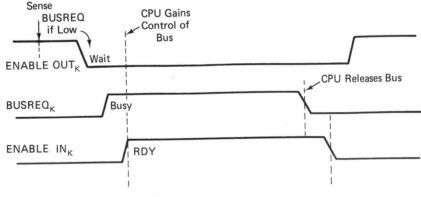

Figure 14-19

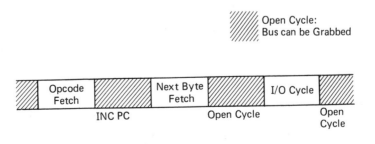

Figure 14-20

or decrement its contents, leaving a copy in the accumulator, and restore the modified contents into the register. These instructions provide the primitives needed in a multi-process system (hardware or software) in which the computer system is viewed as a collection of cooperating, but competing, sequential processes working concurrently (in parallel).

A *process* is defined in this context as the occurrence of a sequence of asynchronous events whose progress is, therefore, independent of the elapsed time between successive events. The two basic coordination requirements have been labeled *Producer/Consumer*, in which one processor produces information that is consumed by another, and *Mutual Exclusion*, in which access to a given resource is allowed to only one process at any given time. Problems of this type were first treated by Dijkstra, who invented coordination primitives that allow *indivisible* or *quantum* operations that, once started, complete their operation without interruption. The coordination primitives operate on integer variables, called *event variables*, that serve as communication and coordination links between the concurrent processes.

A detailed treatment of such coordination techniques is beyond the scope of this text; however, the reader is referred to Presser's excellent review in *Computing Surveys*, or to Dijkstra's work. Suffice it to say that the special SC/MP instructions that do *not* possess open cycles provide the indivisibility required for these basic coordination primitives.

The SC/MP is the first microprocessor with an architecture designed to facilitate multi-process coordination. Possession of these hardware-implemented primitives allows one processor to test and update a location in memory with the assurance that another processor will not interfere with this operation. Most solutions to this problem will have been implemented heretofore in soft-ware.

In addition to the assurance that another processor will not interfere with access to the event variables, each processor should be assured that it will *eventually* gain access to these variables. The problem of the "deadly embrace," in which two processors lock each other out of their critical sections, has been solved by the control-timing relations described above. The problem of lockout, in which a lower priority device is forever denied access to its critical section by higher priority devices, is usually solved via a rotating priority structure, as described in the Intel 8257 DMA controller treatment. A rotating priority for the SC/MP multi-processor system can be implemented in external hardware based around a recirculating shift register.

BACK TO BUNDLED

Uni-processors, which can be adapted to particular applications via the addition of orthogonal TPUs, provide a viable basic architecture in which each subsystem is a highly specialized piece. Multi-processor systems provide, in the extreme, a network of identical hardware pieces that are adapted to particular applications via task-processing software. A significant start in this direction has been seen in the National SC/MP multi-process coordination facilities. There are several microprocessors that contain the CPU, RAM, ROM, and I/O all on one-chip and, therefore, qualify for the term "computer on a chip." The Texas Instruments TMS-1000 and the American Microsystems, Inc. 9209 were the first two such devices and, coincidently, the first devices to sell for less than $10. These microcomputers have not been covered in this book because they are essentially microprogrammed machines, a topic to be covered in a later volume. Additionally, these microcomputers require mask programming of the ROMs during manufacture and, thus, are not "every man's" building blocks, but are practical only for large-volume commercial applications.

This last factor, that of mask programming of ROMs during manufacture, has been the biggest stumbling block in the way of multi-processor systems. This factor is no longer important due to the existence of erasable programmable ROMs. The FAMOS PROMs, invented by Intel and described in the chapter on MSI devices, allow information to be stored by using moderate voltages ($\approx$ 50 volts), retained indefinitely, and erased by ultraviolet radiation. Advances in technology have made it practical to include such a PROM on the CPU chip itself and, in fact, provide a distinguishing feature of the third-generation micro-processor.

An even more desirable ROM is based on the 2K-bit, electrically alterable, read-only memory introduced by Nippon Electric Company (NEC) of Japan. This device can be erased electrically as well as programmed electrically at a speed of approximately 60 msec per byte. The entire memory can be programmed in 15 sec, and electrically erased (i.e., without ultraviolet radiation) in 1 minute. ROMs of this type should retain programs for longer than 10 years.

THE FIRST THREE GENERATIONS

First-generation microprocessors were characterized by slow P-MOS techno-logy, minimal on-chip decoding, and extremely basic architectures. The Intel 8008 typifies the first-generation 8-bit microprocessor. The introduction of the first N-MOS Intel 8080—with on-chip decoding and a respectable instruction set—clearly divides the first generation from the second generation. It becomes more difficult to distinguish clearly between second- and third-generation chips due to the diversity of the types available.

If bipolar (TTL) microprogrammable systems are disregarded and only monolithic microprocessors are considered, the dividing line between second- and third-generation devices centers on the multi-processor coordination of the National SC/MP, the on-board PROM of the Intel 8048, and the memory-to-memory architecture of the TI 9900.

THE FOURTH GENERATION AND BEYOND

As LSI packing densities increase, the inclusion of special TPU subsystems on the CPU chip will accelerate. Electrically alterable ROMs on the CPU chip speed access times and eliminate communication channels between CPU and memory chips, thus freeing more pins for useful I/O functions. The well-developed analog-to-digital and digital-to-analog technologies will provide on-chip analog I/O facilities of remarkable power. The economic factors described earlier portend the development of super-bundled general-purpose chips with on-board PROMs that can be configured, "on-the-spot," to particular applications. The speeds achieved with N-MOS technology have already surpassed TTL, and the limits have not been reached. Exciting new technologies offer vast improvement in every aspect of microprocessor-based system design.

CONCLUSION

Two factors—applications that require raw speed and the development of more powerful automated design techniques—argue for the continued development of special-purpose, highly orthogonal hardware. This topic is best approached via microprogramming and is to be treated in a second volume of *Microprocessor Systems Design*.

Economic considerations in the foreseeable future, combined with high-speed, high-density Grand Scale Integrated (GSI) technology, argue for the evolution of the universal super-building block. Systems implemented with these identical units will be expandable via the extension of the hardware net with all orthogonality manifested in software. When this occurs we will cease to speak of microprocessor system design but will speak instead of cellular automata.

appendix

A mechanics of the assembly process

The mechanics of the assembly process vary only slightly from one machine to another and generally follow this sequence:

1. Load the ASSEMBLER software into "main" storage from auxiliary storage. "Main" storage is addressed directly by the CPU, whereas auxiliary storage can be paper tape, magnetic tape, magnetic disc, or other high-capacity, low-cost-per-bit media that are indirectly addressed via output ports or interfaced device controllers.

2. Transfer control from the Loader program to the Assembler program.

3. Begin Pass 1 of the assembly process that scans the source code for labels and builds the Symbol Table to be used in Pass 2.

4. Begin Pass 2 of the assembly process that translates the source code and produces object code, i.e., the code that will be loaded into the machine and executed. The object code is normally output to some auxiliary storage medium and (optionally) a listing is produced.

NOTE: Many ASSEMBLERs combine steps 3 and 4, while others separate step 4 into a pass for a listing and another pass for the object-only production. These are minor details that are explained more completely in the relevant manufacturers' manuals.

appendix

B *conditional assembly:*
the rationale behind it

The MACRO-facility replaces the user-defined MACRO-instruction with the replacement string. This in-line substitution seems to run contrary to the spirit of subroutines in which repeated strings of inline commands were collected and a copy stored at a known location to be CALLed when needed. Although more time is required for saving return addresses and transferring control to and from the subroutine, this cost is usually more than offset by the savings in memory space.

If a given routine is to be used often, it is almost mandatory that subroutines be used; however, it is highly desirable to retain the ease and convenience of problem-oriented instructions with the MACRO-parameter-passing features. It is possible, via the use of the conditional assembly facility, to preserve both subroutine economy and macro-instruction ease.

"DRIVER" ROUTINES

Although the term DRIVER is often associated with routines that "drive" or operate INPUT/OUTPUT devices, it will be used here to represent that portion of a process that actually performs the desired function, given the necessary data. The driver is contrasted here with the portion of the program that accesses the necessary data, i.e., that passes parameters to the driver. This portion of the process will be termed the "SETUP" routine. Two examples that illustrate the general nature of this division are given next.

Consider a process in which one of several identical motors is to be selected and driven at a specified speed for a specified number of revolutions. The process is easily divisible into the SETUP routine that passes the motor number, speed, and number of revolutions and the DRIVER routine that uses these data to select and control the motor.

Consider a mathematical operation on two or more entities where it is desired that inputs and outputs be referenced symbolically. This process can also be divided into the SETUP routine that specifies the arguments and the location at which the result is to be stored and the DRIVER that performs the operation on these data.

The primary difference in the SETUP and DRIVER portions of any process lies in the fact that the *information* provided to the process constantly changes and must, therefore, be SETUP *every time* the process is invoked, whereas the operation of the process is essentially unaltered from one invocation to the next. This implies that the DRIVER can be written as a subroutine and be called, while the SETUP must be present at every occurrence of the process.

The following treatment will consider a general process that is assumed divided into a SETUP procedure and a DRIVER procedure. Although the number of parameters can range up to 256, the example will use only three: two arguments as input, and a result to be output. The general form of the MACRO will be:

```
PROCESS   MACRO      ARG1,      ARG2,      RESULT
          SETUP code
          DRIVER code
          ENDM
```

The goal of this section is to write a MACRO that will treat the DRIVER as a CALL routine, rather than substitute it inline every time the MACRO is invoked. The DRIVER must be included in the program once, and this will be done during the *first* expansion of the MACRO.

The conditional assembly pair, IF. . ./ENDIF, can be used to accomplish this goal.

```
PROCESS   MACRO   ARG1, ARG2,  RESULT
          SETUP-code                        assembled every
                                            time MACRO is
          CALL      DRIVER                  invoked
          IF        FIRST
          JUMP      ENDDRIVER +1            assembled only the
                                            first time MACRO
                                            is invoked

DRIVER:   DRIVER-code
ENDDRIVER: RETURN
          ENDIF
          ENDM
```

The MACRO above explicitly shows that the SETUP code and the call to the DRIVER are assembled upon each invocation of the MACRO. Although the DRIVER could have been re-ORIGINed out of the main sequence of code, it is usually more desirable simply to place it in line where the MACRO first appears. Thus, upon return to the first call statement, it is necessary to jump over the driver code as shown.

The conditional assembly meta-instruction, IF.., evaluates the accompanying expression to determine whether the following code (to ENDIF) is to be assembled or skipped. In the preceding example, the expression is simply the term FIRST; however, no provision has yet been made for assigning it to proper value. The first time it is encountered, FIRST should equal nonzero (TRUE), and thereafter it should be zero (FALSE). The ability to set and reset values is provided by the SET meta-instruction. For simplicity, we will set the value of FIRST at the beginning of our program. The nature of its use requires that it be reset *within* the MACRO, more specifically with the DRIVER portion of the MACRO. This modification to the MACRO is shown below:

```
PROCESS  MACRO    ARG1,  ARG2,  RESULT
         SETUP-code
         CALL DRIVER
         IF FIRST
         JUMP ENDDRIVER +1
DRIVER:  DRIVER-code
ENDDRIVER RETURN
FIRST    SET Ø
         ENDIF
         ENDM
```

Using a specific process, say MULTIPLY, a sample program will now be analyzed:

```
MULTIPLY  MACRO ARG1,  ARG2,  RESULT
            .
            .

           ·macro                          MACRO definitions
           ·body                           precede program
            .
            .
            .

          ENDM
            .
            .
            .
            .

          ORG 100H              start of program
            .
            .
            .

FIRST SET 1
            .
            .
            .
```

```
        .                        dots represent assembly
        .                        language instructions
        .

MULTIPLY  HOURS, RATE, WAGES . . . . first invocation
        .                                of MULTIPLY
        .                                Macro
        .
        .
        .
        .
        .

MULTIPLY  SPEED, TIME, DISTANCE . . . following
        .                                invocation.
        .

END                               end of program
```

The MACRO-assembler will first "learn" the new instructions, which are defined via the use of the MACRO/ENDM meta-instructions. It will then encounter the ORIGIN instruction and begin assembling the program instruction sequence from location 100H. Upon encountering the FIRST SET 1 meta-instruction, the assembler will add FIRST to its symbol table and bind the value 1 to the symbol, then continue assembling the program. Upon encountering the first MULTIPLY MACRO, the ASSEMBLER will:

1. assemble the SETUP code;

2. assemble the CALL DRIVER instruction;

3. evaluate the expression in the IF field—upon finding a TRUE value (FIRST = 1), it will proceed to

4. assemble the jump over the DRIVER for the return from the first call;

5. assemble the DRIVER proper, including the return statement;

6. reset the value of FIRST to zero (FALSE);

7. return to program code upon encountering ENDM.

The ASSEMBLER will then proceed to translate the intervening program instructions until it reaches the next MULTIPLY command where it will:

1. assemble the SETUP code;

2. assemble the CALL DRIVER instruction;

3. evaluate the expression in the IF field. Upon finding a FALSE value (FIRST = 0) it will proceed to the ENDIF.

4. It will then encounter the ENDM and return to the program code.

This last procedure will occur every time another MULTIPLY is encountered. The results of the ASSEMBLY process are:

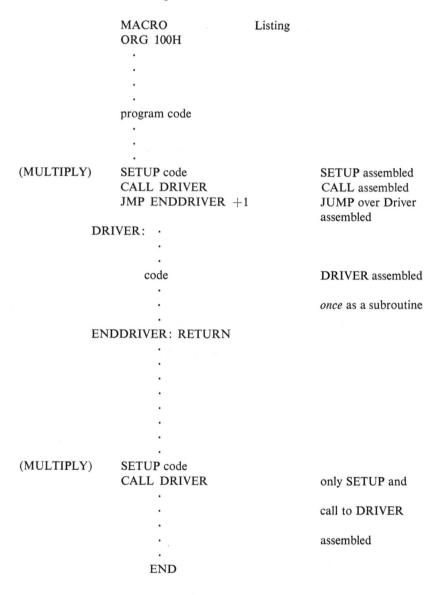

	MACRO	Listing
	ORG 100H	
	.	
	.	
	.	
	.	
	program code	
	.	
	.	
	.	
(MULTIPLY)	SETUP code	SETUP assembled
	CALL DRIVER	CALL assembled
	JMP ENDDRIVER +1	JUMP over Driver assembled
DRIVER:	·	
	.	
	.	
	code	DRIVER assembled
	.	
	.	*once* as a subroutine
	.	
ENDDRIVER:	RETURN	
	.	
	.	
	.	
	.	
	.	
	.	
	.	
(MULTIPLY)	SETUP code	
	CALL DRIVER	only SETUP and
	.	
	.	call to DRIVER
	.	
	.	assembled
	.	
	END	

The preceding example illustrates the way in which the nonchanging portions of a MACRO may be put in subroutine form and called within the MACRO. A question might naturally arise concerning all of this trouble just to get the subroutine into the MACRO: Why not simply write the subroutine externally and call it from the MACRO, forgetting all of the conditional assembly rigamarole? Although this is possible, of course, and sometimes desirable, in general the above procedure is to be preferred. MACROs are not meant for on-the-spot programming, but are designed to enhance the power of a machine via the addition of *well-thought-out* custom instructions.

The system to be *used* (as opposed to dedicated systems to be marketed) should be viewed as an *evolving* system that becomes increasingly sophisticated and increasingly easy to use. The creation of powerful, *self-contained* MACROs that form a growing macro-library is a primary means of achieving such sophistication. If, after a considerable time, we possess 100 or more special-purpose instructions, it would be highly inconvenient to have to remember and access the one or more special subroutines required by each MACRO. It is simpler in the long run to put a little more effort into the creation of the MACRO as a totally self-contained entity and, thereafter, to enjoy the effortless use of these custom instructions. In this light, it would be desirable to include the initialized statement, FIRST SET 1, in the MACRO proper.

appendix
C *local and global variables*

Although MACRO-assemblers can offer many more features then described here, the last topic we will treat is that of local variables. The use of names within a MACRO could present a problem if the same name in two different MACROs resulted in a multiply-defined error condition. For example, many programs have loops, and it would be highly inconvenient if, while writing the 100th MACRO, we had to comb all of the preceding 99 to be sure that LOOP had not been used. This inconvenience is eliminated by treating variables defined within a MACRO as LOCAL, i.e., as defined only with the MACRO proper. Thus, the same names can be used in different MACROs and no problems will result. If it is desired, for any reason, to access a name in a MACRO, then the name can be declared GLOBAL by using *two* colons after the symbol, i.e.,

LOOP:

is treated as a LOCAL variable, whereas

LOOP::

is treated as a GLOBAL variable with the usual rules pertaining to variables applying. GLOBAL declaration overrides locality.

appendix
D   *manufacturers' data*

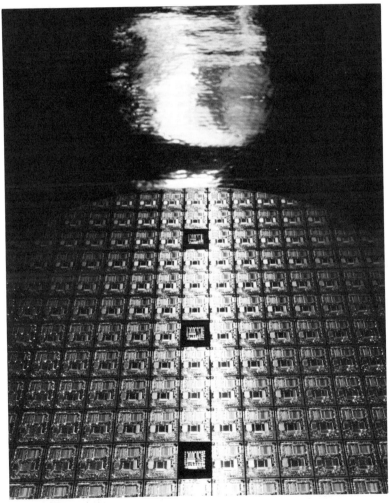

The following product data sheets are used with the permission of the manufacturers.

SINGLE COMPONENT 8-BIT MICROCOMPUTER

8048 Mask Programmable ROM
8748 User Programmable/Erasable EPROM
8035 External ROM or EPROM

INSTRUCTION SET

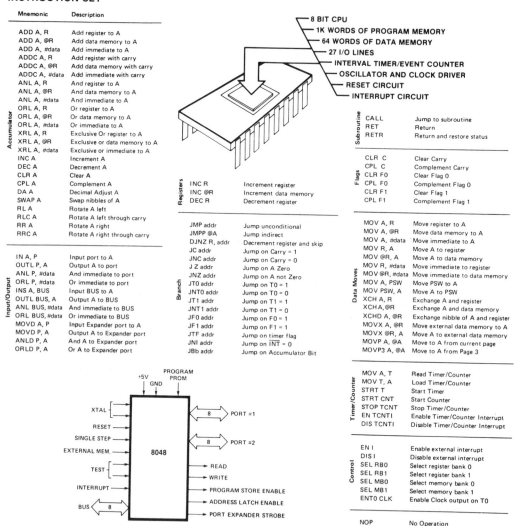

Mnemonic	Description
Accumulator	
ADD A, R	Add register to A
ADD A, @R	Add data memory to A
ADD A, #data	Add immediate to A
ADDC A, R	Add register with carry
ADDC A, @R	Add data memory with carry
ADDC A, #data	Add immediate with carry
ANL A, R	And register to A
ANL A, @R	And data memory to A
ANL A, #data	And immediate to A
ORL A, R	Or register to A
ORL A, @R	Or data memory to A
ORL A, #data	Or immediate to A
XRL A, R	Exclusive Or register to A
XRL A, @R	Exclusive or data memory to A
XRL A, #data	Exclusive or immediate to A
INC A	Increment A
DEC A	Decrement A
CLR A	Clear A
CPL A	Complement A
DA A	Decimal Adjust A
SWAP A	Swap nibbles of A
RL A	Rotate A left
RLC A	Rotate A left through carry
RR A	Rotate A right
RRC A	Rotate A right through carry

Mnemonic	Description
Input/Output	
IN A, P	Input port to A
OUTL P, A	Output A to port
ANL P, #data	And immediate to port
ORL P, #data	Or immediate to port
INS A, BUS	Input BUS to A
OUTL BUS, A	Output A to BUS
ANL BUS, #data	And immediate to BUS
ORL BUS, #data	Or immediate to BUS
MOVD A, P	Input Expander port to A
MOVD P, A	Output A to Expander port
ANLD P, A	And A to Expander port
ORLD P, A	Or A to Expander port

Mnemonic	Description
Registers	
INC R	Increment register
INC @R	Increment data memory
DEC R	Decrement register

Mnemonic	Description
Branch	
JMP addr	Jump unconditional
JMPP @A	Jump indirect
DJNZ R, addr	Decrement register and skip
JC addr	Jump on Carry = 1
JNC addr	Jump on Carry = 0
J Z addr	Jump on A Zero
JNZ addr	Jump on A not Zero
JT0 addr	Jump on T0 = 1
JNT0 addr	Jump on T0 = 0
JT1 addr	Jump on T1 = 1
JNT1 addr	Jump on T1 = 0
JF0 addr	Jump on F0 = 1
JF1 addr	Jump on F1 = 1
JTF addr	Jump on timer flag
JNI addr	Jump on $\overline{INT}$ = 0
JBb addr	Jump on Accumulator Bit

8 BIT CPU
1K WORDS OF PROGRAM MEMORY
64 WORDS OF DATA MEMORY
27 I/O LINES
INTERVAL TIMER/EVENT COUNTER
OSCILLATOR AND CLOCK DRIVER
RESET CIRCUIT
INTERRUPT CIRCUIT

Mnemonic	Description
Subroutine	
CALL	Jump to subroutine
RET	Return
RETR	Return and restore status

Mnemonic	Description
Flags	
CLR C	Clear Carry
CPL C	Complement Carry
CLR F0	Clear Flag 0
CPL F0	Complement Flag 0
CLR F1	Clear Flag 1
CPL F1	Complement Flag 1

Mnemonic	Description
Data Moves	
MOV A, R	Move register to A
MOV A, @R	Move data memory to A
MOV A, #data	Move immediate to A
MOV R, A	Move A to register
MOV @R, A	Move A to data memory
MOV R, #data	Move immediate to register
MOV @R, #data	Move immediate to data memory
MOV A, PSW	Move PSW to A
MOV PSW, A	Move A to PSW
XCH A, R	Exchange A and register
XCH A, @R	Exchange A and data memory
XCHD A, @R	Exchange nibble of A and register
MOVX A, @R	Move external data memory to A
MOVX @R, A	Move A to external data memory
MOVP A, @A	Move to A from current page
MOVP3 A, @A	Move to A from Page 3

Mnemonic	Description
Timer/Counter	
MOV A, T	Read Timer/Counter
MOV T, A	Load Timer/Counter
STRT T	Start Timer
STRT CNT	Start Counter
STOP TCNT	Stop Timer/Counter
EN TCNTI	Enable Timer/Counter Interrupt
DIS TCNTI	Disable Timer/Counter Interrupt

Mnemonic	Description
Control	
EN I	Enable external interrupt
DIS I	Disable external interrupt
SEL RB0	Select register bank 0
SEL RB1	Select register bank 1
SEL MB0	Select memory bank 0
SEL MB1	Select memory bank 1
ENT0 CLK	Enable Clock output on T0
NOP	No Operation

The Intel® 8048/8748/8035 is a totally self-sufficient 8-bit parallel computer fabricated on a single silicon chip using Intel's N-channel silicon gate MOS process.

The 8048 contains a 1K x 8 program memory, a 64 x 8 RAM data memory, 27 I/O lines, and an 8-bit timer/counter in addition to on board oscillator and clock circuits. For systems that require extra capability, the 8048 can be expanded using standard memories and MCS-80™ (8080A) peripherals. The 8035 is the equivalent of an 8048 without program memory.

To reduce development problems to a minimum and provide maximum flexibility, three interchangeable pin-compatible versions of this single component microcomputer exist: the 8748 with user-programmable and erasable EPROM program memory for prototype and preproduction systems, the 8048 with factory-programmed mask ROM program memory for low-cost high volume production, and the 8035 without program memory for use with external program memories.

intel® 8080A MICROPROCESSOR

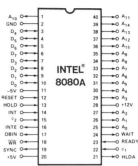

A_{10}	1	40	A_{11}
GND	2	39	A_{14}
D_4	3	38	A_{13}
D_5	4	37	A_{12}
D_6	5	36	A_{15}
D_7	6	35	A_9
D_3	7	34	A_8
D_2	8	33	A_7
D_1	9	32	A_6
D_0	10	31	A_5
−5V	11	30	A_4
RESET	12	29	A_3
HOLD	13	28	+12V
INT	14	27	A_2
ϕ_2	15	26	A_1
INTE	16	25	A_0
DBIN	17	24	WAIT
$\overline{WR}$	18	23	READY
SYNC	19	22	ϕ_1
+5V	20	21	HLDA

INTEL® 8080A

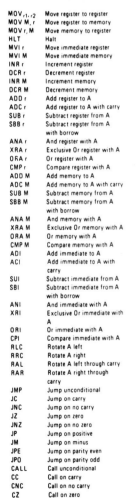

MOV r_1, r_2	Move register to register
MOV M, r	Move register to memory
MOV r, M	Move memory to register
HLT	Halt
MVI r	Move immediate register
MVI M	Move immediate memory
INR r	Increment register
DCR r	Decrement register
INR M	Increment memory
DCR M	Decrement memory
ADD r	Add register to A
ADC r	Add register to A with carry
SUB r	Subtract register from A
SBB r	Subtract register from A with borrow
ANA r	And register with A
XRA r	Exclusive Or register with A
ORA r	Or register with A
CMP r	Compare register with A
ADD M	Add memory to A
ADC M	Add memory to A with carry
SUB M	Subtract memory from A
SBB M	Subtract memory from A with borrow
ANA M	And memory with A
XRA M	Exclusive Or memory with A
ORA M	Or memory with A
CMP M	Compare memory with A
ADI	Add immediate to A
ACI	Add immediate to A with carry
SUI	Subtract immediate from A
SBI	Subtract immediate from A with borrow
ANI	And immediate with A
XRI	Exclusive Or immediate with A
ORI	Or immediate with A
CPI	Compare immediate with A
RLC	Rotate A left
RRC	Rotate A right
RAL	Rotate A left through carry
RAR	Rotate A right through carry
JMP	Jump unconditional
JC	Jump on carry
JNC	Jump on no carry
JZ	Jump on zero
JNZ	Jump on no zero
JP	Jump on positive
JM	Jump on minus
JPE	Jump on parity even
JPO	Jump on parity odd
CALL	Call unconditional
CC	Call on carry
CNC	Call on no carry
CZ	Call on zero

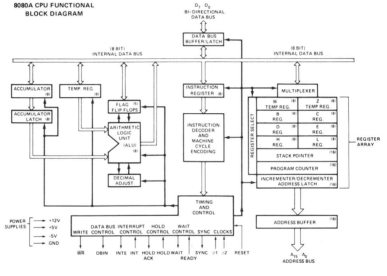

8080A CPU FUNCTIONAL BLOCK DIAGRAM

CNZ	Call on no zero
CP	Call on positive
CM	Call on minus
CPE	Call on parity even
CPO	Call on parity odd
RET	Return
RC	Return on carry
RNC	Return on no carry
RZ	Return on zero
RNZ	Return on no zero
RP	Return on positive
RM	Return on minus
RPE	Return on parity even
RPO	Return on parity odd
RST	Restart
IN	Input
OUT	Output
LXI B	Load immediate register Pair B & C
LXI D	Load immediate register Pair D & E
LXI H	Load immediate register Pair H & L
LXI SP	Load immediate stack pointer

PUSH B	Push register Pair B & C on stack
PUSH D	Push register Pair D & E on stack
PUSH H	Push register Pair H & L on stack
PUSH PSW	Push A and Flags on stack
POP B	Pop register pair B & C off stack
POP D	Pop register pair D & E off stack
POP H	Pop register pair H & L off stack
POP PSW	Pop A and Flags off stack
STA	Store A direct
LDA	Load A direct
XCHG	Exchange D & E, H & L Registers
XTHL	Exchange top of stack, H & L
SPHL	H & L to stack pointer
PCHL	H & L to program counter
DAD B	Add B & C to H & L

DAD D	Add D & E to H & L
DAD H	Add H & L to H & L
DAD SP	Add stack pointer to H & L
STAX B	Store A indirect
STAX D	Store A indirect
LDAX B	Load A indirect
LDAX D	Load A indirect
INX B	Increment B & C registers
INX D	Increment D & E registers
INX H	Increment H & L registers
INX SP	Increment stack pointer
DCX B	Decrement B & C
DCX D	Decrement D & E
DCX H	Decrement H & L
DCX SP	Decrement stack pointer
CMA	Complement A
STC	Set carry
CMC	Complement carry
DAA	Decimal adjust A
SHLD	Store H & L direct
LHLD	Load H & L direct
EI	Enable Interrupts
DI	Disable interrupt
NOP	No-operation

F8 MICROPROCESSOR

3850 CENTRAL PROCESSING UNIT

Fairchild's F8 Central Processing Unit (CPU) contains all of the functions of an ordinary central processor and adds some time and money saving features uniquely its own. For instance, the 64 bytes of scratchpad RAM memory already included on the F8 CPU eliminate the need for external RAM circuits in many applications. Clock and power-on-reset circuitry, normally requiring additional integrated circuit packages, are included on-chip. Fairchild's CPU also contains 16 bits of fully bidirectional input and output lines internally latched (for storing output data) and capable of driving a standard TTL load.

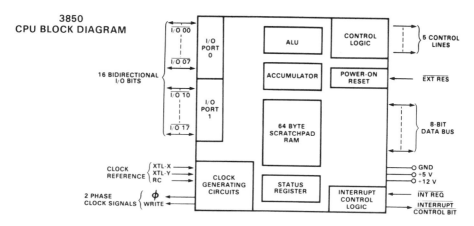

3850
CPU BLOCK DIAGRAM

F8 ADDRESSING MODES

Direct Addressing — In these two-byte instructions, the address of the operand is contained in the second byte of the instruction. The Direct Addressing mode is used in the Input/Output class of instructions.

Short Immediate Addressing — Instructions whose addressing mode is Short Immediate have the instruction op code as the first four bits and the operand as the last four bits. They are all one-byte instructions.

Long Immediate Addressing — In these two-byte instructions, the first instruction byte is the op code and the second byte is the 8-bit operand.

Direct Register Addressing — This mode of addressing may be used to directly reference the Scratchpad Registers. By including the register number in the one-byte instruction, 12 of the 64 Scratchpad Registers may be referenced directly.

Indirect Register Addressing — All 64 Scratchpad Registers may be indirectly referenced, using the Indirect Scratchpad Register in the CPU. This 6-bit register, which acts as a pointer to the scratchpad memory, may either be incremented,

decremented, or left unchanged while accessing the scratchpad register.

Indirect Memory Addressing — A 16-bit Indirect Address Register, the Data Counter, points to either data or constants in bulk memory. A group of one-byte instructions is provided to manipulate this area of memory. These instructions imply that the Data Counter is pointing to the desired memory byte. The Data Counter is self-incrementing, allowing for an entire data field to be scanned and manipulated without requiring special instructions to increment its content. The memory interface circuit contains two interchangeable data counters.

Relative Addressing — All F8 Branch Instructions use the relative addressing mode. Whenever a branch is taken, the Program Counter is updated by an 8-bit relative address contained in the second byte of the instruction. A branch may extend 128 locations forward or 127 locations back.

Implied Addressing — The data for this one-byte instruction is implied by the actual instruction. For example, the POP instruction automatically implies that the content of the Program Counter will be set to the value contained in the Stack Register.

F8 INSTRUCTION SET

ADC	Add Data Counter with Accumulator		JMP	Jump
AI	Add Immediate with Accumulator		LI	Load Accumulator Immediate
AM	Add Binary Accumulator with Memory		LIS	Load Accumulator Short
AMD	Add Decimal Accumulator with Memory		LISL	Load ISAR Lower 3 Bits
AS	Add Binary Accumulator with Scratchpad Register		LISU	Load ISAR Upper 3 Bits
ASD	Add Decimal Accumulator with Scratchpad Register		LM	Load Memory
			LNK	Link Carry into Accumulator
BC	Branch on Carry		LR	Load Register
BF	Branch on False Condition		NI	Logical AND Accumulator Immediate
BM	Branch if Negative		NM	Logical AND from Memory
BNC	Branch if no Carry		NOP	No Operation
BNO	Branch if no Overflow		NS	Logical AND Scratchpad and Accumulator
BNZ	Branch if no Zero		OI	Logical OR Immediate
BP	Branch if Positive		OM	Logical OR Memory with Accumulator
BR	Unconditional Branch		OUT	Output
BR7	Branch if ISAR is not 7		OUTS	Output Short
BT	Branch on True Condition		PI	Push Program Counter into Stack Register
BZ	Branch on Zero Condition			Set Program Counter to New Location
CI	Compare Immediate		PK	Push Program Counter into Stack Register
CLR	Clear Accumulator			Set Program Counter from Scratchpad
CM	Compare with Memory		POP	Put Stack Register into Program Counter
COM	Complement Accumulator		SL	Shift Left
DCI	Load Data Counter Immediate		SR	Shift Right
DI	Disable Interrupt		ST	Store to Memory
DS	Decrement Scratchpad Register		XDC	Exchange Data Counters
EI	Enable Interrupt		XI	Exclusive OR Immediate
INC	Increment Accumulator		XM	Exclusive OR Accumulator with Memory
IN	Input		XS	Exclusive OR Accumulator with Scratchpad
INS	Input Short			

3851 PROGRAM STORAGE UNIT

Fairchild's Program Storage Unit (PSU) is not just a conventional Read Only Memory. In addition to containing 1024 bytes of mask programmable ROM for program and constant storage, the F8 PSU includes the addressing logic for memory referencing, a Program Counter, an Indirect Address Register (the Data Counter) and a Stack Register. A complete vectored interrupt level, including an external interrupt line to alert the central processor, is provided. All of the logic necessary to request, acknowledge and reset the interrupt is on the F8 PSU. The 8-bit Programmable Timer is especially useful for generating real time delays. The PSU has an additional 16 bits of TTL compatible, bidirectional, fully latched I/O lines.

3851 PSU BLOCK DIAGRAM

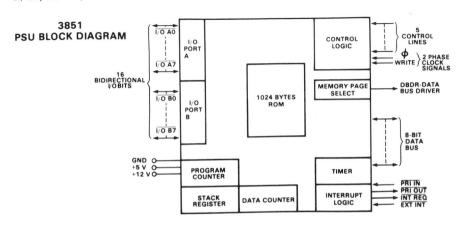

MOS MCS650X–

*ADC	Add Memory to Accumulator with Carry	*JSR	Jump to New Location Saving Return Address
*AND	"AND" Memory with Accumulator	*LDA	Load Accumulator with Memory
*ASL	Shift Left One Bit (Memory or Accumulator)	*LDX	Load Index X with Memory
		LDY	Load Index Y with Memory
*BCC	Branch on Carry Clear	*LSR	Shift One Bit Right (Memory or Accumulator)
*BCS	Branch on Carry Set		
*BEQ	Branch on Result Zero	NØP	No Operation
*BIT	Test Bits in Memory with Accumulator	*ØRA	"OR" Memory with Accumulator
*BMI	Branch on Result Minus	*PHA	Push Accumulator on Stack
*BNE	Branch on Result not Zero	PHP	Push Processor Status on Stack
*BPL	Branch on Result Plus	*PLA	Pull Accumulator from Stack
*BRK	Force Break	PLP	Pull Processor Status from Stack
*BVC	Branch on Overflow Clear	*RØL	Rotate One Bit Left (Memory or Accumulator)
*BVS	Branch on Overflow Set		
*CLC	Clear Carry Flag	*RTI	Return From Interrupt
CLD	Clear Decimal Mode	*RTS	Return From Subroutine
*CLI	Clear Interrupt Disable Bit	*SBC	Subtract Memory from Accumulator with Borrow
*CLV	Clear Overflow Flag	*SEC	Set Carry Flag
*CMP	Compare Memory and Accumulator	SED	Set Decimal Mode
*CPX	Compare Memory and Index X	*SEI	Set Interrupt Disable Status
CPY	Compare Memory and Index Y	*STA	Store Accumulator in Memory
*DEC	Decrement Memory by One	*STX	Store Index X in Memory
*DEX	Decrement Index X by One	STY	Store Index Y in Memory
DEY	Decrement Index Y by One	TAX	Transfer Accumulator to Index X
*EØR	"Exclusive-or" Memory with Accumulator	TAY	Transfer Accumulator to Index Y
*INC	Increment Memory by One	*TSX	Transfer Stack Pointer to Index X
*INX	Increment X by One	TXA	Transfer Index X to Accumulator
INY	Increment Y by One	*TXS	Transfer Index X to Stack Pointer
*JMP	Jump to New Location	TYA	Transfer Index Y to Accumulator

*Instructions similar to MC6800

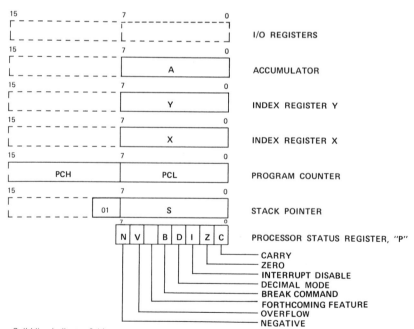

• Solid line indicates 8-bit processors.
  Dashed line indicates 16-bit versions.

456

MOTOROLA MC6800

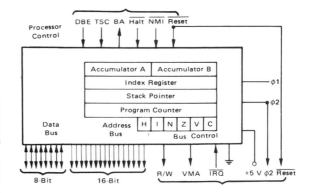

Accumulator (ACCX) Addressing — In accumulator only addressing, either accumulator A or accumulator B is specified. These are one-byte instructions.

Immediate Addressing — In immediate addressing, the operand is contained in the second byte of the instruction except LDS and LDX which have the operand in the second and third bytes of the instruction. The MPU addresses this location when it fetches the immediate instruction for execution. These are two or three-byte instructions.

Direct Addressing — In direct addressing, the address of the operand is contained in the second byte of the instruction. Direct addressing allows the user to directly address the lowest 256 bytes in the machine i.e., locations zero through 255. Enhanced execution times are achieved by storing data in these locations.

Extended Addressing — In extended addressing, the address contained in the second byte of the instruction is used as the higher eight-bits of the address of the operand. The third byte of the instruction is used as the lower eight-bits of the address for the operand.

Indexed Addressing — In indexed addressing, the address contained in the second byte of the instruction is added to the index register's lowest eight bits in the MPU. The carry is then added to the higher order eight bits of the index register. This result is then used to address memory. The modified address is held in a temporary address register so there is no change to the index register.

Implied Addressing — In the implied addressing mode the instruction gives the address (i.e., stack pointer, index

Relative Addressing — In relative addressing, the address contained in the second byte of the instruction is added to the program counter's lowest eight bits plus two. The carry or borrow is then added to the high eight bits. This allows the user to address data within a range of –125 to +129 bytes of the present instruction. These are two-byte instructions.

MOTOROLA
MC6800
MICROPROCESSOR

1	V_{SS}	O Reset	40
2	Halt	TSC	39
3	$\phi 1$	N.C.	38
4	$\overline{IRQ}$	$\phi 2$	37
5	VMA	DBE	36
6	$\overline{NMI}$	N.C.	35
7	BA	R/W	34
8	V_{CC}	D0	33
9	A0	D1	32
10	A1	D2	31
11	A2	D3	30
12	A3	D4	29
13	A4	D5	28
14	A5	D6	27
15	A6	D7	26
16	A7	A15	25
17	A8	A14	24
18	A9	A13	23
19	A10	A12	22
20	A11	V_{SS}	21

MPU INSTRUCTION SET

ABA	Add Accumulators	CLR	Clear	PUL	Pull Data
ADC	Add with Carry	CLV	Clear Overflow	ROL	Rotate Left
ADD	Add	CMP	Compare	ROR	Rotate Right
AND	Logical And	COM	Complement	RTI	Return from Interrupt
ASL	Arithmetic Shift Left	CPX	Compare Index Register	RTS	Return from Subroutine
ASR	Arithmetic Shift Right	DAA	Decimal Adjust	SBA	Subtract Accumulators
BCC	Branch if Carry Clear	DEC	Decrement	SBC	Subtract with Carry
BCS	Branch if Carry Set	DES	Decrement Stack Pointer	SEC	Set Carry
BEQ	Branch if Equal to Zero	DEX	Decrement Index Register	SEI	Set Interrupt Mask
BGE	Branch if Greater or Equal Zero	EOR	Exclusive OR	SEV	Set Overflow
BGT	Branch if Greater than Zero			STA	Store Accumulator
BHI	Branch if Higher	INC	Increment	STS	Store Stack Register
BIT	Bit Test	INS	Increment Stack Pointer	STX	Store Index Register
BLE	Branch if Less or Equal	INX	Increment Index Register	SUB	Subtract
BLS	Branch if Lower or Same	JMP	Jump	SWI	Software Interrupt
BLT	Branch if Less than Zero	JSR	Jump to Subroutine	TAB	Transfer Accumulators
BMI	Branch if Minus			TAP	Transfer Accumulators to Condition Code Reg.
BNE	Branch if Not Equal to Zero	LDA	Load Accumulator	TBA	Transfer Accumulators
BPL	Branch if Plus	LDS	Load Stack Pointer	TPA	Transfer Condition Code Reg. to Accumulator
BRA	Branch Always	LDX	Load Index Register	TST	Test
BSR	Branch to Subroutine	LSR	Logical Shift Right	TSX	Transfer Stack Pointer to Index Register
BVC	Branch if Overflow Clear	NEG	Negate	TXS	Transfer Index Register to Stack Pointer
BVS	Branch if Overflow Set	NOP	No Operation		
CBA	Compare Accumulators	ORA	Inclusive OR Accumulator	WAI	Wait for Interrupt
CLC	Clear Carry				
CLI	Clear Interrupt Mask	PSH	Push Data		

National Semiconductor Corporation

SC/MP-II
microprocessor

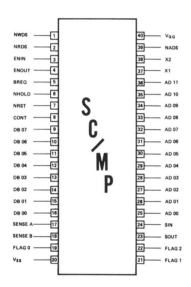

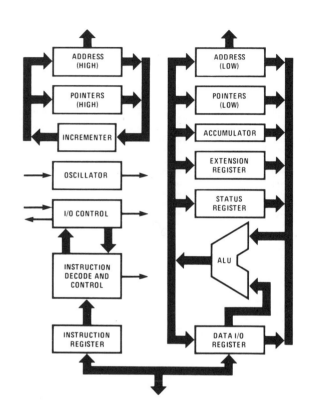

Memory Reference Instructions

LD	Load	$(AC) \leftarrow (EA)$
ST	Store	$(EA) \leftarrow (AC)$
AND	AND	$(AC) \leftarrow (AC)\ (EA)$
OR	OR	$(AC) \leftarrow (AC)\ V\ (EA)$
XOR	Exclusive-OR	$(AC) \leftarrow (AC)\ V\ (EA)$
DAD	Decimal Add	$(AC) \leftarrow (AC)_{10} + (EA)_{10} + (CY/L);(CY/L)$
ADD	Add	$(AC) \leftarrow (AC) + (EA) + (CY/L);(CY/L),(OV)$
CAD	Complement and Add	$(AC) \leftarrow (AC) + \sim(EA) + (CY/L);(CY/L),(OV)$

Memory Increment/Decrement Instructions

ILD	Increment and Load	$(AC), (EA) \leftarrow (EA) + 1$
DLD	Decrement and Load	$(AC), (EA) \leftarrow (EA) - 1$

Immediate Instructions

LDI	Load Immediate	$(AC) \leftarrow data$
ANI	AND Immediate	$(AC) \leftarrow (AC)\ data$
ORI	OR Immediate	$(AC) \leftarrow (AC)\ V\ data$
XRI	Exclusive-OR Immediate	$(AC) \leftarrow (AC)\ V\ data$
DAI	Decimal Add Immediate	$(AC) \leftarrow (AC)_{10} + data_{10} + (CY/L);(CY/L)$
ADI	Add Immediate	$(AC) \leftarrow (AC) + data + (CY/L);(CY/L),(OV)$
CAI	Complement and Add Immediate	$(AC) \leftarrow (AC) + \sim data + (CY/L);(CY/L),(OV)$

Transfer Instructions

JMP	Jump	$(PC) \leftarrow EA$
JP	Jump if Positive	If $(AC) \geqslant 0$, $(PC) \leftarrow EA$
JZ	Jump if Zero	If $(AC) = 0$, $(PC) \leftarrow EA$
JNZ	Jump if Not Zero	If $(AC) \neq 0$, $(PC) \leftarrow EA$

Double-Byte Miscellaneous Instructions

DLY	Delay	count AC to -1, delay $= 13 + 2(AC) +$ $2\,disp + 2^9\,disp$ microcycles

Extension Register Instructions

LDE	Load AC from Extension	$(AC) \leftarrow (E)$
XAE	Exchange AC and Extension	$(AC) \leftrightarrow (E)$
ANE	AND Extension	$(AC) \leftarrow (AC)\ (E)$
ORE	OR Extension	$(AC) \leftarrow (AC)\ V\ (E)$
XRE	Exclusive-OR Extension	$(AC) \leftarrow (AC)\ V\ (E)$
DAE	Decimal Add Extension	$(AC) \leftarrow (AC)_{10} + (E)_{10} + (CY/L);(CY/L)$
ADE	Add Extension	$(AC) \leftarrow (AC) + (E) + (CY/L);(CY/L),(OV)$
CAE	Complement and Add Extension	$(AC) \leftarrow (AC) + \sim(E) + (CY/L);(CY/L),(OV)$

Pointer Register Move Instructions

XPAL	Exchange Pointer Low	$(AC) \leftrightarrow (PTR_{7:0})$
XPAH	Exchange Pointer High	$(AC) \leftrightarrow (PTR_{15:8})$
XPPC	Exchange Pointer with PC	$(PC) \leftrightarrow (PTR)$

Shift, Rotate, Serial I/O Instructions

SIO	Serial Input/Output	$(E_i) \rightarrow (E_{i-1})$, $SIN \rightarrow (E_7)$, $(E_0) \rightarrow SOUT$
SR	Shift Right	$(AC_i) \rightarrow (AC_{i-1})$, $0 \rightarrow (AC_7)$
SRL	Shift Right with Link	$(AC_i) \rightarrow (AC_{i-1})$, $(CY/L) \rightarrow (AC_7)$
RR	Rotate Right	$(AC_i) \rightarrow (AC_{i-1})$, $(AC_0) \rightarrow (AC_7)$
RRL	Rotate Right with Link	$(AC_i) \rightarrow (AC_{i-1})$, $(AC_0) \rightarrow (CY/L) \rightarrow (AC_7)$

Single-Byte Miscellaneous Instructions

HALT	Halt	Pulse H-flag
CCL	Clear Carry/Link	$(CY/L) \leftarrow 0$
SCL	Set Carry/Link	$(CY/L) \leftarrow 1$
DINT	Disable Interrupt	$(IE) \leftarrow 0$
IEN	Enable Interrupt	$(IE) \leftarrow 1$
CSA	Copy Status to AC	$(AC) \leftarrow (SR)$
CAS	Copy AC to Status	$(SR) \leftarrow (AC)$
NOP	No Operation	None

Rockwell International

PPS-8 SYSTEM

Over 90 Instructions
Digit (4-bit) and Byte (8-bit) Manipulation
Decimal and Binary Arithmetic
Bit Setting/Resetting/Testing
Single Byte Subroutine Call
Data Stacking
Common Data "Pools"
2048 x 8 RCM devices
Local Page Addressing to 128 Bytes
Direct Addressing to 16,384 Bytes
Bank Select Addressing to 32K Without External Circuitry
Indirect, Auto-increment Addressing
256 x 8 RAM devices
Direct Addressing to 16,384 Bytes
Bank Select Addressing to 32K
3 RAM Addressing Registers
Auto-Increment and Auto-Decrement Addressing
Priority Interrupt System
- Power-Fail Detect
- Real Time Clock
- I/O Device Service

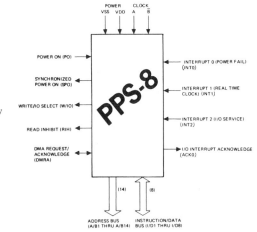

Central Processor Unit

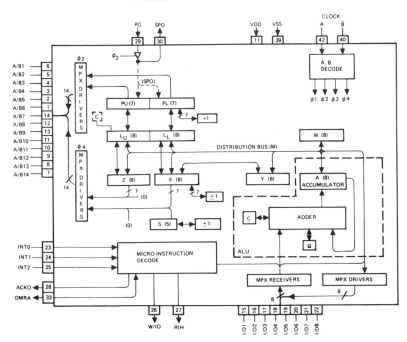

PARALLEL PROCESSING SYSTEM

RCA
Solid State Division

COSMAC Microprocessor

INSTRUCTION

CONTROL INSTRUCTIONS

Instruction	Operation
IDLE	WAIT FOR DMA OR INTERRUPT; M(R(0))→BUS
NO OPERATION	CONTINUE
SET P	N→P
SET X	N→X
SET Q	1→Q
RESET Q	0→Q
SAVE	T→M(R(X))
PUSH X,P TO STACK	(X,P)→T; (X,P)→M(R(2)) THEN P→X; R(2)−1
RETURN	M(R(X))→(X,P); R(X) +1 1→IE
DISABLE	M(R(X))→(X,P); R(X) +1 0→IE

MEMORY REFERENCE

Instruction	Operation
LOAD VIA N	M(R(N))→D; FOR N NOT 0
LOAD ADVANCE	M(R(N))→D; R(N) +1
LOAD VIA X	M(R(X))→D
LOAD VIA X AND ADVANCE	M(R(X))→D; R(X) +1
LOAD IMMEDIATE	M(R(P))→D; R(P) +1
STORE VIA N	D→M(R(N))
STORE VIA X AND DECREMENT	D→M(R(X)); R(X) −1

REGISTER OPERATIONS

Instruction	Operation
INCREMENT REG N	R(N) +1
DECREMENT REG N	R(N) −1
INCREMENT REG X	R(X) +1
GET LOW REG N	R(N).0→D
PUT LOW REG N	D→R(N).0
GET HIGH REG N	R(N).1→D
PUT HIGH REG N	D→R(N).1

LOGIC OPERATIONS♦♦

Instruction	Operation
OR	M(R(X)) OR D→D
OR IMMEDIATE	M(R(P)) OR D→D; R(P) +1
EXCLUSIVE OR	M(R(X)) XOR D→D
EXCLUSIVE OR IMMEDIATE	M(R(P)) XOR D→D; R(P) +1
AND	M(R(X)) AND D→D
AND IMMEDIATE	M(R(P)) AND D→D; R(P) +1
SHIFT RIGHT	SHIFT D RIGHT, LSB(D)→DF, 0→MSB(D)
SHIFT RIGHT WITH CARRY	SHIFT D RIGHT, LSB(D)→DF, DF→MSB(D)
RING SHIFT RIGHT	
SHIFT LEFT	SHIFT D LEFT, MSB(D)→DF, 0→LSB(D)
SHIFT LEFT WITH CARRY	SHIFT D LEFT, MSB(D)→DF, DF→LSB(D)
RING SHIFT LEFT	

ARITHMETIC OPERATIONS♦♦

Instruction	Operation
ADD	M(R(X)) +D→DF, D
ADD IMMEDIATE	M(R(P)) +D→DF, D; R(P) +1
ADD WITH CARRY	M(R(X)) +D +DF→DF, D
ADD WITH CARRY, IMMEDIATE	M(R(P)) +D +DF→DF, D R(P) +1
SUBTRACT D	M(R(X))−D→DF, D
SUBTRACT D IMMEDIATE	M(R(P))−D→DF, D; R(P) +1
SUBTRACT D WITH BORROW	M(R(X))−D−(NOT DF)→DF, D
SUBTRACT D WITH BORROW, IMMEDIATE	M(R(P))−D−(NOT DF)→DF, D; R(P) +1
SUBTRACT MEMORY	D−M(R(X))→DF, D
SUBTRACT MEMORY IMMEDIATE	D−M(R(P))→DF, D; R(P) +1
SUBTRACT MEMORY WITH BORROW	D−M(R(X))−(NOT DF)→DF, D
SUBTRACT MEMORY WITH BORROW, IMMEDIATE	D−M(R(P))−(NOT DF)→DF, D R(P) +1

OPERATION

BRANCH INSTRUCTIONS—SHORT BRANCH

Instruction	Operation
SHORT BRANCH	M(R(P))→R(P).0
NO SHORT BRANCH (SEE SKP)	R(P) +1
SHORT BRANCH IF D=0	IF D=0, M(R(P))→R(P).0 ELSE R(P) +1
SHORT BRANCH IF D NOT 0	IF D NOT 0, M(R(P))→R(P).0 ELSE R(P) +1
SHORT BRANCH IF DF=1	IF DF=1, M(R(P))→R(P).0 ELSE R(P) +1
SHORT BRANCH IF POS OR ZERO	
SHORT BRANCH IF EQUAL OR GREATER	
SHORT BRANCH IF DF=0	IF DF=0, M(R(P))→R(P).0 ELSE R(P) +1
SHORT BRANCH IF MINUS	
SHORT BRANCH IF LESS	
SHORT BRANCH IF Q=1	IF Q=1, M(R(P))→R(P).0 ELSE R(P) +1
SHORT BRANCH IF Q=0	IF Q=0, M(R(P))→R(P).0 ELSE R(P) +1
SHORT BRANCH IF EF1=1	IF EF1=1, M(R(P))→R(P).0 ELSE R(P) +1
SHORT BRANCH IF EF1=0	IF EF1=0, M(R(P))→R(P).0 ELSE R(P) +1
SHORT BRANCH IF EF2=1	IF EF2=1, M(R(P))→R(P).0 ELSE R(P) +1
SHORT BRANCH IF EF2=0	IF EF2=0, M(R(P))→R(P).0 ELSE R(P) +1
SHORT BRANCH IF EF3=1	IF EF3=1, M(R(P))→R(P).0 ELSE R(P) +1
SHORT BRANCH IF EF3=0	IF EF3=0, M(R(P))→R(P).0 ELSE R(P) +1
SHORT BRANCH IF EF4=1	IF EF4=1, M(R(P))→R(P).0 ELSE R(P) +1
SHORT BRANCH IF EF4=0	IF EF4=0, M(R(P))→R(P).0 ELSE R(P) +1

BRANCH INSTRUCTIONS—LONG BRANCH

Instruction	Operation
LONG BRANCH	M(R(P))→R(P).1 M(R(P) +1)→R(P).0
NO LONG BRANCH (SEE LSKP)	R(P) +2
LONG BRANCH IF D=0	IF D=0, M(R(P))→R(P).1 M(R(P) +1)→R(P).0 ELSE R(P) +2
LONG BRANCH IF D NOT 0	IF D NOT 0, M(R(P))→R(P).1 M(R(P) +1)→R(P).0 ELSE R(P) +2
LONG BRANCH IF DF=1	IF DF=1, M(R(P))→R(P).1 M(R(P) +1)→R(P).0 ELSE R(P) +2
LONG BRANCH IF DF=0	IF DF=0, M(R(P))→R(P).1 M(R(P) +1)→R(P).0 ELSE R(P) +2
LONG BRANCH IF Q=1	IF Q=1, M(R(P))→R(P).1 M(R(P) +1)→R(P).0 ELSE R(P) +2
LONG BRANCH IF Q=0	IF Q=0, M(R(P))→R(P).1 M(R(P) +1)→R(P).0 ELSE R(P) +2

SKIP INSTRUCTIONS

Instruction	Operation
SHORT SKIP (SEE NBR)	R(P) +1
LONG SKIP (SEE NLBR)	R(P) +2
LONG SKIP IF D=0	IF D=0, R(P) +2 ELSE CONTINUE
LONG SKIP IF D NOT 0	IF D NOT 0, R(P) +2 ELSE CONTINUE

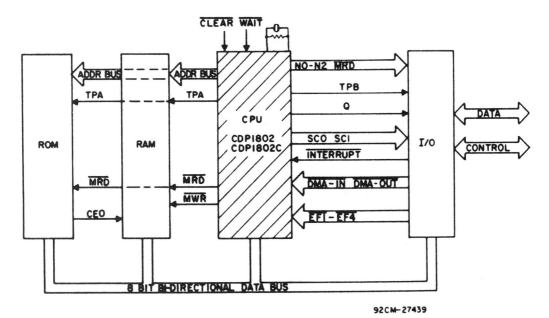

Fig. 1—Typical CDP1802 microprocessor system.

LONG SKIP IF DF=1	IF DF=1, R(P) +2
	ELSE CONTINUE
LONG SKIP IF DF=0	IF DF=0, R(P) +2
	ELSE CONTINUE
LONG SKIP IF Q=1	IF Q=1, R(P) +2
	ELSE CONTINUE
LONG SKIP IF Q=0	IF Q=0, R(P) +2
	ELSE CONTINUE
LONG SKIP IF IE=1	IF IE=1, R(P) +2
	ELSE CONTINUE
INPUT—OUTPUT BYTE TRANSFER	
OUTPUT 1	M(R(X))→BUS; R(X) +1; N LINES = 1
OUTPUT 2	M(R(X))→BUS; R(X) +1; N LINES = 2
OUTPUT 3	M(R(X))→BUS; R(X) +1; N LINES = 3
OUTPUT 4	M(R(X))→BUS; R(X) +1; N LINES = 4
OUTPUT 5	M(R(X))→BUS; R(X) +1; N LINES = 5
OUTPUT 6	M(R(X))→BUS; R(X) +1; N LINES = 6
OUTPUT 7	M(R(X))→BUS; R(X) +1; N LINES = 7
INPUT 1	BUS→M(R(X)); BUS→D; N LINES = 1
INPUT 2	BUS→M(R(X)); BUS→D; N LINES = 2
INPUT 3	BUS→M(R(X)); BUS→D; N LINES = 3
INPUT 4	BUS→M(R(X)); BUS→D; N LINES = 4
INPUT 5	BUS→M(R(X)); BUS→D; N LINES = 5
INPUT 6	BUS→M(R(X)); BUS→D; N LINES = 6
INPUT 7	BUS→M(R(X)); BUS→D; N LINES = 7

Signetics

2650

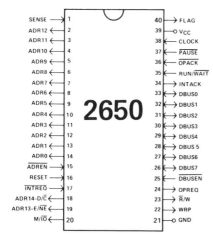

SENSE →	1	40	→ FLAG
ADR12 ←	2	39	O VCC
ADR11 ←	3	38	← CLOCK
ADR10 ←	4	37	→ PAUSE
ADR9 ←	5	36	→ OPACK
ADR8 ←	6	35	→ RUN/WAIT
ADR7 ←	7	34	→ INTACK
ADR6 ←	8	33	←→ DBUS0
ADR5 ←	9	32	←→ DBUS1
ADR4 ←	10	31	←→ DBUS2
ADR3 ←	11	30	←→ DBUS3
ADR2 ←	12	29	←→ DBUS4
ADR1 ←	13	28	←→ DBUS5
ADR0 ←	14	27	←→ DBUS6
ADREN →	15	26	←→ DBUS7
RESET →	16	25	← DBUSEN
INTREQ ←	17	24	→ OPREQ
ADR14-D/C ←	18	23	→ R/W
ADR13-E/NE ←	19	22	→ WRP
M/IO ←	20	21	O GND

2650

PROGRAM STATUS WORD

PSU

7	6	5	4	3	2	1	0
S	F	II	Not Used	Not Used	SP2	SP1	SP0

S Sense SP2 Stack Pointer Two
F Flag SP1 Stack Pointer One
II Interrupt Inhibit SP0 Stack Pointer Zero

PSL

7	6	5	4	3	2	1	0
CC1	CC0	IDC	RS	WC	OVF	COM	C

CC1 Condition Code One WC With/Without Carry
CC0 Condition Code Zero OVF Overflow
IDC Interdigit Carry COM Logical/Arith. Compare
RS Register Bank Select C Carry/Borrow

2650 MICROPROCESSOR INSTRUCTION SET

	MNEMONIC		OP CODE	DESCRIPTION OF OPERATION
LOAD/STORE	LOD	Z	000 000	Load Register Zero
		I	000 001	Load Immediate
		R	000 010	Load Relative
		A	000 011	Load Absolute
	STR	Z	110 000	Store Register Zero (r ≠ 0)
		R	110 010	Store Relative
		A	110 011	Store Absolute
ARITHMETIC	ADD	Z	100 000	Add to Register Zero w/wo Carry
		I	100 001	Add Immediate w/wo Carry
		R	100 010	Add Relative w/wo Carry
		A	100 011	Add Absolute w/wo Carry
	SUB	Z	101 000	Subtract from Register Zero w/wo Borrow
		I	101 001	Subtract Immediate w/wo Borrow
		R	101 010	Subtract Relative w/wo Borrow
		A	101 011	Subtract Absolute w/wo Borrow
	DAR		100 101	Decimal Adjust Register
LOGICAL	AND	Z	010 000	AND to Register Zero (r ≠ 0)
		I	010 001	AND Immediate
		R	010 010	AND Relative
		A	010 011	AND Absolute
	IOR	Z	011 000	Inclusive OR to Register Zero
		I	011 001	Inclusive OR Immediate
		R	011 010	Inclusive OR Relative
		A	011 011	Inclusive OR Absolute
	EOR	Z	001 000	Exclusive OR to Register Zero
		I	001 001	Exclusive OR Immediate
		R	001 010	Exclusive OR Relative
		A	001 011	Exclusive OR Absolute
ROTATE COMPARE	COM	Z	111 000	Compare to Register Zero Arithmetic/Logical
		I	111 001	Compare Immediate Arithmetic/Logical
		R	111 010	Compare Relative Arithmetic/Logical
		A	111 011	Compare Absolute Arithmetic/Logical
	RRR		010 100	Rotate Register Right w/wo Carry
	RRL		110 100	Rotate Register Left w/wo Carry
BRANCH	BCT	R	000 110	Branch On Condition True Relative
		A	000 111	Branch On Condition True Absolute
	BCF	R	100 110	Branch On Condition False Relative
		A	100 111	Branch On Condition False Absolute
	BRN	R	010 110	Branch On Register Non-Zero Relative
		A	010 111	Branch On Register Non-Zero Absolute
	BIR	R	110 110	Branch On Incrementing Register Relative
		A	110 111	Branch On Incrementing Register Absolute
	BDR	R	111 110	Branch On Decrementing Register Relative
		A	111 111	Branch On Decrementing Register Absolute
	ZBRR		100 110 11	Zero Branch Relative, Unconditional
	BXA		100 111 11	Branch Indexed Absolute, Unconditional (Note 5)
SUBROUTINE BRANCH/RETURN	BST	R	001 110	Branch To Subroutine On Condition True, Relative
		A	001 111	Branch To Subroutine On Condition True, Absolute
	BSF	R	101 110	Branch To Subroutine On Condition False, Relative
		A	101 111	Branch To Subroutine On Condition False, Absolute
	BSN	R	011 110	Branch To Subroutine On Non-Zero Register, Relative
		A	011 111	Branch To Subroutine On Non-Zero Register, Absolute
	ZBSR		101 110 11	Zero Branch To Subroutine Relative, Unconditional
	BSXA		101 111 11	Branch To Subroutine, Indexed, Absolute Unconditional (note 5)
	RET	C	000 101	Return From Subroutine, Conditional
		E	001 101	Return From Subroutine and Enable Interrupt, Conditional
INPUT/OUTPUT	WRTD		111 100	Write Data
	REDD		011 100	Read Data
	WRTC		101 100	Write Control
	REDC		001 100	Read Control
	WRTE		110 101	Write Extended
	REDE		010 101	Read Extended
MISC.	HALT		010 000 00	Halt, Enter Wait State
	NOP		110 000 00	No Operation
	TMI		111 101	Test Under Mask Immediate
PROGRAM STATUS	LPS	U	100 100 10	Load Program Status, Upper
		L	100 100 11	Load Program Status, Lower
	SPS	U	000 100 10	Store Program Status, Upper
		L	000 100 11	Store Program Status, Lower
	CPS	U	011 101 00	Clear Program Status, Upper, Masked
		L	011 101 01	Clear Program Status, Lower, Masked
	PPS	U	011 101 10	Preset Program Status, Upper, Masked
		L	011 101 11	Preset Program Status, Lower, Masked
	TPS	U	101 101 00	Test Program Status, Upper, Masked
		L	101 101 01	Test Program Status, Lower, Masked

BLOCK DIAGRAM

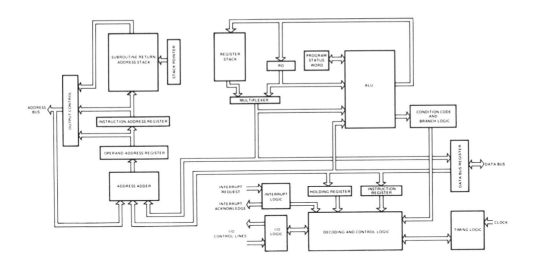

INSTRUCTION FORMATS

(Z) REGISTER ADDRESSING

(I) IMMEDIATE ADDRESSING

(R) RELATIVE ADDRESSING

(A) ABSOLUTE ADDRESSING
   (NON-BRANCH INSTRUCTIONS)

(B) ABSOLUTE ADDRESSING
   (BRANCH INSTRUCTIONS)

INDIRECT ADDRESSING

   MISCELLANEOUS
(E) INSTRUCTIONS

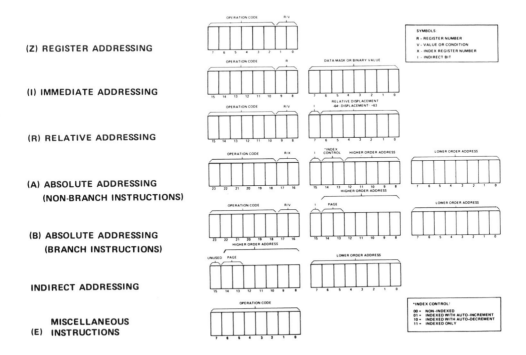

2650 MICROPROCESSOR

TEXAS INSTRUMENTS
INCORPORATED
TMS 9900

GENERAL MEMORY

PROGRAM A

WORKSPACE REGISTER 0

WORKSPACE A

WORKSPACE REGISTER 15

PROGRAM B

WORKSPACE B

TMS 9900

PC (A)

WP (A)

ST (A)

SYMBOLIC (DIRECT) ADDRESSING @ LABEL

The word following the instruction contains the address of the operand.

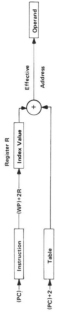

(PC) → Instruction

(PC)+2 → Label

Operand

INDEXED ADDRESSING @ TABLE (R)

The word following the instruction contains the base address. Workspace register R contains the index value. sum of the base address and the index value results in the effective address of the operand.

(PC) → Instruction

(PC)+2 → Table

Register R

(WP)+2R → Index Value

Effective Address

Operand

IMMEDIATE ADDRESSING

The word following the instruction contains the operand.

(PC) → Instruction

(PC)+2 → Operand

PROGRAM COUNTER RELATIVE ADDRESSING

The 8-bit signed displacement in the right byte (bits 8 through 15) of the instruction is multiplied by 2 and added to the updated contents of the program counter. The result is placed in the PC.

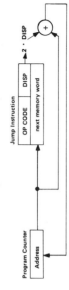

Jump Instruction

OP CODE DISP

2 · DISP

next memory word

Program Counter

Address

CRU RELATIVE ADDRESSING

The 8-bit signed displacement in the right byte of the instruction is added to the CRU base address (bits 3 through 14 of the workspace register 12). The result is the CRU address of the selected CRU bit.

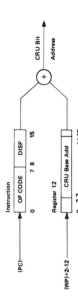

Instruction

(PC) → OP CODE DISP
       0   7 8   15

Register 12

(WP)+2·12 → CRU Base Add
            0 2 3   14 15

CRU Bit

Address

WORKSPACE REGISTER INDIRECT ADDRESSING *R

Workspace Register R contains the address of the operand.

(PC) → Instruction

(WP)+2R → Register R Operand

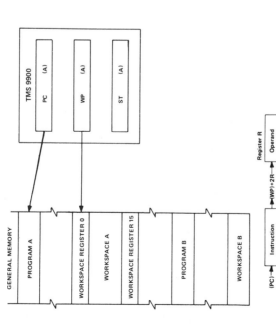

WORKSPACE REGISTER INDIRECT AUTO INCREMENT ADDRESSING *R+

Workspace Register R contains the address of the operand. Upon completion of the operation, the contents of workspace register R are incremented.

(PC) → Instruction

(WP)+2R → Register R Address

Operand

1 (byte) or 2 (word)

Copyright 1976, Texas Instruments, Incorporated

Z80-CPU
Product Specification

FEATURES

- Single chip, N-channel Silicon Gate CPU.
- 158 instructions—includes all 78 of the 8080A instructions with total software compatibility. New instructions include 4-, 8- and 16-bit operations with more useful addressing modes such as indexed, bit and relative.
- 17 internal registers.
- Three modes of fast interrupt response plus a non-maskable interrupt.
- Directly interfaces standard speed static or dynamic memories with virtually no external logic.
- 1.6 μs instruction execution speed.
- Single 5 VDC supply and single-phase 5 volt Clock.
- Out-performs any other single chip microcomputer in 4-, 8-, or 16-bit applications.
- All pins TTL Compatible
- Built-in dynamic RAM refresh circuitry.

Package Configuration

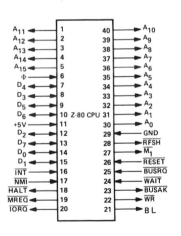

Z80-CPU BLOCK DIAGRAM

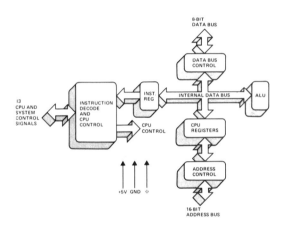

Z80-CPU REGISTERS

MAIN REG SET		ALTERNATE REG SET		
ACCUMULATOR A	FLAGS F	ACCUMULATOR A'	FLAGS F'	
B	C	B'	C'	GENERAL PURPOSE REGISTERS
D	E	D'	E'	
H	L	H'	L'	
INTERRUPT VECTOR I	MEMORY REFRESH R			SPECIAL PURPOSE REGISTERS
INDEX REGISTER	IX			
INDEX REGISTER	IY			
STACK POINTER	SP			
PROGRAM COUNTER	PC			

bibliography

ASHENHURST, R. L., and R. H. VONDEROHE, "A Hierarchical Network," *Datamation*, February 1975.

BARRON, D. W., *Assemblers and Loaders*, second ed. London and New York, MacDonald/American Elsevier, 1972.

BRILLOUIN, L., *Science and Information Theory*, New York, NY, Academic Press, 1962.

BROWN, P. J., *Macro Processors and Techniques for Portable Software*, London, John Wiley & Sons, 1974.

CARR, WILLIAM N., and JACK P. MIZE, *MOS/LSI Design and Application*, Texas Instruments Electronic Series, New York, NY, McGraw-Hill Book Co., 1972.
Another "must" for serious designers.

CHU, YAOHAN, ed., *High-Level Language Computer Architecture*, New York, NY, Academic Press, 1975

CLARE, CHRISTOPHER R., *Designing Logic Systems Using State Machines*, New York, NY, McGraw-Hill Book Co., 1973.
A classic treatise recommended to the serious designer.

"COS/MOS Integrated Circuits Manual," Somerset NJ, RCA Solid State Division, 1974.
A superb text which is the first of its kind. I believe that *all* processors designed in future should be influenced by the principles outlined in this text. An *absolute must* for computer architects.

DAHL, O. J., E. W. DIJKSTRA, and C.A.R. HOARE, *Structured Programming*, London, Academic Press, 1972.
Dijkstra is a major force in the world of programming who has worked long and hard for clarity in this field. He is one of the leading exponents of structured programming.

Digital-Linear-MOS Data Book, Signetics Corporation, Sunnyvale, CA, 1973.

DIJSKTRA, E. W. "Co-operating Sequential Processes," *Programming Languages: NATO advanced study institute*. F. Genuys, ed., London, Academic Press, 1968

EADIE, DONALD, *Introduction to the Basic Computer*, Englewood Cliffs, NJ, Prentice-Hall, Inc., 1968.
Written about 1967, this text treats SSI and early MSI circuits in detail and serves as a refresher for Boolean algebra and binary arithmetic.

"8008 8-Bit Parallel Central Processor Unit" *MCS-8 User's Manual*, Intel Corp., Santa Clara, CA, March 1973.

FARBER, DAVID J., "A Ring Network," *Datamation*, February 1975

FRASER, A. G., "A Virtual Channel Network," *Datamation*, February 1975.

FROST, DAVID, "Designing for Generality," *Datamation*, December 1974.

GALLER, B. A. and A. J. PERLIS, *A View of Programming Languages*, Reading, MA., Addison-Wesley Publishing Co., 1970.
An in-depth, highly abstract analysis of some of the primitive elements of programming.

GILBERT, PHILIP, and W. J. CHANDLER, "Interface Between Communicating Parallel Processes," *Communications of the ACM*, **15**, 6, June 1972.

GRIES, DAVID, *Compiler Construction for Digital Computers*, New York, NY, John Wiley & Sons, 1971.
Although not easily readable, this book is becoming a classic text.

IM 6100 CMOS 12-Bit Microprocessor Handbook, Intersil Inc., Cupertino, CA., 1976.

KATZ, SHMUEL, and ZOHAR MANNA, "Logical Analysis of FPrograms," The Weizmann Institute of Science, *Communications of the ACM*, **19**, 4, April 1976.

KENT, "Assembler-Language Macroprogramming: A Tutorial Oriented Toward the IBM 360," *ACM Computing Surveys*, **1**, 4, Dec. 1969.

KORN, G. A., *Minicomputers for Engineers and Scientists*, New York, NY, McGraw-Hill Book Co., 1973.
An excellent reference for most topics dealing with minicomputers and particularly good treatment of interfacing and I/O timing.

LEE, JOHN A. N. *The Anatomy of a Compiler*, second ed. New York, NY, Van Nostrand-Reinhold Co., 1974.
An easily readable book which avoids heavy theoretical treatments in favor of a "how to" approach.

MCS-84 Microcomputer Users' Manual, Intel Corp., Santa Clara, CA, 1976.

MCS-80 Microcomputer System Users Manual, Intel Corp., Santa Clara, CA, 1976.

MCS-85 Microcomputer System Users Manual, Intel Corp., Santa Clara, CA, 1976.

MARTIN, JAMES, *The Design of Real-Time Computer Systems*, Englewood Cliffs, NY, Prentice-Hall, Inc., 1967.

MILLS, HARLAN D. "The New Math of Computer Programming," *Communications of the ACM*, **18**, 1, January 1975.

MORRIS, ROBERT L. and J. R. MILLER, eds., *Designing with TTL Integrated Circuits*, New York, NY, Texas Instruments Electronic Series, The McGraw Hill Book Co., 1972.
A "must for the serious digital designer."

NEWELL, ALLEN, and HERBERT A. SIMON, "Computer Science as Empirical Inquiry: Symbols and Search," *Communications of the ACM*, **19**, 3, March 1976.

PEATMAN, JOHN B., *The Design of Digital Systems*, New York, NY, The McGraw-Hill Book Co., 1972.
Probably the best treatment of small and medium-scale integrated circuit design available.

————Microcomputer-Based Design, New York, NY, The McGraw-Hill Book Co. February 1977.

PRESSER, LEON, "Multiprogramming Coordination," *ACM Computing Surveys*, **7**, 1, March 1975.

RATHER, ELIZABETH D., and CHARLES H. MOORE, "Forth High-Level Programming Technique on Microprocessors," Electro*76* Professional Program, May 1976.
Further information on this technique can be obtained from Forth, Inc. 815 Manhattan Ave., Manhattan Beach, CA 90266.

REDDI, S. S., and E. A. FEUSTEL, "A Conceptual Framework for Computer Architecture," *ACM Computing Surveys*, **8**, 2, June 1976.

REYLING, GEORGE, Jr., "Performance and Control of Multiple Microprocessor Systems," *Computer Design*, March 1974.

ROSS, DOUGLAS T., and JOHN B. GOODENOUGH, "Software Engineering: Process, Principles, and Goals," *Computer*, May 1975.

SIMON, HERBERT A. *The Science of the Artificial*, Cambridge, MA, The M.I.T. Press, 1969.

TTL Applications Handbook, Mountain View, CA Fairchild Semiconductor, 1972.

TTL Data Book, Mountain View, CA, Fairchild Semiconductor, 1972.

The TTL Data Book for Design Engineers, Texas Instruments, Inc., Dallas, TE, 1973.

THOMAS, A. THAMPY, "Design Techniques for Microprocessors Memory Systems," *Computer Design*, August 1975.

TOU, J. T. and R. C. GONZALEZ, Pattern Recognition Principles, Reading, MA, Addison-Wesley Publishing Co., 1974.
An excellent summary text of approaches to pattern recogntion which will prove useful for any application of microprocessors in this area.

WATANABE, SATOSI, "Creative Learning and Propensity Automaton," *IEEE Transactions on Systems, Man, and Cybernetics*, SMC-**5**, 6, Nov. 1975.

————, "Learning Process and Inverse H-Theorem," *IRE Trans*. PGIT IT-8, **5**, 246, 1962.

WEISSBERGER, ALAN J. "Distributed Function Microprocessor Architecture," *Computer Design*, November 1974.

WIRTH, NIKLAUS, *Algorithm + Data Structures = Programs*, Englewood Cliffs, NJ, Prentice-Hall, Inc., 1976.

YOURDON, EDWARD, *Techniques of Program Structure and Design*, Englewood Cliffs, NJ, Prentice-Hall, Inc. 1975.
An easy-to-read text treating top-down design, modular and structured programming, as well as programming style and program testing and debugging.

index